HISTORY OF THE GUARDS DIVISION IN THE GREAT WAR, 1915-1918

Vol. II

All rights reserved

A GUARDSMAN, 1918

HISTORY OF
THE GUARDS DIVISION IN THE GREAT WAR 1915–1918

BY
CUTHBERT HEADLAM, D.S.O.
(LATE LIEUT.-COLONEL, GENERAL STAFF, B.E.F.)

VOLUME II

LONDON
JOHN MURRAY, ALBEMARLE STREET, W.

First Edition 1924

Printed and bound in Great Britain by
Antony Rowe Ltd, Eastbourne

CONTENTS

CHAPTER XI

THE CAMBRAI OPERATIONS (*continued*)—THE GERMAN COUNTER-ATTACKS, 30TH OF NOVEMBER TO 3RD OF DECEMBER, 1917.

(1) Opening of the German counter-attacks—capture of Gouzeaucourt by the enemy, 29th of November. (2) Orders to the Guards Division, 30th of November. (3) Recapture of Gouzeaucourt by the 1st Guards Brigade. (4) Movements of the 2nd and 3rd Guards Brigades, 30th of November. (5) Preparations for the attack on Gonnelieu and Gauche Wood. (6) Attack by the 1st Guards Brigade on the Quentin ridge and Gauche Wood, 1st of December. (7) Attack by the 3rd Guards Brigade on Gonnelieu, 1st of December. (8) Relief of the Guards by the 9th Division, 4th–6th of December. (9) Work of the Divisional Artillery in the Cambrai operations. (10) Work of the Divisional R.E. and 4th Bn. Coldstream Guards (Pioneers) during the Cambrai operations. (11) Casualties of, and record of prisoners taken by, the Guards between the 25th of November and 6th of December . . . . (pp. 1–22)

CHAPTER XII

THE WINTER OF 1917–1918—THE GUARDS IN THE ARRAS SECTOR OF THE LINE—FORMATION OF THE 4TH GUARDS BRIGADE.

(1) The Guards in rest billets in the Arras area—policy for the winter months. (2) Relief of the 15th Division north and south of the Scarpe—description of the new line. (3) Three months of trench warfare. (4) Work of the Divisional R.E. and 4th Bn. Coldstream Guards (Pioneers) on the Scarpe front. (5) Work of the Divisional Artillery and Trench-Mortar Batteries during the winter months. (6) Formation of the 4th Guards Brigade.
(pp. 23–40)

CONTENTS

CHAPTER XIII

THE GERMAN OFFENSIVE, 1918—EVENTS ON THE FRONT HELD BY THE GUARDS DIVISION AND THE 4TH GUARDS BRIGADE (31ST DIVISION) BETWEEN THE 21ST AND 31ST OF MARCH.

(1) Opening days of the German offensive. (2) The German attack on the front of the VI Corps, 21st of March—the 2nd Guards Brigade moved to Mercatel. (3) Continued progress of the enemy on the 22nd of March—movements of the Guards Division. (4) Withdrawal of the front of the VI Corps on the night of the 22nd–23rd of March—the Guards Division and the 4th Guards Brigade (31st Division) in the line. (5) Steady German pressure between Mory and Henin, 23rd of March. (6) The enemy breaks through the British line near Mory, 24th of March—measures for the protection of Ervillers by the 4th Guards Brigade—a quiet day on the front of the Guards Division. (7) Withdrawal of the Guards and the 31st Division, 25th of March. (8) The 4th Guards Brigade and the Guards Division withdrawn to the line Ayette—Boisleux-St. Marc — loss of Moyenneville, 26th of March. (9) The night of the 26th–27th of March—relief of the 2nd Guards Brigade by the 1st Guards Brigade—awkward position occupied by the Division. (10) Withdrawal of the 92nd and 93rd Infantry Brigades west of Ayette — the 4th Guards Brigade holds the front of the 31st Division—German attacks on the front of the Guards Division. (11) The night of the 27th–28th of March—the 4th Guards Brigade secures touch with the 42nd Division on its right. (12) Unsuccessful attempts by the enemy to break through the line of the 4th Guards Brigade and of the Guards Division, 28th of March—the 3rd Division north of the Guards Division driven back to the "Army line." (13) The 29th of March—a quiet day on the front held by the Guards—work of the Divisional Artillery. (14) The enemy attacks in strength along the Divisional front and is beaten back, 30th of March. (15) Relief of the 4th Guards Brigade—reorganization of the line on the front of the Guards Division, 31st of March

(pp. 41–77)

CHAPTER XIV

THE GERMAN ADVANCE IN THE VALLEY OF THE LYS—THE BATTLE OF HAZEBROUCK, 12TH–15TH OF APRIL, 1918—THE 4TH GUARDS BRIGADE (31ST DIVISION) IN THE DEFENCE OF NIEPPE FOREST.

(1) Opening of the German offensive in the Valley of the Lys—the 31st Division sent to reinforce the British front in the Hazebrouck area. (2) The task assigned to the 4th Guards Brigade

CONTENTS

—the fighting north of Merville, 12th of April. (3) Continuance of the German advance towards Hazebrouck—stubborn resistance by the Guards—the British line secured. (4) Share of the 4th Guards Brigade in the defence of Hazebrouck. (5) Subsequent history of the 4th Guards Brigade . . (pp. 78–93)

CHAPTER XV

APRIL–AUGUST, 1918—CLOSE OF THE GERMAN OFFENSIVE.

(1) Cessation of the enemy's attacks on the front of the VI Corps—strengthening of the defences on the Guards Divisional front—relief of the Guards by the 2nd Division, 13th–15th of April. (2) The Guards return to the line, 24th–26th of April. (3) Work of the Divisional Artillery during the month of April. (4) Events on the Divisional front during the month of May. (5) Relief of the Guards, 6th–7th of June—the Division in rest billets in the Bavincourt area. (6) The Guards return to the line, 5th–7th of July—the opening of the British counter-offensive, 8th of August. (7) Work of the Divisional Artillery during the months of May, June and July . . . . . (pp. 94–111)

CHAPTER XVI

THE ADVANCE TO VICTORY, 1918—OPENING OF THE BRITISH COUNTER-OFFENSIVE ON THE FRONT OF THE THIRD ARMY—THE ST. LEGER FIGHTING IN AUGUST.

(1) Opening of the offensive on the front of the Third Army. (2) Dispositions of the Guards Division for the attack on Moyenneville. (3) Assembly of the 2nd Guards Brigade for the attack, 20th–21st of August. (4) Attack by the 2nd Guards Brigade, 21st of August. (5) Events of the night of the 21st–22nd of August. (6) German counter-attack in the morning of the 22nd of August—preparations for the renewal of the advance by the 2nd Guards Brigade. (7) Attack by the 2nd Guards Brigade, 23rd of August. (8) Attack by the 3rd Guards Brigade, 24th of August. (9) Continuance of the attack, 25th of August. (10) The 1st Guards Brigade in the line, 26th of August—orders for the renewal of the attack on the 27th of August. (11) Attack by the 1st Guards Brigade, 27th of August. (12) Events of the 28th of August—steady progress of the 1st Guards Brigade—relief of the Division by the 3rd Division—work of the Divisional R.E. and 4th Bn. Coldstream Guards (Pioneers) during the advance. (13) Work of the Divisional Artillery with the 3rd Division . . . . (pp. 112–142)

CHAPTER XVII

THE BREAKING OF THE HINDENBURG LINE—ADVANCE OF THE GUARDS TOWARDS THE CANAL DU NORD.

(1) Effects of the Allied offensive—the Germans thrust back across the old battle-field of the Somme—capture of the Drocourt—Quéant Line by the First Army. (2) The Guards relieve the 3rd Division west of Lagnicourt—advance of the 2nd and 3rd Guards Brigades towards the Canal du Nord, 3rd of September—retreat of the enemy to the Hindenburg Line. (3) Stiffening of the enemy's resistance between Boursies and Mœuvres—continuous pressure maintained along the line by the Guards Division, 4th–7th of September. (4) Organized attack by the troops of the VI Corps—rôle of the Guards Division in the battle of Havrincourt, 12th of September—Major-General Feilding leaves the Division on his appointment to command the London district—Major-General Matheson appointed to command the Guards Division. (5) The battle of Havrincourt—local fighting on the front of the VI Corps, 12th–27th of September . . (pp. 143–160)

CHAPTER XVIII

THE BREAKING OF THE HINDENBURG LINE (*continued*)—THE BATTLE OF THE CANAL DU NORD, 27TH OF SEPTEMBER, 1918.

(1) Final preparations for the crossing of the Canal du Nord and assault on the Hindenburg Line. (2) Task of the Guards Division and flanking divisions in the general scheme of operations. (3) Plan of operations on the Guards Divisional front. . (4) Artillery arrangements. (5) Assembly of the troops on the night of the 26th–27th of September. (6) Attack of the 2nd Guards Brigade, 27th of September. (7) Attack of the 1st Guards Brigade, 27th of September. (8) Attack of the 3rd Guards Brigade, 27th of September—Brig.-General Follett killed. (9) Work of the Divisional R.E. and 4th Bn. Coldstream Guards (Pioneers) throughout the day's fighting. (10) Relief of the Division by the 2nd Division on the night of the 27th of September—the achievements of the Guards in the Battle of the Canal du Nord . . . . (pp. 161–181)

CHAPTER XIX

PURSUIT OF THE ENEMY TO THE SELLE RIVER—THE BATTLE OF THE SELLE, 17TH–25TH OF OCTOBER, 1918.

(1) Progress of the Allied advance during the early days of October.

CONTENTS

(2) The Guards Division returns to the line—attack of the 3rd and 2nd Divisions towards the Selle river, 8th of October—arrangements for the attack on Wambaix. (3) Advance of the 1st and 2nd Guards Brigades, 9th of October—capture of Wambaix—the line Fontaine au Tertre Farm—St. Hilaire reached. (4) Continuance of the advance of the 1st and 2nd Guards Brigades, 10th of October. (5) Advance of the 3rd Guards Brigade, 11th of October—capture of St. Vaast. (6) Progress made by the Guards, 12th of October. (7) Events of the 13th of October—relief of the 3rd Guards Brigade. (8) Events of the 14th–15th of October. (9) Haussy taken and lost—the 1st Bn. Coldstream Guards in action—orders issued for the passage of the Selle river. (10) Resumption of the general Allied advance. (11) The crossing of the Selle river, 20th of October. (12) Work of the Divisional Artillery and Trench-Mortar Batteries during the month of October. (13) Work of the Divisional R.E. and 4th Bn. Coldstream Guards (Pioneers) during the month of October—their share in the crossing of the Selle river

(pp. 182–216)

CHAPTER XX

THE BATTLE OF THE SAMBRE AND THE OCCUPATION OF MAUBEUGE, 4TH–9TH OF NOVEMBER, 1918—THE ARMISTICE.

(1) Growing effects of the Allied victories—opening of the final British advance. (2) The Guards return to the line—the new front west of Villers Pol—arrangements for the resumption of the advance on the 4th of November. (3) Advance of the 1st and 2nd Guards Brigades, 4th of November. (4) Advance of the 3rd Guards Brigade, 5th and 6th of November. (5) The 2nd Guards Brigade resumes the advance—events of the 7th and 8th of November—occupation of Maubeuge. (6) The Armistice, 11th of November—achievements of the Guards Division in the final stages of the war. (7) Work of the Divisional R.E. and 4th Bn. Coldstream Guards (Pioneers) and of the Divisional Signal Company and the Administrative services during the closing days of the advance . . . . . (pp. 217–236)

CHAPTER XXI

THE MARCH INTO GERMANY—THE GUARDS AT COLOGNE—THE TRIUMPHAL MARCH THROUGH LONDON, 22ND OF MARCH, 1919.

(pp. 237–248)

CONTENTS
APPENDICES

APPENDIX		PAGE
I.	Composition of the Guards Division on its Formation	251
II.	Succession of Officers, Staffs and Commands	253
III.	Victoria Crosses won by Officers and Other Ranks	269
IV.	Guards Division Operation Orders	278
V.	Note on the Reserve Battalions of the Guards Regiments	311
VI.	Origin and History of the Guards Machine-Gun Regiment	314
VII.	Household Brigade Officer Cadet Battalion	318
VIII.	Guards Entrenching Battalion	320
IX.	Guards Division Base Depôt at Harfleur	322
X.	Foreign Service of the Bands of the Regiments of Guards	324
XI.	Address by the Major-General Commanding the Guards Division on Armistice Day, 1918	326
XII.	Notes on Dress and Equipment of the Foot Guards during the War, 1914–1918	329
XIII.	Race Card. The Calais First Spring Meeting	333
INDEX		336

FRONTISPIECE: A Guardsman, 1918.
From a coloured sketch by OLIVE SNELL.

LIST OF MAPS

	FACING PAGE
Guards Division: Operations, Nov. 30th and Dec., 1917	22
Guards Division and 4th Guards Brigade: Operations, March 21st–31st, 1918	76
4th Guards Brigade: Operations, April 12th and 13th, 1918	92
Guards Division: Operations, August 21st–29th, 1918	142
Guards Division: Operations, Sept. 1st–6th, 1918	160
Guards Division: Operations, Sept. 27th, 1918	180
Guards Division: Operations, October, 1918	216
Guards Division: Advance to Maubeuge, November, 1918	236
The Western Front	*End of Volume*

HISTORY OF THE GUARDS DIVISION IN THE GREAT WAR, 1915—1918

CHAPTER XI

THE CAMBRAI OPERATIONS (*continued*) — THE GERMAN COUNTER-ATTACKS, 30TH OF NOVEMBER TO 3RD OF DECEMBER, 1917.

(1) OPENING OF THE GERMAN COUNTER-ATTACKS—CAPTURE OF GOUZEAUCOURT BY THE ENEMY, 29TH OF NOVEMBER.

THE course of the fighting from the 21st of November onwards, especially the failure of the attack upon the Bourlon ridge on the 27th, made it clear that the enemy had been reinforced and that he was determined to regain the ground which had been taken from him. For some days before the great German counter-offensive the III Corps, which was holding the line to the south of the IV Corps, had been expecting a hostile attack,* but no one was really prepared for the strength and suddenness with which the storm actually burst. It was a fine feat of arms for which General von der Marwitz, commanding the Second German Army, and his troops deserve the greatest credit.

The enemy's attack was launched between 7 and 8 a.m. on the 30th of November. That which was probably intended to be the main offensive movement was delivered from the

* " During the last days of November increased registration of hostile artillery, the movements of troops and transport observed behind the German lines, together with other indications of a like nature, pointed to further efforts by the enemy to regain the positions we had wrested from him." *See* " Sir Douglas Haig's Despatches, 1915–1918," p. 162.

north,* and had, for its principal objective, the complete recapture of the Bourlon ridge.† But the thrust which was unfortunately attended with so much success, was delivered along the British front between Vendhuille and Masnières—a distance of about ten miles. The line in this area was held from south to north by the 55th, the 12th, the 20th and 29th Divisions, the first-named of which, in particular, was holding a dangerously extended line. Between Masnières and Marcoing the German attack failed to penetrate the British front, but farther south it succeeded in breaking through the defences. So swift, indeed, was the enemy's advance that, within an hour and a half after the assault had been made, he had captured Villers-Guislain, Gonnelieu and the Bonavis ridge, and had made his way as far as Gouzeaucourt. The position of the Third Army in the Cambrai salient, therefore, was seriously endangered.

(2) Orders to the Guards Division, 30th of November.

At about 8 a.m. on the 30th of November, a telegram was received at divisional headquarters, stating that the Germans were attacking the III Corps in great strength, and that the Guards were to be prepared to move at a moment's notice. The three brigadiers were immediately warned to be in readiness, and the bearers of Field Ambulances were ordered to get into touch with the headquarters of brigades. At 10 a.m., upon instructions received from the IV Corps, the

* The weight of troops employed in the northern attack would appear to prove that the enemy meant it to be his principal effort, but General Ludendorff asserts that it was only a subsidiary attack. *See* " My War Memories, 1914–1918," vol. ii. p. 496. The General's assertion may have been influenced by the failure of the northern attack and the success of the southern one.

† With the story of the fighting on this portion of the line this book has no concern as the Guards were not engaged in the defence. But no military record of the battle can pass over in absolute silence the magnificent resistance of the 47th, 2nd and 56th Divisions which, from east to west in the order named, held the line from Bourlon Wood to a point just west of Mœuvres. They held their ground against the repeated attacks of seven German divisions. Their stubborn defence undoubtedly saved the situation for the Third Army, so far as its northern flank was concerned.

1st Guards Bde. was ordered to move to Heudecourt and the 2nd and 3rd Guards Bdes. to the neighbourhood of Metz-en-Couture. Twenty minutes later definite news was received from the IV Corps that the enemy had taken Gonnelieu and Villers-Guislain, and that the Guards Division was to come under the orders of the VII Corps.

Upon the receipt of this information the G.S.O.3 was at once sent off to the headquarters of the VII Corps in order to get in touch with the situation. But scarcely had he left divisional headquarters before fresh orders were received from the IV Corps cancelling the previous orders and instructing the 1st Guards Bde. to move on Gouzeaucourt in order to hold the high ground—known as Quentin ridge—east of that village. The 3rd Guards Bde. was ordered to advance on the right of the 1st Guards Bde., while the 2nd Guards Bde. was to move forward on the right of the former brigade to Revelon, a hamlet on the high ground beyond the railway line a little to the north-east of Heudecourt.

At 11 a.m. yet another message was received from the IV Corps informing Major-General Feilding that his division was to come under the orders of the III Corps instead of the VII Corps, and he himself at once started off for III Corps headquarters.

Shortly after midday the Major-General sent a telephone message to divisional headquarters ordering an advanced headquarters to be established as soon as possible at Metz-en-Couture. This order was promptly carried out and, by 2 p.m., the new headquarters was satisfactorily linked up by telephonic communication with the headquarters of the brigades.

Meanwhile, about 12.30 p.m., information had been received that the enemy was holding a line Villers Plouich—Gouzeaucourt, and, as the 1st Guards Bde. was already marching upon the latter place, a staff officer was dispatched to stop the 3rd Guards Bde. from moving too far to the south and to direct it to come up on the left of the 1st Guards Bde., with the object of driving the enemy northward from the line which he was then reported to be holding. At the same time the 2nd Guards Bde. was ordered to move into reserve in the neighbourhood of Queen's Cross, a little to the west of Gouzeaucourt, whilst " H " Bn. Tanks was directed to make its way to Gouzeaucourt Wood and to get in touch with the 1st Guards Bde.

In order to follow the somewhat complicated incidents of the subsequent fighting, it will now be best to relate in detail the movements of each of the Guards brigades.

(3) RECAPTURE OF GOUZEAUCOURT BY THE 1ST GUARDS BRIGADE.

The battalions of the 1st Guards Bde., which were in billets at Metz-en-Couture, were just about to march southward in order to carry out their original instructions when the order to occupy the high ground east of Gouzeaucourt reached Brig.-General de Crespigny. He at once rode forward with his commanding officers to acquaint himself with the situation. He found the roads crowded with retreating transport, while men belonging to every arm of the Service—many of them without their rifles and equipment—were streaming westward across country in a state of great disorder and panic. Upon reaching Gouzeaucourt Wood, it became obvious to the reconnoitring officers, both from what they could themselves see and also from what they learned from stragglers, that the enemy was already in possession of Gouzeaucourt and that his patrols were on the high ground to the west of that village. The Brigadier at once made up his mind to launch a counter-attack without any loss of time in order to recapture the village and then to establish a line on the rising ground just east of it.

The Metz-Gouzeaucourt road gave the general direction for the attack, and two battalions of the brigade—the 2nd and 3rd Bn. Coldstream Guards each with four machine guns—were ordered to effect their entry into the village from the south, whilst one battalion—the 1st Bn. Irish Guards with two machine guns—was ordered to assault it from the north.

The head of the brigade reached Gouzeaucourt Wood

about noon and the three attacking battalions prepared for action in the shelter of the low ground just east of it. About half an hour later they moved forward in artillery formation, each battalion on a frontage of about 500 yards, with two companies in line and two in support, the intention being to deploy as soon as the advance brought them under heavy fire. The 2nd Bn. Grenadier Guards, with six machine guns, remained in reserve in the vicinity of Gouzeaucourt Wood.

The advance was carried out in splendid order, and good progress was made, although the troops were met by heavy machine-gun fire—chiefly from a southerly direction—the moment they appeared on the top of the ridge west of Queen's Cross.

On the right of the brigade front the 2nd Bn. Coldstream Guards had to advance for some distance with its right flank in the air as the 3rd Guards Bde., which it had originally been intended should cooperate on this flank, had, as already related, been diverted to the north of the 1st Guards Bde. This change of plan was of course unknown to the officer in command of the Coldstream, but he made the best dispositions he could for the safety of his battalion by sending forward two of his machine guns with the leading waves—one in the centre and one on the right flank—whilst he detailed his two remaining guns to accompany the right rear of the battalion. Upon arriving within about 1,000 yards of Gouzeaucourt the 2nd Bn. Coldstream Guards came upon some R.E. and pioneers belonging to the 20th and 29th Divisions, who were still holding out in a trench, and some of this party gallantly accompanied the battalion in its attack, while, just about the same time, the 20th Hussars appeared upon the scene, and, advancing on foot in conjunction with the Guards, prolonged the line on the right.

The three battalions of the 1st Guards Bde. reached the slope down into Gouzeaucourt almost simultaneously and at this stage in the advance the German machine-gun fire became intense; but the brigade swept on down the hill, through the village and up the slope on its eastern side. Here it became exposed to heavy artillery fire from the eastern edge of Quentin ridge, the enemy, who appeared to be holding the ridge in some strength, making effective use of some captured British guns and firing at very short range. By 1.30 p.m., however, the whole objective—Gouzeaucourt and the rising ground just east of it—had been secured and the work of consolidation was in progress.

The 1st Guards Bde. line now ran approximately along the western side of the railway line from the northern end of Gouzeaucourt, where touch was obtained with the 4th Bn. Grenadier Guards, round the village, and thence southward again.

The action had been well planned and was admirably carried out. The machine gunners had greatly assisted the infantry. The 3rd Bn. Coldstream Guards, in particular, just as it was forcing its way into Gouzeaucourt, was helped materially by the covering fire of the subsection of guns on the flank of the Irish Guards. This subsection, owing to the prompt initiative of its commanding officer, engaged the enemy's machine guns posted in the village, the fire of which had momentarily checked the advance of the Coldstream.

After the brigade had made its way into Gouzeaucourt few Germans remained to resist its farther progress, but a good many of the enemy were killed and about 100 prisoners were captured. Numerous batteries of British howitzers, 60-pdrs. and other guns were also recovered.

About 3.50 p.m., by which time the brigade was fairly comfortably installed in its new position, eleven tanks which had been detailed for the recapture of Gouzeaucourt began to arrive on the scene of action. They immediately became targets for the enemy's gunners, and four of them soon became casualties. Their crews, however, acting with great promptitude and presence of mind, retrieved their Lewis guns from the wreckage of their machines and joined forces with the 2nd Bn. Coldstream Guards in order to resist a threatened German counter-attack. But no counter-attack was attempted and, when darkness began to set in, the battle died down.

(4) Movements of the 2nd and 3rd Guards Brigades, 30th of November.

The 2nd Guards Bde., which, it will be remembered, was in billets in Bertincourt and Ruyaulcourt on the morning of the 30th of November, advanced to Neuville at 11.30 a.m., where it halted for an hour. It then moved forward again across country to Gouzeaucourt Wood, where it remained in reserve positions on the eastern side of the wood for the rest of the day.

The headquarters of the 3rd Guards Bde. was at Trescault on the morning of the 30th of November, and its battalions were bivouacked along the eastern edge of Havrincourt Wood. At 8.40 a.m. the brigade received orders to be ready to move at short notice and in the meantime to take up a defensive line covering Havrincourt Wood from the south-east. But, at about 10.15 a.m., a second order reached Brig.-General Corkran instructing him to move south via Metz-en-Couture in order to prolong the line of the 1st Guards Bde. in a southerly direction.

The brigade, accordingly, moved off from Havrincourt Wood and its leading battalion—the 2nd Bn. Scots Guards—had almost reached Dessart Wood, about 2,000 yards south of Metz-en-Couture, when, at about 2.30 p.m., a staff officer from the division gave the brigadier verbal instructions to take up a line covering Gouzeaucourt—Villers Plouich. The brigade, therefore, changed its direction, and, after adopting artillery formation, advanced northward between Havrincourt and Gouzeaucourt Woods, and took up a position west of Gouzeaucourt—Villers Plouich, a continuation of the line held by the 1st Guards Bde. The 4th Bn. Grenadier Guards on the right was in touch with the 1st Bn. Irish Guards, and the 2nd Bn. Scots Guards with the 59th Division on the left. The 1st Bn. Welsh Guards was in support and the 1st Bn. Grenadier Guards in reserve. All the units of the brigade were in their respective positions by 3.50 p.m.

(5) Preparations for the Attack on Gonnelieu and Gauche Wood.

At 10.30 p.m., on the night of the 30th of November, verbal orders were given to Major-General Feilding from the III Corps commander that the Guards Division, in conjunction with the tanks and cavalry on its right, was to be prepared to attack Gonnelieu, Gauche Wood and the Quentin ridge the following morning in the event of an attack, which was being arranged by the 20th Division, proving unsuccessful. The actual written orders for this operation were not received from the III Corps until 12.15 a.m. on the 1st of December, just after the divisional orders for the attack had been issued to the brigades.

The 1st Guards Bde. on the right and the 3rd Guards Bde. on the left were detailed by the Major-General to carry out the attack. The former brigade was to storm the Quentin ridge and the latter brigade to recapture Gonnelieu. The cavalry was to attack south of the 1st Guards Bde. The tanks, the cooperation of a number of which was promised, were ordered to precede the infantry as in this case the advance was uphill and they would not be exposed, therefore, to direct fire from the enemy's guns.* Instructions were given to the 70th and 235th Bdes., R.F.A., the only two artillery brigades which appear to have been available for the purpose, to put down a heavy barrage at zero hour upon "Twenty-two" ravine with the object of preventing any concentration of hostile reinforcements in that area. Arrangements were also made for the provision of overhead machine-gun fire to cover the advancing troops.

At 2.45 a.m., on the 1st of December, the news was received at divisional headquarters that the hurriedly prepared attack of the 20th Division had ended in failure. It was left, therefore, to the Guards to retrieve the situation.

* The officer in command of the tanks, in anticipation of an order being received for the Guards to attack on the 1st of December, had been detained at divisional headquarters and was given his orders verbally. *See* Narrative of Operations of the Guards Division, 9th of November to the 6th of December, 1917, W.D., Guards Division.

(6) ATTACK BY THE 1ST GUARDS BRIGADE ON THE QUENTIN RIDGE AND GAUCHE WOOD, 1ST OF DECEMBER.

The 2nd Bn. Grenadier Guards on the right and the 3rd Bn. Coldstream Guards on the left received orders to cross the line at 6.20 a.m. They were to be preceded by twenty tanks and were to capture the Quentin ridge and Gauche Wood.

Up to zero hour everything went according to plan, except that the tanks which were to operate on the front of the right battalion, and the cavalry which was to carry out the attack on the right of the front held by the Guards Division, were both late in arriving. The tanks, which had been ordered to act in conjunction with the left battalion, made their appearance just in time and took part in the attack as arranged, but those which were to have led the 2nd Bn. Grenadier Guards had not arrived upon the scene of action ten minutes after zero hour. The Grenadiers, therefore, had no alternative but to go forward to the attack without them.

Losses from machine-gun fire were heavy from the start and many officers became casualties, but, nevertheless, the battalion, much assisted by the indirect fire of the 1st Guards Bde. Machine-Gun Company, made good progress, Gauche Wood being reached by 7 a.m. The Grenadiers then rushed the wood, overpowering some of the enemy's machine gunners, who still remained in it. The company on the right of the attacking force had then to swing round to the right in order to repel two German counter-attacks—a task in which it was completely successful, inflicting heavy losses on the enemy.

Meanwhile, the tanks, which were so late in arrival, had been following the infantry and had all been ditched or put out of action by the German artillery fire. Their crews, however, now came up with their Lewis guns and were of great assistance on the right flank which until the cavalry— the 7th Dragoon Guards and the 18th Lancers (Indian Army) —appeared on the scene had been entirely in the air.

The new line which had been gained by the Grenadiers on the eastern edge of Gauche Wood was consolidated as rapidly as possible, but it was much exposed to the enemy's snipers and also to shell fire from Villers-Guislain, with the result that there were a good many casualties, especially amongst officers. The Germans, however, attempted no more counter-attacks, and, by the evening, the position was fairly secure; but, as it was found necessary to refuse the right flank along the southern edge of Gauche Wood, a company of the 2nd Bn. Coldstream Guards was sent up in close support of the Grenadiers.

On the left of the attack, the 3rd Bn. Coldstream Guards, preceded by four tanks, captured their objective without much difficulty, although it is doubtful whether its task would have been a possible one without the cooperation of the tanks which proved of the greatest assistance to the infantry. Touch with the 1st Bn. Welsh Guards on the left flank of the Coldstream could not be effected, however, until late in the day, and then not until a company of the 1st Bn. Irish Guards had been sent up to fill the gap between the two brigades.

As soon as the Coldstream were in possession of their objective, two machine guns were mounted on the Quentin ridge, and their fire, as well as that of one of the enemy's captured guns, was directed with considerable effect upon the Germans who were still holding out against the troops of the 3rd Guards Bde. in Gonnelieu.

During the day's operations on this part of the front over 300 prisoners were captured, as well as 3 field guns and 31 machine guns, whilst about 100 British guns, which had been parked ready for removal near Gouzeaucourt station, also fell into the possession of the Guards.*

(7) ATTACK BY THE 3RD GUARDS BRIGADE ON GONNELIEU, 1ST OF DECEMBER.

At 4 a.m., on the 1st of December, the 3rd Guards Bde. was informed that nine tanks would be available to assist the infantry in the attack on Gonnelieu, but, as a matter of

* *See* Narrative of Operations of the Guards Division, 9th of November to the 6th of December, 1917. W.D., Guards Division.

fact, the majority of these promised machines arrived too late to be of any real help to the assaulting troops, at any rate in the initial stages of the advance. One tank, however, later on in the day, materially assisted the 1st Bn. Welsh Guards, and was largely responsible for the clearing of a party of the enemy's machine gunners out of a piece of trench from which they were checking the forward progress of the battalion.

The attack was launched punctually at 6.20 a.m.—the 1st Bn. Welsh Guards on the right, the 4th Bn. Grenadier Guards on the left.* On the right, from the moment the troops crossed the line, they were subjected to a withering fire from the enemy's machine guns in Gonnelieu. But, although the German resistance was very obstinate, the Welsh Guards went steadily forward, and, with the assistance of a tank, as already mentioned, fought their way to the high ground just south-west of Gonnelieu.

On the left, the three companies of the 4th Bn. Grenadier Guards, which had been detailed to capture the village of Gonnelieu, crossed the railway line east of Gouzeaucourt during the night of the 30th of November–1st of December and established themselves in a more convenient starting off position for their attack.

The following morning at zero hour they pushed forward from their new line in perfect order up the gradual slope which led to their objective. The enemy took the fullest advantage of the fine field of fire afforded to him by the configuration of the ground, and the Grenadiers, who were not accompanied by any tanks, were met by a hail of machine-gun bullets. The leading company on the right appears to have lost direction, inclining too much towards the Welsh Guards, and its exact movements are somewhat difficult to follow. It is certain, however, that it had very heavy casualties.† The other companies, after halting for a few minutes along

* The 1st Bn. Grenadier Guards was in support on the left, its task being to protect the left flank as the attacking force advanced. The 2nd Bn. Scots Guards was already in occupation of the high ground in the neighbourhood of Villers Plouich.

† One platoon was practically wiped out. *See* "The Grenadier Guards in the Great War, 1914–1918," vol. ii. pp. 310, 311.

the Gouzeaucourt—Masnières road, pushed on towards Gonnelieu. In front of the village they came upon a trench which was still occupied by men belonging to the 20th Division. After crossing the northern portion of this trench, the left leading company of the Grenadiers entered the village and a few men, led by a subaltern, penetrated as far as the cemetery where they succeeded in getting a Lewis gun into action. Unfortunately this gun, the fire of which was effectively enfilading the enemy, jammed, and the little party was overwhelmed by a German counter-attack—only two survivors, the subaltern and a sergeant, managing to find their way back from the village.

Meanwhile, the remainder of this company had forced its way to the eastern edge of the village, but its strength by this time was so much reduced that it was greatly outnumbered by the Germans and surrounded. After a very gallant struggle, in which the company commander was wounded and taken prisoner, seven men belonging to the company succeeded in fighting their way back to the battalion. It was clear, after this bitter struggle, that the capture of Gonnelieu could not be effected with the force still available, more especially as the situation on the left flank of the brigade was giving cause for considerable anxiety, while touch with the Welsh Guards on the right had not been obtained.* At about 9 a.m., consequently, Viscount Gort, commanding the Grenadiers, after collecting the remnants of the attacking companies, decided to utilize the trench just west of Gonnelieu, to which reference has already been made, and to organize a defensive position outside the village.† This movement was carried out quite successfully,

---

* " It was now clear that without considerable reinforcements and unlimited sacrifices the village could not be taken. The enemy's machine guns were too strong. The Germans were counter-attacking, and were able to overpower any parties that had gained a footing in the village. Only one of the fourteen tanks that had been expected appeared, and, although it was undoubtedly a great help to the Welsh Guards, it was quite inadequate by itself. The Brigade on the left and the Welsh Guards on the right had been held up, so that even had the Battalion taken the village they would not have been able to hold it." *See* " The Grenadier Guards in the Great War," vol. ii. pp. 313, 314.

† After supervising the consolidation of this new line Lord Gort

but the situation was still far from satisfactory as the Grenadiers were much reduced in numbers and both their flanks were in the air. Three companies of the 1st Bn. Grenadier Guards were sent forward, therefore, to strengthen the front. These companies made a vigorous counter-attack upon the Germans, who were moving forward north of the Gouzeaucourt—Masnières road, and, after some hard fighting, which cost them over 100 casualties, were successful in driving back the enemy and securing the safety of the left flank of the 4th Bn. Grenadier Guards.

This action brought to a close the day's fighting on this part of the front, for, although the enemy continued shelling the new line held by the Guards on and off throughout the remainder of the day, he attempted no further counter-attack, and by the evening the captured position was fairly well consolidated. It ran along the Quentin ridge from just north-west of Gonnelieu round the eastern edge of Gauche Wood.

The attacking troops, therefore, did not quite succeed in capturing the entire objective which had been assigned to them on the 1st of December, but the recapture by the Guards on the previous day of Gouzeaucourt, followed by the seizure of the important high ground to the east of it in the engagement which has just been described, undoubtedly brought to a standstill the great German counter-offensive in the Cambrai salient.*

The magnificent fighting qualities displayed by all ranks thoroughly deserved the warm tribute of praise which was accorded to them by the Commander-in-Chief and the III Corps commander.

---

went forward to make a personal reconnaissance of the situation on the left of the line now occupied by his battalion. Whilst engaged upon this task he was severely wounded, and the command of the battalion devolved upon Major W. S. Pilcher.

* The young officer of the Scots Guards who, in a letter dated the 7th of December, 1917, stated :—" The Division have been *absolutely superb*, and absolutely saved the situation—a thing that the papers of course hardly suggest at all "—was scarcely overstating the case. *See* " Henry Dundas, Scots Guards—A Memoir," William Blackwood & Sons, 1921.

"I desire," said Sir Douglas Haig in a telegram to Major-General Feilding on the 5th of December, " to congratulate the Guards Division most warmly on their fine counter-attacks at Gouzeaucourt and Gonnelieu. The promptness of decision and rapidity of action displayed by them was successful in dealing with a difficult situation."

The message of the III Corps commander was equally complimentary :—

" The corps commander wishes to express to all ranks of the Guards Division his high appreciation of the prompt manner in which they turned out on the 30th November, counter-attacked through a disorganized rabble and retook Gouzeaucourt. The very fine attack which they subsequently carried out against Quentin ridge and Gauche Wood, resulting in the capture of these important positions, was worthy of the highest traditions of the Guards."

(8) RELIEF OF THE GUARDS BY THE 9TH DIVISION, 4TH–6TH OF DECEMBER.

During the night of the 1st–2nd of December the 1st Guards Bde. was relieved by the 2nd Guards Bde. without much difficulty as the enemy's gunners had ceased their activity when darkness set in.* On the front of the 3rd Guards Bde. Major-General Feilding had been assured that the 1st Bn. Grenadier Guards and the 2nd Bn. Scots Guards would be relieved by troops of the 183rd Infantry Bde. so that these two battalions might take over the line from the two battalions which had been engaged in the day's attack and which were still holding the front. For some reason, however, this anticipated relief did not take place and, as a consequence, the 4th Bn. Grenadier Guards and the 1st Bn. Welsh Guards had to remain in the line for a further twenty-four hours—a severe strain upon troops who had been through such severe fighting and suffered such heavy losses.

Luckily, the 2nd of December was a comparatively

* During the two days' fighting the 1st Guards Bde. had lost 36 officers and 765 other ranks.

quiet day on this part of the front, and, on the night of the 2nd–3rd the relief of the two battalions was safely effected by the 1st Bn. Grenadier Guards and the 2nd Bn. Scots Guards—the 4th Bn. Grenadier Guards and the 1st Bn. Welsh Guards moving into bivouacs near Gouzeaucourt Wood. The following night the 1st Guards Bde. took over the line held by the 3rd Guards Bde., the actual relief of the Guards Division only beginning on the night of the 4th–5th of December, when the 2nd Guards Bde. was replaced in the line by a brigade of the 9th Division. But the Guards were not to go back to their well-earned rest without another fight.

In the morning of the 5th of December the enemy made two determined bombing attacks on the front now held by the 1st Guards Bde. and succeeded in one of them in gaining a foothold in the trenches held by the 1st Bn. Irish Guards. This battalion, the strength of which was only 450 men, was holding a frontage of about 1,200 yards west and north-west of Gonnelieu. North of the Gouzeaucourt—Masnières road the position was fairly easy to defend, but south of this road there were barricaded communication trenches leading into the enemy's line. At 6.30 a.m. the Germans put down a heavy artillery barrage in rear of the Guards position which effectually cut off all communications, and bombarded the front line with trench mortars. They then attacked in considerable force just south of the Gouzeaucourt—Masnières road. A shell from a trench mortar had demolished one of the barricades and the enemy's bombers rushed into the trenches defended by the Irish Guards. They were promptly counter-attacked and the line was soon re-established, whilst another hostile advance from the direction of Gonnelieu was driven back with heavy loss to the enemy by Lewis-gun and rifle fire.*

On the night of the 5th–6th of December the 1st Guards Bde. was relieved by the 26th Infantry Bde., and, at 10 a.m. on the 6th, Major-General Feilding handed over the command of the sector to the G.O.C. the 9th Division. The Guards Division, on relief, was moved by train to the Fosseux area

* The Irish Guards lost 1 officer and 34 other ranks in this affair.

west of Arras—travelling over the track which had been laid by its own troops through Morval, Lesbœufs and Ginchy earlier in the year after the German retreat.

(9) Work of the Divisional Artillery in the Cambrai Operations.

The Artillery of the Guards Division left the Boesinghe sector on the 3rd of November, and, after only two days' rest, started on its southward march.*

The 74th Bde., R.F.A., reached Caucourt and Hermin on the 9th of November, and was called upon to make no farther advance until the 18th, but, although the rest was a welcome one, there was no opportunity for obtaining fresh clothing or equipment of both of which after its long sojourn in the line the brigade was in great need. The 75th Bde., R.F.A., spent a similar period of waiting at Villers Chatel.

The two brigades and the D.A.C. eventually reached the battle area after four night marches, and, on the 24th of November, arrived at Ribécourt, the D.A.C. taking over an ammunition dump and bomb store in Havrincourt Wood from the 51st Division.

On the night of the 25th of November the batteries of the 74th Bde. went into action along the Graincourt—La Justice road, and those of the 75th Bde. in the vicinity of Orival Wood. In addition to his own brigades, the C.R.A., Guards Division, had under his command six other R.F.A. brigades with which to cover the front held by the Guards. The artillery barrage provided for the attack by the 2nd Guards Bde. on the 27th of November crept forward at the rate of 100 yards in 5 minutes, the howitzers firing on a line which was kept 200 yards in advance of that of the 18-pdrs. This barrage, it will be remembered, was not entirely satisfactory,† but, in fairness to the gunners, it must be borne in mind that all their guns were in the open, that there had been practically no time in which to carry out registration, and that the facilities for observation of fire were very poor.

* *See* Vol. I, p. 293.
† *See* Vol. I, p. 312.

When the troops of the 2nd Guards Bde. were compelled to withdraw to their original positions, the batteries harassed the high ground east and north-east of Bourlon Wood and Fontaine-Notre-Dame, and continued to do so throughout the 28th of November.* On the 29th, when the infantry of the Guards Division was relieved by the 59th Division, the same artillery brigades as had covered the Guards Division remained in the line and the command was still retained by the C.R.A., Guards Division.

At 6.30 a.m. that day the enemy put down a heavy artillery barrage on, and in rear of, the British front line in the Bourlon Wood area, and all batteries were called upon to fire on their S.O.S. lines for an hour, after which harassing fire on the enemy's positions was resumed and kept up for the remainder of the day.

On the 30th of November, the day of their great counter-attack on the two flanks of the Cambrai salient, the Germans began their assault in the Bourlon Wood area at 9 o'clock in the morning after a very severe artillery bombardment. Their infantry, advancing in dense formation, attacked in great strength and suffered terrible casualties, but for a time, nevertheless, the situation on this part of the front was precarious owing to the swift progress made by the enemy on the front between Masnières and Vendhuille. All the batteries under the command of the C.R.A., Guards Division, therefore, made arrangements to withdraw at short notice should the necessity arise. Luckily, no such retirement was found necessary; for, although some temporary success was achieved by the enemy, the defence of the northern sector of the British line held firm,† while farther to the south the prompt and effective counter-attack of the Guards at Gouzeaucourt checked the German advance. The batteries

* Losses to battery *personnel* during the 27th–28th of November were surprisingly few considering the exposed positions of the guns.

† "In the north he (the enemy) practically had no success at all, for though he pierced our line for a second he was immediately driven out. The gunners say that they could fire into the brown, it was not necessary to select targets, the enemy formations being so dense; in fact it was like the early days of the war when they attacked arm-in-arm." *See* "The Press and the General Staff," by Neville Lytton, pp. 131, 132.

of the Guards Division were withdrawn from the line as darkness set in on the evening of the 30th of November, and the following day the C.R.A., Guards Division, relinquished the command of the gunners on this part of the front, taking over the control of the artillery which was covering the line held by the Guards from the north-east corner of Gauche Wood to the northern outskirts of Gonnelieu.*

On leaving the Bourlon Wood area, the 74th Bde., R.F.A., moved to positions just south of Flesquières, where they remained for the next few days ready to open fire on the enemy should he succeed in breaking through the northern sector of the line.† The 75th Bde., R.F.A., went into action on the 1st of December in the neighbourhood of Heudecourt, where it formed part of the right artillery group.

On the 4th of December the guns of the 74th Bde. were swung round in order to cover Marcoing, the orders to the battery commanders being to put down a barrage west of that village should the Germans succeed in breaking their way through the British line. The evacuation of the positions, which had been gained during the Cambrai offensive north of the Flesquières ridge, began on the night of the 4th, and was completed by the 7th of December.‡ The following day the 74th Bde. withdrew to positions immediately south of Havrincourt, whence harassing fire was opened and continued until the 15th of December when the guns were handed over in position to the 298th Bde., R.F.A., and the *personnel* of the batteries went back to Montenescourt for a well-earned rest.

* During the fighting on the 30th of November about 350 rounds was fired by each gun in the Guards Division batteries, practically no ammunition being left at the gun-positions when the brigades went out of action. Between the 25th of November and the end of the month the D.A.C., Guards Division, handled over 54,000 rounds of ammunition. The Column detached 17 wagons to supply S.A.A. to the Guards brigades for the attack on Gouzeaucourt.

† Just before this brigade was withdrawn from the line the commanding officer of A/74, Major Blathwayt, was killed and two other officers wounded.

‡ Before their withdrawal from the line the batteries of the 74th Bde. were in positions within 1,100 yards of the front line.

Meanwhile, activity on the southern sector of the line was dying down after the attack on Gonnelieu and the Quentin ridge by the Guards on the 1st of December. But, on the 2nd, during the course of the afternoon, the cavalry in the trenches on the right of the Guards, sent up the S.O.S. and the batteries of the 75th Bde., R.F.A., at once put down a barrage on the Villers-Guislain—Gonnelieu road, where the enemy was reported to be massing. If a counter-attack had been intended, its development was effectually checked.

When the infantry of the Guards Division was relieved in the line on the 6th of December, the 75th Bde., R.F.A., came under the orders of the 9th Division, and a programme of steady shooting on specified areas was carried out. On the 13th of December the relief of the Brigade, which had begun the previous day, was completed and the batteries moved back to Habarcq.*

(10) WORK OF THE DIVISIONAL R.E. AND 4TH BN. COLD-
STREAM GUARDS (PIONEERS) DURING THE CAMBRAI
OPERATIONS.

The story of the Field Companies, R.E., and the 4th Bn. Coldstream Guards (Pioneers) during the Cambrai offensive has little to do with that of the infantry of the Guards Division. It is a story of incessant and hard manual work, well carried out in most trying conditions.

The 4th Bn. Coldstream Guards was at Doignies on the 23rd of November, and was allotted the task of clearing of obstruction a section of the Canal du Nord. A party of 300 men was employed on this work for three days, whilst other

* During the Cambrai offensive the D.A.C., Guards Division, in addition to its other activities, supplied many wagons for work with the Field Companies, R.E. On the 4th of December No. 2 Section, which was attached to the 74th Bde., R.F.A., provided six teams and limbers to collect German guns in the recaptured area round Gouzeaucourt. This work continued for several days, and was extremely arduous. The camps of the D.A.C. in Havrincourt Wood were heavily shelled on the 8th and 9th of December, 7 men and 18 animals being killed or wounded.

parties belonging to the battalion mended the roads leading from the canal towards Flesquières. When the Guards went into the line on the night of the 24th of November all three Field Companies, R.E., assisted by detachments of the 4th Bn. Coldstream Guards (Pioneers), were used to keep the road from Trescault to La Justice fit for wheeled traffic. This road, it should be remembered, crossed the whole of the Hindenburg defensive system, and there was consequently much bridging work to be done in addition to the ordinary repairs.* This work was continued until the evening of the 29th of November, and was surprisingly little interfered with by the enemy's fire.

A fine electric lighting plant was found in the catacombs of Flesquières, and put in working order by the 75th Field Company, R.E., and to an officer belonging to the same company belongs the credit of the clearing and repairing of the German light railway which ran from Flesquières to Fontaine-Notre-Dame. This line was blocked by trucks, but two German tractors were found near Anneux and one of these was put into working order and used successfully to clear the line. This line proved of great value on the 27th of November for the evacuation of the wounded.

On the 30th of November every available sapper was called upon to work on the Flesquières defences and the task of constructing machine-gun emplacements and wiring continued incessantly until nightfall, when the three Field Companies were withdrawn to Trescault. The 4th Bn. Coldstream Guards (Pioneers) moved back to the vicinity of Lechelle the same day.

On the 1st of December, as soon as the Guards had established their position on the Gouzeaucourt front, the Field Companies and Pioneers set to work upon the construction of a reserve line. This work was continued until the 10th of December when the Field Companies and Pioneers rejoined their division. During these ten days they had constructed a front and support system of trenches, with the necessary wire, "T" heads and machine-gun emplacements, which extended not only behind the front actually

* A tank was employed to clear away wire where necessary.

A RESERVE LINE COMPLETED

held by the Guards, but also northward to the vicinity of Beaucamp and southward towards Heudecourt. Nearly the whole of this reserve line, which followed the high ground about midway between Gouzeaucourt Wood and Gouzeaucourt and thence stretched north and south, was completed and ready for defence by the 10th of December. Much of the work had to be done during the nights and their achievement was one of which the men might well be proud. In his report the C.R.E., Guards Division, mentions that one of the Field Companies dug, on an average, 130 cubic feet per man during one shift, and that the Pioneers did even better than this when digging one of the trenches.*

(11) CASUALTIES OF, AND RECORD OF PRISONERS TAKEN BY, THE GUARDS BETWEEN THE 25TH OF NOVEMBER AND 6TH OF DECEMBER.

The losses suffered by the Guards during the battle of Cambrai, as set out in the table below, were naturally very heavy. Both the attacks in which they were called upon to take part were soldiers' battles, carried out hurriedly and with little or no effective artillery preparation. In both cases, too, the ground over which the infantry had to advance was under the direct observation of the enemy's artillery and machine guns and lacking in cover. That the division came through its trying ordeal with so much credit was almost entirely due to the self-sacrificing gallantry and prompt initiative of its regimental officers, and to the splendid discipline and dogged determination displayed by all ranks.

* *See* W.D., Guards Division, December, 1917. The normal task in easy soil is laid down as 80 cubic feet. In a report to the XVII Corps, dated the 14th of December, Major-General Feilding says of the 4th Bn. Coldstream Guards (Pioneers) and the Field Companies, R.E.: "Considering that they have not had a rest since June 16th (the date on which the Guards took over the Boesinghe sector before the Ypres offensive) I am of opinion that they should have a rest of not less than 14 days." *See* W.D., Guards Division, December, 1917, App. 625.

Those who fell did not die in vain, for they had magnificently maintained the tradition of their regiments.*

The nature of the fighting in which the Guards were engaged on the 27th and 30th of November and the 1st of December precluded any chance of the capture of a large number of prisoners. At Fontaine-Notre-Dame the 2nd Guards Bde. was too weak in numbers even to retain possession of many of the prisoners who had surrendered to it, whilst in the fighting at Gouzeaucourt the Germans retreated so quickly after the battalions of the 1st Guards Bde. had entered the village, that few remained to be captured. The total return of prisoners taken by the division during the operations of Cambrai amounted to 13 officers and 743 other ranks, while the German war material captured included three 77-mm. guns, as well as 5 others destroyed in Fontaine-Notre-Dame, 66 machine guns and 1 heavy trench mortar. In addition to these captures, it will be remembered that at Gouzeaucourt the Guards recaptured many British guns which had fallen into the hands of the enemy.

* The casualties of the division between the 25th of November and the 6th of December were as follows :—

1st Guards Bde.	Officers 44	Other ranks	820
2nd Guards Bde.	,, 40	,,	1,136
3rd Guards Bde.	,, 34	,,	928
Divisional Artillery	,, 4	,,	49
Royal Engineers	,, 2	,,	10
R.A.M.C.	,, 1	,,	19
4th Guards M.-G. Coy.	,, —	,,	4
Total	125		2,966

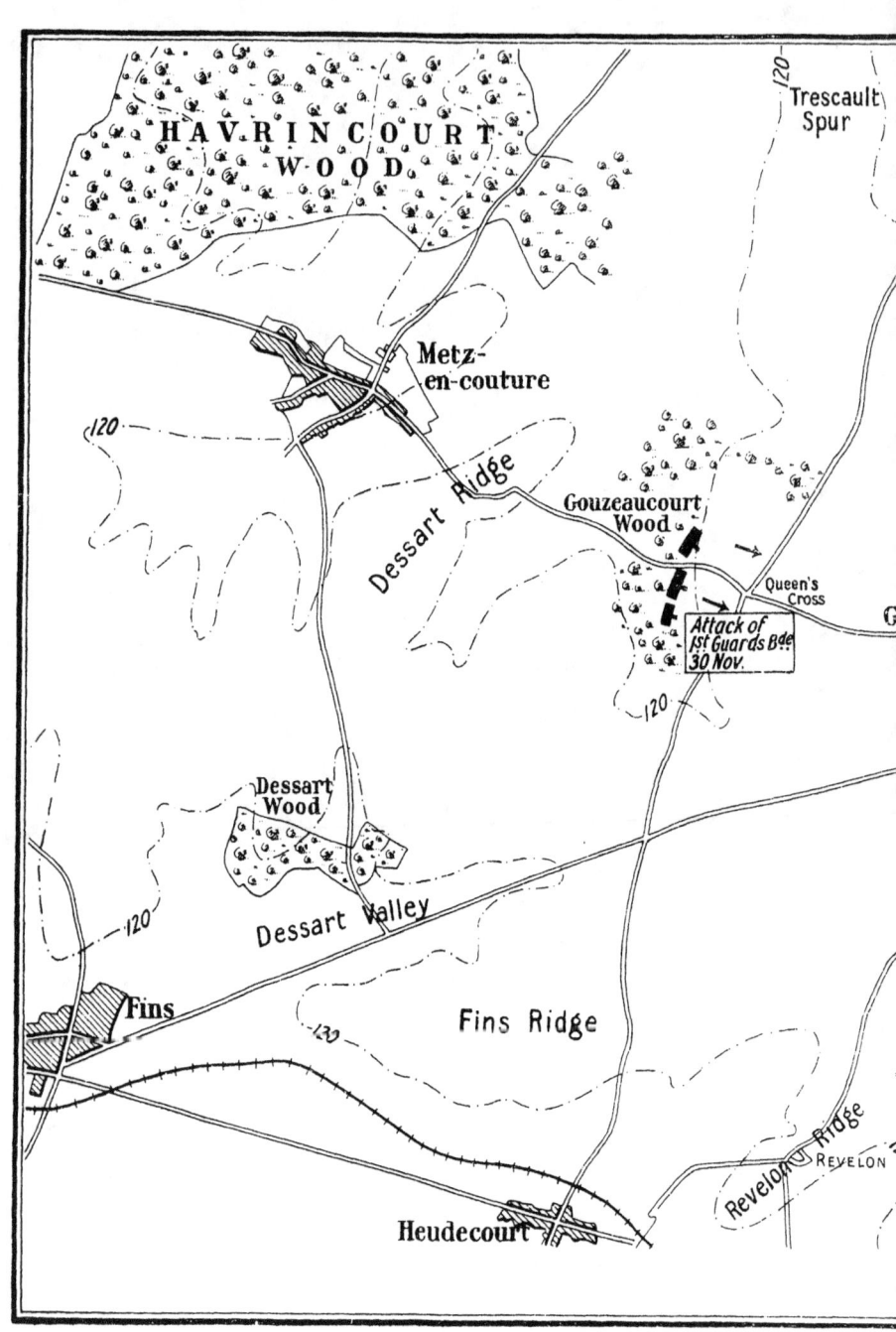

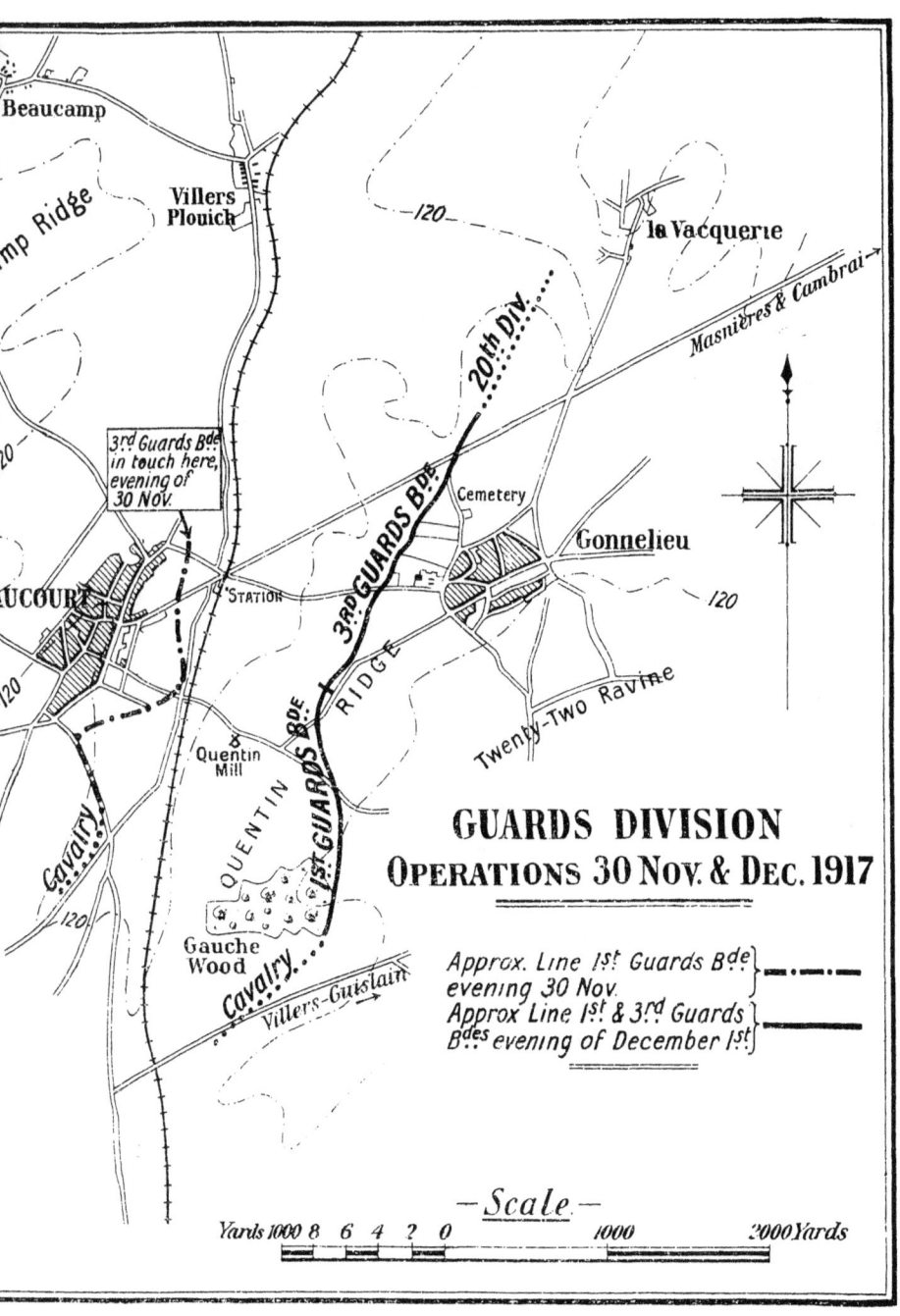

CHAPTER XII

THE WINTER OF 1917-1918—THE GUARDS IN THE ARRAS SECTOR OF THE LINE—FORMATION OF THE 4TH GUARDS BRIGADE (31ST DIVISION).

(1) THE GUARDS IN REST BILLETS IN THE ARRAS AREA—POLICY FOR THE WINTER MONTHS.

SHORTLY after leaving the Cambrai front, the Guards were attached to the XVII Corps (Lieut.-General Sir Charles Fergusson) and spent the remainder of the month of December resting and training in the area in and round Arras.* The casualties amongst instructors and trained soldiers had been exceptionally heavy during the Cambrai operations, and these repeated losses amongst experienced non-commissioned officers and men, following so soon after the losses in the Ypres offensive, proved a severe strain even for the Guards—a fact which Major-General Feilding pointed out in a report to the III Corps dated the 8th of December. He stated that the constant reorganizing of the *personnel* of

* Divisional headquarters was moved from Fosseux to Arras on the 12th of December. The 1st Guards Bde. was billetted in Berneville; the 2nd Guards Bde. in and round Simencourt; and the 3rd Guards Bde. in Arras and Dainville. The 4th Bn. Coldstream Guards (Pioneers) was moved by rail from Ytres to the Fosseux area on the 10th of December on which day also the Field Companies, R.E., rejoined the division. The divisional Artillery, on its withdrawal from the Cambrai front on the 14th of December, was billetted in and round Beaulencourt, and the trench-mortar batteries on their return from Moyenneville, where they had been training, were accommodated at Duisans. The Reinforcement Bn., which had been quartered at Bus-les-Artois, was moved by train to Arras on the 15th of December and thence marched to a camp at Agnez-les-Duisans. The remaining units of the division were billetted in Arras and its environs, the divisional Train taking over its winter horse-lines at Baudimont on the 29th of December.

companies rendered necessary during the operations scarcely made for efficiency, and, with his usual frankness, gave it as his opinion that the level of training in the division for the time being could not be considered a high one.*

The period of rest now allowed to the Guards before they were again sent into the line was not a long one, but in the few weeks at their disposal commanding officers and company commanders were able to supervise the reorganization and refitment of their battalions and companies, as well as to see to the general welfare and comfort of their men and to make arrangements for a fitting celebration of Christmas. The Third Army seized the occasion of this anniversary to inquire anxiously whether the desirability of peace was being seriously discussed by the troops, to which a reply was sent by the Guards Division to the effect that there was no more peace talk than there had been the year before.†

The weather at the close of 1917 was bitterly cold, but, except for some occasional snowstorms, it was generally fine and the time passed quickly, as all periods of time out of the line invariably seemed to pass, amid the usual routine of work and play. Cleaning up, refitting, drill and football were the order of the day. During these weeks in the Arras area the divisional Signal Company established a Signalling School at Agnez-les-Duisans, which was kept in being when the division again went into the line as the instruction given at the school was mainly intended for the training of the men in the Reinforcement Battalion. The Signal Company at this time was also employed in the task of tracing out and putting in order the telephone lines laid in the sewers of Arras—a piece of work which was to prove of value during the next few months.

Major-General Feilding soon after the Division joined the XVII Corps had been informed that it was to relieve the 15th Division in the line early in the New Year. In view of the altered situation of the Allied forces caused by the total collapse of the Russians and the German-Austrian successful campaign in Italy, a defensive policy on the Western

* *See* W.D., Guards Division, App. 618, December, 1917.
† *See* W.D., 2nd Guards Bde., December, 1917.

POLICY FOR THE WINTER 25

Front was now inevitable. But the Major-General emphasized the importance of an active defence in order to maintain the self-confidence of the troops whilst in the front line. He also pointed out that a hostile attack in force was almost certain in the near future now that the enemy could make use of so many divisions released from their Eastern Front, and that such an attack would probably be launched with little or no preliminary advertisement. He impressed upon his subordinate commanders, therefore, the urgent importance of keeping a close watch upon the enemy's movements so that as much warning as possible might be obtained of the coming blow. At the same time, he made it clearly understood that whenever a raid was considered advisable it must be properly prepared and organized, and that it was his wish that the troops, both artillery and infantry, should be given as much rest as could be arranged for them during the winter months.*

(2) RELIEF OF THE 15TH DIVISION NORTH AND SOUTH OF THE SCARPE—DESCRIPTION OF THE NEW LINE.

On the 1st of January, 1918, the 3rd Guards Bde. moved forward from Arras and relieved the 46th Infantry Bde. in the left sector of the front held by the 15th Division.† The following night the 2nd Guards Bde., which had already moved into Arras, took over the right sector of the line. Both these reliefs were carried out without any interruption from the enemy, and, by an early hour on the 3rd of January, the command of the left divisional sector of the XVII Corps front had been transferred to Major-General Feilding. The 1st Guards Bde. remained in Arras in divisional reserve.

The divisional Artillery went into the line on the 3rd of

* For Major-General Feilding's outline of policy for the winter 1917–1918, see W.D., Guards Division, Apps. 641 and 645, December, 1917.
† A few days before the Guards went into the line—on the 24th of December—Lieut.-Colonel the Honble. A. Hore-Ruthven vacated his appointment as G.S.O.1 upon his promotion to be B.G.G.S. VII Corps. Lieut.-Colonel R. MacClintock, R.E., succeeded him as G.S.O.1 of the Guards Division.

January, where it took over the guns of the 15th Division covering the front now held by the Guards Division.

The sector of the British line in which the Guards now found themselves marked the farthest limit of the advance made during the battle of Arras. It extended northward from a point slightly north-east of Monchy-le-Preux to a point about 500 yards from the south-eastern outskirts of Gavrelle—a front of rather more than 5,000 yards. It was divided into two distinct parts by the Scarpe owing to the fact that that river was unfordable and bordered by wide lagoons. South of the river the front of the divisional area was situated in low-lying ground, and, although machine guns in position north of the stream could play an important rôle in the defence of the southern sector of the line, its security in the event of a hostile attack on a large scale really depended upon the retention by the defenders of the more commanding positions round the village of Monchy which lay in the area of the right division of the XVII Corps south of the Guards.

North of the Scarpe the front line was sited about 1,000 yards more to the east than it was south of the river, and ran in a northerly direction, along the western slopes of Greenland Hill. From their trenches some distance higher up on this same hill the Germans could look down upon the Guards defences in this part of the line, but on the British front the little detached hill, lying between the Arras—Douai railway line and the Scarpe, on which stood Mount Pleasant Wood afforded excellent observation, besides forming a tactical feature of considerable importance in the defence of the sector. Distant observation of some of the enemy's positions, too, could be obtained from the high ground west of the Fampoux—Gavrelle road, although the country round Plouvain was hidden from view.

The plan laid down for the defence of the British line at this period in the war—a plan largely based on the defensive methods employed by the Germans in the Ypres operations—provided for (1) a forward zone or outpost line to be held by a limited number of troops whose task was to hold on as long as possible in order to break down the impetus of a

THE DEFENCES IN THE SCARPE SECTOR 27

hostile attack in force; (2) a main line of resistance on which the battle was to be contested; and (3) a rear zone in which the reserves were to concentrate and to which the defenders could withdraw in the last resort.*

The main line of resistance in this defensive organization was usually fixed some distance in rear of the forward zone, well out of reach of the enemy's preliminary bombardment, the idea being that, by the time a hostile attack succeeded in penetrating so far, the attacking troops would have lost cohesion and would be less able consequently to resist an organized counter-attack, whilst at the same time they would have lost the protection of a great number of their guns.

The line north-east and east of Arras when the Guards went into it did not in many respects meet the requirements of this new system of defence in depth. South of the Scarpe the forward zone and the main line of resistance had perforce to coincide, as it was not considered possible to give ground on this part of the front. North of the river the two zones were clearly defined, these being an outpost line, consisting of a system of front and support trenches, and a main line of resistance from 800 to 1,000 yards in rear, the front edge of which included Mount Pleasant Wood and thence stretched northward to meet the battle zone of the XIII Corps west of Gavrelle. But both north and south of the river the trenches had not been laid out to the best tactical advantage and they also required an immense amount of labour spent on them. They had been hastily and unsystematically constructed during and after the Arras fighting earlier in the year, and were not designed as a permanent line of defence or to withstand the climatic conditions in winter. The Guards, therefore, were called upon to work very hard during their occupation of this sector of the line, for the British Army had once again assumed a defensive rôle and the time available for the strengthening of the front was all too short in view of the coming German onslaught. But, notwithstanding its many disadvantages, there were countervailing

* A division in the line was not responsible for the defence of the the rear zone.

advantages in this sector which appealed to all ranks. When reliefs had to be carried out, for instance, the incoming and outgoing battalions were saved much marching as there was a Decauville railway line in use between Arras and Fampoux, while rations could be conveyed up the river in barges.* Hot meals, too, could easily be taken to the front line as there was a large kitchen in the caves at Rœux, in which later on drying rooms were fitted up. And, in addition to these amenities, Arras, which at this time had been comparatively little damaged by the enemy's artillery, provided comfortable billets and the cheerful town surroundings so dear to the heart of the British soldier after a spell in the trenches.

(3) Three months of Trench Warfare.

During the first fortnight of the occupation by the Guards of their new front the enemy lay very low, and, except for the intermittent activity of his trench mortars and the occasional bursts of gas-shelling on both banks of the Scarpe, little occurred to disturb the equanimity of the troops in the line who worked steadily upon the improvement of their defences. This period of peace was all to the advantage of the Guards as a sudden thaw set in about the 10th of January, and, although it did not last long and was succeeded by a spell of fine weather, its effect upon the trenches in the divisional area was catastrophic. Few of them had been revetted, and they simply crumbled away under the rain, sometimes collapsing so suddenly and completely that their occupants had to be dug out. So wholesale, indeed, was the havoc wrought by the weather that it was found necessary considerably to reduce the number of men in the front line and to hold it by a chain of sentry posts, while, for the time being, the use of communication trenches had to be entirely abandoned.† Mercifully, the Germans were in the same

---

* *See* W.D., Guards Division, " Q," January, 1918.

† In commenting upon the unpleasant condition of the line at this time the writer of the War Diary of the 2nd Bn. Scots Guards somewhat sarcastically remarks that " if our predecessors had not been so

plight, and their working parties, which could be plainly seen, were several times successfully engaged by the divisional Artillery. When the weather improved towards the latter part of January the enemy's patrols began to display some activity and several prisoners, all belonging to the 236th Division, were captured by the Guards. Hostile trench-mortar fire also increased considerably, and special arrangements were made by the artillery and trench-mortar batteries to deal with it. This preparation by the enemy's trench mortars turned out to be the preliminary to an attempt by the Germans to raid the divisional front. At 2.45 a.m. on the 29th of January a heavy hostile bombardment, which appeared to extend southward as far as Guemappe two and a half miles away, was opened by all calibres of guns on the sector of the line held by the 3rd Guards Bde. south of the Scarpe. At 3.10 a.m. this barrage was lifted and a body of the enemy's infantry, about 50 strong, belonging to the storm troops of the 24th Division, attempted to rush a post held by a non-commissioned officer and six men of the 1st Bn. Grenadier Guards. The raiders managed to cut a path through the wire, but were driven off by the Lewis-gun and rifle fire of the various posts in the vicinity. A patrol was then sent forward which collected two prisoners of whom one only could be brought back alive.*

At the beginning of February a reorganization of the line was rendered necessary owing to the reduction in the strength of the division caused by the formation of the 4th Guards Bde. and its transference to the 31st Division.† The 4th Bn. Grenadier Guards, the 3rd Bn. Coldstream Guards and

---

ambitious when they dug 36 miles of trenches in a 5,000 yards divisional front without revetting any, this *débacle* might not have occurred." See W.D., 2nd Bn. Scots Guards, January, 1918.

* During the month of January the 1st Guards Bde. lost 2 officers and 95 other ranks. Of these 24 of the other ranks were the victims of mustard gas shelling while waiting for the train at Fampoux after being relieved in the line. They belonged to the 2nd Bn. Grenadier Guards. The 2nd Guards Bde. reported 1 officer and 30 other ranks as casualties during the same period of time, and the 3rd Guards Bde., 1 officer and 62 other ranks.

† For the reasons which led to the reduction in strength of infantry brigades, *see* note, p. 37.

the 2nd Bn. Irish Guards were withdrawn from the division to form the new brigade under the command of Brig.-General Lord Ardee. The loss of a battalion from each brigade made it impossible to continue the policy of keeping one brigade always in divisional reserve and henceforward the front was held with all three brigades in the line—the 3rd Guards Bde. on the right, the 1st Guards Bde. in the centre astride the Arras—Douai railway line, the 2nd Guards Bde. on the left. Each brigade had one battalion in the front trenches, one in support positions and one in reserve in Arras. Each battalion now did, in turn, four days in the line, four days in support and four days in reserve.

The Household Battalion was also disbanded about this time and a draft from it was sent to reinforce the 1st Bn. Irish Guards—an official recognition regretfully noticed in the battalion War Diary that even the Irish Guards could no longer be kept up to strength by recruits from Ireland.*

On the 9th and 10th of February a further reorganization of the front took place which considerably simplified the defence of the sector. A brigade of the 15th Division took over the line south of the Scarpe, thus enabling the 3rd Guards Bde. to relieve the 1st Guards Bde. of about 600 yards of its front.

By this time the trenches had been much improved, and the divisional sector was beginning to be in reality and no longer in theory an area defended in depth.† When once the whole trench system had been remodelled and largely reconstructed, the main exertions of the three Guards brigades were turned to the construction of defensive localities between the forward zone and the main line of resistance. From right to left of the line these strong points were formed in the village of Rœux, Rœux Château,

---

* See W.D., 1st Bn. Irish Guards, February, 1918.

† On the 9th of February the War Diary of the 1st Guards Bde. records that it was at last possible to walk round the brigade front in daylight without being exposed to rifle or machine-gun fire. The approximate trench strength per company in the brigade at this time is given as :—2nd Bn. Grenadier Guards, 140 ; 2nd Bn. Coldstream Guards, 150 ; 1st Bn. Irish Guards, 90. See W.D., 1st Guards Bde., February, 1918.

the Chemical Works and the inn on the Rœux—Gavrelle road.

From the middle of February onwards the Guards patrols became more than usually active, as in view of the enemy's threatened offensive it was now of vital importance to obtain identifications and to keep the higher authorities constantly informed of the enemy's " Order of Battle " on the divisional front. About this period the Germans had again become very inactive, but, at 5 a.m. on the 21st of February, one of their patrols showed a little more enterprise and approached a post held by the 1st Bn. Scots Guards. It was fired on and hastily retired, leaving behind four of its number who were made prisoners. Their capture identified the presence of the 5th Bavarian Reserve Division, which, the prisoners stated, had relieved the 236th Division a few days previously. On the 23rd of February the Welsh Guards captured two more Bavarians who confirmed this information. They also stated that the battalions in their division were very strong as large drafts had recently arrived from Russia, and that tanks were to be employed by the enemy on the Scarpe front.* This latter information, however, was contradicted by prisoners captured on the night of the 27th–28th of February. On that night the 1st Bn. Coldstream Guards carried out an organized raid under an artillery barrage. The attack was an unqualified success. The enemy was completely surprised and the raiders succeeded in rushing one of his machine-gun posts before the gun could be brought into action. After a short fight the garrison of the trench surrendered, and 11 prisoners, belonging to the 5th Bavarian

* See W.D., Guards Division, App. 726, February, 1918. On the 11th of January Major-General Feilding, who anticipated the possible employment of tanks by the Germans in this sector of the line, had sent a memorandum to the XVII Corps, in which he pointed out that he did not consider that the two 18-pdr. guns already in position between the Gavrelle road and Fampoux were sufficient for the anti-tank defence, while they were required for the purposes of the ordinary artillery protection of the line. He suggested that pom-poms, 6-pdrs., 3-pdrs., or French 38-mm. guns would be better suited for anti-tank work, or, if they could not be provided, he asked that two male tanks might be detailed for the purpose. See W.D., Guards Division, App. 657, January, 1918.

Reserve Division,* and 1 machine gun were brought back by the Coldstream, who themselves had no casualties until they were once again in their own line when three of them were killed and one wounded by a shell which unluckily fell into a communication trench. The planning and execution of this raid were alike excellent. The enemy's wire was perfectly cut and the artillery, trench-mortar and machine-gun barrage was most effective.†

At the beginning of March the Guards Machine-Gun Regiment came into being,‡ the command of which was given to Major R. C. Bingham, Coldstream Guards. The machine-gun companies, however, remained in the line where they formed an important factor in the defensive organization of the fortified localities in the area behind the forward zone.

With the advent of March, too, the raiding and patrolling activities of the Guards still further increased. It was known that the beginning of the long expected German offensive was now only a matter of days and the troops were on the *qui vive* in readiness to resist the coming assault. The enemy was kept under the closest observation night and day and his movements were harassed as much as possible.

On the night of the 5th–6th of March, the 2nd Bn. Grenadier Guards carried out a carefully planned raid with the assistance of the gunners. Several Germans were bayoneted, a machine gun was captured, two dug-outs were bombed and two prisoners, belonging to the 19th Bavarian Regiment, were brought back by the raiding party which

---

* *See* W.D., Guards Division, App. 734, February, 1918. Most of these prisoners were quite young boys or men who had been called up from civil occupations. Their moral was bad. They knew little about their own front or about what was going on in rear. They had heard nothing about a coming offensive or the employment of tanks.

† During the month of February the losses in the division were principally due to the enemy's gas-shelling which was very severe. The 2nd Guards Bde. had 91 men gassed out of a total of 127 casualties. In the 1st Guards Bde. there were 69 casualties, but only 4 men were killed. The losses in the 3rd Guards Bde. amounted to 59.

‡ The establishment of the regiment was 52 officers and 774 other ranks with 217 animals and 60 vehicles. *See* Appendix VI.

A FALSE ALARM

had no casualties.* On the night of the 9th–10th of March the 1st Bn. Welsh Guards raided the enemy's line, but this attack was not attended with so much success. The Germans, who were anticipating the visit, adopted the policy of retiring a short distance behind their front line and then attacked the raiders with bombs. After some hard fighting the Welsh Guards withdrew, having captured a prisoner. On their way back to their own line they came under the fire of the enemy's machine guns and 1 officer and 12 other ranks became casualties. The utmost gallantry was displayed in bringing in the wounded.†

Reports now reached divisional headquarters, founded on statements made by prisoners captured on the Cambrai front, that a German attack on a large scale had been timed to take place on the Scarpe front on the 13th of March. Although the most vigilant patrolling failed to disclose any signs of such an operation being prepared by the enemy opposite the Guards, every possible precaution was taken by the divisional staff to be in readiness for the offensive. The reserve battalion of each brigade was moved forward from Arras, the bridges over the Scarpe and the caves at Rœux were prepared for demolition should occasion arise, and the artillery bombarded the enemy's lines and the approaches to them on the night of the 12th of March and again on the following night. The 13th of March was an exceptionally quiet day and there were no indications of the much talked about attack before the relief of the Guards Division began on the night of the 19th. The relief was successfully completed on the morning of the 21st of March when Major-General Feilding handed over the command of the sector to the G.O.C. the 4th Division, the Guards being concentrated in Arras and Berneville as XVII Corps reserve.‡

---

* *See* W.D., Guards Division, App. 740, March, 1918.
† *See* W.D., Guards Division, App. 745, March, 1918.
‡ During the month of March to the date of this relief the casualties in the three Guards brigades amounted to 3 officers and 170 other ranks.

(4) Work of the Divisional R.E. and 4th Bn. Coldstream Guards (Pioneers) on the Scarpe front.

The Field Companies, R.E., and the 4th Bn. Coldstream Guards (Pioneers) went into the line at the end of December shortly before the infantry of the division.* When they first arrived in the area the frost-bound condition of the chalky ground made any kind of work exceedingly difficult, and, during the period of thaw which followed, the task of renovating and revetting the trenches became even harder. But, nevertheless, an immense amount of work was actually accomplished. New trenches were dug and vast quantities of wire were laid,† fortified localities were constructed, a big dressing station was erected at the Triple Arch bridge where the railway line crossed the river south-east of Fampoux, the roads and tramway lines throughout the divisional area were repaired and kept in order, gas curtains for the dug-outs were supplied and inspected by the R.E., much screening and camouflage work was put up and a water supply system installed. Assistance was also given to the New Zealand Tunnelling Company which was working in the sector.

But the urgent and special preparations, which had to be made to meet the coming German attack, naturally delayed the ordinary routine work in the line and throughout the whole of the divisional area. Towards the middle of January these preparations began in earnest. All the trees on Mount Pleasant—over a hundred in number—were either cut down or blown up. Arrangements for the demolition of the bridges over the Scarpe were put in hand about the middle of February, and, by about the 10th of March, charges of gun cotton had been placed in position under the bridges

---

* In February, 1918, pioneer battalions throughout the Army in France were reduced to three companies. The 4th Bn. Coldstream Guards conformed with this new regulation by absorbing its 4th company into the three other companies.

† During the months of January and February the 55th Field Company estimated that it had put out about 6 miles of wire (low) 9 feet in width, and dug a mile of trenches 6 feet deep, 6 feet wide at the top and 2 feet wide at the bottom.

PREPARATIONS FOR GERMAN ATTACK

over the river in the forward area. From the 12th to the 14th of March a party of sappers with an officer was posted at each bridge ready to blow the charge as soon as the order was received. Meanwhile, a pontoon and the materials required for carrying a bridge over the Scarpe west of Fampoux had been brought up in readiness for any eventuality. Both the R.E. and the 4th Bn. Coldstream Guards (Pioneers) remained in the line under the orders of the 4th Division until the 22nd of March when they rejoined the Guards.

(5) Work of the Divisional Artillery and Trench-Mortar Batteries during the Winter Months.

The divisional Artillery was divided into two groups. The right group was formed by the 75th Bde., R.F.A., with three batteries in positions round Feuchy and Fampoux, and one battery farther to the right in a position south-east of Broken Mill. The 74th Bde., R.F.A., with its batteries in positions on the high ground north of the Scarpe,* together with an 18-pdr. battery belonging to another division temporarily attached to it, formed the left group. The two Guards Bdes., R.F.A., took over the guns of the outgoing brigades of the 15th Division.

The artillery at the disposal of the Guards Division was not strong enough to enable each brigade to have permanent S.O.S. lines. Alternative lines, therefore, were given to the gunners according to the part of the front on which artillery assistance might be required. The usual programme of shooting incidental to trench warfare was regularly carried out during these months. Hostile machine guns and trench mortars which were a cause of annoyance to the infantry were destroyed; wire was cut and the gaps kept open; the enemy's communications were subjected to harassing fire whenever a relief was suspected and his working parties were constantly engaged.

But the main task of the gunners, like that of other units

---

* Excellent observation was available from an O.P. within 1,000 yards of all the batteries of the 74th Bde. over the whole of the enemy's front as far back as Vitry. Each battery had a silent position in addition to its active one.

in the division, was that of preparing for the German offensive. Arrangements for the close defence of battery positions, the digging and wiring of alternative and reinforcing positions and the construction of new positions for the artillery defence of the main line of resistance kept busy all the available artillery *personnel*.

The batteries belonging to the northern group were not much disturbed by the enemy, at any rate during their first weeks in the line, but those belonging to the southern group in the valley of the Scarpe were a good deal worried by the enemy's gas-shelling, which was very persistent throughout these months.

The barrages provided by the artillery in conjunction with the trench-mortar batteries and machine guns, gave the greatest satisfaction to the infantry, and in one of them—during the raid made by the 2nd Bn. Grenadier Guards on the 5th–6th of March—B/74, commanded by Major G. N. C. Martin, actually fired with complete accuracy the astonishing number of 18 rounds per gun in one minute.*

In February the 9·45 trench mortars and their R.G.A. *personnel* were transferred to " V " Heavy-Mortar Battery administered by the XVII Corps. " X " and " Y " T.M. Batteries, each of 6-in. mortars, remained with the Guards Division and were in action until the Guards left the line. Their principal task was the cutting of the enemy's wire—a task which they carried out with great efficiency.

The relief of the divisional Artillery was postponed in view of the expected German attack on the 13th of March, but, as this attack did not take place, orders were given for its relief by the artillery of the 4th Division on the 21st of March. At 1 a.m. that day an attack south of the Scarpe was anticipated and the 74th Bde., R.F.A., put down a protective barrage. The enemy opened his initial bombardment from south of Monchy to St. Quentin at 5.15 a.m. and his

* " The brigade (74th Bde. R.F.A.) received the warmest and most felicitous congratulations from the G.O.C. of each infantry brigade and from the C.O. 1st Coldstream Guards and the O.C. 2nd Grenadier Guards ; it may be said that the thanks of battalion commanders were so warm as to be almost embarrassing." Extract from the diary of Lieut.-Colonel C. Vickery, commanding 74th Bde., R.F.A.

infantry came forward to the attack about three hours later. The shelling, however, of the area occupied by the divisional Artillery was never very severe and died away towards midday, about which time orders were received for the relief to be carried out as speedily as possible. Two hours later the artillery of the 4th Division had taken over the command of the sector and half the Guards batteries had been safely withdrawn to Arras, the remainder following during the night of the 21st–22nd of March.

(6) FORMATION OF THE 4TH GUARDS BRIGADE.

As already stated in this narrative, the 4th Guards Bde. came into being in the early days of February,* and, on the 8th of that month, the 3rd Bn. Coldstream Guards bade a sad farewell to its comrades of the 1st Guards Bde. and marched out of Arras to join the 31st Division.† Its destination was Ecurie Wood Camp, west of Roclincourt, where the next day the battalion was inspected by its new divisional

---

* The staff of the new brigade was as follows :—Brig.-General Lord Ardee, Irish Guards, in command ; Captain O. Lyttelton, Grenadier Guards, brigade-major ; Captain E. D. Mackenzie, Scots Guards, staff captain ; 2nd Lieutenant D. L. Carnegie, R.E., signals officer. The 4th Bn. Grenadier Guards was commanded by Lieut.-Colonel W. S. Pilcher ; the 3rd Bn. Coldstream Guards, by Lieut.-Colonel F. Longueville ; the 2nd Bn. Irish Guards, by Lieut.-Colonel the Honble. H. R. Alexander.

† After the strenuous fighting and severe losses of 1917 it was deemed necessary by the War Cabinet, in view of the shortage in manpower, to reduce the establishment of an infantry brigade from four to three battalions. Each British division in France was thus called upon to relinquish three of its thirteen battalions ; as a general rule, these battalions were broken up and used as reinforcements for the remaining battalions of the regiments to which they belonged. But of the "surplus" Guards battalions a new brigade was formed. In their case, therefore, except for the severance from their own division, the change was not such a drastic one as with other less fortunate battalions. Nevertheless, as Sir Douglas Haig pointed out in his despatch of the 20th of July, 1918, the reduction in the strength of brigades was not conducive to military efficiency. "An unfamiliar grouping of units was introduced thereby, necessitating new methods of tactical handling of the troops and the discarding of old methods to which subordinate commanders had become accustomed." *See* "Sir Douglas Haig's Despatches," p. 179.

commander, Major-General R. J. Bridgford.* The 4th Guards Bde. took the place of the 94th Infantry Bde. the units of which were dispersed among other divisions, portions of its *personnel* and equipment being handed over to the Guards.†

On the 11th of February the 4th Bn. Grenadier Guards and the 2nd Bn. Irish Guards left the Guards Division, being played out of Arras by all the pipes and drums of the division,‡ and joined the 4th Guards Bde.§

A few days later Lieut.-General Congreve, commanding the XIII Corps, inspected the brigade which was still in reserve and carrying out training, although the 3rd Bn. Coldstream Guards had already been called upon to furnish large working parties for the burying of cable.

On the 17th of February the brigade relieved the 93rd Infantry Bde. in the right sector of the line held by the 31st Division, the three battalions being distributed in depth on a frontage of about 2,000 yards.

The Grenadiers took over the front line from the 18th Bn. Durham Light Infantry. It ran north-east, east and south-east of Arleux-en-Gohelle, and consisted of a series of posts, the derelict trenches between them being filled in with wire. The support positions between Bailleul and Willerval were well situated and comfortable. The relief was accomplished without incident, the troops going up by train almost as far as the support line.

---

* The 31st Division belonged at this time to the XIII Corps which held the right front of the First Army and was in the line on the immediate left of the XVII Corps, Third Army, to which the Guards Division then belonged.

† The 94th Signals Section joined Lord Ardee's headquarters on the 11th of February, and the 94th Machine-Gun Company and the 94th Trench-Mortar Battery (Stokes guns) were also attached to the 4th Guards Bde. as complete units.

‡ " I watched the 4th Battalion Grenadiers marching out to-day ... they were perfectly superb. The Irish Guards followed them— headed by ' Alex ' [Major H. R. Alexander], looking supreme. But as I looked at all the things that Eric [Lieut.-Colonel E. Greer] used to be so fond of—their drums and one or two things like that—I wept quite properly." Extract from a letter of Henry Dundas, Scots Guards.

§ The 4th Guards Bde. received its drafts from the Guards Reinforcement Bn. and all postings of officers were from the Guards Division.

The enemy held an irregular series of trenches opposite the brigade front and touch in consequence with the troops on the flanks could only be satisfactorily maintained by constant patrolling. The Germans appeared to be very inactive and unenterprising when the Guards first went into the line, but the Grenadiers were warned by the outgoing troops that a prisoner recently captured had stated that the presence of the Guards in the sector was already suspected, and that a raid for the purpose of obtaining an identification was being prepared by the enemy. All ranks, therefore, were very much on the alert, and, on the 19th of February, the expected blow came. At about 9 p.m. that day a heavy hostile artillery bombardment by all calibres of guns was directed on the forward posts held by the Grenadiers. The British artillery opened fire in response to the S.O.S. signal, but was not successful in checking the assault of the enemy's infantry, as, when the German barrage was lifted, a determined attack was made between the Fresnoy Park road and Fresnoy road by a party of about 60 picked men belonging to the 469th Regiment. Making their way down the front British trench from the left of the Guards line, the Germans first came in contact with a post of six Grenadiers commanded by a non-commissioned officer. This post, being greatly outnumbered, fell back in good order towards the right. Fierce hand to hand fighting then ensued both in the front line and also in a communication trench before the enemy was ejected from this part of the sector. Meanwhile, an equally vigorous struggle was taking place in a machine-gun post farther to the left in which the gun had been put out of action by a shell from one of the enemy's trench mortars. Eventually, the Germans were driven back all along the line without having obtained the identification which they came to seek—unless, indeed, the nature of their reception were a sufficient justification of their suspicions. They left 2 dead and 5 wounded behind them. Their raid had been well planned and was carried out with great daring and determination. Its failure can only be attributed to the gallantry and fine fighting qualities of the Grenadiers who displayed great eagerness to get to grips with their assailants and well deserved the congratulations which they received from the Third Army commander. The 4th Guards Bde. had made a good beginning.

The remainder of this tour in the line was devoid of any particular incident, but much work was done in the improvement of the defences which were considerably stronger when the Guards left the line than they had found them when they went in.*

On the 1st of March the 31st Division was relieved by the 62nd Division and the 4th Guards Bde., after handing over its sector of the line to the 187th Infantry Bde., was moved next day by train to the Tinques area east of St. Pol. The 31st Division was now in G.H.Q. Reserve and full advantage was taken by Lord Ardee of the opportunity afforded to him of training his battalions, although one of them was kept in the forward area for a short time to work on the Farbus—Bailleul line.

The 4th Guards Brigade was busily engaged in an open warfare scheme on the 21st of March—the day on which the bombardment began heralding the opening of the great German offensive.

* The casualties of the 4th Guards Bde. during its first month of existence amounted to 33.

CHAPTER XIII

THE GERMAN OFFENSIVE, 1918—EVENTS ON THE FRONT HELD BY THE GUARDS DIVISION AND THE 4TH GUARDS BRIGADE (31ST DIVISION) BETWEEN THE 21ST AND 31ST OF MARCH.

(1) OPENING DAYS OF THE GERMAN OFFENSIVE.

ON the 21st of March the long expected storm broke and sixty-four German divisions were hurled against the British line held by the Third and Fifth Armies on a front of approximately fifty-four miles. To oppose this gigantic attack in its initial stages the British Commander-in-Chief had available either in the line or in close reserve, twenty-nine infantry divisions and three cavalry divisions. For the defence of the front of the Third Army, with which this narrative is concerned, there were eight infantry divisions in the line, and seven, including the Guards Division, in reserve.*

In describing the doings of the Guards during the period between the opening of the offensive and the end of March, it seems to be the simplest and most convenient plan to set out the story of their movements and achievements in the form of a daily diary. These days were so much crowded with incident, so dramatic in their happenings, that no other

---

* See "Sir Douglas Haig's Despatches," p. 185. "Launched on a front of about fifty-four miles on the 21st March, the area of the German offensive spread northwards on the 28th March, until from La Fère to beyond Gavrelle some sixty-three miles of our former line was involved. On this front a total of seventy-three German divisions were engaged during March against the Third and Fifth Armies and the right of the First Army, and were opposed in the first place by twenty-two British infantry divisions in line, with twelve infantry divisions and three cavalry divisions in close reserve." *Ibid.*

way of dealing with them appears satisfactory, while this method has the additional advantage of making it possible to record the work of the 4th Guards Bde. at the same time, and in the same narrative, as that of the Guards Division, for the exigences of the situation brought the 31st Division into the line on the right of the Guards.

(2) THE GERMAN ATTACK ON THE FRONT OF THE VI CORPS, 21ST OF MARCH—THE 2ND GUARDS BRIGADE MOVED TO MERCATEL.

On the 21st of March the front held by the XVII Corps was not attacked by the enemy's infantry, but that held by the VI Corps, commanded by Lieut.-General Sir J. A. L. Haldane, in the Third Army area immediately to the south, did not escape so lightly. The 59th Division, which was holding the right sector of this corps front, was driven back with heavy losses to a line some distance west of Ecoust-St.-Mein,* with the result that the 34th Division, on its left, found its right flank seriously threatened by the enemy's troops who had broken through the British front near Bullecourt. This division succeeded in throwing back its exposed flank through Croisilles where, on the night of the 21st, it is reported to have been in touch with the left brigade of the 59th Division.

The 3rd Division, on the left of the VI Corps front, successfully resisted all the attacks made upon it during the day, but its right brigade was compelled to relinquish its front line positions and to form a defensive flank facing south-east.

Throughout the course of the day bad news and even more alarming rumours kept pouring into Arras, where the Guards continued to carry on their usual routine of training, although the shelling of the town by the enemy's high velocity guns proved somewhat disconcerting.

* This division suffered so severely during the day's fighting that it had to be withdrawn from the line during the night of the 21st–22nd of March. Its place was taken by the 40th Division, commanded by Major-General J. Ponsonby, which moved forward from reserve south-west of Arras.

THE 2ND GUARDS BDE. CALLED UPON 43

In the evening, orders were received for the 2nd Guards Bde., with the 4th Guards Bde. Machine-Gun Company, to proceed to Mercatel, a village about four miles south of Arras on the Bapaume road, where it was to come under the orders of the VI Corps commander. The brigade moved at once and reached its destination about 9 p.m., where it found some deserted huts in which the troops spent the night. Up to that time the only casualties sustained were due to the long distance shelling of Arras from which the 3rd Bn. Grenadier Guards had suffered more than the other battalions in the brigade.

(3) Continued Progress of the Enemy on the 22nd of March—Movements of the Guards Division.

In the morning on the 22nd of March the enemy renewed his attacks with great vigour on the front of the VI Corps, and, during the course of the day, met with a large measure of success. On the right he gained possession of Vaulx-Vraucourt, and, by means of strong pressure at the point of junction between the 40th and 34th Divisions, he succeeded in making himself master of St. Leger. He also captured the greater part of Henin Hill.*

During the morning, while the Guards Division was still waiting upon events, the precaution was taken of sending parties from the 1st and 3rd Guards Bdes. to reconnoitre the portion of the " third system " of defence, running west of Wancourt southward to the western outskirts of Henin-sur-Cojeul †—for it was now fully apparent that the German

---

* *See* VI Corps Narrative.

† It may be convenient here to set out briefly the various lines of defence which were constructed or in course of construction at this time and to which allusion is made in this narrative :—

The " front system "—the front line.
The " second system "—a line running east of Monchy-le-Preux and
    Guemappe—south-west along the Wancourt ridge, parallel
    with the Cojeul river to a point due east of Henin and due south
    of Wancourt—thence due south to a point east of Boyelles—
    thence south-east to Ecoust. In this system there were the
    following switches :—(i) from east of Henin to the vicinity of

attack was a formidable one, and that the successful continuance of the hostile pressure might necessitate a withdrawal by the Third Army to its rear lines of defence.

About noon a message reached Major-General Feilding stating that the German infantry was already on the high ground lying between Croisilles and Henin, and that the enemy's cavalry was reported to be advancing farther to the south. Very soon after the receipt of this news at divisional headquarters, the 2nd Guards Bde. was ordered by the VI Corps commander to move forward immediately in order to occupy the " third system " of defence from a point east of Boyelles to Henin, and, before 3 p.m., this brigade, which was commanded by Lieut.-Colonel Follett, Coldstream Guards,* was in position in the line—the 1st Bn. Scots Guards on the right and the 1st Bn. Coldstream Guards on the left, with the 3rd Bn. Grenadier Guards in support.

The situation had now become a somewhat serious one, for, although elements of the 34th Division were known still to be holding out in the " second system " of defence on the slopes of Henin Hill, the enemy's pressure was very great and it was obvious that at any moment the Germans might succeed in forcing back or in turning the line immediately in front of that held by the Guards. Towards evening this

> Heninel; (ii) from Ecoust towards Vraucourt; (iii) from Croisilles to St. Leger ; and (iv) from Noreuil towards Vraucourt.
>
> The " third system "—a line running half-way between Feuchy Chapel and Monchy-le-Preux—just west of Wancourt—south-west round the western outskirts of Henin-sur-Cojeul—thence about 800 yards east of Boiry-Becquerelle—thence south-east and round the east side of St. Leger—thence south-east in front of Vraucourt.
>
> The " Army line "—a line covering Tilloy—Neuville Vitasse—the eastern side of Mercatel—the eastern side of Boisleux-St.-Marc—the eastern side of Hamelincourt thence south-east to Mory Copse and thence east of Mory.

* Brig.-General Sergison-Brooke had been obliged temporarily to relinquish the command of the brigade owing to gas poisoning. " A great disaster—the Brigadier has had to go sick—gassed. He must have got a mouthful up in our last place, where it used to lie about for days. Anyway his voice went completely, and yesterday he got so bad that he had to go, though he said it would be only forty-eight hours—but I'm afraid it will be longer than that." *See* " Henry Dundas, Scots Guards, A Memoir," p. 211.

latter contingency happened. The enemy, after having been repeatedly driven back with heavy losses by the troops of the 3rd Division, at last contrived to find a gap on the right flank of that division, and promptly pushed forward some posts between it and the 34th Division. This movement led to a withdrawal by the troops of the latter division in front of the 2nd Guards Bde. and left the Guards confronting the German advance.

As soon as darkness set in, the 1st Bn. Coldstream Guards sent out patrols to gain touch with the enemy. They drew fire after advancing about 250 yards from the British line.*

Meanwhile, the battalions of the 3rd Guards Bde., with the 3rd Guards Bde. Machine-Gun Company, had been sent forward from Berneville in buses, and, early in the afternoon, had taken over the huts vacated by the 2nd Guards Bde. Orders had also been given to the Guards divisional Artillery to go into the line. The 75th Bde., R.F.A., accordingly moved from Arras in the evening to positions of observation at Beaurains, ready to fire east or south-east as the occasion might require. It was followed at 10 p.m. by the 74th Bde., R.F.A., which went to positions near Mercatel. Both brigades were instructed to go into action in support of the 3rd Division.

(4) WITHDRAWAL OF THE FRONT OF THE VI CORPS ON THE NIGHT OF THE 22ND–23RD OF MARCH—THE GUARDS DIVISION AND THE 4TH (GUARDS) BRIGADE (31ST DIVISION) IN THE LINE.

The steady progress made by the Germans during the course of the fighting on the 22nd of March made imperative a speedy withdrawal to the "third system" of defence by the VI Corps. The front which its troops were still occupying when darkness set in had become dangerously extended, and it was beyond the powers of the two divisions in the line— the 3rd and the 34th—which by this time had been much

* At this time the left flank of this battalion was entirely in the air and its position was by no means comfortable until some tanks appeared on the exposed flank. See W.D., 1st Bn. Coldstream Guards, March, 1918.

reduced in strength, to continue holding it against the steady and unremitting pressure of the enemy.

Orders were accordingly given for these two divisions to fall back, the 15th Division, the right division of the XVII Corps on the immediate left, being instructed to conform with this movement. No ground, however, was given up north of the Scarpe.

Advantage was also taken of the hours of darkness to relieve the remnants of the 34th Division by troops of the 31st Division who had been brought up from the Tinques area where, it will be remembered, the division was in G.H.Q. Reserve.

During the night, as soon as the 3rd Division began to withdraw its front to the "third system" of defence, the 3rd Guards Bde. moved forward from Mercatel, and went into the positions until then occupied by the 2nd Guards Bde.—the latter brigade side-slipping to the right.*

Major-General Feilding now assumed the command of the sector of the front held by the two Guards brigades and established his headquarters at Bretencourt, a few miles to the west of Mercatel.†

At 12.30 a.m. on the 23rd of March the 1st Guards Bde., with the remainder of the Guards Machine-Gun Regiment, went into occupation of the "Army line" between Hamelincourt and Boisleux-St.-Marc. Meanwhile, as already stated, the 31st Division had relieved the 34th Division in the line. The 4th (Guards) Bde. was the leading brigade of the division. Its battalions were brought up in buses from the Tinques area, passing through St. Pol under long distance German shell-fire, and thence through Frevent, Doullens and Blaireville to the battle area. The troops left their buses at the cross-roads north-west of Boisleux-St. Marc, and from that point made their way to their appointed positions in the line near St. Leger.‡

* When this movement was made, the 3rd Bn. Grenadier Guards relieved the 1st Bn. Coldstream Guards on the left of the line of the 2nd Guards Bde.

† See W.D., Guards Division, March, 1918.

‡ "On the 21st March they [the 2nd Bn. Irish Guards, 4th Guards Bde.] finished the finals in the Divisional sports—Tug-of-war and

(5) STEADY GERMAN PRESSURE BETWEEN MORY AND HENIN, 23RD OF MARCH.

At dawn on the 23rd of March, therefore, as a result of this rearrangement, the front of the VI Corps, which extended from a little north of Mory northward to Henin, was held from right to left by the 40th, 31st, Guards and 3rd Divisions. The 2nd and 3rd Guards Bdes. were holding the Guards divisional front which lay between Bank Copse just north of the Courcelles—Croisilles road and the southern outskirts of Henin, while the 1st Guards Bde. had two battalions disposed in support positions north-west of Boyelles and its remaining battalion—the 2nd Bn. Grenadier Guards—in reserve at Boiry-St.-Rictrude.*

The 4th Guards Bde. was holding the right sector of the 31st divisional front from a point on the Ervillers—St. Leger road about midway between the two villages to Judas Copse, where it was in touch with troops of the 34th Division who were still in the line as the 93rd Infantry Bde. (31st Division), which had been ordered to relieve them, had not yet arrived on the scene of action. The 4th Bn. Grenadier Guards was on the right and the 2nd Bn. Irish Guards on the

Boxing against the 15th West Yorkshires. At one o'clock in the morning came word that the Battalion would probably move by bus at eight directly into the battle which promised to be hot. As a matter of fact they and their Brigade found themselves on the outskirts of it almost as soon as they left billets. The enemy had begun a comprehensive shelling of all back-areas and they could hear the big stuff skying above them all round St. Pol. Their buses picked them up at St. Pol Frevent and headed for Beaumetz, where they were met by a member of the General Staff who explained the local situation so far as they had been able to overtake it. There was no accurate news, but any amount of rumour, none comforting." *See* "The Irish Guards in the Great War," vol. ii. pp. 191, 192.

* The excitement which prevailed behind the line at this time is well illustrated by a quotation from this battalion's War Diary—" many people seem to have taken leave of their senses, and not only have innumerable camps full of every kind of stores been incontinently abandoned, but in this village alone a large Expeditionary Force canteen has been set on fire with all its contents and a water reservoir supplying the surrounding districts has been blown up, though neither is in the slightest danger of immediate capture." *See* W.D., 2nd Bn. Grenadier Guards, March, 1918.

left of the front held by the 4th Guards Bde., the Sensée river—which at this time was practically dry in many places—being the dividing line between the two battalions. Each battalion had two companies in the front line and two in support in the "Army line" east of the Arras—Bapaume road, while the 3rd Bn. Coldstream Guards remained in reserve south-east of Hamelincourt.

During the course of the morning the 74th Bde., R.F.A., came under the orders of the Guards Division and moved into positions near the railway line north of Boisleux-au-Mont. The 75th Bde., R.F.A., which had moved to Mercatel, supported the 3rd Division throughout the day, but rejoined the Guards Division at nightfall.*

The brunt of the fighting on the front of the VI Corps on the 23rd of March fell upon the troops of the 40th Division, for, as St. Leger was already in their possession, the Germans were able to rush their batteries as far forward as Hally Copse, a position a little to the south of that village from which the fire of the guns could be used effectively to cover the advance of the attacking troops.†

As a result of the continuous hostile pressure which was brought to bear on this part of the line, the situation round Mory was rendered critical in the extreme, and, in despite of the gallant defence, it looked as if the 40th Division would be compelled to give ground.‡ The 92nd Infantry Bde. (31st Division), therefore, which had now reached the battle zone, was ordered to occupy the ground to the north of Ervillers in order to strengthen the front in this part of the line as the capture by the enemy of the high ground north-west and south-west of Mory would have seriously endangered the whole of the front held by the 4th Guards Bde.

---

* C/75 was completely successful in destroying a German battery just as it was coming into action on the front of the 3rd Division.

† The enemy's attack on this part of the front was being carried out by the 111th Reserve Division and the 2nd Guard Reserve Division.

‡ The enemy appears to have actually gained possession of Mory at one period in the day, but was driven out of the village again by a counter-attack made by troops belonging to the 40th Division. *See* " Sir Douglas Haig's Despatches," p. 197.

During the morning news reached the 4th Bn. Grenadier Guards that the enemy had broken through at Mory.* This information was subsequently contradicted, but, nevertheless, the situation from morning to night was a harassing one for the 4th Guards Bde. Its positions were continually shelled not only by the enemy's artillery, but also by the British heavy guns, and the battalions in the front line, if not actually attacked in great force by the German infantry, were kept constantly employed in preventing parties of hostile troops from massing for the assault or from penetrating round their flanks. All such attempts were frustrated with heavy losses to the enemy.

On the front of the Guards Division the day passed in a manner very similar to that passed on the 4th Guards Bde. front. The line from Bank Copse to Henin looked across an open valley to the Henin—Croisilles ridge, but the sunken roads in the valley provided the enemy with excellent positions of assembly and gave him a covered line of approach to the left flank of the Guards. The troops in the front line, however, were very much on the alert and their rifle and machine-gun fire was so promptly brought to bear on the German infantry the moment it began to move across the front in the direction of Henin that every attempt made by the enemy to advance in strength was nipped in the bud and he undoubtedly suffered very severe casualties. In despite, therefore, of the vigorous hostile shell and machine-gun fire to which the Guards were subjected throughout the day, the 23rd of March was accounted a tolerably quiet day

---

* "During the morning the news reached the Battalion [the 4th Bn. Grenadier Guards] that the enemy had broken through at Mory, and that the right flank of the Brigade was in danger; this was contradicted later. An order issued to the Battalion to feel its right, and take over ground occupied by the Fortieth Division was never carried out, as the troops on the right refused to move, stating that they had received no orders. Then commenced a most harassing shelling of our trenches by our own guns which every effort on the part of the Commanding Officer failed to stop. . . . Nor was the shelling the only annoyance: the men in the front trench were constantly employed in repelling attacks, and fired off no less than 80,000 cartridges, inflicting continual losses on the advancing enemy." *See* "The Grenadier Guards in the Great War," vol. iii. pp. 9, 10.

on the divisional front. But the general situation was still so precarious on the front of the Third Army, and the news which came from the Fifth Army was so disquieting, that no precautions could be neglected, and consequently the Divisional Field Companies, R.E., and the 4th Bn. Coldstream Guards (Pioneers) * were ordered to reconnoitre the ground with a view to the preparation of a " fifth system " of defence west of Boiry-St.-Rictrude.

(6) THE ENEMY BREAKS THROUGH THE BRITISH LINE NEAR MORY—MEASURES FOR THE PROTECTION OF ERVILLERS BY THE 4TH (GUARDS) BRIGADE, 24TH OF MARCH—A QUIET DAY ON THE FRONT OF THE GUARDS DIVISION.

On the 24th of March the Germans continued their onslaught upon the front of the VI Corps, their main efforts, as on the previous day, being directed against the southern flank in the neighbourhood of Mory, where the exhausted troops of the 40th Division were again compelled to give ground.

On the front of the 31st Division the sector of the line held by the 4th Guards Bde. was heavily bombarded by the enemy's artillery in the early hours of the morning, but an infantry attack north of the Sensée river which followed the bombardment was beaten back without much difficulty by the 2nd Bn. Irish Guards.†

Shortly after this engagement, the Irish Guards were relieved by troops of the 93rd Infantry Bde. and ordered to move into the line on the right of the 4th Bn. Grenadier Guards—the purpose of this manœuvre being to extend the front of the 31st Division in a south-easterly direction from the Ervillers—St. Leger road for the better defence of the approaches to Ervillers in the event of the anticipated breaking of the line at Mory. With this same object in view, the 3rd Bn. Coldstream Guards had already dug a

---

* The Field Companies and Pioneers had been concentrated in Arras on the 22nd of March.
† See W.D., 2nd Bn. Irish Guards, March, 1918.

trench to cover the right flank of the 4th Guards Bde., while the 42nd Division, on the right of the 40th Division, had thrown back a defensive flank along the Achiet-le-Grand—Bihucourt road.*

The 4th Bn. Grenadier Guards which, after the withdrawal of the Irish Guards, had become the left battalion of the 4th Guards Bde., notwithstanding the fact that it was heavily shelled by both British and German guns,† maintained a vigilant watch on its front and was successful in breaking up several hostile concentrations during the day. Farther to the north, the 93rd Infantry Bde. was heavily attacked, but held its ground, although its troops like the Guards complained bitterly that they were fired upon by British guns, as well as from British aeroplanes flying low over their trenches.‡ During these strenuous days of retreat, when the positions of troops were changing from hour to hour and when the progress of the enemy was so disconcertingly rapid, reports of this kind were common all along the British line and no doubt were often accurate. It was a difficult task for the gunners and airmen to distinguish friends from foes, whilst at the same time the situation was so critical that they could afford to take no risks—naturally, however, it was no easy matter for the long-suffering infantry to appreciate the difficulties of the other arms, and, even in the general confusion which prevailed, the much tried battalions found time to record their protests against the treatment they were receiving.

Late in the evening it was at length found possible to extricate from the line the remaining troops of the 40th Division—the remnants of two battalions §—and to replace them with three companies of the 2nd Bn. Irish Guards. The remaining company of this battalion, which was to occupy a support position some 400 yards in rear of the other companies, was still in the neighbourhood of battalion headquarters, at the cross-roads north-east of Ervillers,

---

* *See* VI Corps Narrative.
† *See* W.D., 4th Bn. Grenadier Guards, March, 1918.
‡ *See* W.D., 31st Division, March, 1918.
§ The 13th Bn. Yorkshire Regt. and the 21st Bn. Middlesex Regt.

when bursts of rifle and machine-gun fire were heard from the direction of Mory. Soon afterwards troops began streaming back from the front saying that the Germans had broken through in force at Mory Copse and were advancing upon Ervillers. This was at about 10 p.m., and such additional measures as were possible were at once taken to ensure the defence of the right flank of the 4th Guards Bde. The two companies on the right of the 2nd Bn. Irish Guards were swung back and linked up with the reserve company, and the men set to work to dig themselves in on the high ground north-east of Ervillers.*

By 12.30 a.m. on the 25th of March the position of the Irish Guards was for the time being tolerably secure, although as it became light the enemy could be seen pressing forward down the valley below them towards Ervillers.†

The Germans made no really serious attempt to break through the front held by the Guards Division on the 24th of March, but, at about 11 a.m., they advanced in considerable force to attack the sector of the line held by the 8th Infantry Bde. (3rd Division) on the immediate left of the 3rd Guards Bde. This advance crossed the front of the 1st Bn. Grenadier Guards and the company on the left of the battalion took the enemy in enfilade very effectively, whilst his troops, as they moved down the slope between St. Martin-sur-Cojeul and Henin, also afforded an excellent target for eight of the Guards machine guns.‡ The enemy suffered very heavily, but his tactics greatly impressed the Grenadiers. In the battalion's report the excellence of the training of the attacking troops is commented upon. The men "dribbled" forward to their places of assembly and then advanced in waves; all their movements were

---

* *See* W.D., 2nd Bn. Irish Guards, March, 1918.

† The Germans actually entered Ervillers, but were driven out again by a counter-attack delivered by troops of the 92nd Infantry Bde. This brigade was now on the immediate right of the 4th Guards Bde. *See* VI Corps Narrative. *Cf.* also "The Irish Guards in the Great War," vol. ii. p. 193.

‡ Twenty thousand rounds were fired by the machine gunners into the attacking Germans, who belonged to the 180th Reserve Infantry Regiment. *See* W.D., M.-G. Regiment, March, 1918.

performed quickly and with precision, flags and discs being used to mark the flanks and to ensure the right direction of the advance. There was no protective fire during the advance, but there were light machine guns in rear to cover a retirement.*

After this attack had been driven back, nothing happened until late in the afternoon when a party of about 100 Germans, advancing by twos and threes, attempted to work its way forward on the front of the 3rd Bn. Grenadier Guards, the right battalion of the 2nd Guards Bde. The Grenadiers had no difficulty in dealing with this attack,† and at the close of the day the line of the Guards Division remained intact. All ranks in the division were in good spirits and quite confident of their ability to hold their own against the enemy, who, it was reported by patrols sent out in the evening, was massing for another attack.‡ It was clear, however, that the successful advance made by the Germans farther south must soon necessitate a withdrawal on the part of the Guards and so the staff of the division set to work to reconnoitre the new defensive system running through Gomiecourt, Blaireville and Ficheux, which had been christened the "purple line," while commanding officers seized the opportunity of sending back officers to make sure of the routes running westward.

Throughout the day the 1st Guards Bde., in reserve, was busily engaged in improving its trenches and the divisional Artillery was constantly called upon to break up concentrations of hostile troops. The 75th Bde., R.F.A., came into

---

* *See* W.D., 1st Bn. Grenadier Guards, March, 1918. Major-General Feilding issued a memorandum to brigades, on the 24th of March, with regard to the tactics to be employed against the "dribbling" methods of advance employed by the enemy. He pointed out that such a system of advance must be countered by rifle, Lewis-gun and machine-gun fire as artillery fire was clearly ineffective until the enemy's concentration was complete. *See* W.D., Guards Division, March, 1918, App. 767. He also issued to his troops the special message of encouragement sent to the Army by the Commander-in-Chief. *Ibid.*, App. 768.

† The Germans lost about 30 of their number, but, as they managed to carry off their dead and wounded, no identifications were obtained.

‡ *See* "The Grenadier Guards in the Great War," vol. ii. p. 377.

action about 4 a.m. in positions at Boisleux-au-Mont and in the valley midway between that village and Hamelincourt, from which it could cover the whole of the divisional front, while the 74th Bde., R.F.A., took over the S.O.S. lines. The Field Companies, R.E., and the 4th Bn. Coldstream Guards (Pioneers) spent the day working steadily on the " fifth system " of defence.

(7) Withdrawal of the Guards and the 31st Division, 25th of March.

Early in the morning on the 25th of March there was a readjustment of the line by which the sector of the front of the VI Corps hitherto held by the 40th Division, which had by this time been almost entirely relieved by the 42nd Division, was handed over to the IV Corps.* Before this change in the organization of the line took place, the 31st Division had been ordered by the VI Corps to retire to the Ervillers line; but, owing to the importance of the retention of the high ground to the west of the Mory—St. Leger road for the defence of the line farther to the north, the withdrawal had been delayed.† South of Ervillers, however, the troops of the Third Army had been forced back although the fire of the British artillery on the front of the 31st Division was so effective that the enemy was unable to launch an attack on any large scale, his troops as they kept collecting in the valley east of Ervillers being continually dispersed by shell fire. So successful, indeed, were the gunners that it is recorded that the 4th Guards Bde. complained that the excellence of their shooting prevented the infantry from taking its full toll of the advancing Germans with its rifle and machine-gun fire.‡

* *See* VI Corps Narrative.
† *See* W.D., 31st Division, March, 1918. It appears to have been Lord Ardee, commanding the 4th Guards Bde., who pointed out to the 31st divisional commander that the ground which would have to be evacuated commanded the British line to the north.
‡ The Guards on this front still complained, however, that their trenches were shelled by the British heavy guns. *See* W.D., 4th Guards Bde., March, 1918.

But if the situation on this part of the line was tolerably safe, things were by no means so satisfactory farther south. During the morning British troops could be seen from north of Ervillers retiring into Gomiecourt with the enemy pressing close behind them and during the course of the day Sapignies, Behagnies and Gomiecourt fell into the hands of the Germans. By dusk, therefore, it was obvious that the 31st Division and the Guards Division would have to withdraw in conformity with the retirement of the troops of the IV Corps on their right, and orders were given to the 31st Division to take up a line running from Ablainzeville, west of Courcelles, to Moyenneville. The 4th Guards Bde. was the first brigade of its division to move back to its new positions. It began its withdrawal shortly after 8 p.m., its troops moving round the northern outskirts of Hamelincourt—a wise precaution in view of the fact that the Germans were known to be in some strength to the north-east of Ervillers.* The brigade reached its new line about midnight and at once went into the positions assigned to it—the 3rd Bn. Coldstream Guards on the right, the 2nd Bn. Irish Guards in the centre and the 4th Bn. Grenadier Guards on the left. The front extended for about 3,000 yards on the high ground lying between Courcelles and Moyenneville, and, as there were no trenches in this area, the troops spent a busy night digging themselves in.†

On the front of the Guards Division the day passed tolerably quietly, for, although the line was shelled intermittently, no infantry attack of any magnitude was launched against the Guards. In the morning, in view of the alarming reports which came from farther south, the 3rd Bn. Grenadier Guards set to work to dig a defensive flank astride the railway line north-west of Bank Copse for the protection of the right flank of the 2nd Guards Bde., but this new line was never actually manned.‡

Later on in the day, small parties of Germans made an attempt to attack the line held by this battalion, but, in

---

* See W.D., 4th Guards Bde., March, 1918.
† See W.D., 2nd Bn. Irish Guards, March, 1918.
‡ See W.D., 3rd Bn. Grenadier Guards, March, 1918.

order to do so, they had to cross the front of the 1st Bn. Scots Guards—the left battalion of the 2nd Guards Bde.—and were met by such effective rifle and machine-gun fire that they beat a hasty retreat. Both the Grenadiers and Scots Guards sent out patrols to keep in touch with the enemy's movements, but otherwise the men were given as little to do as possible.

On the front of the 3rd Guards Bde. a patrol belonging to the 1st Bn. Grenadier Guards came across some German infantry on the outskirts of Henin and captured a prisoner ; * but, although the enemy could be observed throughout the day in considerable strength moving along the Henin—Croisilles road, no serious fighting developed.

The 1st Guards Bde. remained in reserve on the 25th of March, but, at about 6 p.m., upon the receipt of the news that the Germans had taken Gomiecourt and were advancing on Courcelles, the 2nd Bn. Grenadier Guards with a section of machine guns was sent to hold the high ground lying between Boiry-St. Martin and Hamelincourt.†

About the same time as this battalion reached its appointed position, the 2nd and 3rd Guards Bdes. began their withdrawal. In the general scheme of operations it was intended that the Guards and 31st Divisions should pivot on the right of the 3rd Division and that the Guards should fall back fighting as far as the "purple line." The first stage in this retirement was to be the "Army line" which ran west of Boyelles and the Guards Division was ordered to throw back its right flank north-west of Hamelincourt in order to keep in touch with the 31st Division.‡

The artillery had been the first unit of the Guards Division to move. The two brigades R.F.A., which had maintained a steady fire upon the enemy throughout the day, withdrew at dusk to positions north-west and south-west of Ransart, from which they could cover the "purple line" from Adinfer

---

* *See* W.D., 1st Bn. Grenadier Guards, March, 1918.

† The Field Companies, R.E., and the 4th Bn. Coldstream Guards (Pioneers) were employed during the day in digging and wiring a new defensive line south and south-west of Blaireville and east of Adinfer.

‡ *See* W.D., Guards Division, March, 1918.

to Ficheux. The infantry followed, its movements being carried out in good order and with perfect steadiness throughout the night. The Germans, except on the left of the line where they exchanged shots with the rear guards of the 1st Bn. Grenadier Guards * and 1st Bn. Welsh Guards, showed little or no inclination to interfere in the proceedings.

(8) The 4th Guards Bde. and the Guards Division withdrawn to the line Ayette—Boisleux-St. Marc—Loss of Moyenneville, 26th of March.

At 2 a.m. on the 26th of March the 4th Guards Bde. (31st Division) was digging in on the line Courcelles—Moyenneville and was in touch on the left with the Guards Division, the 2nd Guards Bde. having taken up a position on the right front of the 2nd Bn. Grenadier Guards † of the 1st Guards Bde., while the 3rd Guards Bde. did likewise on the left flank. But orders soon came for the 4th Guards Bde. to move back to reserve positions round Ayette and for the front of the 31st Division to be held by the 92nd Infantry Bde. on the right and the 93rd Infantry Bde. on the left. Before daybreak the majority of the troops of these two brigades had managed to find their way to the positions in the line assigned to them, although, owing to the difficulty of transmitting messages and the close pressure of the enemy, various units did not reach their positions until later in the day. On the arrival of the 4th Guards Bde. at Ayette, the 3rd Bn. Coldstream Guards was stationed on the high ground to the south-west of the village with the 4th Bn. Grenadier Guards in rear and the 2nd Bn. Irish Guards on the spur of hilly country which runs to the north-east.

The line now held by the Guards Division extended

---

* Viscount Gort, commanding this battalion, remained in rear with two platoons until 1.20 a.m. on the 26th of March in order to make quite certain that no troops were left east of the Arras—Bapaume road, and to ensure that the left flank was properly adjusted in touch with the 3rd Division. *See* W.D., 1st Bn. Grenadier Guards, March, 1918. *Cf.* also " History of the Welsh Guards," p. 206.

† *See* p. 56.

from about 500 yards north of Moyenneville to the Arras—Bapaume road north-west of Boiry-Becquerelle.* The 2nd Guards Bde. was on the right with the 1st Bn. Coldstream Guards and the 1st Bn. Scots Guards in the front line and the 3rd Bn. Grenadier Guards in close support. The 3rd Guards Bde., on the left, had the 2nd Bn. Scots Guards and the 1st Bn. Grenadier Guards in the front line and the 1st Bn. Welsh Guards in support. The 1st Guards Bde., which remained in reserve throughout the day, now had two of its battalions in positions south-east of Boiry-St.-Martin and its remaining battalion at the sugar factory a little to the south-west of that village.

The day was a strenuous one for the 4th Guards Bde., for, although the troops were not called upon to do much actual fighting, they were kept on the alert from morning to night, while the constant reports of the enemy's successes on the front of the 31st Division and farther to the south which came pouring into brigade headquarters necessitated incessant work in the construction and the strengthening of the defences. The village of Ayette was left unoccupied, the cross-fire of machine guns sited on the high ground on each flank and in rear being relied upon for its defence. One company of Irish Guards, however, was ordered to dig itself in on the south-west outskirts of the village forming one of a chain of posts by means of which the battalion held a front of about 2,000 yards.†

Before midday the brigadier received a message from 31st divisional headquarters stating that the Germans had broken through at Hébuterne, a village about five miles south-west of Ayette, and were pushing forward in armoured cars towards Souastre, a village some considerable distance in rear.‡ The 4th Bn. Grenadier Guards was at once moved to the threatened right flank and Quesnoy Farm on the Bucquoy—Monchy-au-Bois road was rapidly put into a state of defence, while three companies of Grenadiers dug themselves in on a line running eastward from the farm.

* *See* Guards Divisional Narrative.
† *See* W.D., 2nd Bn. Irish Guards, March, 1918.
‡ *See* W.D., 4th Guards Bde., March, 1918.

THE LOSS OF MOYENNEVILLE

Soon after this, all communication with the division failed for a time and Lord Ardee assumed the command of the 92nd and 93rd Infantry Bdes. as well as of his own brigade. Later on in the day, however, a despatch rider from the division succeeded in reaching his headquarters with orders for the defensive flank on the right to be still further extended. But Lord Ardee decided that, with the troops at his disposal, any further extension of this line was out of the question, and shortly afterwards the urgent need for its construction was removed as another message arrived contradicting the story of the break-through at Hébuterne. Meanwhile, however, news had arrived that Moyenneville was definitely in the hands of the enemy, and that the troops of the 31st Division who had been defending the place were retiring through the line held by the Guards Division. A company of the 2nd Bn. Irish Guards was immediately sent forward to fill the gap, its orders being to gain touch with the Guards Division and to dig in on a line to the west of Moyenneville. During the course of this operation this company lost one of its officers and 16 men from machine-gun fire. It was eventually relieved at 8 p.m. by troops of the 93rd Infantry Bde. and rejoined the battalion.*

On the front of the Guards Division the 26th of March was also a day of some anxiety. The piquets which had been left, when the withdrawal of the previous night began, to cover Boyelles and Boiry-Becquerelle, were driven in early in the morning, and the German batteries then set to work to shell the new positions held by the Guards.† Throughout the day the enemy's infantry kept "dribbling" forward into the deserted villages, whilst his field guns came into action in the open on the forward slopes east of Moyenneville. His guns could also be seen coming over the ridge south-west

---

* *See* W.D., 2nd Bn. Irish Guards, March, 1918. It would appear that the loss of Moyenneville was due to misadventure, the defending troops of the 93rd Infantry Bde. receiving an order, given in error, to withdraw. In spite of hard fighting, it was found impossible to recapture the village, although the Germans were prevented from pressing their advantage by the stubborn resistance they encountered.

† *See* Guards Division Narrative.

of Boyelles. There were all the indications of an attack in force, but only minor engagements actually occurred.

On the right, the 2nd Guards Bde. found it by no means an easy task to maintain touch with the troops of the 31st Division, whose dispositions were continually changing. The loss of Moyenneville and the failure of the 93rd Infantry Bde. to regain possession of it rendered the situation on the right somewhat uncertain until touch was effected with the 4th Guards Bde. Large bodies of German infantry were visible moving about Moyenneville and Hamelincourt, and the enemy's patrols were active on the Brigade front all day, the outposts of the 1st Bn. Scots Guards inflicting numerous casualties among them with their Lewis-gun fire.*

In the evening the 1st Bn. Coldstream Guards drove back a German bombing attack made on its line up a sunken road. On the left of the divisional front, the 3rd Guards Bde. passed through a day very similar to that passed by the 2nd Guards Bde. Parties of the enemy could be seen moving about the country, but no infantry attack was attempted. The artillery support on this part of the line was reported to be inadequate, the Germans advancing in large bodies from the Henin—Croisilles ridge without much hindrance from the British guns. Upon the receipt of this information, Major-General Feilding complained to the VI Corps with regard to the withdrawal of all the heavy artillery to positions about 6,000 yards behind the " purple line " and asked that some batteries, at any rate, should be moved forward again in order to take advantage of the splendid targets afforded by the general advance of the Germans.† This suggestion was adopted by the corps commander and some of the large howitzers were moved into more forward positions.

The Guards divisional Artillery was busily at work all day. The 74th Bde., R.F.A., went into action at 4 a.m. near Ficheux. The 75th Bde., R.F.A., and the 155th Bde., R.F.A., which was now assisting in the task of covering the Division, were in action during the morning in the neighbour-

* See W.D., 1st Bn. Scots Guards, March, 1918.
† See W.D., Guards Division, App. 772, March, 1918.

hood of Hendecourt. But in the afternoon the former of these two brigades moved into positions east of the Adinfer—Ransart road in order to cover the threatened point of the line between Moyenneville and Ayette.

Throughout the day the Guards machine gunners were actively engaged, but their work appears to have been severely handicapped by the difficulty of communication. There was no signalling officer with the unit and consequently most messages had to be sent by runners.* The Field Companies, R.E., and the 4th Bn. Coldstream Guards (Pioneers) worked from morning to night on the " purple line " defences between Adinfer and Hendecourt, the monotony of their labours being relieved by some hostile shelling and the never-ceasing rumours of an alarming nature—rumours which, as a rule, turned out to be false or, at any rate, a too intelligent anticipation of events.

(9) The night of the 26th–27th of March—Relief of the 2nd Guards Brigade by the 1st Guards Brigade —Awkward position now occupied by the Division.

The relief of the 2nd Guards Bde. by the 1st Guards Bde. was begun as soon as it was dark on the night of the 26th of March. On the right, astride the Arras—Albert railway line, the 2nd Bn. Grenadier Guards took over the sector of the front held by the 1st Bn. Coldstream Guards and the 1st Bn. Irish Guards relieved the 1st Bn. Scots Guards on the right. In consequence of the loss of Moyenneville, the right of the Guards Division now rested on the Moyenneville—Boiry road well to the north-west of the first named village, while farther to the south troops belonging to the 93rd Infantry Bde. were still struggling manfully to maintain their line. The front of approximately three and a half miles held by the Guards, especially the sector of it occupied by the 2nd Bn. Grenadier Guards,† was badly adapted for

* *See* W.D., Guards Machine-Gun Regiment, March, 1918.
† " The new position (of the 2nd Bn. Grenadier Guards) was difficult to hold, for, not only did it include three sunken roads and a

the purposes of defence. The trenches were mainly on the forward slopes of the hills and were much overlooked from the high ground in the immediate vicinity of Moyenneville. So awkward, indeed, was the situation on the right found to be as a result of the steady forward movement of the enemy on the front of the 31st Division,* that it was found advisable during the night to refuse the right flank of the 2nd Bn. Grenadier Guards towards the positions occupied by the 2nd Bn. Coldstream Guards in support—this latter battalion being ordered to push out posts to fill a gap caused by a subsequent withdrawal by the 93rd Infantry Bde.

(10) THE 27TH OF MARCH—WITHDRAWAL OF THE 92ND AND 93RD INFANTRY BDES. WEST OF AYETTE—THE 4TH GUARDS BRIGADE HOLDS THE FRONT OF THE 31ST DIVISION—GERMAN ATTACKS ON THE FRONT OF THE GUARDS DIVISION.

The enemy's attacks on the front held by the 31st Division continued on the 27th of March, but the troops of the 92nd and 93rd Infantry Bdes. managed to hold their own until early in the afternoon when the Germans succeeded in pene-

---

railway, but it was also overlooked from the outskirts of Moyenneville and from high ground all along the front, where a number of deserted huts could give cover to snipers and machine guns." *See* "The Grenadier Guards in the Great War," vol. ii. p. 369.

* " By this time, though it would not be easy to trace their various arrivals in the confusion, the Guards Brigades had got into line between Boisleux-St. Marc and Ayette, on a front of roughly three and a half miles, while battalions of exhausted and withdrawing Divisions, hard pressed by the enemy, passed through them each with its burden of bad news. It was not an inspiriting sight, nor was the actual position of the Guards Brigades one to be envied. High ground commanded them throughout, and a number of huts and half-ruined buildings gave good cover to the gathering machine guns. The German advance on that quarter resembled, as one imaginative soul put it, an encompassment of were-wolves. They slouched forward, while men rubbed tired eyes, in twos and threes, at no point offering any definite target, either for small-arm or artillery, and yet, in some wizard fashion, always thickening and spreading, while our guns from the rear raged and tore uselessly at their almost invisible lines." *See* " The Irish Guards in the Great War," vol. ii. pp. 272, 273.

THE 31ST DIVISION DRIVEN BACK

trating the line between Ablainzeville and Courcelles. The troops of the two brigades were then compelled to fall back fighting on the positions occupied by the 4th Guards Bde. round Ayette.

A heavy hostile bombardment in the morning which preceded the enemy's advance had warned the 4th Guards Bde. that a strenuous day might be in store for it, and in the afternoon it was called upon to hold the whole of the 31st divisional front, the units of the 92nd and 93rd Infantry Bdes. passing through its line to reorganize in rear. The enemy's infantry, following closely behind these troops, succeeded in reaching the aerodrome situated near the cross-roads west of Courcelles, but here a vigorous concentration by the British artillery practically wiped out two German battalions and temporarily brought the hostile advance to a standstill.* Two companies of the 4th Bn. Grenadier Guards, with which it had originally been intended to reinforce the 92nd Infantry Bde., were now attached to the 2nd Bn. Irish Guards and used to strengthen the line round Ayette.† The day passed without much incident, but, at about 7.30 p.m., a message arrived from the 2nd Guards Bde. stating that it was no longer in touch with the 2nd Bn. Irish Guards. Troops belonging to the 93rd Infantry Bde. were brought up as soon as possible to close the gap which was now found to exist between the 4th and 2nd Guards Bdes. During the course of the evening, too, the maintenance of touch with the 42nd Division (the left division of the IV Corps) on the right became a matter of some difficulty, but, at about 11 p.m., it was definitely ascertained that the troops of this division were still holding on east of Bucquoy, their left being at a point some little distance to the south-east of Ablainzeville.‡

At 11.30 a.m. on the 27th of March the enemy opened

---

* *See* W.D., 4th Bn. Grenadier Guards, March, 1918.

† Lord Ardee was unfortunately gassed during the course of the afternoon and was compelled to relinquish the command of the 4th Guards Bde., which devolved upon Lieut.-Colonel the Honble. H. Alexander, 2nd Bn. Irish Guards, Major P. S. Long-Innes coming up to take the command of the Irish Guards.

‡ *See* W.D., 4th Guards Bde., March, 1918.

a heavy artillery bombardment on the centre and left of the area held by the Guards Division,* the fire of his guns being mainly directed against the front and support lines but also searching the country as far back as Boisleux-au-Mont. After this bombardment had been in progress for about an hour and a half, the German infantry, covered by an overhead machine-gun barrage, assaulted the line held by the 3rd Guards Bde. on a front of about 500 yards between Boyelles and Boiry-Becquerelle, while small groups of men crawled forward into dead ground on the flanks of the main advance, and thence endeavoured to make their way through the defences. This attack, the brunt of which fell upon the 2nd Bn. Scots Guards on the left of the line, was beaten back without much difficulty, and with but few casualties among the defending troops. The enemy attempted no further aggressive action on this part of the front during the day, but at one time late in the afternoon it looked as if another attack were in course of preparation as his infantry was observed to be concentrating in Boyelles. This information was immediately reported to the gunners by the 1st Bn. Grenadier Guards and the 74th Bde., R.F.A., concentrated its fire upon the village with what appeared to be the most satisfactory results. In the evening the 1st Bn. Welsh Guards relieved the Grenadiers in the front line.

On the front held by the 1st Guards Bde., although the trenches were shelled fairly heavily throughout the day and the enemy's machine gunners showed great activity, the Germans launched no infantry attack until the evening. Then, at about 8.30 p.m., about 40 or 50 Germans tried to push their way through a gap in the wire opposite the 1st Bn. Irish Guards. They were quickly dispersed by Lewis-gun and rifle fire, leaving behind them 8 dead—all belonging to the 451st Regiment—and 2 machine guns.

The divisional Artillery had a busy and successful day. The 75th Bde., R.F.A., gave splendid support to the 1st Guards Bde., while the 74th Bde., R.F.A., covered the 3rd Guards Bde., effectually preventing, as already related, the German infantry from concentrating in Boyelles. The

* *See* Guards Division Narrative.

THE LINE TO BE HELD AT ALL COSTS

machine gunners also did valuable service in the defence, engaging the enemy with great effect at ranges varying from 2,000 yards to point blank. Three of their guns were knocked out during the day, but were promptly replaced by the Ordnance.

But although at the end of the day the Guards themselves were in fine spirits and still quite confident of their ability to hold their ground, the actual situation of the division in the evening of the 27th of March was an anxious one for its commander. The withdrawal of the 31st Division to Ayette had had the effect of lengthening the VI Corps line to such an extent that the 2nd Guards Bde., which was now the supporting brigade of the Guards Division, had been obliged to push forward first the 3rd Bn. Grenadier Guards, and then the 1st Bn. Coldstream Guards, in order to prolong the line on the right of the 1st Guards Bde.* and to keep in touch with the troops of the 93rd Infantry Bde. As a consequence of this necessary movement of troops, all three brigades of the Guards Division were now in the line—a line which extended over a front of 8,000 yards. Major-General Feilding not unnaturally was of the opinion that this was too wide an area for his troops to hold in the circumstances, more especially as he no longer had any reserve at his disposal. He strongly urged upon the VI Corps commander, therefore, the advisability of a withdrawal during the night to the " purple line " on the construction of which good progress had been made from Adinfer to Hendecourt, and which was now manned by the Field Companies, R.E., and the 4th Bn. Coldstream Guards (Pioneers). The matter was referred by the corps to the Third Army. The reply was that the extended right flank of the Guards Division was to be held at all costs, and the only answer, which was vouchsafed to further protests from Major-General Feilding, was that this was an Army order which must be complied with.† The Major-General's representations, however, had some effect upon

---

* *See* W.D's., 3rd Bn. Grenadier Guards and 1st Bn. Coldstream Guards, March, 1918.

† *See* W.D., Guards Division, March, 1918.

the higher authorities, for the 97th Infantry Bde. (32nd Division) was placed under his orders as a reserve to be used for the purposes of counter-attack should the necessity arise. This brigade reached Ransart about midnight on the 27th of March.*

(11) THE NIGHT OF THE 27TH–28TH OF MARCH—THE 4TH GUARDS BRIGADE SECURES TOUCH WITH THE 42ND DIVISION ON ITS RIGHT.

The apparent determination of the Germans to drive a wedge through the British line in the area occupied by the 31st Division made it a matter of imperative importance that the point of junction between that division and the 42nd Division on its right should be rendered secure. As soon, therefore, as it was clear that the left flank of the 42nd Division was still a little to the south-east of Ablainzeville, measures were taken to link up the two divisional fronts. The 3rd Bn. Coldstream Guards moved forward from Douchy-les-Ayette at about 1 a.m. on the 28th of March to occupy some already existing trenches on the Ayette—Bucquoy road, where it gained touch with the 10th Bn. Manchester Regiment (42nd Division) just west of Ablainzeville on its right, and with the 2nd Bn. Irish Guards on its left. Two companies of the 4th Bn. Grenadier Guards were still attached to this last-named battalion, and its two remaining companies were moved into the trenches running south-west of Douchy-les-Ayette which had just been vacated by the Coldstream.

(12) UNSUCCESSFUL ATTEMPTS BY THE ENEMY TO BREAK THROUGH THE LINE OF THE 4TH GUARDS BRIGADE AND OF THE GUARDS DIVISION, 28TH OF MARCH— THE 3RD DIVISION NORTH OF THE GUARDS DIVISION DRIVEN BACK TO THE " ARMY LINE."

The troops of the 4th Guards Bde., as a result of the rearrangement of the previous night, found themselves, on the morning of the 28th of March, holding a front of

* *See* W.D., Guards Division, App. 774, March, 1918.

FRESH ATTACK ON 4TH GUARDS BDE.

over 3,000 yards. They were soon called upon to resist the enemy's further progress. Before daylight the Germans began moving forward and forced back the small posts of Irish Guardsmen which had been placed on the eastern outskirts of Ayette.* At 9 a.m. a heavy hostile artillery bombardment was put down along the Ayette—Bucquoy road and on the village of Ayette, and the enemy's infantry could be observed concentrating north of Ablainzeville and west of Courcelles. At 10.30 a.m. the whole front of the brigade was attacked, but the assaulting troops simply withered away in face of the deadly British artillery and machine-gun fire. Only on the right did any of the German infantry succeed in getting anywhere near the Guards line, and then the steady and accurate Lewis-gun and rifle fire of the 3rd Bn. Coldstream Guards proved too much for them. Further hostile concentrations south of Ayette later in the day were broken up by the British artillery, and, when evening came, the line held by the 4th Guards Bde. was much the same as it had been in the morning, except for the fact that a few Germans had succeeded in effecting a lodgment in Ayette.† The 31st divisional commander was now anxious for the line to be advanced east of Ayette and placed the 12th Bn. K.O.Y.L.I. (Pioneers) at the disposal of the 4th Guards Bde. for counter-attack purposes.‡ But it was eventually decided to deny the western exits of the village to the enemy—a policy which, it was considered, would be equally effective for the defence of the sector whilst imposing far less strain upon the troops.

On the front of the Guards Division a hostile artillery bombardment in the early hours of the morning was followed, at about 8 a.m., by an infantry attack upon the advanced posts of the 2nd Guards Bde. held by the 3rd Bn. Grenadier Guards at its point of junction with the 93rd Infantry Bde.

---

* *See* W.D., 4th Guards Bde., March, 1918.

† These Germans in Ayette proved rather troublesome, their sniping tactics occasioning numerous casualties especially among the Coldstream. In the evening a trench-mortar battery was moved up to deal with them, but, as no ballastite rings or Allways fuzes were available, the mortars could not be fired.

‡ *See* W.D., 31st Division, March, 1918.

The Germans met with some temporary success, but were speedily counter-attacked and driven back by the Grenadiers and men belonging to the York and Lancaster Regiment, leaving many dead behind them.* This was the only infantry attack delivered on this part of the front during the day,† but the troops were kept continuously on the alert and were a good deal harassed by the fire of the enemy's guns, whilst his aeroplanes with Allied markings on them are reported to have flown low over the trenches dropping bombs. When night came, the 1st Bn. Scots Guards moved up from support and relieved the 3rd Bn. Grenadier Guards on the right of the Brigade line.

The 1st Guards Bde., in the centre of the divisional front, also had an early encounter with the enemy. Before daybreak patrols of the 2nd Bn. Grenadier Guards discovered the Germans assembling in the open barely a 100 yards in front of the brigade line. These were quickly dispersed by the fire of the British guns, but, at 9.45 a.m., after a short preliminary bombardment, the enemy's infantry again tried to move forward. This attempt at an attack was also nipped in the bud by the British gunners, and various offensive movements made by the Germans during the afternoon under the cover of machine-gun fire were similarly checked. But, although they were themselves not called upon to do much fighting, the day was a trying one for the troops in the line. The Grenadiers were persistently and accurately shelled—the enemy's gunners having direct observation—and lost a considerable number of men. The 1st Bn. Irish Guards, on their left, was rather more lucky, but it, too, suffered a good deal from the German artillery and trench-mortar fire in the late afternoon and evening.

On the front of the 3rd Guards Bde. a British artillery bombardment, carried out quite early in the morning, provoked a fierce retaliation and the troops in the line suffered severely. However, even the infantry admitted

* *See* W.D., 3rd Bn. Grenadier Guards, March, 1918.
† At about 11.15 a.m. a German retirement was reported from the front line. But this proved to be a relief among the enemy's foremost troops. *See* W.D., 2nd Guards Bde., March, 1918.

that the artillery support received on this occasion was "rather better than it had been," * and Boyelles, where two German battalions were reported to be assembling for an attack, was clearly shelled with great effect.

On the left of the Guards Division the day was more crowded with incident. After an artillery bombardment, lasting from 7 a.m. to 11.30 a.m., the enemy carried out a strong attack on the front of the 3rd Division, the results of which at one time threatened the left flank of the 3rd Guards Bde.

The troops of the 3rd Division were forced back to the "Army line" defences running behind the Arras—Bapaume road south-east of Mercatel.† A company of the 1st Bn. Welsh Guards on the extreme left of the 3rd Guards Bde. front was vigorously attacked by the advancing Germans. It drove them back with its Lewis-gun and rifle fire, and, later in the evening, the battalion by refusing its left was successful in keeping intact the junction between the Guards and the 3rd Division.‡

Throughout the day the majority of the Guards machine guns were employed in the front line, it being found impossible—even had time and materials been available—to site concealed positions in rear as the line lay on a forward slope. The guns were in action almost continuously, and, in consequence, were easily located by the enemy, who succeeded in damaging four of them. The casualties in the machine-gun companies up to this date amounted to nearly 50 of the *personnel*, and, as all available reinforcements were now up in the line, it was becoming a matter of some difficulty to man all the guns. As a precautionary measure the Field Companies, R.E., and the 4th Bn. Coldstream Guards

---

* *See* W.D., 2nd Bn. Scots Guards, March, 1918.

† On the left of the 3rd Division the 15th Division, which was in the line immediately south of the Scarpe, was also obliged to make a short withdrawal. North of the Scarpe the 4th Division was able to keep its front intact in despite of heavy German pressure, the work which the Guards had put in on the defences in this area earlier in the year proving of the greatest value in the emergency.

‡ *See* W.D., 1st Bn. Grenadier Guards, March, 1918. *Cf.* " History of the Welsh Guards," p. 207.

(Pioneers) stood to arms in the " purple line " between Adinfer and Hendecourt during the day, but, as soon as darkness set in, work on the defences was resumed, covering parties being provided by the Pioneers.

Owing to the continuance of the enemy's pressure southward from Ayette, it was deemed advisable in the morning on the 28th of March to transfer the 97th Infantry Bde., which, it will be remembered, had been placed under Major-General Feilding's orders, to the 31st Division. But the Guards Division was strengthened later on in the day by the arrival of the Guards Reinforcement Bn. behind the " purple line " ready to occupy it should the occasion arise.*

(13) THE 29TH OF MARCH—A QUIET DAY ON THE FRONT HELD BY THE GUARDS—WORK OF THE DIVISIONAL ARTILLERY.

Although the fire of the enemy's snipers and machine gunners in Ayette proved rather troublesome, the 29th of March may be described as a quiet day on the front of the 4th Guards Bde., where the troops were mainly employed in the work of consolidating their line. Two companies of the K.O.Y.L.I. (Pioneers) were sent up in close support of the 3rd Bn. Coldstream Guards on the right, and various minor readjustments of the front were carried out.† At night the left sector of the 31st divisional front was taken over by the 97th Bde. (32nd Division). The day, too, passed more or less uneventfully on the front of the Guards Division. Except for the usual activity of their artillery, the Germans remained inactive, being busily employed, as subsequent events were to prove, on their preparations for another forward movement. On the right the 2nd Guards Bde. reported that its junction with the 93rd Infantry Bde., which had hitherto not been considered entirely satisfactory, was now firmly secured, and the 1st Bn. Coldstream Guards was able to put out a good deal of new wire in front of its positions.

* See W.D., Guards Division, March, 1918.
† See W.D., 4th Guards Bde., March, 1918.

A BRIEF RESPITE

In the 1st Guards Bde. a plan was now adopted by which men who were considered to be in urgent need of rest could be sent to the rear. Four sergeants, four corporals and forty rank and file were brought up from the Reinforcement Bn. to relieve the same number of men in the front line.* This method of relief was continued daily until the brigade left the line, but there is no record of its having been adopted systematically by the two other brigades, although it appears to have been carried out by some of the battalions.†

On the 3rd Guards Bde. front the 1st Bn. Grenadier Guards relieved the 2nd Bn. Scots Guards on the right of the line.

The divisional Artillery was kept busily employed throughout the day and some idea of the activity of the gunners in this strenuous period may be gathered from the fact that, during the course of the forty-eight hours ending at 9 a.m. on the 29th of March, the 74th Bde., R.F.A., which, together with the 178th Army Bde. (less one battery), now formed the left group covering the front of the 3rd Guards Bde., fired no less than 12,000 rounds into Boiry-Becquerelle and Boyelles.‡ The concentration of the enemy's infantry must have been far from an easy task.

The work on the defences in the "purple line" continued without interruption all day. The Field Companies, R.E., and the 4th Bn. Coldstream Guards (Pioneers) still retained small posts in the forward system of trenches, but the majority of the men were now busily engaged in the construction of support positions.

(14) THE ENEMY ATTACKS IN STRENGTH ALONG THE DIVISIONAL FRONT AND IS BEATEN BACK, 30TH OF MARCH.

The trenches held by the 3rd Bn. Coldstream Guards on the front of the 4th Guards Bde. were shelled intermittently from morning to night on the 30th of March, but,

---

* *See* W.D., 1st Guards Bde., March, 1918.
† *E.g.* the 1st Bn. Welsh Guards. *See* "History of the Welsh Guards," p. 208.
‡ *See* W.D., 74th Bde., R.F.A., March, 1918.

except for this artillery fire and the persistent sniping from Ayette, the day passed as uneventfully as the preceding one, so far as the 31st Division was concerned.* It was a very different one on the front of the Guards Division, where the infantry was called upon to resist the heaviest attack made upon it since the division went into the line.

According to the reports of the 1st and 3rd Guards Bdes. a hostile artillery bombardment of the most intense and accurate description was put down upon the centre and left of the divisional front about 8.30 a.m., and was continued until about 11.14 a.m., when the enemy launched his infantry attack.†

In the sector of the line held by the 3rd Guards Bde. the brunt of the German attack fell upon the battalion on the right—the 1st Bn. Grenadier Guards. During the previous night the enemy's machine guns on this part of the front had been unpleasantly active, their fire coming principally from the high ground north-west of Boyelles, but the patrols which had been sent out had brought back no information tending to show that an attack was to be expected. When the bombardment first began, *minenwerfer* fire from the direction of Boyelles did terrible damage to the Grenadiers' trenches, while, later on, at about 9 a.m., when the enemy's barrage became thicker, the area of bombardment spread as far in rear as Boisleux-au-Mont. About 10 a.m. the barrage was still further thickened by machine-gun fire, with which the Germans also swept the valley between Boisleux-au-Mont and Boisleux-St.-Marc. Three-quarters of an hour later their guns lifted from the front line which was then enfiladed by machine-gun fire while no less than fourteen German aeroplanes are reported as having bombed the Grenadiers' trenches.

* The sniping from Ayette became so annoying as the day wore on that in the evening a battery of field howitzers was called upon to fire a fifteen minutes' concentration into the village. The results are said to have been satisfactory, and at 10 p.m. a sniper belonging to the 466th Regiment decided that the situation in the village was so far from comfortable that he walked into the lines of the Irish Guards. *See* W.D., 2nd Bn. Irish Guards, March, 1918.

† The divisional narrative states that this bombardment began at 9.30 a.m.

Under cover of this storm of shot and shell the enemy's infantry now moved forward to the assault. The Germans in a dense mass swarmed up the sunken road from Boyelles north-east of the railway line; farther to the north they advanced in waves; south-west of the sunken road they attempted a local flanking movement in scattered parties. They met with a stout and full-blooded resistance. Their ranks were raked by the fiercest machine-gun, Lewis-gun and rifle fire, while the British gunners working on their S.O.S. lines poured shell into them with relentless persistency. Nevertheless, the attackers continued to struggle forward with the utmost determination. Some of their main body actually succeeded in making their way into the Grenadiers' trenches at the spot where the sunken road crossed the line. Here they were promptly counter-attacked and almost immediately hurled out again. At no other point in the line did they succeed even in reaching the Guards' wire. Their losses in the attack were seen to be very heavy, while numbers of them were shot down as they retired, but their retreat was so effectively covered by machine-gun and rifle fire that no pursuit could be attempted and they were thus enabled to carry off most of their wounded.*

An attack on the 1st Guards Bde. was delivered simultaneously with that on the front of the 3rd Guards Bde. The enemy advanced up the railway line between Hamelincourt and Moyenneville, but were unable to stand up against the deadly fire of the 2nd Bn. Grenadier Guards whose trenches bestrode the track in this area, and, after suffering many casualties, beat a hasty retreat. Only in one part of the line did any Germans succeed in getting to grips

* The General Staff (Intelligence) of the VI Corps established the fact that this attack on the Guards Division was made by the 234th Division with the 452nd and 453rd Regiments, each of which had one battalion in the assault, one in close support and one in local reserve. The 451st Regiment was in divisional reserve and was held in readiness to support any success that might be obtained. A prisoner divulged the information that it had been the enemy's intention to sweep on to Boisleux-St. Marc by sheer weight of numbers and then to turn westward to effect a junction with troops advancing up the railway line towards Boisleux-au-Mont. He admitted that the assaulting battalions had been practically annihilated in the attack.

with the Grenadiers. Taking advantage of the cover afforded by a sunken road west of the railway line a party of them stormed a post most of the occupants of which were either killed or wounded. A counter-attack was immediately organized and the Germans, attacked with the bayonet from both flanks, were speedily ejected from the line.*

From a report of the 74th Bde., R.F.A., it would appear that the enemy used smoke to conceal the concentration of his infantry for these two attacks. The British counter-artillery preparations was put down at 8.50 a.m. and all the available batteries began firing at half rate on the S.O.S. lines at 9.5 a.m., increasing to the full rate one hour and a quarter later. This rate of fire was maintained for forty minutes, while twice during the course of the afternoon a ",rake" of 200 rounds was fired into Boiry-Becquerelle and Boyelles. Altogether the group of guns employed on this front fired 6,000 rounds; it had 5 guns knocked out and suffered many casualties both at the battery positions and also at the wagon lines.†

The work of the Guards machine gunners in this engagement also deserves notice. Notwithstanding the terrific bombardment to which they were subjected,‡ the teams kept their guns working all day and contributed materially to the success of the defence.

In the evening various reliefs and readjustments of troops were carried out. All three brigades § still remained in the line, but, with the object of saving his men as much as was

---

* *See* W.D.'s, 1st Guards Bde. and Guards Division, App. 776, March, 1918.

† *See* Report of the 74th Bde., R.F.A., also W.D., 74th Bde., R.F.A. The battery commander of A/75 was wounded, but the battery was kept in action throughout the day, although it was very heavily shelled. The 74th Bde. lost 37 horses, killed and wounded, during the action.

‡ One gun was riddled with machine-gun bullets; another was buried in the explosion of a trench-mortar bomb, but was dug out and again brought into action. Only three men of these two teams came through the day unscathed. *See* W.D., Guards M.-G. Regiment, March, 1918.

§ The 2nd Guards Bde., although it suffered a good deal from the enemy's bombardment, was not involved in the fighting on the 30th of March.

THE ACHIEVEMENT OF THE GUARDS 75

practicable, Major-General Feilding decided that the front battalions should be distributed in depth so that one battalion in each brigade might occupy a reserve position.*

The performance of the Guards Division on the 30th of March, and indeed throughout the previous ten days, was one to which all arms and all ranks in the division could look back upon with pride and satisfaction, and which thoroughly deserved the congratulations which it drew from the Third Army commander. The enemy's advance had received a decided check, and the Guards had once again amply justified the confidence which was placed in them to face any emergency. If they had not been called upon during the critical days of the March offensive to endure the tremendous strain to which some other divisions were subjected, they had, nevertheless, passed through a period of great anxiety and danger. Had the front of the Third Army been broken, the result might well have been disastrous for the Allies. But the line held and the share of the Guards in the successful defence was no insignificant one.

"Under conditions that made rest and sleep impossible for days together, and called incessantly for the greatest physical exertion and quickness of thought, officers and men remained undismayed, realizing that for the time being they must play a waiting game, and determined to make the enemy pay the full price for the success which for the moment was his." †

(15) Relief of the 4th Guards Brigade—Reorganization of the line on the front of the Guards Division, 31st of March.

On the front of the 4th Guards Bde. the day was again a tolerably quiet one except for spasmodic bursts of hostile shelling, and in the evening the brigade was relieved by the

* On the 30th of March Lieut.-Colonel E. W. M. Grigg, Grenadier Guards, succeeded Lieut.-Colonel R. S. McClintock, R.E., as G.S.O.1 of the Guards Division, the latter having been appointed a G.S.O.1 on the Lines of Communication.

† See "Sir Douglas Haig's Despatches," p. 236.

96th Infantry Bde. (32nd Division) and withdrew to Bienvillers. Since the 23rd of March its battalions had fought magnificently against five German divisions,* and its casualties during this period amounted to 14 officers and 372 other ranks.†

The day was also a restful one on the front of the Guards Division, and it was possible, therefore, to continue the work of reorganizing the line. The War Diary of the 1st Guards Bde. records that the troops were tired, but in the best of spirits, and that 80 was the average strength of companies. No attempt was any longer made to keep the trench mortars in action, as it was found that the strain and labour entailed in the carrying forward of the Stokes ammunition was too arduous. The teams of the mortars were employed, therefore, in bringing up wire and other materials required for the defence. Commanding officers and their seconds-in-command, and adjutants and assistant-adjutants, henceforward divided duty in the front line, doing forty-eight hours alternately.

When darkness set in, the 2nd Canadian Division, which had already relieved the 3rd Division, on the left, took over about 1,000 yards of the front held by the Guards. This relief greatly facilitated the organization of the Guards' front in depth as it released a battalion in the line.

During the ten days' fighting the D.A.C., in addition to supplying S.A.A. and gun ammunition, had provided wagons for R.E. fatigues. Except on one occasion—on the evening of the 28th of March, when it appears that gun ammunition began to run low—no complaints are recorded as to the adequacy either of S.A.A. or shells.

As the Guards were more or less stationary through this period, there was little difficulty in providing the troops with rations, forage and ordnance stores, although the issue of the latter was naturally confined to essentials,‡ and the appear-

---

* The 11th and 239th Divisions, the 16th Bavarian Division, and the 1st and 2nd Guard Reserve Divisions.
† *See* W.D., 31st Division, March, 1918.
‡ *See* W.D's., Guards Divisional Train and D.A.D.O.S., March, 1918.

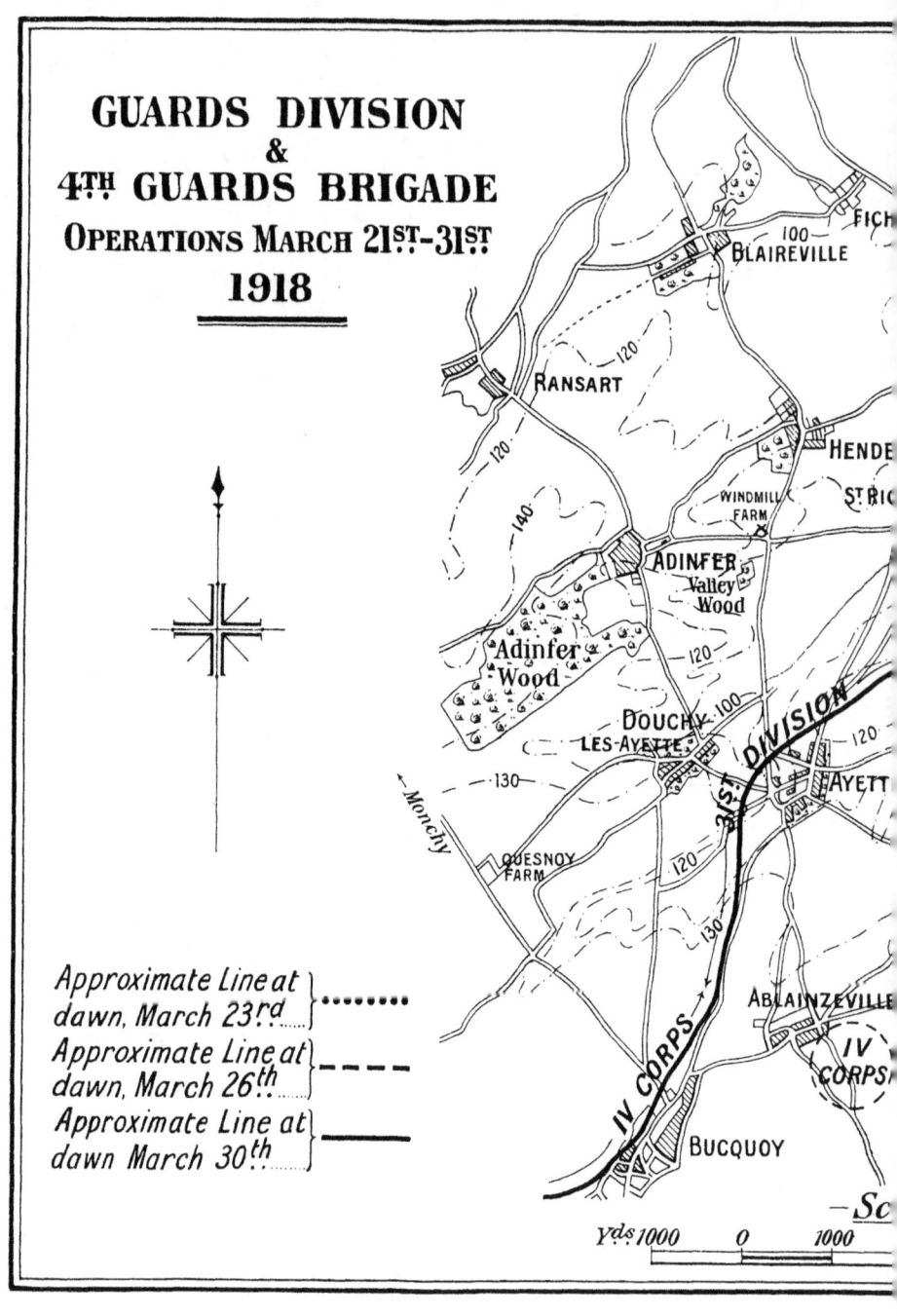

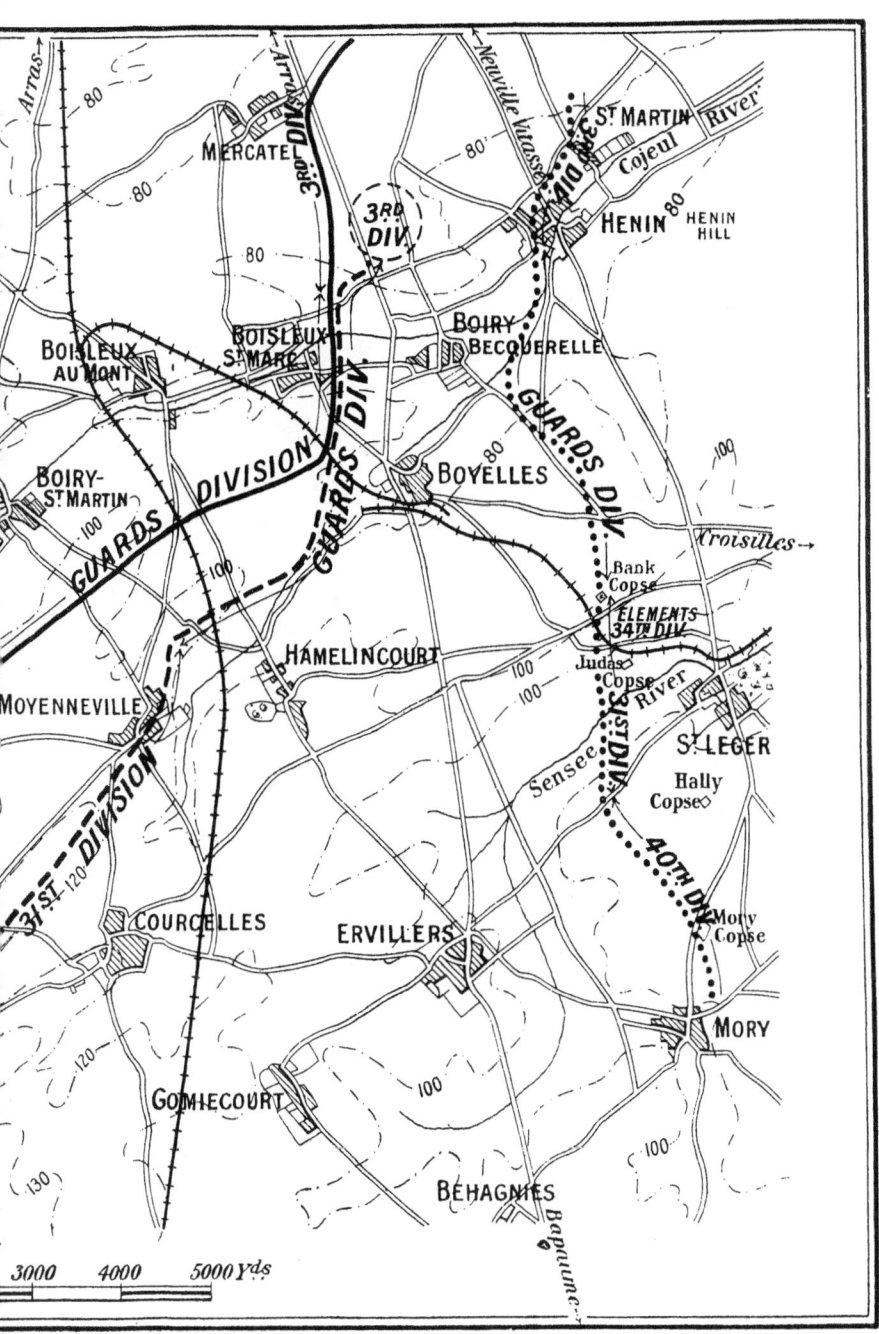

CASUALTIES

ance of officers and men was somewhat ragged and woebegone at the end of their ten days' fighting.* The casualties in the division between the 21st and 31st of March are recorded as 59 officers and 1,080 other ranks.†

---

* " I have men now who are ragged about the trousers to the extent of indecency, and many have their bare toes sticking through their boots." Extract from the diary of Major C. H. Dudley Ward. *See* " History of the Welsh Guards," p. 213.

† The 1st Guards Bde. lost 16 officers and 321 other ranks. There appears to be no separate return for this period by the 2nd Guards Bde. The 3rd Guards Bde. lost 12 officers and 332 other ranks. The Guards Machine-Gun Regiment lost 8 officers and 82 other ranks.

CHAPTER XIV

THE GERMAN ADVANCE IN THE VALLEY OF THE LYS —THE BATTLE OF HAZEBROUCK, 12TH TO 15TH OF APRIL, 1918—THE 4TH GUARDS BRIGADE (31ST DIVISION) IN THE DEFENCE OF NIEPPE FOREST.

(1) OPENING OF THE GERMAN OFFENSIVE IN THE VALLEY OF THE LYS—THE 31ST DIVISION SENT TO REINFORCE THE BRITISH FRONT IN THE HAZEBROUCK AREA.

IT is now necessary, before proceeding further with the story of the Guards Division, to describe in some detail the magnificent part played by the 4th Guards Bde. in stemming the tide of German success in the Lys offensive. The record of the brigade in this fighting is one of which all Guardsmen are justly proud and no history of the Guards in the Great War would be complete, or even adequate, which failed to relate the epic deeds performed just north of Merville by the 4th Bn. Grenadier Guards, the 3rd Bn. Coldstream Guards and the 2nd Bn. Irish Guards while forming part of the 31st Division.

After its relief at the beginning of April * the 31st Division was withdrawn to rest and to refit in the Monchy-le-Breton area, the troops of the 4th Guards Bde. being conveyed in buses on the 2nd of April *via* Frevent and St. Pol to Tinques cross-roads from which point they marched to billets in and near Chelers.† Here they remained until the night of the 10th–11th of April, Brig.-General the Honble. L. J. P. Butler arriving from England on the 4th and taking over the command of the brigade from Lieut.-Colonel the Honble.

---

* *See* p. 75.
† *See* W.D., 4th Guards Bde., April, 1918.

H. Alexander, who resumed the command of the 2nd Bn. Irish Guards.

The enemy's offensive in the valley of the Lys was opened with dramatic suddenness on the 9th of April when General von Quart with a force of 9 divisions, after overwhelming the Portuguese east of Laventie in the early hours of the morning, succeeded during the course of the day in pressing back nearly the whole of the British front lying between Givenchy and Rue du Bois—the new German salient at nightfall roughly following a line east of Festubert, Vieille Chapelle, Lestrem station, the outskirts of Estaires, Sailly-sur-La Lys, Croix-du-Bac, Fleurbaix. By the evening of the following day (10th of April) Lestrem, Estaires and Armentières were in the possession of the enemy, and his troops had made their way westward as far as Steenwerck on the Armentières—Hazebrouck railway line.*

Among the reinforcements which were hurried to this part of the battlefront was the 31st Division, and the advanced troops of the 92nd and 93rd Infantry Bdes. arrived in the line east and south of Outtersteene, a little to the east of Merris, early in the morning on the 11th of April.†

The 4th Guards Bde., the remaining brigade in the division, did not reach the scene of action until late in the evening of the same day. The brigade received orders to "embus" at midnight on the 10th of April, but for some reason the buses did not put in an appearance until about 9 a.m. on the 11th and the troops were obliged to spend the night on the Arras—St. Pol road waiting for them—a disagreeable

---

* On the 10th of April the area of the Lys offensive was extended north of Armentières. Under cover of a thick mist the outpost lines of the 25th and 19th Divisions were driven in early in the morning, and by midday the enemy had gained the village of Ploegsteert, part of Ploegsteert Wood and Messines. Later in the day, the area of the fighting was still further enlarged, and, by the evening, the British line had been pushed back as far as the crest of the Wytschaete ridge. As a result of this northern advance of the Germans, the position of the 34th Division in Armentières became precarious, and it was deemed advisable to evacuate that town. The evacuation was successfully effected and the bridges over the Lys destroyed by 9.30 p.m. See "Sir Douglas Haig's Despatches," p. 224.

† See W.D., 31st Division, April, 1918.

beginning to that which was to prove a particularly disagreeable expedition.* When the buses actually did arrive, it took them twelve hours to convey the troops to their destination, and it was not until about 9 p.m. on the 11th of April that the leading battalion reached Strazeele. In ruined houses and shelters just south of that village the brigade bivouacked for the few hours of darkness which remained, a company of the 2nd Bn. Irish Guards being sent forward along the Strazeele—Vieux Berquin road to reconnoitre a suitable position to be taken up the following morning.†

(2) THE TASK ASSIGNED TO THE 4TH GUARDS BRIGADE—THE FIGHTING NORTH OF MERVILLE, 12TH OF APRIL.

The course of the battle in the area east of Merville on the 11th of April had been distinctly unfavourable to the British. The German advance had been pressed with great determination throughout the day; the troops of the 50th Division, worn out and much reduced in strength after three days of exceptionally heavy fighting, had been steadily forced back and, by 6 p.m., the enemy had reached Neuf Berquin and penetrated into the eastern outskirts of Merville. It was then decided, in view of the fact that fresh troops were not yet available for the defence of the town, to withdraw the defending force just west of Merville, and this movement was successfully carried out late in the evening.‡

---

* The experience of the 4th Bn. Grenadier Guards, which was typical of that of the other battalions in the brigade, was as follows:—
"The Battalion was in billets at Villers Brulin on April 10th, when Lieut.-Colonel Pilcher received orders to move up in omnibuses to Strazeele station *via* St. Pol. According to instructions it should have started 'embussing' at 11.30 that night, but owing to some mistake the buses were twelve hours late, and all ranks spent the night and half the next day waiting by the roadside. It was impossible to cook any proper breakfasts, and too cold to sleep, so that when at last a start was made the men were already tired out. Then for twelve hours they jolted along in the buses, terribly cramped and without any opportunity for real rest." *See* "The Grenadier Guards in the Great War," vol. iii. p. 34.

† *See* "The Irish Guards in the Great War," vol. ii. pp. 198, 199.
‡ *See* "Sir Douglas Haig's Despatches," pp. 224, 225.

THE 4TH GUARDS BDE. TAKES UP ITS FRONT

The task entrusted to the 4th Guards Bde. by the XV Corps (Lieut.-General Sir B. de Lisle) on its arrival at Strazeele was to restore the situation between Merville and the right of the 29th Division which was reported to be somewhere in the neighbourhood of Vieux Berquin, but its exact location like that of most units and formations during these hectic days was by no means certain. The task, therefore, of Brig.-General Butler and his men, as Mr. Rudyard Kipling has so tersely expressed it, was really to " discover and fill the nearest or widest gap," and " to get into touch with the Divisions on their right and left, whose present whereabouts were rather doubtful."

After a hurried consultation with his commanding officers, Brig.-General Butler issued his orders, and, before daylight on the 12th of April, the 4th Guards Bde. moved south from Strazeele and took up a line extending from l'Epinette to La Couronne, west of the Vieux-Berquin—Neuf-Berquin road. The 3rd Bn. Coldstream Guards held the right of the line from l'Epinette to le Cornet Perdu whence it was continued by the 4th Bn. Grenadier Guards to the road junction due east of Gars Brugghe. The 2nd Bn. Irish Guards remained in reserve about Verte Rue. A little later in the morning this front was extended to the right—to the junction of the Arrewage—l'Epinette roads—with the result that the length of line held by each battalion was slightly increased.

The Guards' position was by no means an ideal one from the point of view of defence, but it was the best available. On the east it was bounded by the long, straight road that runs from Strazeele to Estaires through a succession of straggling villages—Vieux-Berquin, La Couronne, Pont Rondin. On the west stretched the outskirts of Nieppe Forest. In front and in rear of the line lay an expanse of dead flat, highly cultivated country, cut up into fields by fences or, more usually, by broad ditches, intersected by lanes and tracks running mainly from east to west, and dotted with small farm-houses and cottages.

The exact line reached by the Germans was still uncertain, but the company of Irish Guards, which had been sent forward during the night, had been fired upon in the neighbourhood of Vieux-Berquin, and the fire of hostile machine guns had been visible all round the horizon from that village to Vierhouck.

As soon as it became light the enemy's artillery came into action and the whole line and the area in rear were heavily shelled,* whilst any attempt at movement by the Guards was met with fierce bursts of machine-gun fire. About 8 a.m. strong bodies of German infantry moved forward to the attack, but they were driven back by rifle and machine-gun fire before they reached the trenches of the Grenadiers and Coldstream.

Soon after this successful beginning to the day's fighting, Brig.-General Butler received orders to advance in order to secure the line Vieux Moulin—the College, and to prevent the enemy from moving along the Merville—Neuf-Berquin road. He was told that troops belonging to the 50th Division were still in the neighbourhood of les Puresbecques as well as in the area lying between Vierhouck and Pont Rondin. He was also definitely assured that les Puresbecques was not occupied by the Germans. He accordingly gave his commanding officers verbal instructions to advance at 11 a.m. with patrols thrown well out on all forward roads. He told them, at the same time, to impress upon their subordinate commanders the importance of exploiting to the full all patrol successes, and emphasized the urgent necessity for the occupation by the brigade of les Puresbecques and Vierhouck, where he hoped to gain touch on each of his flanks with the 50th Division and so to close a dangerous gap in the British line. Events, however, soon proved that the information given to the 4th Guards Bde. was entirely incorrect. The 3rd Bn. Coldstream Guards, on the right of

* " The morning of April 12th broke hot and sunny, under a sky full of observation-balloons that seemed to hover directly above them. These passed word to the German guns, and the bombardment of heavies and shrapnel began—our own artillery not doing much to keep it down—with a careful searching of all houses and shelters, and specially for Battalion Headquarters. The Battalion, imperfectly dug in, or to the more leeward of cottages and fences, suffered ; for every movement was spotted by the balloons." *See* " The Irish Guards in the Great War," vol. ii. p. 199.

4TH GRENADIER GUARDS HEAVILY ENGAGED

the advance, almost as soon as it moved forward encountered a heavy cross fire from the enemy's riflemen and machine gunners stationed in the houses in les Puresbecques and in an orchard south-west of Vierhouck. In despite of a good many casualties, the battalion succeeded in pushing on for about 400 yards. Meanwhile, however, the right company of the 4th Bn. Grenadier Guards advancing upon Vierhouck had been brought to a standstill owing to the intensity of the German artillery and machine-gun fire, which swept the only road by which the stream in front of the village could be crossed.

The left company of the Grenadiers, under the command of Captain T. T. Pryce, which was directed on Pont Rondin, was more successful. This operation was conducted with a determination and precision which carried all before it, and Captain Pryce and his men, after some fierce hand to hand fighting, succeeded in taking possession of several houses in Pont Rondin.*

It was now about 3 p.m. and the situation in which the Guards found themselves, if not actually critical, was a peculiarly awkward one. The Coldstream had found no British troops on their right, while there was a gap between them and the Grenadiers on their left. The right and centre of the Grenadiers were suffering very severely from the close-range fire of the German field guns and trench mortars,†

---

* " In the houses down the road, by which the Grenadiers had to come, the Germans were posted with light machine guns, and before any progress could be made these houses had to be cleared. Slowly and systematically, No. 2 Company worked from house to house, and silenced the machine guns. Thirty Germans were killed in this way—Captain Pryce alone accounted for seven—and were found afterwards in the houses or near by. Two machine guns were taken as well as a couple of prisoners. During the whole operation, this company was under heavy fire, not only from machine guns but also from a battery of field guns, which was firing with open sights from a position some 300 yards down the road." See " The Grenadier Guards in the Great War," vol. iii. p. 37.

† Battalion headquarters (4th Bn. Grenadier Guards) in a farm a little behind the line, also suffered a good deal from the fire of these guns. It was kept down to some extent with the assistance of the 152nd Bde., R.F.A., whose guns did heavy execution among the advancing Germans. See " The Grenadier Guards in the Great War," vol. iii. p. 39.

while Captain Pryce, on the extreme left of the brigade front, reported that his left flank was in the air and that he could see the enemy 1,000 yards in his rear. All that it was possible, however, for the brigadier to do in the circumstances was to send forward two companies of the Irish Guards, one to reinforce the Coldstream, the other the Grenadiers, in the event of a fresh German attack. This came a little later in the afternoon when a determined effort was made to envelop the right flank of the Coldstream. The company on this flank was by this time only about 40 strong, but the sergeant in command managed to extricate his men very skilfully, and brought them to Pont Tournant by stages after inflicting heavy losses on the enemy. But this movement enabled parties of Germans to penetrate between this company and the company on its left. An immediate counter-attack, in which the supporting company of Irish Guards on its own initiative participated, quickly restored the situation, and so keen was the fighting spirit of the men that they could with difficulty be restrained from following up the enemy as he retreated.

While this engagement was in progress, Brig.-General Butler, finding himself unable to reinforce the left flank of the Grenadiers, withdrew it to the road junction east of Gars Brugghe. About this time in the day, too, the 12th Bn. K.O.Y.L.I., the Pioneer Bn. of the 31st Division, which was holding the line from La Couronne in a north-easterly direction, was placed under the orders of the 4th Guards Bde. and a company of the 2nd Bn. Irish Guards was sent forward to link up the Pioneers with the left of the Grenadiers.

These arrangements had hardly been completed when, at 4.30 p.m., after a short but intense artillery preparation, the Germans again attacked all along the Guards' line. They were met with a withering rifle and Lewis-gun fire and flung back with heavy losses. A little later, however, at about 6 p.m., a fresh attack was made at Bleu, a hamlet a little to the north of La Couronne held by troops of the 29th Division. This resulted in a slight gain of ground by the enemy and compelled the 12th Bn. K.O.Y.L.I. to form a defensive flank to the north—nevertheless, at the end of an arduous day's fighting the front of the 4th Guards Bde. held firm all along the line. The casualties had been heavy—those of the 4th Bn. Grenadier Guards alone amounting to 8 officers and 250 other ranks—and the men were worn out ; but their spirit and discipline remained unshaken. Few of them probably realized the full gravity of the situation or the immense responsibility which rested upon them, but the majority understood well enough that their task was to delay the German advance until fresh British troops could be brought to the battle area—and they knew that they had carried out this task successfully from morning to night against an attacking force vastly superior to them in numbers.

(3) Continuance of the German advance towards Haze-brouck—Stubborn resistance by the Guards—The British Line secured.

During the night Brig.-General Butler received orders from the 31st Division to reorganize his troops on a line running from Pont Tournant through l'Epinette and le Cornet Perdu to La Couronne.

In view of the reduced strength of his battalions and the exposed condition of his flanks, the Brig.-General requested that this front might be somewhat reduced and was told that the 5th Division had been ordered to take over the line as far as l'Epinette. To what extent this relief was carried out, or whether it actually took place, are matters with regard to which reports differ.* In either case, however, the troops

* According to the narrative of the 31st Division, 13th of April, 1918, the 4th Guards Bde. reported at 3.30 a.m. that day that the 5th Division had taken over the line from Pont Tournant to the Arrewage—l'Epinette road junction. In Appendix 16 of the W.D., 1st Australian Division (April, 1918), it is stated that a staff officer of the 31st Division rang up on the telephone at 5 p.m. on the 13th of April to say that the Guards Bde. was on a line Pont Tournant—Arrewage road east of Bois d'Aval corner ; and that elements of the brigade might still be fighting, though surrounded, in front of this line. In reply to a question this officer said that the 5th Division had previously taken over the Guards' line as far north as Arrewage, and that he could not account for the Guards being still in the vicinity of Pont Tournant unless they had fallen back behind the 5th Division. On the 12th of April the W.D., of the 5th Division do not appear to have moved farther in the direction of l'Epinette than the junction of the Arrewage—l'Epinette roads, for, at an early hour in the morning of the 13th of April, the front of the 4th Guards Bde. ran from the junction of these roads in a north-easterly direction through l'Epinette and le Cornet Perdu to a point a little north of La Couronne.* The 3rd Bn. Coldstream Guards was holding the right, the 4th Bn. Grenadier Guards the centre, and the 12th Bn. K.O.Y.L.I. the left of the line; while the bulk of the 2nd Bn. Irish Guards and a company of the 3rd Bn. Coldstream Guards were in brigade reserve in and about the orchards at Caudescure and Arrewage.

During the night the exhausted troops, with the assistance of the 210th Field Company, R.E., had done what they could to dig themselves in on their new line; but their numbers were so much reduced, their weariness so great, that all that was possible was to dig small detached posts in which groups of four or five men could obtain some slight cover.† Any kind of patrolling in front of the battalion positions during the night was out of the question as no men could be spared for the purpose, and the enemy was quick to take advantage of this opportunity, as well as of the thick mist which hung over the ground during the early hours of the morning, to push forward his machine guns.‡

About 6.30 a.m. the fighting was resumed; it was to

5th Division, places the left of the divisional front as being about Pont Tournant. It also states that in the evening the left battalion of the division was in touch with the Guards in this vicinity. The following day there is an entry in the W.D. (5th Division) saying that its left battalion (1st D.C.L.I.) withdrew in order to conform with the Guards' retirement until its left was at Arrewage orchard.

See W.D., 31st Division, App. 347, April, 1918. 4th Guards Bde. Narrative.

† See " The Grenadier Guards in the Great War," vol. iii. pp. 40–42.

‡ " Our people did not attach much importance to the enemy's infantry, but spoke with unqualified admiration of their machine gunners. The method of attack was uniformly simple. Machine-gun working to a flank enfiladed our dug-in line, while field guns hammered it flat frontally, sometimes even going up with the assaulting infantry. Meanwhile, individual machine guns crept forward, using all shelters and covers, and turned up in rear of our defences." *See* " The Irish Guards in the Great War," vol. ii. p. 205.

continue with little intermission throughout the day. The German infantry attacked the front of the Coldstream in conjunction with an armoured car,* which came up from the direction of les Puresbecques and engaged with its machine guns a post on the extreme right of the line, firing at a range of about 10 yards. Assisted by the fog, too, small parties of the enemy dribbled their way between the thin line of posts round l'Epinette, and a company of Irish Guards was sent forward to restore the line in this area, as the position of the right company of the Grenadiers appeared to be somewhat precarious.

At 9.15 a.m. a further determined assault was made by the Germans, who attacked in strength along the whole brigade front. But the defence was magnificent; the line stood firm.† Farther to the north, however, some time between 9 and 10 a.m., the enemy unfortunately succeeded in working his way into Vieux-Berquin, and the withdrawal of the British troops from this village uncovered the left flank of the 4th Guards Bde. The situation immediately became extremely critical. The Germans were still exerting a strong pressure on the brigade front; they had succeeded in penetrating round the flanks and were now in considerable strength in rear of the line, whilst a fresh column of hostile infantry, estimated at two battalions, could be observed advancing from Bleu. It was at about this time, too, that the enemy brought his field guns into action at close range, the fire of which quickly flattened out the defences on the northern portion of the brigade front. A little later, at about 12.30 p.m., the 12th Bn. K.O.Y.L.I., whose men had fought with the utmost gallantry throughout the morning, was literally blown out of its positions at La Couronne by trench-mortar fire and was forced back as far as la Becque. The left flank company of the 4th Bn. Grenadier Guards

* *See* " Sir Douglas Haig's Despatches," p. 227.
† It is recorded that Private Jacotin, 3rd Bn. Coldstream Guards, the sole survivor in the left post of the centre company of his battalion, single-handed kept the enemy at bay for 20 minutes until he was killed by a bomb. When the left company of the Coldstream was attacked near le Cornet Perdu the Germans came forward through the mist shouting that they were " The King's Company Grenadier Guards."

was thus practically isolated, and a message from Captain Pryce, its commander, which was received at brigade headquarters at 3.30 p.m., stated that it was partially surrounded and that the men were fighting back to back. Brig.-General Butler at once ordered a company of the Irish Guards to go to Captain Pryce's assistance and to endeavour to form a defensive flank about Verte Rue. This relief force moved forward along the La Couronne road and was heavily attacked by the enemy from la Becque and also from the south-east. Surrounded, outnumbered, and exposed to a deadly machine-gun fire from the houses in Vieux-Berquin, the Irish Guards could only hope to delay the German advance for a time. They could do no more. Only one non-commissioned officer and six men were left to rejoin their battalion at night. But the defence of the Guards in this area of the fighting was not yet broken. The enemy's thrust towards Hazebrouck was now confronted by the battalion headquarters of the 4th Bn. Grenadier Guards and the 3rd Bn. Coldstream Guards, and their stubborn resistance successfully held him at bay until darkness set in.*

Meanwhile, the hostile pressure from the south and south-east along the brigade front had been kept up throughout the afternoon. The numbers of the defenders grew fewer and fewer. Broken up in small parties, Grenadiers and Coldstream and Irish Guards still clung tenaciously to the positions which they had been ordered to defend at all costs, contesting every yard of ground and exacting a heavy toll from the advancing Germans.

On the right of the line the remnants of the Coldstream—whose right and centre companies had been practically wiped out—were still fighting at 6.15 p.m. with the enemy attacking on all sides. Later in the evening, the survivors endeavoured to withdraw upon the 5th Division and the 1st Australian Division, but few succeeded in doing so. The Grenadiers fought with a similar gallantry and suffered equally severely —only very few of them being able to make their way back to the Australian line.† The story of the last heroic stand

* See " The Grenadier Guards in the Great War," vol. iii. p. 45.
† Even then the fighting spirit of the survivors appears to have

made by Captain Pryce and his company on the extreme left of the line, who died fighting to the last man after holding up the advance of an overwhelmingly superior force of the enemy until late in the evening, is one that ranks with the finest episodes in military history and has added a glorious page to the records of the Grenadier Guards.*

(4) SHARE OF THE 4TH GUARDS BRIGADE IN THE DEFENCE OF HAZEBROUCK.

By about 6 o'clock in the evening of the 13th of April the front of the 1st Australian Division had been firmly established and ran from Arrewage, in front of Caudescure, thence northward from the east corner of Bois d'Aval towards Vieux-Berquin. The way to Hazebrouck was definitely closed.† The survivors of the 4th Guards Bde. were collected

been undiminished. The story related by Lieut. C. Kerr, 8th Bn. Australian Infantry, of the Grenadier sergeant who, on reaching the Australian line, proceeded to collect his men and then asked permission to remain in the line until he received instructions to rejoin his battalion, illustrates a spirit of discipline and a sense of duty beyond all praise. The report of Lieut. Kerr is printed in "The Grenadier Guards in the Great War," vol. iii. p. 52, and the following extract from it shows the effect which the fighting qualities of the men of the 4th Guards Bde. had upon all those who witnessed their deeds on the 13th of April :—
"The men of my company and battalion are full of admiration for the manner in which the Guards fought. We watched the fighting in the village and farms whilst consolidating the new line. The moral effect on our troops of the stubborn resistance offered by these troops in denying ground to the enemy, the orderly withdrawal to our line, and the refusal of the sergeant to leave the line when offered the choice of comfortable quarters was excellent."

* Captain Pryce was awarded the Victoria Cross for his magnificent courage and fine leadership on this occasion. *See* Appendix II. The story of the last stand made by him and his comrades is admirably told by Sir Frederick Ponsonby in "The Grenadier Guards in the Great War," pp. 45–47.

† The entries in the W.D. of the 31st Division with regard to this soul-stirring and eminently critical day's fighting are meagre and decidedly misleading. They show how difficult a task it is for the historian to give anything like an accurate or worthy account of a battle from the official sources. The Diary states that the 4th Guards Brigade was pushed back during the day to the line Arrewage—south-east corner of Bois d'Aval—la Becque—about Vieux-Berquin; and that the relief of the Guards by the Australians was carried out in

on the right portion of this front, where they remained in the line under the command of Lieut.-Colonel Alexander until relieved on the night of the 14th–15th of April. Between the 12th and 14th of that month the total casualties of the brigade amounted to 39 officers and 1,244 other ranks.*

But these losses had not been in vain. The Guards had once again saved the situation. As at Loos and at Cambrai they had set an example of courage, discipline and tenacity of purpose which was an inspiration to all who witnessed it. In recording his appreciation of the splendid services of the troops who withstood the German drive towards Hazebrouck on the 13th of April the Commander-in-Chief gives the chief credit to the 4th Guards Bde. :—

"The performance of all the troops engaged in this most gallant stand, and especially that of the 4th Guards Brigade, on whose front of some 4,000 yards the heaviest attacks fell, is worthy of the highest praise. No more brilliant exploit has taken place since the opening of the enemy's offensive, though gallant actions have been without number." †

In forwarding to the Second Army commander a special "narrative of the action of the 4th Guards Brigade during the operations of the 11th to the 14th of April, 1918," Lieut.-General Sir Beauvoir de Lisle, commanding the XV Corps, stated that in his opinion nothing finer was recorded in the annals of the British Army than "the glorious stand against overwhelming odds" made by the 4th Guards Bde.‡ In a special letter addressed to Brig.-General Butler, General Sir Herbert Plumer, the Second Army commander, said that he considered the performance of the brigade "under very trying circumstances to be worthy of all praise. Such results are only obtained by troops that have gained the

good order although one company on the right of the Guards had to fight its way back to the Australian line—indeed, the Diary even speaks of the line " handed over " to the Australians.

* The Grenadiers lost 15 officers and 504 other ranks; the Coldstream 15 officers and 490 other ranks; the Irish Guards 9 officers and 250 other ranks.

† *See* " Sir Douglas Haig's Despatches," p. 227.

‡ *See* W.D., 31st Division, April, 1918. XV Corps, No. 608/13/70.

highest standard of training and discipline, and they reflect the highest credit on all officers, non-commissioned officers and men."

(5) Subsequent History of the 4th Guards Brigade.

On leaving the line the 4th Guards Bde. went into billets in the Borre area, a little to the north-east of Hazebrouck where, on the 15th of April, Brig.-General Butler reorganized it again in three battalions—the 2nd Bn. Irish Guards, a composite battalion of Grenadiers and Coldstream and the 12th Bn. K.O.Y.L.I. This amalgamation of the Grenadiers and Coldstream was necessary as neither the 4th Bn. Grenadier Guards nor the 3rd Bn. Coldstream Guards could muster more than two companies, and, as the Brig.-General was aware that he might be called upon to take over a brigade sector in the Hazebrouck defences at very short notice, he decided that each of his three battalions must be up to strength.* Two days later, on the 17th of April, the Guards were set to work on this defensive system, and, on the 19th, relieved the 2nd Australian Bde. in the line on the eastern edge of Nieppe Forest at the south-eastern corner of Bois d'Aval. The 12th Bn. K.O.Y.L.I. and the 2nd Bn. Irish Guards on the right and left respectively occupied the front trenches with the composite battalion in support. The British and German lines were extremely close together at this point, the enemy's positions being in Ferme Beaulieu and just north of the Verte Rue—La Couronne road.

The first two days in the line passed quietly, neither side displaying any anxiety to make itself conspicuous, but on the night of the 21st of April, and again on the 22nd, the day on which the composite battalion relieved the K.O.Y.L.I.

* The 31st Division was instructed to man the Hazebrouck defences should the reserve Australian brigade have to move forward. *See* W.D's., 31st Division and 4th Guards Bde., April, 1918. It is interesting to note that this was the first occasion in the history of the two Regiments that any such amalgamation had ever taken place. *Cf.* "The Grenadier Guards in the Great War," vol. iii. p. 54. Lieut.-Colonel Pilcher assumed the command of the composite battalion, with Major Gillilan, Coldstream Guards, as his second-in-command.

in the line, the enemy bombarded Nieppe Forest with gas, which made conditions in that thickly wooded area almost unendurable.*

The following night, the 23rd–24th of April, 2 officers and 80 men of the Irish Guards, supported by an artillery, trench-mortar and machine-gun barrage, carried out a highly successful raid on Beaulieu Farm. They brought back 25 prisoners and a machine gun, killed 30 of the enemy and put 2 more machine guns out of action. They had themselves only 7 slight casualties.†

The next day the Guards were relieved in the line and moved into billets at Hondeghem, a village lying between Hazebrouck and Cassel. Here they remained for the next three weeks, and were employed in the work of constructing and strengthening the defences in this area.‡

On the 6th of May Major-General Bridgford, commanding the 31st Division, bade farewell to the brigade, and, on the 15th, General Sir Herbert Plumer presented medal ribbons at a highly successful ceremonial parade. Five days later, by which time all danger from the Lys offensive was at an end and the Germans were already beginning to experience the unmitigated misery of inhabiting a low-lying salient exposed to the incessant fire of a powerful artillery, the 4th Guards Bde. was moved in buses and by rail into the Third Army area where it was located at Grenas, Saulty, Thievres and Barly. It was now in G.H.Q. Reserve and was used to provide reinforcements for the Guards Division whenever the necessary officers and men were not forthcoming from the Guards Base.

The rest of the story of the 4th Guards Bde. can be

---

* Both the brigade-major and the staff captain of the 4th Guards Bde. were evacuated gassed on the 22nd of April. On the 24th Brig.-General Butler was also gassed, the command of the brigade once again devolving upon Lieut.-Colonel Alexander until the arrival from England on the 27th of April of Lieut.-Colonel R. J. B. Crawford, Coldstream Guards.

† *See* " The Irish Guards in the Great War," vol. ii. pp. 208, 209. The brigade received the congratulations of the Army commander and the corps commander.

‡ The total casualties of the 4th Guards Bde. for the month of April amounted to 48 officers and 1,379 other ranks.

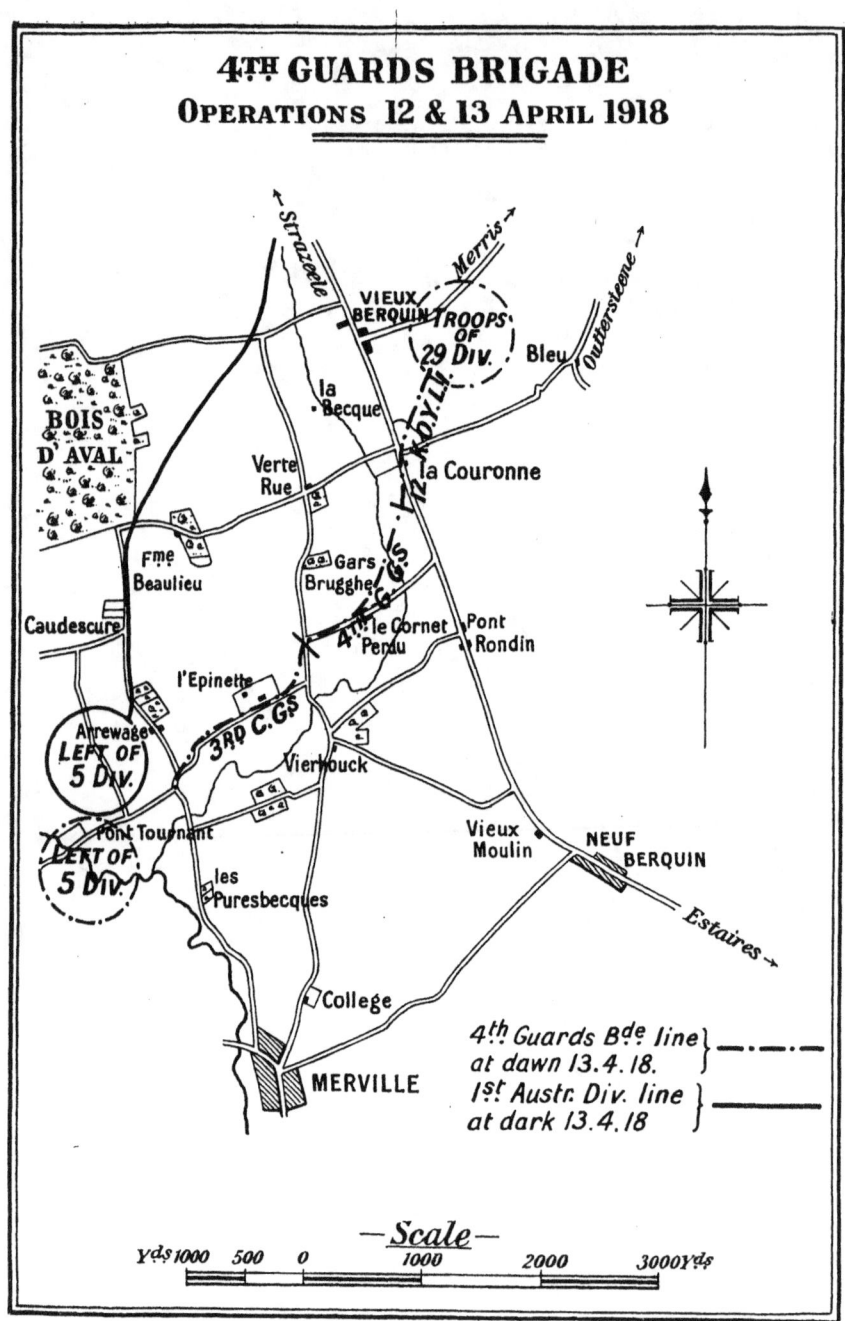

told very briefly. On the 11th and 12th of June it was transferred to the La Cauchie area, where its troops worked on the Berles-au-Bois—Gouy defences until the 6th of July. Three days later the brigade was sent to Criel Plage, a pleasant seaside resort on the coast between Dieppe and Le Treport, where a school for young officers was established under the supervision of the brigade commander.

In September, when the Allied advance had begun, the 4th Bn. Grenadier Guards and the 3rd Bn. Coldstream Guards were moved to Auxi-le-Château, the 2nd Bn. Irish Guards remaining at Criel Plage to furnish all the duties for the Young Officers' School.

The Grenadiers and Coldstream now came under the orders of the Cavalry Corps, and for a time formed part of a mobile column of all arms which, it was intended, should advance in lorries and cars and be entirely independent of horse transport.*

Before the end of September this column—which was known as the 4th Guards Bde. Column—had moved forward to Bray-sur-Somme, and the idea of its being sent into action with Le Cateau as its objective, was seriously considered. Even when all hope of a cavalry advance had to be abandoned the idea of the employment of this mobile column appears to have still been considered feasible, for, on the 9th of October, the column was pushed forward along the Montbrehain—Brancourt—Premont road, where it came under the enemy's artillery fire. It reached Gouy-le-Catelet on the 11th, but took no part in the operations, and, on the 26th, it was broken up. The two Guards battalions then returned to Criel Plage, where the 4th Guards Bde. remained until it rejoined the Guards Division at Maubeuge after the Armistice.

* The 1st Bn. H.A.C. and A/58 Battery, R.F.A., and a bridging train also formed part of this column.

CHAPTER XV

APRIL TO AUGUST, 1918—CLOSE OF THE GERMAN OFFENSIVE.

(1) CESSATION OF THE ENEMY'S ATTACKS ON THE FRONT OF THE VI CORPS—STRENGTHENING OF THE DEFENCES ON THE GUARDS DIVISIONAL FRONT—RELIEF OF THE GUARDS BY THE 2ND DIVISION, 13TH–15TH OF APRIL.

WITH the failure of the attack on the Guards Division on the 30th of March the enemy's attempts to press forward his advance on the front of the VI Corps really came to an end.* But, although for the next few months the war was once again to become stationary on this part of the British line, a speedy resumption of the hostile offensive in the area south of the Scarpe was generally anticipated at the beginning of April. Every measure compatible with the prevailing scarcity of men and guns was accordingly put in hand by Major-General Feilding for the strengthening and developing of the defensive organization in his divisional sector. In view of the great strain to which his troops had been exposed,† his principal anxiety was to bring about some reduction in the number of men in the forward area, and a plan for the withdrawal of one of the Guards brigades into the back

---

* The line held by the VI Corps, after the recapture of Ayette by the 32nd Division on the 3rd of April, ran from Bucquoy east of Ayette, round the northern edge of Moyenneville and west of Boyelles, northward to Mercatel. See W.D., 1st Guards Bde., April, 1918.

† Although the moral of the troops left nothing to be desired the battalions in all three Guards brigades were in need of rest and reorganization. This point is emphasized in the following passage from the diary of the 3rd Guards Bde. :—" a large number of experts having been knocked out in the recent heavy fighting and all ranks very tired and done." See W.D., 3rd Guards Bde., April, 1918.

area was carefully examined. It was found, however, that the readjustment of the line involved by this redistribution of troops would necessitate too great a shortening of the front and the scheme had to be abandoned. The Major-General then decided to hold the forward area as lightly as possible and to keep battalions ready in rear for counter-attack purposes. The attachment to the Guards Division on the 2nd of April of the 265th Machine-Gun Company, newly arrived from England, materially assisted this scheme of defence as it enabled the Major-General to strengthen considerably the flanks of his position by the reorganization in depth of his machine guns, some of the guns of the 1st and 3rd Guards Bdes. being moved back from the front line in order to conform with the new dispositions.* The defensive situation from an artillery point of view was less satisfactory as the C.R.A. informed the divisional commander that with the guns now left at his disposal he could not provide a barrage to cover more than 2,000 yards of the 5,500 yards forming the divisional front. The infantry brigadiers, therefore, were called upon to report to the Major-General in which particular area they considered that the provision of a barrage would be most generally useful,† and a scheme of artillery support was drawn up more or less in conformity with their suggestions. It was admittedly by no means a complete or satisfactory system of artillery defence, but it was the best that could be devised in the circumstances and its efficiency was luckily not put to any really serious test.

On the 4th of April the Germans began their final desperate effort to break through the Allied line on the Somme front, making their principal attack at the point of junction between the British and French Armies south of the river.‡ During this day there was a good deal of

---

* *See* W.D., Guards Division, App. 779, April, 1918.
† *Ibid.* App. 780.
‡ " On the 4th and 5th of April the enemy made a final effort to prevent the French and British line becoming stable. The principal attack on the 4th of April was made south of the Somme, and involved the whole of the British front between the river and Hangard, where we joined the French, and also the French Army on our right." *See* " Sir Douglas Haig's Despatches," p. 215.

hostile shelling on the front of the VI Corps, the enemy's trench-mortar fire being particularly severe between Moyenneville and Boyelles, but no infantry attack developed. On the 5th and 6th of April this artillery and trench-mortar activity rather increased, and as the enemy's aircraft was also continually over the line, the Third Army commander fully expected that the anticipated attack was about to begin. The Guards accordingly were more than usually on the alert, and, notwithstanding the wet weather which prevailed about this period in the month, carried out vigilant patrol work all along their front.* But no signs of hostile activity were observed, nor did the enemy make any attempt to advance in this area; and, as the days passed by, his artillery became less aggressive—the opening of his offensive in the valley of the Lys no doubt necessitated the withdrawal of a certain number of his guns from the region south of the Scarpe.† The chief local effect, however, of the opening of this northern offensive was that it led to the departure of the 5th Division, which was to have relieved the 2nd Canadian Division on the left of the Guards, and so lengthened the period of time spent by troops in the front line. But except for this not unusual inconvenience nothing occurred to disturb the ordinary routine of trench life before the welcome relief of the Guards by the 2nd Division on the nights of the 13th–14th and 14th–15th of April. Divisional headquarters was then opened at Bavincourt.‡ The 1st Guards Bde. was quartered round Bavincourt and Saulty; the 2nd Guards Bde. in the Larbret area and the 3rd Guards Bde. at Barly. The divisional Artillery remained in the line.

The division was now in Third Army reserve and was under orders to move at three hours' notice, its allotted

---

* It poured with rain on the night of the 5th–6th of April, and the state of the ground became very bad. The troops suffered considerably as there was little shelter in the area and it was almost impossible for the men to get dry.

† The attack on the Portuguese south-east of Laventie, which heralded the Lys offensive, was launched early in the morning on the 9th of April.

‡ While divisional headquarters was at Bavincourt the Major-General was visited by the Commander-in-Chief, and also by General Lemaistre, commanding the Tenth French Army.

task being to carry out a counter-attack should the enemy succeed in penetrating the "purple line." But luckily no such untoward event took place, and so, for a period of ten days, the Guards were enabled to rest and to refit, as well as to obtain some useful rifle practice at a range near Barly. Some of the commanding officers also made a gallant attempt to give their men some field training, but the area in which they found themselves was closely cultivated and the usual restrictions as to growing crops were still in force. The French farmers, magnificently unperturbed by the possible coming of the Germans, were steadily pursuing their usual agricultural work, and, consequently, little really useful practice in moving across country was possible.* But, nevertheless, even this abortive effort to resume field training was a sign of the times, the meaning of which was not lost on the men. Possibly, also, the breaking up of the Reinforcement Battalion †—a step which was taken about this time in order that drafts might be trained with their respective units—and the reorganization of the infantry transport for the purposes of moving warfare ‡ did something to countenance a more cheerful view of the situation.

(2) THE GUARDS RETURN TO THE LINE, 24TH–26TH OF APRIL.

On the 24th and 25th of April and the following night the Guards, much benefited by their short rest, relieved the 32nd Division in the right sector of the VI Corps front, the 37th Division (IV Corps) being on their right and the 2nd Division on their left. Major-General Feilding established his headquarters at Humbercamp, and all three brigades—the 3rd, 1st and 2nd Guards Bdes. in the order named from right to left—went into the line, each brigadier placing two battalions in the front system of trenches and keeping his remaining battalion in reserve.

The forward area was held by means of a series of posts with short lengths of support and reserve trenches in rear.

* *See* " History of the Welsh Guards," pp. 214, 215.
† *See* Appendix VIII.
‡ *See* W.D., Guards Division, April, 1918, Apps. 790 and 793.

Behind these lay the " purple line," which by this time had been developed into a regular defensive system.* It consisted of front and rear trenches at a distance apart varying from 1,200 to 2,000 yards between which ran an intermediate line of defences that included the fortified Quesnoy Farm and an old German trench running west of the farm and south-east of Adinfer Wood. The machine-gun defence was arranged so as to sweep the valley approaches and thus to force the enemy, if he decided to embark upon a fresh advance in this area, to move forward over the high ground on which the artillery could fire to better advantage. The divisional front was covered by six R.F.A. brigades, five 6-in. howitzer and two 60-pdr. batteries, while more heavy artillery protection was available for S.O.S. and counter-preparation calls.†

Although the weather was wet at the end of April, and the ground in consequence very heavy, all the battalions in the line displayed great energy in patrolling and several prisoners were taken. There were no signs of a German advance—indeed, the enemy showed a greater inclination to retreat—and when, on the 28th of April, a patrol of the 1st Bn. Grenadier Guards made the discovery that he had vacated some of his forward trenches south of Ayette, the question of pushing forward the Guards line towards the Ablainzeville—Moyenneville ridge began to be seriously considered.‡

---

* This satisfactory result was largely due to the steady and unremitting labours of the Field Companies, R.E. Guards Division, and of the 4th Bn. Coldstream Guards (Pioneers) who had continued working on these defences throughout the month of April.

† When the Guards relieved the 32nd Division their Trench-Mortar *personnel* took over eight mortars in the line, and had four more in reserve west of Ayette. Three tanks were allotted to the division for counter-attack purposes, and were stationed at a point a little to the south-east of Quesnoy Farm. Battalions were at about this period made up to a strength of 120 rifles per company, a number which was shortly afterwards increased to 150 for companies in the line.

‡ The casualties of the three Guards brigades during the month of April amounted to 19 officers and 464 other ranks. *See* W.D's., 1st, 2nd and 3rd Guards Bdes., April, 1918. There were various changes in commands about this time. Early in April Brig.-General Lord Henry Seymour relinquished the command of the 3rd Guards Bde. Lieut.-

(3) Work of the Divisional Artillery during the month of April.

The artillery covering the front of the Guards Division at the beginning of April consisted of two groups. The right group comprised the 75th Bde., R.F.A., and the 155th Army Bde., while the left group was formed by the 74th Bde., R.F.A., and the 178th Army Bde. (less one battery). The guns in both groups were continually employed in harassing fire and in special concentrations on specified areas.* On the 3rd of April the right group shelled Moyenneville in support of the successful attack carried out by the 32nd Division on Ayette. On the 16th, after the Guards had left the line, the Germans made another attempt to capture the high ground north of Boyelles and the left group of guns was busily employed in assisting the infantry of the 2nd Division.† Two days later the 75th Bde., R.F.A., was transferred to the left group, its S.O.S. lines being altered so as to cover the left infantry brigade on this divisional front.

On the 28th of April, a few days after the Guards relieved

Colonel N. A. Orr-Ewing, Scots Guards, upon whom the command devolved, commanded the brigade until the 21st of April, when Lieut.-Colonel G. B. S. Follett, Coldstream Guards, was appointed to succeed Lord Henry Seymour. Brig.-General B. N. Sergison-Brooke was sufficiently restored to health to resume the command of the 2nd Guards Bde. on the 25th of April. *See* W.D., " A " & " Q," Guards Division, April, 1918.

On the 21st of May Lieut.-Colonel Orr-Ewing was appointed to the command of the 45th Infantry Bde. and was succeeded in the command of the 2nd Bn. Scots Guards by Major J. A. Stirling. On the 4th of June Lieut.-Colonel R. V. Pollok was appointed commandant of the VI Corps School, and the command of the 1st Bn. Irish Guards devolved upon Major R. R. C. Baggallay.

* The casualties among the artillery *personnel* in the early days of the month were heavy. They included Lieut.-Colonel J. B. Biddulph, commanding the 75th Bde., R.F.A. The command of the brigade devolved upon Major Houseden until the arrival of Lieut.-Colonel W. C. E. Rudkin on the 24th of April.

† "The 2nd Division was most complimentary in its references to help received from the brigade." Extract from the diary of Lieut.-Colonel C. Vickery, commanding 74th Bde., R.F.A.

the 32nd Division, the two divisional brigades, R.F.A., were withdrawn from the 2nd Division and moved into positions behind Adinfer Wood from which they could cover the front of their own division. During the weeks that followed the gunners gave the enemy but little respite either by night or by day, some of the batteries being pushed forward to within 1,000 yards of the front line trenches, where they were employed in searching far in rear of the enemy's forward positions and in enfilading his communications.*

(4) Events on the Divisional front during the month of May.

During the month of May the enemy's infantry opposite the Guards displayed no great offensive spirit, but when attacked was usually found to be on the alert; his artillery was continually active, more especially so towards the end of the month. Its fire, however, did not prevent the accomplishment of a great deal of useful work on the trenches. Tank traps were also constructed on several of the roads running westward and a new switch line was dug from the " purple " system of defences to the southern outskirts of Ayette along the spur which lies to the east of Douchy-les-Ayette.

On the night of the 30th of April–1st of May the 3rd and 1st Guards Bdes., on the right and in the centre respectively of the divisional sector, pushed out their line in order to obtain better observation. Forward posts were established and fresh trenches dug without any opposition from the Germans, although, later on, the new positions came in for a good deal of hostile shelling. Two nights after this successful piece of work a patrol of the 1st Bn. Scots Guards rushed a German post and killed or captured its garrison. The

* The D.A.C., which, notwithstanding the severe strain put upon its resources during the early days of the German offensive, had yet contrived to carry out a great deal of valuable salvage work, was heavily shelled at Beaumetz-les-Loges early in April, and suffered some casualties. It moved to Gouy-en-Artois on the 11th of April, and thence to Gaudiempré, on the 28th, in relief of the 32nd D.A.C.

prisoners belonged to the 451st Regiment (234th Division), and, from the information obtained from them, it was thought that the enemy was contemplating another attack in this area at an early date.* But no such attack developed. On one occasion only during the month is there any record of an attempt by the Germans to attack the Guards and this raid was easily driven back. The real truth of the matter appears to have been that, far from having any intention of continuing his advance in this area, the enemy was fearful that the Guards were contemplating an offensive movement. Prisoners belonging to the 2nd/89th Grenadier Regiment (17th Division) who were captured by the 1st Bn. Irish Guards on the 28th of May, gave this information and the nervous intensity of the German artillery fire towards the end of the month rather tended to confirm it. So far as the Guards Division was concerned, the great German onrush had come to an end.†

(5) Relief of the Guards Division, 6th–7th of June— In rest billets in the Bavincourt area.

On the 6th and 7th of June the Guards were relieved by the 2nd Division and went out of the line for a month's rest and training. Divisional headquarters was once again established at Bavincourt and the three Guards brigades were billetted in the Couterelle, Bazeque and Barly areas.

The enemy's advance in the north had been fought to a

---

* "There were frequent warnings of impending attacks. The warnings were received with equanimity by the troops, who had seen the massed artillery behind Adinfer Wood, and could also look over the top of their trenches and see miles of enemy country which offered little protection to any attacking troops; Ablainzeville, well covered with trees, and standing on a spur which shot out from the ridge the British were holding was the only dangerous spot." See "History of the Welsh Guards," p. 218.

† The casualties in the three Guards brigades during this " quiet " month in the line amounted to 35 officers and 621 other ranks. Four officers belonging to the 1st Bn. Grenadier Guards were killed on the 18th of May when a German aeroplane bombed the 3rd Guards Bde. details at Warlincourt.

standstill.* The Lys offensive had brought the Germans no nearer final success than had their offensive on the Somme. Their progress on the Aisne front had also been definitely checked.† They had gained ground and inflicted much material damage on the Allies, but their losses had been very heavy and the Allied line was still intact. The feeling that a storm of unexceptional magnitude had been safely weathered now began to pervade all ranks. A spirit of optimism was once again in the air.

In the Guards Division, although there had never been any real doubt as to the eventual outcome of the fighting, officers and men had seen enough of the March offensive and its effects to realize the extent of the danger which had been successfully overcome. They felt that Hindenburg and Ludendorff had done their worst against the British—that their bolt was shot—and that the time must shortly arrive when the Allies would once again be in a position to resume the offensive—and this time against a disheartened and much weakened opponent.‡ This feeling of confidence

* "After their capture of Kemmel Hill from the French on the 25th of April the Germans made a series of desperate efforts to gain possession of the Scherpenberg and Mont Rouge. These efforts culminated in a fierce attack on the Allied positions from west of Dranoutre to Voormezeele on the 29th of April. This onslaught was successfully withstood by the French and British, while another attack made in concert with it against the Belgian positions astride the Ypres—Staden railway line was driven back by the Belgians. The following day the French retook Locre and the month closed with the enemy definitely held on both southern and northern battle fronts."
See " Sir Douglas Haig's Despatches," p. 234.

† The German attack on the Aisne front was launched on the morning of the 27th of May. It had been foreseen by the Allied commanders, and, after about ten days' fierce fighting, its progress was definitely checked. The German Higher Command then decided to make one more bid for victory and selected the area east and south-west of Reims for its next attack. This offensive began on the 15th of July, and, "after making some progress at first and effecting the passage of the Marne, was held by the French, American and Italian forces on those fronts." Three days later " Marshal Foch launched the great counter-offensive which he had long been preparing on the front between Château Thierry and Soissons, supporting this successful stroke by vigorous attacks also on other parts of the German salient."
See " Sir Douglas Haig's Despatches," p. 255.

‡ In his picture of the " collective mind " of the 1st Bn. Irish Guards in the early days of July, 1918, Mr. Rudyard Kipling has

among the troops was still further increased by the exercises in open warfare which were now given to them. Training in the art of attack and pursuit, in which all the most recent lessons learnt from the enemy were incorporated and improved upon in light of their own experience, were sedulously practised by all three Guards brigades.* Officers and men were also given an opportunity of studying the methods of the Dominions troops, as a party from the 2nd Canadian Division during the month of June gave a series of demonstrations to the Guards in the art of patrolling and raiding by daylight as practised in the Canadian Corps—demonstrations which appear considerably to have impressed the onlookers.† In June, too, the Guards were called upon to impart instruction to, as well as to receive instruction from, the Britons overseas, as a number of New Zealand non-commissioned officers were attached to various battalions in the division for training as company and regimental sergeant-majors. Reciprocity in military ideas and teaching was a marked characteristic in the British Armies in France. But the steady work in the field and on the parade ground was not allowed to interfere unduly with the recreation and amusement of the troops. During these weeks out of the line various inter-brigade and battalion sports and matches were held. At a gymkhana organized by the 1st Guards

succeeded admirably in describing the general feeling which prevailed among the Guards and other fighting troops at this period of the war. "... the strain of the Push and its bewilderment had given place to the idea that great things were preparing ... as the summer of 1918 grew warmer in the wooded and orchard country behind the Amiens—Albert line, and our lines there held and were strengthened, and those who had been home or on the seas reported what they had heard and seen, hope, of a kind not raised before, grew in the talks of the men and the officers. ('Understand, I do *not* say there was any of the old chat regardin' that the war would finish next Chuseday, the way we talked in '16. But, whatever they said acrost the water, *We* did not hould 'twould endure those two more extra years all them civilians was dishin' out to us. *What* did we think? That '19 would see the finish? 'Twud be hard to tell what we thought. Leave it this way: we was no more than waitin' on mercies to happen an'—'twas mericles that transpired!'") See "The Irish Guards in the Great War," vol. i. pp. 287, 288.

   * See " History of the Welsh Guards," p. 220.
   † *Ibid.* pp. 222, 223.

Bde. at La Bazeque on the 2nd of July Major-General Feilding, riding his own horse, had the satisfaction of winning the 13-stone Hurdle Race. A highly successful divisional Horse Show was held on the 22nd of June between Saulty and Couterelle at which the 2nd Bn. Grenadier Guards carried off the cup given by Major-General Matheson to the unit securing the most prizes. On the 30th of June H.R.H. the Duke of Connaught lunched at divisional headquarters. He inspected the prize winners at the divisional Horse Show, and the commanding officers of all units in the division were presented to him. He was then taken to Barly, where he witnessed a " mass football match " between the 1st Bn. Grenadier Guards and the 1st Bn. Welsh Guards in which each battalion played 25 men and 4 footballs were used. Victory rested with the Grenadiers. After seeing this Homeric struggle, the Duke presented British decorations to French officers at Hesdin and expressed himself as much pleased with the Guard of Honour supplied by the 2nd Bn. Grenadier Guards—so smart, indeed, were the appearance and turn-out of the men forming this Guard that many of the onlookers at the ceremony refused to believe that any of them ever went into the trenches. The battalion received the congratulations of the Third Army commander.*

The casualties of the division during the first few days of June spent in the line, caused mainly by the enemy's shell fire, amounted to about 12 officers and 150 other ranks, but at this period the so-called " Spanish " influenza was taking a great toll of the troops, although luckily there were comparatively few fatal cases. The 3rd Bn. Grenadier Guards had about 150 men sick with this complaint on the 29th of June, and the 1st Bn. Coldstream Guards also alludes in its War Diary to the extraordinary severity of the outbreak. At about the same date all the officers, the sergeant-major and the majority of the men in the 55th Field Company, R.E., were laid low with the same malady.† Every unit in the division was more or less in similar straits.

* *See* W.D., 2nd Bn. Grenadier Guards, July, 1918.
† *See* W.D's., 3rd Bn. Grenadier Guards, 1st Bn. Coldstream Guards and 55th Field Company, R.E., June, 1918.

THE GUARDS ON THEIR OLD FRONT

Fortunately, the epidemic had decreased considerably by the end of the first week in July when the Guards were called upon to return to the line, but even then the trench strength of some of the battalions was considerably reduced.*

(6) THE GUARDS RELIEVE THE 32ND DIVISION IN THE LINE, 5TH–7TH OF JULY—THE OPENING OF THE BRITISH COUNTER-OFFENSIVE, 8TH OF AUGUST.

On the nights of the 5th, 6th and 7th of July the Guards Division once again relieved the 32nd Division, this time in the centre sector of the VI Corps front—the sector which the Guards had held during the middle of April.† All three Guards brigades went into the line—the 2nd, 1st and 3rd Guards Bdes. in the order named from right to left—each brigade with its three battalions disposed in depth.

The Guards found the Germans extremely unenterprising and the reports of patrols made it evident that they were more than ever apprehensive of a British attack.‡ There was, however, a certain amount of hostile artillery fire and on the 22nd of July the enemy put down a gas bombardment which caused 16 casualties in a party engaged in the burying of a cable. This bombardment was probably in retaliation for a projection of 680 drums of gas into Boyelles about ten days earlier. But this tour of duty in the line was, on the whole, a singularly quiet and uneventful one for the division, and " little shelling and no casualties " was not

---

* When the 1st Bn. Irish Guards, for instance, went into the line all battalion headquarters except the commanding officer and all the officers of No. 2 Company were down with influenza. A third of the men of this battalion are also reported to have been incapacitated by reason of the disease. See " The Irish Guards in the Great War," vol. i. p. 287.

† The 4th Bn. Coldstream Guards (Pioneers) had already moved forward—on the 1st of July—to Berles-au-Bois to work under the orders of the C.R.E., 32nd Division.

‡ A patrol of the 1st Bn. Coldstream Guards captured 8 Germans belonging to the 452nd Infantry Regiment north-west of Moyenneville on the 13th of July.

infrequently the order of the day, at any rate until quite the end of the month.*

On the 28th of June troops belonging to the Army of the United States of America had joined the division. They went into the line to gain with the Guards their first experience in active warfare. The visitors belonged to the 80th American Division and included the headquarters of the 160th Infantry Bde., the 320th Regiment and a machine-gun company. The spirit in which they were received may be gauged from the following correspondence :—

"Guards Division ' Q ' to Transport Officer, 1st Guards Bde.—Draw 6 bottles of whisky from divisional Soldiers' Club and deliver to Bde. H.Q. for American officers attached."
—"G.O.C. 1st Guards Bde. to Guards Division ' Q.'—On behalf of all officers of the American Army attached to brigade under my command I wish to express my deepest thanks for the courteous present of whisky foreshadowed in your message. I am requested to add that these officers accept the gift as a proof of the solidarity of the union existing between the American and British nations, which will endure till the whisky runs out." †

The Americans, who displayed a great keenness to learn,‡ were soon called upon to prove their mettle. On the 4th of August the Germans, who no doubt were anxious to obtain an identification of the new-comers, attempted to raid a post belonging to the 2nd Guards Bde., but the Americans in occupation of it had no difficulty in driving off the raiders.

In the early hours of the morning of the 13th of August the enemy made a rather more ambitious attack, this time on a post on the 3rd Guards Bde. front which was also held

---

* See "The Irish Guards in the Great War," vol. i. p. 288. The casualties of the division for the month of July, not including those due to influenza, amounted to 2 officers and 209 other ranks.

† See "The Grenadier Guards in the Great War," vol. iii. p. 81.

‡ The 1st Bn. Coldstream Guards record that "the Americans gave a good deal of extra work, but we were thoroughly recompensed by the keenness they showed and their appreciation of anything we were able to do for them." See W.D., 1st Bn. Coldstream Guards, July, 1918.

by Americans. After a hostile artillery barrage, lasting for about half an hour, a small party of German infantry succeeded in entering the post, but the raiders were quickly driven out again by the defenders.*

This attack turned out to be the last offensive action of the German Army on the front of the Guards Division. The following day, the 14th of August, the enemy was reported to be withdrawing opposite the 2nd Division on the immediate right of the Guards,† and, although it was soon found that no such withdrawal was as yet taking place opposite the Guards and that German troops were still in Moyenneville and Hamelincourt, it was evident that the enemy was no longer in an aggressive mood—even the projection of 680 gas drums into Moyenneville provoking but little artillery retaliation. The whole situation on the Western Front had now changed finally in favour of the Allies.

The British counter-offensive had been successfully opened on the 8th of August—the day, described by General Ludendorff as "the black day" for the German Army in the history of the war, on which Sir Henry Rawlinson's Fourth Army began its famous attack on the Amiens front.‡

The battle of Amiens (8th–12th of August), in addition to its discouraging moral effect upon the German troops and its material gains, threw the enemy definitely on the defensive and compelled him " to straighten out the salients in his line." But by the 13th of August the British Commander-in-Chief, finding that the Germans east of Amiens had been strongly reinforced and that their opposition was

* See W.D., 3rd Guards Bde., August, 1918.

† Patrols of the 2nd Division made their way into the German outpost line, but speedily located the enemy in his main line of resistance.

‡ " Within the space of five days the town of Amiens and the railway centring upon it had been disengaged. Twenty German divisions had been heavily defeated by thirteen British infantry divisions and three cavalry divisions, assisted by a regiment of the 33rd American Division and supported by some four hundred tanks. Nearly 22,000 prisoners and over four hundred guns had been taken by us and our line had been pushed forward to a depth of some twelve miles in a vital sector. Further, our deep advance, combined with the attacks of the French Armies on our right, had compelled the enemy to evacuate hurriedly a wide extent of territory to the south of us." See " Sir Douglas Haig's Despatches," p. 263.

stiffening, decided to break off the battle on this front and to transfer the offensive without any delay to the front of the Third Army north of the Somme, his intention being to strike at the enemy in an unexpected quarter and " to operate in the direction of Bapaume, so as to turn the line of the old Somme defences from the north." *

It was decided that the main attack by the Third Army should be delivered on the 23rd of August in conjunction with some divisions belonging to the Fourth Army north of the Somme, but that a limited attack should be launched two days earlier north of the Ancre in order to gain the line of the Arras—Albert railway along which it was known lay the enemy's main line of resistance. The task of carrying out this preliminary attack on the 21st of August was given to the divisions of the IV and VI Corps which were then holding the line.

Major-General Feilding determined to utilize the 2nd Guards Bde. for this attack and accordingly he withdrew this brigade from the line on the 16th of August to Saulty.† The positions on the right of the divisional front which it vacated were taken over by the 2/320th U.S.A. Regiment and two battalions of the 1st Guards Bde.—the 2nd Bn. Grenadier Guards and the 2nd Bn. Coldstream Guards—under the command of Brig.-General de Crespigny. The officer commanding the 320th U.S.A. Regiment then assumed the command of the centre sector of the line with the 1st Bn.

---

* *See* " Sir Douglas Haig's Despatches," p. 263.

† " There was much conjecture as to what this (the withdrawal from the line of the 2nd Guards Bde.) meant, the official explanation given out being that the enemy was massing opposite us and a new attack was imminent and therefore it had been decided that each division should have one complete brigade in reserve for counter-attacking purposes, and that the 2nd Guards Brigade had been selected to be in reserve for the Guards Division. Well, everyone believed this at first, but personally I rather suspected something different, chiefly because we were told to practise counter-attacking and that if we did have to counter-attack we should be required to go past our original line and capture the village of Moyenneville, and therefore as we already knew the features of the ground behind our own lines, special study must be made of that between our old line and Moyenneville . . . this looked to me much more like a plan for an offensive from our side." *See* " Reminiscences of a Grenadier," pp. 185, 186.

THE DIVISIONAL ARTILLERY 109

Irish Guards in the front line and two American battalions in support and reserve.

This arrangement, however, only lasted for two days, as on the 18th of August the American troops were withdrawn from the divisional front and the three brigade sectors were then each held by two battalions, Brig.-General de Crespigny being responsible for the defence of the right and centre sectors.

(7) WORK OF THE DIVISIONAL ARTILLERY DURING THE MONTHS OF MAY, JUNE AND JULY.

There is little to relate with regard to the doings of the divisional Artillery during the months of May, June and July, its work like that of the infantry mainly consisting in the monotonous routine of trench warfare. The gunners, however, were kept busily employed for the greater part of the time. During May both the 74th and 75th Bdes., R.F.A., were continuously in action, and, in addition to the usual harassing tactics, were often called upon to put down counter-preparation in anticipation of the German infantry attack which never actually matured.*

There were repeated complaints from the troops in the line about this time of short shooting by the British heavy guns as a result of which there were several casualties in the 1st Guards Bde.† Upon investigations being made, the short shooting was accounted for to some extent by the discovery that three 4·5 howitzers were worn out.

The divisional Artillery remained in the line when the Guards were relieved on the 6th–7th of June. But, on the

* The battery positions of both brigades were shelled fairly regularly, the enemy employing both gas and high explosive shell, and there were some casualties. B/75 was unlucky enough to lose two commanders—Major F. H. Corbett, who was killed by a German sniper on the 5th of May, and his successor, Major Foley, who was wounded later in the month.

† *See* W.D., 1st Guards Bde., May, 1918. " Guns still shooting short. Everybody much exasperated." *See* W.D., 2nd Bn. Grenadier Guards, May, 1918.

16th, the 74th Bde., R.F.A., went back into corps reserve at Humbercamp, where it rested and carried out training until early in July. The divisional Trench-Mortar Batteries were also relieved about this date by the trench-mortar batteries of the 32nd Division. The 75th Bde., R.F.A., remained in the line and came in for a good deal of hostile shelling on the 8th of June when several of its guns were badly damaged. The influenza epidemic " caught by the signallers from the infantry " laid low most of the *personnel* of the batteries, and also in the wagon lines.*

On the 4th of July the 74th Bde., R.F.A., went back into the line into positions between Blaireville and Boisleux-au-Mont from which its guns covered the left sector of the divisional front. Meanwhile, the 75th Bde., R.F.A., remained in action under the command of the C.R.A., 2nd Division, and assisted in the carrying out of two successful raids by the troops of that division. On the 16th, however, the brigade was withdrawn into mobile reserve at Berles-au-Bois, where it enjoyed some well-earned rest and was also able to do some useful training. Gun positions were reconnoitred east of Ransart which were to be occupied in case of emergency, but no such emergency arose and the brigade commander found it possible to send his batteries in turn to the calibration range at Occoches.

During the first week in July the reorganization of the D.A.C. to comply with the latest war establishment, which effected a certain economy in artillery *personnel*, was begun, and completed by the 16th.

The trench-mortar batteries took over their old positions in the Boisleux sector on the 8th of July. They had six mortars in the line and six in reserve, and, in addition to a considerable amount of shooting, constructed some new emplacements and dug-outs in preparation for a winter campaign which was never to arrive.

On the 7th–8th and 8th–9th of August the 75th Bde., R.F.A., returned to the line relieving the 72nd Bde., R.F.A., which was at that date covering the centre sector of the

* Some gun detachments could only muster three men. *See* W.D., 75th Bde., R.F.A., June, 1918.

Guards divisional front opposite Hamelincourt, its gun-positions lying between Ficheux and Boiry-St. Martin.*

The contemplated attack by the troops of the VI Corps was now in course of preparation and some of the guns in each brigade, R.F.A., were moved into more forward positions, while the D.A.C. and all the batteries were busily engaged in the work of bringing up ammunition into the Cojeul valley. By the night of the 19th of August 600 rounds for each gun, all of which had been carefully camouflaged, were in position.

* *See* W.D., 75th Bde., R.F.A., August, 1918. On the 17th of August Lieut.-Colonel W. E. Rudkin was appointed C.R.A., 57th Division, and the command of the 75th Bde. again devolved temporarily on Major E. J. Housden.

CHAPTER XVI

THE ADVANCE TO VICTORY, 1918 — OPENING OF THE BRITISH COUNTER-OFFENSIVE ON THE FRONT OF THE THIRD ARMY — THE ST. LEGER FIGHTING IN AUGUST.

(1) Opening of the offensive on the front of the Third Army.

The general situation on the front of the Third Army as a result of the battle of Amiens and the nature of the task assigned to the troops of the VI Corps on the 21st of August have already been outlined in a previous chapter. It will be remembered that a tendency had been observed on the part of the enemy to withdraw from his advanced positions on this portion of the line and that the British Commander-in-Chief, determined to give the Germans no respite after their defeat south of the Somme, had instructed Sir Julian Byng, the Third Army commander, to attack on a front of about 9 miles from Miraumont to Moyenneville with the object of turning the line of the old Somme defences from the north. The main offensive was to be launched on the 23rd of August, but it was to be preceded, on the 21st, by a separate attack designed to capture the Ablainzeville—Moyenneville spur and so to gain the line of the Arras—Albert railway north of the Ancre. On the front of the VI Corps, troops belonging to the 2nd Division on the right and the Guards on the left were ordered to carry out this preliminary attack, while the 3rd Division, in rear of the 2nd Division, and the 5th Infantry Bde. (2nd Division), in rear of the Guards, were held in readiness to support the operation.

TASK OF THE 2ND GUARDS BDE.

(2) Dispositions of the Guards Division for the attack on Moyenneville.

Major-General Feilding ordered the 2nd Guards Bde., which, it will be remembered, had been withdrawn to Saulty on the 16th of August,* in conjunction with tanks and a company of the Guards Machine-Gun Regiment, to capture Moyenneville and the line of the Arras—Albert railway north and south-east of that village. The attack was to be delivered from the right sector of the Guards divisional front a little to the north-west of Moyenneville, and on the left the advance was to pivot on the existing line which was held by the 1st Guards Bde. This latter brigade was instructed to take advantage of the operation by seizing the German trenches opposite its front, and, if possible, to establish posts in Hamel switch, should that trench be found to be unoccupied by the enemy. Farther to the north, the 3rd Guards Bde. was to endeavour to gain ground by means of patrols. Sixteen tanks were detailed to accompany the 2nd Guards Bde. in its advance, which was to be covered by the fire of seven brigades, R.F.A., and of the heavy artillery.†

By the 20th of August all the artillery arrangements had been completed. The 75th Bde., R.F.A., had moved into forward positions in the vicinity of Boiry-St. Martin and Boiry-St. Rictrude, and, together with the 74th Bde., R.F.A., and the 72nd (Army) Bde., formed the left group of guns under the command of Lieut.-Colonel C. Vickery.‡

---

* *See* p. 108.
† *See* W.D., Guards Division, August, 1918.
‡ *See* W.D., 75th Bde., R.F.A., August, 1918. Special tasks were assigned to the howitzer batteries and one 18-pdr. battery in each brigade, R.F.A., was employed to fire smoke-shell. The barrage on the 21st of August was extremely effective, but there was rather too much smoke—in conjunction with the mist, it made the fog of battle rather too dense.

(3) Assembly of the 2nd Guards Brigade for the attack, 20th–21st of August.

The night of the 20th–21st of August was a fine one and the troops of the 2nd Guards Bde., who were brought up from Saulty in lorries, reached their positions of assembly without any difficulty.*

Brig.-General Sergison-Brooke's plan of operation was to initiate the attack with the 1st Bn. Scots Guards on the right and the 1st Bn. Coldstream Guards on the left, and then, after the capture of the first and second objectives, to push the 3rd Bn. Grenadier Guards through the Scots Guards in order to take the third and final objective—the Arras—Albert railway line.

Owing to the line of direction which the attacking troops were obliged to follow, the two leading companies of the Scots Guards on the right of the line had to form up in positions about 300 yards in front of the British line. In order to secure this ground, the 1st Guards Bde. established two posts early in the night, which were only withdrawn when strong covering patrols of the Scots Guards arrived on the scene. There was a certain amount of hostile gas-shelling when this relief took place, but, owing to the prompt use of respirators, there was only one casualty.†

On the left of the line, the 1st Bn. Coldstream Guards formed up for the attack close behind the front trenches, almost due north of Moyenneville.

The 3rd Bn. Grenadier Guards assembled in a sunken road at Boiry-St. Martin.

---

* During their few days at Saulty all ranks in the 2nd Guards Bde. had done their best to prepare themselves for the coming operation. "We had all learnt our parts as best we could; there had been many conferences and much poring over maps. We all knew our objectives on the map; those of us who had taken part in big offensives before were less sanguine of finding them easily on the actual ground." *See* "Reminiscences of a Grenadier," p. 187.

† *See* W.D., 1st Bn. Scots Guards, August, 1918.

(4) ATTACK BY THE 2ND GUARDS BRIGADE, 21ST OF AUGUST.

At 4.35 a.m., zero hour, on the 21st of August, there was a very thick mist, which much handicapped the work of the F.O.O.'s and the contact aeroplanes ; it also caused delay in the arrival of the tanks at the infantry starting positions and made it extremely difficult for the advancing troops to maintain their direction.* At the same time, no doubt, it interfered equally with the defence.

On the right of the attack the Scots Guards, although only one tank was available to accompany them, reached their objective south-east of Moyenneville without much incident or difficulty. The mist caused some little confusion, at first, but it was soon overcome by the skilful leadership of the subordinate commanders, and touch was well maintained with the troops on the right and the 1st Bn. Coldstream Guards on the left. Some nests of German machine gunners caused a little trouble, but the hostile shelling although heavy was scattered and comparatively ineffective. Many of the enemy were killed and about 100 prisoners were taken, together with 70 machine guns and much material.†

On the left, most of the tanks detailed to cooperate with the Coldstream arrived in time to advance with the infantry. But, as it happened, their assistance was scarcely required. The enemy offered little resistance, and by 6.30 a.m. Moyenneville had fallen and about 30 prisoners had been captured.‡ Up to this time the losses of the Coldstream had been few, but the Germans now turned the fire of their guns and trench mortars on to Moyenneville, and many casualties were the result.§

At 5.40 a.m. the 3rd Bn. Grenadier Guards moved up from its position south of Boiry-St. Martin, but the tanks, which were to have advanced with it, were delayed by gas in the Cojeul valley and consequently the infantry had to

---

* *See* W.D., Guards Division, August, 1918.

† *See* W.D., 1st Bn. Scots Guards, August, 1918. The casualties of the battalion during this advance amounted to about 50.

‡ The prisoners belonged to the 451st and 452nd Regiments, 234th Division.

§ *See* W.D., 1st Bn. Coldstream Guards, August, 1918.

attack without them.* The task of locating the positions reached by the Scots Guards and of carrying on the advance in the mist and smoke proved by no means an easy one,† and it was not until 11.15 a.m. that a report from Lieut.-Colonel Thorne reached 2nd Guards Bde. headquarters to say that the right of his battalion was on the railway line and in touch with troops of the 3rd Division. A quarter of an hour later, 11.30 a.m., by which time the mist had practically cleared away and the weather had become very warm and fine, a message was received at divisional headquarters from Brig.-General Sergison-Brooke saying that his brigade line ran from a point a little north-east of Moyenneville, thence along the outskirts of that village to a point on the railway opposite Hamel Work, thence along the railway line to the Halte. He also stated that all the tanks co-operating with the 2nd Guards Bde. appeared to have been drawn away to the south-east.‡ Major-General Feilding then warned the Brig.-General not to advance east of the railway without the cooperation of tanks or cavalry.§

About 2 p.m. the 3rd Division was reported to have crossed the railway and to be meeting with stiff opposition. About this hour in the day too, the cavalry, which up till then had been kept in readiness to exploit the situation, was withdrawn, as the ground was found to be too much broken up and covered with wire for the operations of mounted troops.

Meanwhile, early in the afternoon, the left of the 3rd Bn. Grenadier Guards, which had advanced towards Moyenneville, had driven the enemy across the railway line and seized the quarries just west of Hamel Work. This movement was reported by observers, but it was not until 6.30 p.m. that the position of the Grenadiers was definitely known at divisional headquarters. It was then clear that the 2nd

* *See* " The Grenadier Guards in the Great War," vol. iii. p. 96.
† *See* " Reminiscences of a Grenadier," pp. 190–194.
‡ About the same time as this information was received from the 2nd Guards Bde. a message reached divisional headquarters stating that the 2nd Division had captured Courcelles and that the 3rd Division had reached the railway line south of the Halte.
§ *See* W.D., Guards Division, August, 1918.

HEAVY GERMAN BOMBARDMENT

Guards Bde. had gained all its objectives and that its units were in touch with each other and with the troops on their flanks.* Orders were immediately issued for the consolidation of the ground gained and for a vigorous patrolling of the line preparatory to the renewal of the advance on the morning of the 23rd of August. The artillery was ordered to maintain a harassing fire on the enemy's communications and to engage his guns north-west of Ervillers.† On the fronts of the 1st and 3rd Guards Bdes. the day had passed without much incident, but the patrols sent out along the divisional front established the fact that the enemy was still holding the line opposite the Guards.‡

(5) Events of the night of the 21st–22nd of August.

During the night of the 21st–22nd of August § the 1st Bn. Coldstream Guards, which had spent an exceedingly unpleasant day sitting still under heavy shell fire in the ruins of Moyenneville, advanced its line by nearly 500 yards and established strong posts on the outskirts of Hamelin-

---

* The total number of prisoners taken by the 2nd Guards Bde. during the day's fighting amounted to 5 officers and 352 other ranks. One of these prisoners, belonging to the 21st Reserve Division, stated that his Division had intended to attack the British on the night of the 21st of August, as it was believed that the Guards had been relieved by tired troops. Another prisoner, captured by the 3rd Guards Bde., stated that the British attack had been anticipated as the Germans had been warned by a deserter belonging to the 2nd Division, that it was being prepared. *See* W.D's., Guards Division and 3rd Guards Bde., August, 1918.

† *See* W.D., 75th Bde., R.F.A. One battery of this brigade was moved forward at 6.25 p.m. to a position behind Ape Copse.

‡ Early in the morning Viscount Gort, who was in temporary command of the 1st Guards Bde., was instructed to prepare a plan for the capture of Hamelincourt in the evening. He allotted this task to two companies of the 1st Bn. Irish Guards in cooperation with some tanks. This operation was first postponed until the morning of the 22nd and eventually abandoned. *See* W.D., Guards Division, August, 1918.

§ The night was fine and there was a bright moon. The enemy's aeroplanes were very active, bombing mainly behind the lines. They did much damage in the artillery wagon lines. D/75 had 17 horses killed and 7 wounded out of 25 picketed in the open.

court in face of a determined resistance on the part of the enemy.

The 3rd Bn. Grenadier Guards also pushed forward posts east of Hamel Work, whilst on the front of the 1st Guards Bde. patrols of the 1st Bn. Irish Guards made their way into Hamel switch trench and gained touch with the posts of the 1st Bn. Coldstream Guards in Hamelincourt trench. During the course of the night, too, the 3rd Guards Bde. was relieved by the 179th Infantry Bde. (59th Division) and was withdrawn into divisional reserve.

(6) GERMAN COUNTER-ATTACK ON THE MORNING OF THE 22ND OF AUGUST—PREPARATIONS FOR THE RENEWAL OF THE ADVANCE BY THE 2ND GUARDS BRIGADE.

Between 4 and 5 a.m. on the 22nd of August the enemy's artillery heavily bombarded Moyenneville, the railway line and the western side of Hamelincourt trench, and shortly afterwards the German infantry was observed moving forward to the attack. The S.O.S. signal was sent up all along the Guards' front. The prompt and effective reply made by the British guns, combined with the steady rifle, Lewis-gun and machine-gun fire of the infantry, proved too much for the attacking troops who were driven back with heavy losses.* For the remainder of the day, however, the enemy's artillery and machine guns were active. The 1st Bn. Coldstream Guards in Moyenneville again suffered severely,† and the Irish Guards in Hamel switch were so

* This counter-attack was carried out by the 40th (Saxon) Division, which had been specially brought up for the purpose. *See* W.D., Guards Division, August, 1918.

† Lieut.-Colonel J. Brand, the commanding officer of the battalion, was of the opinion that " the battalion could have taken Hamelincourt without a casualty on the afternoon of the 21st, and, further, could have advanced the whole of the 22nd (if only the tactical situation had allowed it) with very much fewer casualties than we had sitting still acting as a target to the enemy's guns." *See* W.D., 1st Bn. Coldstream Guards, August, 1918. In view of the nature of the enemy's opposition on this part of the line, this opinion is probably correct. But the attack on the 21st of August was designedly for a limited purpose and any extension of its objectives might have complicated the arrangements for the main attack on the 23rd.

DISPOSITIONS FOR FURTHER ADVANCE

much harassed by machine-gun fire from three sides during the afternoon that it was thought best to withdraw them at dusk.*

Meanwhile, the final arrangements in connexion with the resumption of the attack on the morrow were completed at divisional headquarters and the operation orders issued to the Guards brigades.

The 2nd Guards Bde. was to continue its advance in conjunction with the 56th Division on its left and the 3rd Division on its right. This attack was to form part of the main operation of the Third Army in the general British offensive which was to extend from the junction with the French south of the Somme to Mercatel—a distance of about 33 miles.† So far as the VI Corps was concerned, this initial attack was to be confined to the capture of certain limited objectives and the exploitation of any success that might be gained.

Upon the receipt of these orders, Brig.-General Sergison-Brooke at 5 p.m. gave verbal instructions to Lieut.-Colonel MacKenzie for the 1st Bn. Scots Guards to seize Hamelincourt the following morning, while the 3rd Bn. Grenadier Guards was to gain possession of the German trenches south of that village.‡

During the night of the 22nd–23rd of August, therefore, the 1st Bn. Scots Guards relieved the 1st Bn. Coldstream Guards in the left sector of the 2nd Guards Bde. line, and, as the converging attack to be carried out by the 56th Division from the north would cover the front held by the 1st Bn. Irish Guards, that battalion was withdrawn from the line without relief.§ Major-General Feilding thus had two of his brigades out of the line, ready to carry on the attack as occasion might require.

* *See* W.D., 1st Guards Bde., August, 1918.
† *See* " Sir Douglas Haig's Despatches," p. 266.
‡ On the right of the 2nd Guards Bde., the 3rd Division was to take Gomiecourt, after which the 2nd Division was to pass through it to the next objective. On the left of the Guards, the attack was entrusted to the 56th Division.
§ *See* W.D., 1st Guards Bde., August, 1918.

(7) ATTACK BY THE 2ND GUARDS BRIGADE, 23RD OF AUGUST.

At 4 a.m. on the 23rd of August, a very fine morning, the 3rd Bn. Grenadier Guards, preceded by the usual artillery barrage, advanced from the line of the railway upon Hamerville trench south of Hamelincourt. The Grenadiers gained their objective with little difficulty; the Germans appeared to be taken completely by surprise and surrendered freely.* But no touch was established with the troops who had attacked at the same hour on the right of the battalion.†

The attack on the left of the 2nd Guards Bde. front was not timed to begin until 4.55 a.m., and, while waiting for the order to advance, the 1st Bn. Scots Guards suffered a good many casualties as a result of a heavy artillery bombardment put down by the Germans as soon as the Grenadiers left their trenches. But when the moment arrived for them to attack, the Scots Guards, accompanied by three tanks, moved forward in splendid order upon Hamelincourt. They attacked with three companies in line and one company in close support, and, in despite of a good deal of opposition, especially in the centre—where, it is reported, the attacking company cleared the village in the face of heavy machine-gun fire "which the tanks did little to subdue" ‡—quickly succeeded in gaining their objectives. The work of consolidation was then promptly put in hand, and touch was gained with the Grenadiers on the right and with the troops of the 56th Division on the left, a section of No. 4 Company of the Guards Machine-Gun Regiment covering the new front with great effect from a position in Hamel switch.§

* ". . . the earth seemed to open and give up Germans; the front companies captured many times their own number." See "Reminiscences of a Grenadier," p. 204.

† See W.D., 2nd Guards Bde., August, 1918.

‡ See W.D., 1st Bn. Scots Guards, August, 1918. The right attacking company, on the other hand, found a tank of the greatest assistance in its advance.

§ The two brigades, R.F.A., Guards divisional Artillery supported the attack of the 56th Division on the 23rd of August, moving to more forward gun positions as the advance progressed. B/75 suffered severely from a hostile gas concentration which caused 20 casualties.

PROGRESS BY THE 1st COLDSTREAM

At 9.25 a.m. Major-General Feilding received a telegram from the VI Corps giving him his objective for the day—a line from the high ground west of Hally Copse on the right to St. Leger Mill on the left. He immediately sent orders to the 2nd Guards Bde. to push forward in order to seize the ridge from Judas Farm to St. Leger Mill, and instructed Brig.-General Follett to move forward the 3rd Guards Bde. from the area round Boiry-St. Martin with the object of relieving the 2nd Guards Bde. in the evening.*

Brig.-General Sergison-Brooke, as soon as he had received the order to resume the attack, ordered the 1st Bn. Coldstream Guards, which had already been concentrated south of Moyenneville, to carry out the operation.† This battalion began its advance at 11 a.m. from the line of the Arras—Albert railway, moving forward in conjunction with troops of the 2nd Division farther south and of the 56th Division to the north. All four companies were soon in full view of the enemy's gunners who put down a heavy barrage through which the battalion steadily made its way, notwithstanding numerous casualties.

At noon its leading companies began to arrive on their objective and a line from Judas Farm to the Boisleux—Cambrai railway in the vicinity of Boyelles reserve trench was quickly established. During the course of the advance the support and reserve companies, in order to deal with the resistance of some of the enemy's machine gunners on that flank, diverged too far to the right, but both companies succeeded in resuming their proper direction before they reached the objective and were put into the line to fill a gap which existed between the two leading companies.‡ For some hours, however, the new front of the Coldstream was by no means secure as the battalion was not in touch with the troops on either flank. Patrols were sent out to try and locate the position reached by the troops of the 56th Division on the northern flank, while machine guns were posted to strengthen the defence on the southern flank.

* *See* W.D., Guards Division, August, 1918.
† *See* W.D., 1st Bn. Coldstream Guards, August, 1918.
‡ *Ibid.*

Subsequently, at 2 p.m., as the situation on the right still remained uncertain, a company of the 1st Bn. Scots Guards was sent forward to form a defensive flank facing south from Judas Farm to Hamel switch trench.*

Meanwhile, Major-General Feilding had ordered the 3rd Guards Bde. to move two battalions and one machine-gun company to positions of readiness west of Moyenneville, and Brig.-General Follett had detailed the 1st Bn. Grenadier Guards and the 1st Bn. Welsh Guards for this purpose. At noon the first named of these battalions was ordered to advance east of Moyenneville and placed at the disposal of the 2nd Guards Bde.†

As early as possible in the afternoon Brig.-General Sergison-Brooke explained verbally to Major the Honble. W. R. Bailey, the officer commanding the 1st Bn. Grenadier Guards,‡ the state of things on the right flank of the 2nd Guards Bde. front and told him to gain touch with the troops of the 2nd Division in the neighbourhood of Ervillers, and, in conjunction with them, to capture the trench known as Mory switch.

Soon after 4 p.m. the 1st Bn. Grenadier Guards moved forward through its own 3rd Bn. in Hamerville trench,§

---

* See W.D., 1st Bn. Scots Guards, August, 1918. Later in the afternoon the line held by the Scots Guards was readjusted so as to run from Judas Farm to Hamel switch, thence along Hamel switch south of Hamelincourt back to Hamel Work. It is not easy to understand why so much uncertainty should have prevailed until quite late in the evening as to the position of the troops of the 2nd Division. As early as 10.10 a.m. the commanding officer of the 3rd Bn. Grenadier Guards, finding that his right was no longer in touch with the 2nd Division, had reported the fact to brigade headquarters and pushed forward patrols in the direction of Ervillers and the Ervillers—Boyelles road. It was then discovered that the 5th Infantry Bde. (2nd Division) had advanced to attack Ervillers and the 3rd Bn. Grenadier Guards was ordered to conform with the movement.

† See W.D., Guards Division, and W.D., 3rd Guards Bde., App. 17, August, 1918.

‡ Viscount Gort, the commanding officer, was still with the 1st Guards Bde.

§ " . . . our 1st Battalion came through in perfect formation and attacked the Mory switch trench ; there was no more wonderful sight than watching that battalion go up in artillery formation, and then deploy and attack ; later still, gunners galloped up and actually

ADVANCE OF THE 1st GRENADIER GUARDS 123

and, by 5.45 p.m., had gained its objective—Mory switch—without a check ; touch with the 5th Infantry Bde., however, was not established until later in the evening.* Throughout this operation the Grenadiers were handled with the utmost skill and precision ; they captured 197 prisoners and 15 machine guns, while their own losses amounted to 3 officers and 40 other ranks.†

While this attack was still in progress, at about 5 p.m., orders for the relief of the 2nd by the 3rd Guards Bde. were issued from divisional headquarters.‡ This relief proved to be a difficult and rather lengthy proceeding as the line reached by the 2nd Guards Bde. was hardly defined until quite late in the evening. However, by 8.55 a.m., the 3rd Guards Bde. was able to report that the 2nd Bn. Scots Guards had relieved the 3rd Bn. Grenadier Guards and part of its own 1st Battalion on the general line of Hammerville trench and that the 1st Bn. Welsh Guards had taken over the positions occupied by the 1st Bn. Coldstream Guards near Judas Farm. The 1st Bn. Grenadier Guards remained in occupation of Mory switch.§

At midnight on the 23rd of August, therefore, the Guards divisional line ran from a point in Mory switch trench a little to the north-west of Mory Copse, thence along Mory switch

---

went in front of where we started the day, and we really began to think things were getting a move on." *See* " Reminiscences of a Grenadier," p. 204.

* The 5th Infantry Bde. captured Ervillers before the advance of the 1st Bn. Grenadier Guards began.

† In a letter addressed to Sir Henry Streatfeild, the lieut.-colonel commanding the regiment, Brig.-General Follett, described this attack as " the finest exhibition that has ever been made in the war. . . . Starting about 3.45 p.m. they [the Grenadiers] had taken all objectives before 6 p.m.—that is, advancing 5,000 yards from their starting point ! Having been very highly trained by Gort during the past month or two, they proceeded to put their training into practice, with the result that it was a wonderful success. Commanded by Bailey (Gort was with the 1st Guards Brigade), they were magnificently manœuvred by their company and platoon commanders, moving in great depth on a very wide extension. . . . I say again, the finest attack in open warfare that has ever been made." *See* " The Grenadier Guards in the Great War," vol. iii. p. 78.

‡ *See* W.D., 3rd Guards Bde., August, 1918.

§ *Ibid.*

to its junction with Judas trench, thence due north across the Sensée river just east of Judas Farm to the junction of Judas and Boyelles reserve trenches. By this time the Guards were in touch with the 56th Division on their northern flank, but there was still a gap between their right and the 2nd Division on the southern flank.

The 2nd Guards Bde. was now withdrawn from the line to the Ayette area where it spent the remainder of the month resting, reorganizing and training. Its battalions had outfought and outmanœuvred the ·enemy, and during their three days' fighting had captured 24 officers and 1,234 other ranks as well as many machine guns, several heavy trench mortars and much material.*

(8) ATTACK BY THE 3RD GUARDS BRIGADE, 24TH OF AUGUST.

Before the relief of the previous night, orders had been given by Major-General Feilding for the 3rd Guards Bde. to carry on the advance on the 24th of August towards Ecoust St. Mein and Longatte in conjunction with the 2nd Division on the right and the 56th Division on the left.† The brigade's first task was the capture of the village of St. Leger.

Brig.-General Follett ordered the 1st Bn. Welsh Guards to attack on the north side of this village and the 2nd Bn. Scots Guards on its southern side—his intention being to force the enemy out of St. Leger by means of pressure on his flanks and then to complete any clearing up that might be required with the southern attacking force. The right flank of the brigade was to be protected by the advance of the 1st Bn. Grenadier Guards with its left on Hally Avenue. Two sections of machine guns were to move with each of the flank battalions and one section with the Scots Guards in the centre.‡

* The number of machine guns captured ran into hundreds, the 1st Bn. Scots Guards alone claiming 200 in addition to 4 heavy trench mortars. *See* W.D's., 2nd Guards Bde. and 1st Bn. Scots Guards, August, 1918.
† *See* W.D., Guards Division, August, 1918.
‡ *See* W.D., 3rd Guards Bde., August, 1918.

Punctually at 7 a.m., zero hour, the artillery barrage came down and the infantry went forward to the attack. On the right of the line the Grenadiers, who advanced on a front of about 1,000 yards, after making their way forward for some little distance without much difficulty, came under an intense machine-gun fire from Hally Copse on their front and from Mory Copse on their right and were brought to a standstill. It soon became evident that any attempt to continue the advance until the troops of the 2nd Division had cleared the enemy out of Mory Copse and the village of Mory had no chance of success and must inevitably result in very heavy casualties. There was no alternative, therefore, but for the troops to remain in the position which they had reached and to make it as secure as was possible in the circumstances.* The two sections of machine gunners with the Grenadiers were most useful throughout the day, their fire doing something to keep down that of the German machine guns and trench mortars.

The advance of the 2nd Bn. Scots Guards, in the centre of the 3rd Guards Bde. line, went well until the attacking troops reached Crucifix road running south from St. Leger. Up to this point in the engagement 100 prisoners and several machine guns had been taken. But now further progress became impossible in face of the bold and skilful opposition offered by the enemy's machine gunners posted in St. Leger Wood and the broken ground immediately to the south of it. The fact, too, that the advance of the Grenadiers had been checked on their right flank made the position still more difficult for the Scots Guards, who, for the time being, were

* " Nothing could be done but to wait until the situation on the right developed, and the difficulty of the position was increased by the fact that all communication with the leading companies was cut off for the remainder of the day. During the morning Germans could be seen dribbling forward small parties to Mory Copse, and the sniping and machine-gun fire from this direction became more intense." *See* " The Grenadier Guards in the Great War," vol. iii. p. 74. The Grenadiers had 7 officers and 150 other ranks casualties during this day's fighting. Major Bailey was wounded and for a time the battalion was under the command of Lieut.-Colonel J. Stirling, 2nd Bn. Scots Guards. In the evening Viscount Gort arrived from 1st Guards Bde. headquarters and resumed the command of his battalion.

out of touch with the F.O.O.'s and consequently without artillery assistance. Every effort was made, nevertheless, to work round the German machine-gun positions under covering fire, but without success—as soon as one hostile gun was silenced or rushed, another gun echelonned in rear opened fire.* The losses of the Scots Guards among the hedges and ditches south-east of St. Leger began to be so heavy that it was decided not to continue to press the attack, but to hold on to the ground that had been gained. Lieut.-Colonel Stirling now sent two platoons of the Scots Guards to support the Grenadiers in Hally Avenue, and moved back the reserve platoons of the Grenadiers to Iscariot Work from the neighbourhood of Mory switch where they were being shelled by the British artillery.† For the rest of the day there was no change in the situation on this part of the front, but the position of the troops was extremely unpleasant as the slightest movement east of Hally Avenue or Mory switch immediately drew fire from the hostile machine guns in Mory Copse, Camouflage Copse and Hally Copse—in fact, it was not until the 2nd Division had taken Mory Copse and Mory that conditions became tolerable on the right and in the centre of the 3rd Guards Bde. front.‡

Meanwhile, on the left of the attack, the experiences of the Welsh Guards had been very similar to those of the two other attacking battalions.§ Their first objective was

* It was almost entirely a machine-gun defence which reflected the greatest credit upon the enemy's machine gunners. They were left to withstand the attack while the remainder of the German troops, who had not been killed, wounded or taken prisoner, made good their escape.

† It will be remembered that when Major Bailey was wounded Lieut.-Colonel Stirling took command of the 1st Bn. Grenadier Guards until the arrival of Lord Gort later in the day. *See* note on p. 125.

‡ The troops of the 2nd Division attacked these two hostile *points d'appui* in the course of the afternoon. The Guards Division was informed of their capture at 6.12 p.m. *See* W.D., Guards Division, August, 1918.

§ Lieut.-Colonel H. Dene, commanding the 1st Bn. Welsh Guards, was wounded before the attack was actually launched, and the battalion was commanded throughout the engagements on the 24th and 25th of August by Captain W. Bonn, as Major Luxmoore Ball, the second-in-command, was with the details at Berles. This latter officer was given the command of the battalion on the 27th of August.

Leger reserve trench. They moved forward to the attack on a one-company front of about 870 yards in conjunction with troops of the 56th Division on their left at 7 a.m. From the first they met with a stout resistance, but they were able to drive the enemy out of Judas Copse, Judas trench and Windmill lane, rushing the machine-gun posts from the flanks. On reaching the northern outskirts of St. Leger, however, the advance was checked for a short time as the attacking troops were caught in the British artillery barrage and suffered several casualties. As soon as they had been reorganized, the attack was resumed along the St. Leger—Croisilles road north of the railway line. But here the fire of the enemy's machine guns, combined with that of the British artillery and the failure of the Scots Guards to make progress farther to the south, caused another check in the advance, and the leading platoons of the Welsh Guards were obliged to fall back to the sunken road west of Leger trench taking their wounded with them. After a further reorganization, two companies—one leading, the other in close support—again pressed forward to the attack and succeeded in capturing Leger reserve trench. They at once set to work to consolidate their new line, while patrols were sent out on the left towards Croisilles to find out what was happening on the front of the 56th Division. These patrols were soon driven back by hostile machine-gun fire and for some time the situation on the left flank remained obscure. From Leger reserve trench, too, the Welsh Guards could see the difficult position in which the 2nd Bn. Scots Guards was placed on their right, and an attempt was made to assist this latter battalion. A platoon of Welsh Guards was pushed out along the railway line north of St. Leger Wood to try and turn the enemy's position in this area. This movement ended in failure and the platoon was forced to withdraw with half its number casualties. Its retirement was skilfully and effectively covered by the fire of a Lewis gun which was brought into action with great promptitude.*

About this period in the day information was received that the troops of the 56th Division, who had made but little

* See " History of the Welsh Guards," pp. 236, 237.

progress towards Croisilles, had been ordered to attempt no further advance during the day.* It was clearly useless, therefore, for the Welsh Guards to try and reach their remaining objectives, and the remainder of the day was spent, consequently, in the work of reorganizing the line and putting Leger reserve trench into a good state of defence.

The day's fighting had not been particularly successful. The casualties were heavy in comparison with the slight gain of ground.† But the attack was a difficult one for the battalions concerned. The larger part of the front on which they were called upon to advance was almost entirely commanded from positions outside the 3rd Guards Bde. sector of the line, and the success or failure of the Guards was thus dependent to a great extent upon that of the other attacking troops on their flanks. The enemy, too, was in considerable strength ‡ and ready for the attack, whilst his machine gunners clung to their positions with a tenacity of purpose worthy of the highest praise.

(9) CONTINUANCE OF THE ATTACK, 25TH OF AUGUST.

Soon after midnight on the 24th–25th of August orders were issued by Major-General Feilding for the 3rd Guards Bde. to resume its advance at 4.30 a.m., on the 25th, in conjunction with the 62nd Division, which had relieved the 2nd Division on the right, and the 56th Division on the left. The Guards were to make a fresh attempt to reach Ecoust and Longatte, capturing Banks and Banks reserve trenches on their way.§

* This division and other divisions operating to the north of the Guards were transferred to the XVIII Corps during the course of the day; the Guards Division then became the left division of the VI Corps.

† At the end of the day the Welsh Guards were in possession of Leger reserve trench south of the railway line, and the Scots Guards had cleared St. Leger of Germans, but Banks trench and Banks reserve trench were still in the enemy's hands. 220 Germans, including 3 officers, had been captured as well as some machine guns and a few field guns.

‡ Two fresh German divisions appear to have been brought into the line opposite the Guards. *See* " The Grenadier Guards in the Great War," vol. iii. p. 78.

§ *See* W.D., Guards Division, August, 1918.

A DAY OF LITTLE SUCCESS

A thick mist covered the landscape at zero hour on the 25th of August when five brigades, R.F.A., put down the covering barrage and the 1st Bn. Grenadier Guards, the 2nd Bn. Scots Guards and the 1st Bn. Welsh Guards, from right to left, once more went forward to the attack.

The Grenadiers, who had the assistance of three tanks, made good progress at the start, and their leading troops, moving up Mory switch, reached the sunken road to the south-west of L'Homme Mort in front of Banks trench. Here they suffered severely from the enemy's machine-gun fire which was incessant from the front and both flanks. The fog had lifted by this time, two of the accompanying tanks had been put out of action,* and the enemy was in force, especially on the right flank. After holding on to the ground which they had reached for some time, therefore, the Grenadiers were given the order to retire and withdrew to Mory switch.†

In the centre of the line the 2nd Bn. Scots Guards made a dogged attempt to seize Banks trench, although only one of the tanks detailed to accompany it in the attack was ever seen by the infantry. The fighting in the rough bush-covered country south of St. Leger was as obstinate and fierce as that on the preceding day, and the gallant effort of the Scots Guards ended in failure. They did not succeed in reaching Banks trench. But if the enemy's defence was successful, he failed in his turn when he counter-attacked near the Crucifix about 9 a.m., his troops being driven back by the steady fire of the Scots Guards assisted by that of the British guns.‡

North of St. Leger no tank arrived in time to cooperate with the 1st Bn. Welsh Guards, which attacked with two companies from Leger reserve trench. At first the enemy's troops on this portion of the front appeared to be taken by surprise, and either surrendered or beat a hasty retreat under cover of the mist. But the advance of the Welsh Guards was soon checked by uncut wire, and, as the mist began

---

* *See* "The Grenadier Guards in the Great War," vol. iii. pp. 76, 77.
† *See* W.D., 3rd Guards Bde., App. 17, August, 1918.
‡ *See* W.D., 2nd Bn. Scots Guards, August, 1918.

to clear away, the troops, both of whose flanks were in the air, came under a heavy machine-gun fire from three sides. In these circumstances, after waiting for an hour to collect his scattered parties, the officer in command ordered a withdrawal to Leger reserve trench, an attempt by the Germans to follow up this movement being easily driven back.*

During the afternoon both infantry and artillery observers reported that the enemy, whose strength was estimated as at least a regiment, was moving across the front of the 3rd Guards Bde. in a south-westerly direction, and, at about 4 p.m., after a short artillery bombardment, a hostile counter-attack was launched at the junction of the Guards Division and the 62nd Division in the vicinity of Mory Copse. All possible fire was brought to bear upon the Germans who were driven back with heavy losses by the troops of the 62nd Division. The 1st Bn. Grenadier Guards seized the opportunity to improve their position in Mory switch, while the 2nd Bn. Scots Guards pushed out a platoon to Hally Copse and established a post in some gun-pits just beyond it.†

At dusk the Scots Guards also succeeded in rushing some of the enemy's posts in front of Banks trench on the northern portion of their sector, and their line then ran from the road junction north-east of Hally Copse, thence north to the Crucifix through St. Leger Wood to the railway at Leger reserve trench where they were in touch with the Welsh Guards.

Throughout the day the Guards Machine-Gun Companies gave the utmost assistance to the infantry. Nos. 2 and 4 Companies on the right of the line effectively covered the withdrawal of the 1st Bn. Grenadier Guards in the morning, and did much execution among the enemy when the Germans counter-attacked in the afternoon. They also covered a gap in the line south of the junction of Hally Avenue with Mory switch. A section of guns attached to the Welsh Guards was gassed west of St. Leger Mill, but four guns were eventually brought into action on this part of the front,

* See W.D., 1st Bn. Welsh Guards, August, 1918.
† See " The Grenadier Guards in the Great War," vol. iii. p. 77. W.D., 2nd Bn. Scots Guards, August, 1918.

two being used to cover the left flank and two to cover St. Leger Wood.*

The batteries of the divisional Artillery, after they had fired the opening barrage, were kept in readiness to move forward, the limbers and wagons being stationed only 500 yards from the guns.† As things turned out, however, the gunners were kept busy throughout the day repelling counter-attacks and, at 6 p.m., it was decided to send the horses to the rear. The enemy's fire on the gun positions was heavier on the 25th of August than it had been on the previous day and so much gas-shell was used that the British gunners were obliged to wear their respirators all the evening.‡

During the night of the 25th–26th of August the 1st Guards Bde. took over the line from the 3rd Guards Bde., the latter being withdrawn first to bivouacs in the Boiry-St. Martin area, and then to the Ransart—Berles-au-Bois area, where the necessary rest was given to the troops and the work of reorganization was carried out by the battalions.

The 3rd Guards Bde. received the congratulations of the divisional commander for the excellence of its work in the line. He realized to the full the difficulty of the task which had been set the troops in view of the determined character of the enemy's defence, and he appreciated their gallant attempts to push forward to their objectives in the face of the enemy's withering machine-gun fire. He knew that they had done all that was humanly possible.§

---

* *See* W.D., Guards Machine-Gun Regiment, August, 1918.

† Major W. E. Mann commanded the 74th Bde., R.F.A., Lieut.-Colonel Vickery being in command of the " advanced group " formed by the two Bdes., 74th and 75th.

‡ *See* W.D., 75th Bde., R.F.A., August, 1918. Lieut.-Colonel F. Kirkland assumed the command of the 75th Bde. this day (25th of August).

§ The casualties of the 3rd Guards Bde. in these two days' fighting amounted to 19 officers and 507 other ranks, the 1st Bn. Grenadier Guards losing 13 officers and 258 other ranks out of this total. The brigade took 506 prisoners, 3 field guns, 58 machine guns, a searchlight and other war material. *See* W.D., 3rd Guards Bde., App. 17, August, 1918.

(10) THE 1ST GUARDS BRIGADE IN THE LINE, 26TH OF AUGUST—ORDERS FOR THE RENEWAL OF THE ATTACK ON THE 27TH OF AUGUST.

The 1st Guards Bde. took over the line with two battalions—the 2nd Bn. Grenadier Guards on the right and the 2nd Bn. Coldstream Guards on the left. The 1st Bn. Irish Guards remained in brigade reserve in Hamel switch and Jewel trench.

In the early hours of the morning the Germans evidently were expecting the resumption of the attack as all the likely places of assembly were kept continuously under fire. Nevertheless, during the course of the morning, posts were successfully established in the southern portion of Leger reserve trench, although any attempt to approach Banks trench was at once greeted with heavy bursts of machine-gun fire. The enemy was clearly very much on the alert, but the day passed more or less uneventfully.

In the evening orders were issued from divisional headquarters for the attack to be renewed the following morning.* The objectives were to be the same as before, namely, the high ground north and south of Longatte and Ecoust, but the advance was not to be pressed if the enemy's resistance proved obstinate The 62nd Division was to advance on the right and the 56th Division on the left of the 1st Guards Bde. This latter division, which took over 500 yards of the Guards' frontage, was to envelop Croisilles. Five brigades R.F.A., and one brigade R.H.A., were to provide the barrage for the Guards. Zero hour was fixed at 7 a.m.†

(11) ATTACK BY THE 1ST GUARDS BRIGADE, 27TH OF AUGUST.

The line from which the attack of the 1st Guards Bde. was launched on the 27th of August—a brilliantly fine and very hot day—ran from Camouflage Copse to the Crucifix

---

* These orders did not reach the battalions in the line until early in the morning on the 27th, so that very little time was available for commanding officers to make their arrangements for the attack.

† *See* W.D's., Guards Division and 1st Guards Bde., August, 1918.

NO COOPERATION ON THE LEFT

and thence bent north-eastward through St. Leger Wood at the northern extremity of which the line of the 56th Division began. This division, it will be remembered, was to attack at 7 a.m. in conjunction with the Guards, but, at 5 a.m., 1st Guards Bde. headquarters was informed that the advance of the 56th Division had been postponed until 9.30 a.m.* In the short time still remaining before zero hour it was impossible for Brig.-General De Crespigny to change the time fixed for his brigade to attack. Most of the units of the two attacking battalions were already in their starting positions and it was out of the question to get in touch with them all quickly enough to prevent some of them at any rate from advancing at the time originally ordered. There was no alternative, therefore, but for the Guards to begin their attack as arranged at 7 a.m., although it was realized that their left flank would be more or less in the air.

The British artillery barrage came down punctually at zero hour,† and crept forward at the rate of 100 yards in 2 minutes. On the right the Grenadiers attacked with one company in the front line, two companies in support and one company in reserve, and only a few minutes after the advance began the leading company came under a well-directed machine-gun fire from Banks and Banks reserve trenches. Casualties were numerous, every movement instantly drawing fire. Nevertheless, the right half of this

---

* *See* W.D., 1st Guards Bde., August, 1918. This sudden change of plan is supposed to have been due to the fact that the Germans had captured some prisoners on the front of the 56th Division during the night and that consequently it was thought wiser to postpone the hour of an attack for which the enemy would probably be in readiness if it took place at the time originally intended. But, whatever good reason may have led to the decision to postpone the attack, it was an unfortunate decision for the success of a combined advance by two divisions.

† The counter-barrage of the enemy's guns was mainly directed in rear of the forming-up positions of the attacking troops, but one hostile shell unfortunately landed amongst a platoon of the reserve company of the Grenadiers, mortally wounding the officer in command and putting all but 3 men in the platoon out of action. It was an unlucky beginning to the day's fighting. *See* W.D., 2nd Grenadier Guards, August, 1918.

company, which was most gallantly led, after rushing a German machine-gun post, managed to make some progress. It was splendidly assisted by the nearest support company which, after losing all its officers, came up to reinforce it. This force struggled forward and succeeded in entering Banks trench at a point just north of l'Homme Mort. Here the survivors of this half of the battalion were raked by machine-gun fire from Banks reserve trench as well as from their left flank, with the result that any kind of reorganization or consolidation of the new position was out of the question until darkness set in—yet, in despite of every difficulty, a post was established and held at this point in Banks trench throughout the day, the enemy remaining in the trench on either flank.

Meanwhile, the supporting company of Grenadiers which moved on the extreme right had worked its way for some distance along Mory switch and had effected an entry into Banks trench at its southern extremity. It continued to advance until it reached Vraucourt trench—thus penetrating to a depth of about 2,000 yards into the enemy's defensive system.*

Here, after capturing a German battalion commander and 180 other prisoners, this company contrived to establish itself. But it was completely isolated, well in advance of any other British troops, and, although it clung stubbornly to its position for several hours, its numbers became so much reduced that it was ultimately obliged to withdraw to the battalion line.

The remaining company of Grenadiers, which started its advance from Hally Copse, suffered very heavy casualties almost immediately it appeared in the open, losing all but one of its officers. The company then made a desperate effort to reinforce the leading troops on the left, following the sunken road west of Banks trench. But by the time it succeeded in getting anywhere near them, it had lost 50 per

---

* This company appears to have met with less opposition than the other companies and so managed to keep well up with the barrage, not only to Banks trench, but also in its farther advance to Vraucourt trench. *See* " The Grenadier Guards in the Great War," vol. iii. p. 89.

THE HARD TASK OF THE COLDSTREAM 135

cent. of its *personnel*, and was finally checked by the intensity of the enemy's machine-gun fire.

The machine-gun section which accompanied the Grenadiers in the attack suffered as severely as the infantry; but, although its officers were killed, its four guns did good service throughout the day and were still in action under the command of non-commissioned officers when night set in, protecting with their fire the right flank of the brigade.*

The Guards' line on this sector of the front then ran about 200 yards west of and parallel to Banks trench, and was held by the remnants of the 2nd Bn. Grenadier Guards and a company of the 1st Bn. Irish Guards which was brought up to fill a gap between the left of the Grenadiers and the right of the Coldstream.†

It now remains to relate the fortune which attended the attack of the 2nd Bn. Coldstream Guards on the left of the 1st Guards Bde. front. The battalion, like the Grenadiers, advanced with one company in the front line, two companies in support and one company in reserve. Its task was a particularly arduous one. Its advance had to be started from St. Leger Wood where the thick undergrowth and fallen trees greatly interfered with the movements of the troops, thus adding to their difficulty in maintaining touch and preventing them from keeping up with the barrage. But, in addition to the awkward nature of the ground in the early stages of the advance, practically the whole of the area on the left and in the centre of the line of attack was commanded from Croisilles. The postponement of its attack by the 56th Division thus enabled the Germans in this village to give their undivided attention to the work of resisting the Coldstream.

The leading company of the battalion attacked at 7 a.m., but, after advancing for about 200 yards, was checked on the right by machine-gun fire from Banks trench which appears to have been little damaged by the British shell fire. In the centre the assaulting troops gained the crest line beyond Leger reserve trench, but could not get any farther owing

* *See* W.D., Guards Machine-Gun Regiment, August, 1918.
† *See* W.D., 2nd Bn. Grenadier Guards August, 1918.

to enfilade fire from the right. On the left the advance was more successful. Many prisoners were taken on the sunken roads running south from Croisilles. Bunhill trench was gained and consolidated under heavy fire which came from Croisilles, east of that village and also from Bunhill reserve trench.

In the centre the Coldstream, who were counter-attacked down the sunken roads south of Croisilles at about 10 a.m.,* were compelled to fall back on Leger reserve trench. The casualties in this part of the line were very heavy, all the officers being either killed or wounded. About the time that this withdrawal took place, the force in Bunhill trench, which by then had been reduced to 1 officer and 18 other ranks, was in grave danger of being cut off, and it, too, fell back.

It was now found that the battalion could only muster 140 rifles, and a company of the 1st Bn. Irish Guards, therefore, had to be put in on the right of the line to hold Leger reserve trench as far as its junction with Banks trench. The Germans were still in this trench system and it was deemed advisable for the time being to form a defensive flank.

The machine gunners with the Coldstream, as with the Grenadiers, shared to the full in the stress and strain of the day's fighting. One team with its gun went forward on the left with the party which reached Bunhill trench. The team of another gun were all either killed or wounded. Four guns were used on the exposed left flank of the battalion for protective purposes and two were posted in Hally Avenue north-west of Hally Copse as a defensive measure in the event of a counter-attack.†

The 1st Bn. Irish Guards, the battalion in reserve, had a long and trying day—the duty which devolved upon it being to reinforce with its platoons the attacking battalions at any point in the line where their advance was checked.

---

* *See* W.D., 1st Guards Bde., August, 1918. It is stated that this counter-attack was the reason for the withdrawal of the Coldstream to Leger reserve trench. It is also stated that the British heavy guns put down a concentration on these sunken roads for the rest of the morning and did great execution among the enemy. The evidence of patrols the following day confirmed these statements.

† *See* W.D., Guards Machine-Gun Regiment, August, 1918.

As soon as the attack was launched, two companies of Irish Guards followed the Grenadiers and two companies the Coldstream. The two former companies came under heavy hostile shell fire and dug themselves in east of Hally Copse as soon as it was evident that no great advance could be effected. Here their stretcher-bearers worked hard until nightfall bringing in the wounded, "their own, those of the Battalions ahead and of the Guards machine-guns." * Of the two other companies one was employed on the left to hold Leger reserve trench after the Coldstream went forward to the attack, and the other, as already related, was put into the line on the right of the Coldstream later on in the morning.

The enemy made no attempt during the remainder of the day to counter-attack the Guards. But, in view of the situation in the centre of the brigade line, it was decided, later in the afternoon, to subject the portion of Banks trench immediately south of its junction with Leger reserve trench to an artillery bombardment. At about 7 p.m., therefore, the British artillery concentrated its fire for a period of fifteen minutes upon this point in the line, at the conclusion of which a party of about 150 Germans surrendered. The trench was then occupied by the Coldstream and Irish Guards.†

During the day the 74th and 75th Bdes., R.F.A., again formed an advanced artillery group under the command of Lieut.-Colonel Vickery.‡ This group was pushed boldly forward in support of the infantry, its orders being to advance to positions just west of Banks trench. In the circumstances these positions were never reached by the gunners. Some of the batteries, however, galloped forward over the crest of the high ground south of St. Leger where they came under direct machine-gun fire.§ The group was

---

* See "The Irish Guards in the Great War," vol. i. p. 299.
† See W.D., 1st Guards Bde., August, 1918.
‡ See W.D., C.R.A., Guards Division, App. XXIV, August, 1918.
§ "The guns came over the crest and into the valley . . . in full view, affording magnificent support to the infantry, both moral and material. The enemy was not slow to turn his artillery on to the Brigade, but they could not be denied and swung into action and got the teams away with only few casualties." Extract from the diary of Lieut.-Colonel C. E. Vickery.

subsequently in action south of Judas trench, then near Jewel trench, where D/75 had three howitzers knocked out. Later in the day, after the infantry attack had come to an end, the guns were withdrawn northward to positions in the Sensée valley. Both brigades, R.F.A., had been almost continuously under fire throughout the day and had behaved with the utmost gallantry and dash. They suffered numerous casualties, which included several officers and experienced non-commissioned officers.

The fighting on the 27th of August thus ended much in the same way as that on the 25th. It had resulted in heavy losses to the Guards Division,* and had led to no appreciable gain of ground. But, nevertheless, the 1st Guards Bde., like the 3rd Guards Bde., had carried out its appointed task in the general scheme of operations of the British advance. It had held a considerable force of the enemy on the Mory—Croisilles front while the attack by the XVII and Canadian Corps developed farther to the north.†

In a hilly area such as that in which they were fighting—with its scattered villages, woods, copses and sunken roads—with its endless lines of old and new trenches and wire entanglements stretching across the country in all directions—the Guards knew well enough from their own experiences in the March offensive how difficult it was for attacking troops to advance with any rapidity when opposed by a determined and skilfully organized defence. On the 27th of August the 1st Guards Bde., advancing from a singularly awkward and exposed line with no support on its left flank, was called upon to attack a series of positions admirably designed for a machine-gun defence held by an expectant enemy in great strength. Its battalions succeeded in inflicting heavy losses on the Germans in killed, wounded

---

* The 2nd Bn. Grenadier Guards lost 12 officers and 279 other ranks; the 2nd Bn. Coldstream Guards 10 officers and 296 other ranks; the 1st Bn. Irish Guards 8 officers and 170 other ranks. The number of prisoners taken, according to the divisional record, amounted to 5 officers and 276 other ranks. But the 1st Guards Bde. claimed 500 prisoners as well as many machine guns and other war material.

† *See* Major-General Feilding's message of congratulation to the 1st Guards Bde., p. 140.

and prisoners, with the result that on the following day the enemy's resistance had perceptibly weakened.

(12) EVENTS ON THE 28TH OF AUGUST—STEADY PROGRESS OF THE 1ST GUARDS BRIGADE—RELIEF OF THE DIVISION BY THE 3RD DIVISION—WORK OF THE DIVISIONAL R.E. AND 4TH BN. COLDSTREAM GUARDS (PIONEERS) DURING THE ADVANCE.

The enemy's machine-gun fire died away as soon as it became dark on the 27th of August, and indications of a German withdrawal opposite the Guards were reported to 1st Guards Bde. headquarters.*

The night passed quietly on the brigade front which was held from right to left by the 2nd Bn. Grenadier Guards, the 1st Bn. Irish Guards and the 2nd Bn. Coldstream Guards.

As soon as it was light in the morning of the 28th of August patrols were sent forward with orders to gain as much ground as possible, and a slow but steady progress was made throughout the day.

The Grenadiers reached and consolidated Banks reserve trench in conjunction with the Irish Guards on their left; but machine-gun fire from the trenches covering Ecoust, where the enemy appeared to be in great strength, prevented any farther advance on this part of the front. On the left of the line, the Coldstream could do little until the troops of the 56th Division on their left had worked their way through Croisilles, but eventually touch was gained with them south of that village.

At 7.45 p.m. Major-General Feilding ordered the 1st Guards Bde. to consolidate the line which it had then reached and to push out patrols to establish connexion with the 62nd Division at the junction of Banks reserve and Vraucourt reserve trenches, and with the 56th Division at the junction of Bunhill trench and Leg lane.† These orders were successfully carried out.

During the day the 74th Bde., R.F.A., moved into forward

* *See* W.D., 1st Guards Bde., August, 1918.
† *See* W.D., Guards Division, August, 1918.

positions near Bank Copse, where it was heavily shelled in the course of the evening.*

The 75th Bde., R.F.A., reconnoitred gun positions south of Hally Copse, but was unable to occupy them as the enemy's artillery opened fire whenever any attempt was made to get forward the batteries.†

At nightfall, on the 28th, the relief of the Guards Division by the 3rd Division began, the 1st Guards Bde. handing over its positions to the 76th Infantry Bde.‡ The command of the line passed to the 3rd Division at 1.20 a.m. on the 29th of August, and the 1st Guards Bde. then moved back to the reserve area east of Adinfer Wood.§

---

* The brigade lost 1 officer and 18 other ranks casualties. *See* W.D., 74th Bde., R.F.A., August, 1918.

† *See* W.D., 75th Bde., R.F.A., August, 1918.

‡ During August the total number of prisoners captured by the Guards Division is given as 30 officers and 1,479 other ranks. *See* W.D., Guards Division, August, 1918.

§ Brig.-General de Crespigny received the following congratulatory message from Major-General Feilding in recognition of the gallant conduct of his brigade :—

" When the 1st Guards Bde. relieved the 3rd Guards Bde. in the line the enemy was fighting hard with fresh troops to maintain his positions on the high ground between Mory and Croisilles, while countering the thrust delivered to the north by the XVII and Canadian Corps. The Guards Division had been ordered to press him continually and to gain all ground possible towards Ecoust so as to prevent him from disengaging troops and guns while the attack of the XVII and Canadian Corps was being pressed on our left flank.

" All battalions of the 1st Guards Bde. discharged this duty splendidly. The attack was delivered by the 2nd Grenadiers and 2nd Coldstream Guards. On August 27th they not only inflicted heavy loss on the enemy and brought in large number of prisoners, but also compelled him next day to relax his hold upon the high ground south of Croisilles. The 1st Irish Guards did most valuable work under trying conditions in taking over part of the line after the attack on the 27th, and distinguished themselves by their vigorous patrolling forward on the following day. The full result of the hard fighting done by the Bde. was gathered only after its relief on the night of August 28/29, for, on the morning of the 29th, the patrols of the relieving Division were able to push right forward into the outskirts of Ecoust. Nos. 1 and 3 Coys., 4th Bn. Guards Machine-Gun Regt., deserve full share of credit for their work while attached to the 1st Guards Brigade.

" The 1st Guards Brigade has never fought more gallantly and I wish to thank all ranks most warmly for the endurance and devotion which they displayed."

THE GUNNERS LEFT IN ACTION

Before closing this narrative of the part played by the Guards Division in the first stage of the Third Army's advance to victory, a short reference must be made to the work of the R.E. and 4th Bn. Coldstream Guards (Pioneers). The maintenance of roads was a fairly simple matter as the weather remained fine. But the water supply during the first four days of the advance was a far from easy problem. The Field Companies, R.E., carried out a systematic reconnaissance for water as the line went forward, and water tanks were erected in various central positions and replenished by lorries.

The work on the caves at Blaireville, where it was intended to provide underground accommodation for one battalion, had been practically completed before the advance began.*

The divisional Signal Company had little difficulty in the construction and maintenance of forward communications, although the passage of tanks is reported to have caused damage to cable in some instances.†

As usual the 4th Bn. Coldstream Guards (Pioneers) provided the bulk of the labour in the divisional area, and the battalion was steadily employed during the advance in the maintenance of roads and tracks, in the loading and unloading of wagons and in burial duties.‡

(13) WORK OF THE GUARDS DIVISIONAL ARTILLERY WITH THE 3RD DIVISION.

After the Guards left the line, the divisional Artillery remained with the 3rd Division and covered its operations until the end of the month.

On the 29th, 30th and 31st of August the 74th and 75th Bdes., R.F.A., were almost continuously in action covering the advance of the infantry in its severe struggle to capture Ecoust, Longatte and Lagnicourt.§

---

* *See* W.D., C.R.E., Guards Division, August, 1918.
† *See* W.D., Signals, Guards Division, August, 1918.
‡ *See* W.D., 4th Bn. Coldstream Guards, August, 1918.
§ *See* W.D's., 74th and 75th Bdes., R.F.A., August, 1918. "Many magnificent targets during this time of enemy in the open were engaged

The horses of the gunners suffered severely during the course of these August operations. Long hours in harness in the hot weather combined with the shortage of water,* together with casualties caused by the enemy's shell fire and bombing, took a heavy toll of horse-flesh and added considerably to the difficulties of getting forward the guns.

Needless to say, too, the resources of the D.A.C. were severely taxed. But the Column worked with splendid energy and success, and, in addition to maintaining the supply of ammunition to the artillery, infantry and machine gunners, it salved many thousands of rounds from abandoned gun positions.† The *personnel* of the trench-mortar batteries were employed at ammunition dumps and on salvage operations.‡

with heavy casualties to the Boche." Extract from the diary of Lieut.-Colonel Vickery. The good work done by the F.O.O.'s during these days' fighting is recorded in the brigade War Diaries.

* Some water supplies in the captured area are reported to have been poisoned.

† *See* W.D., D.A.C., Guards Division, August, 1918.

‡ *See* W.D., T.-M.B.'s, Guards Division, August, 1918.

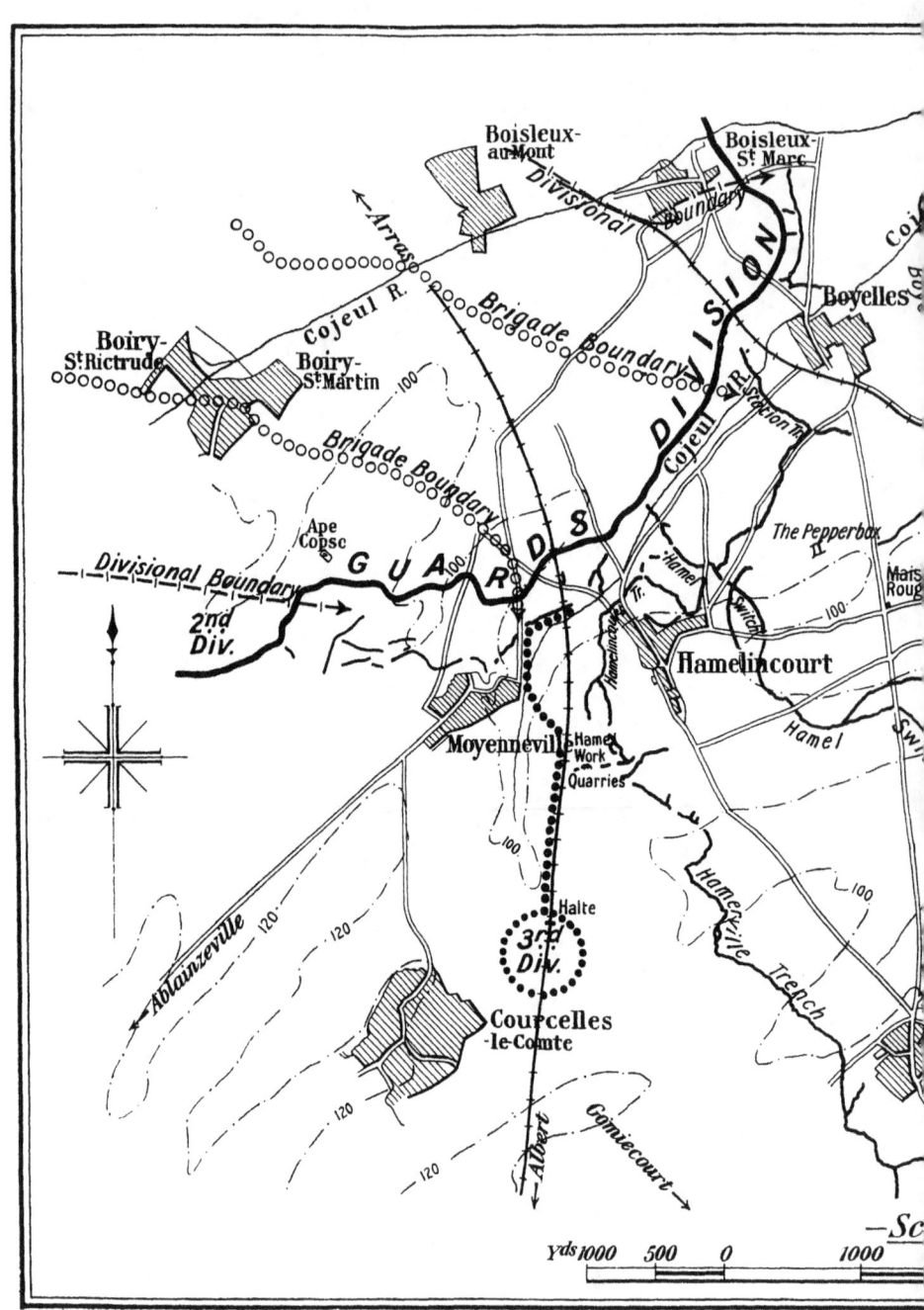

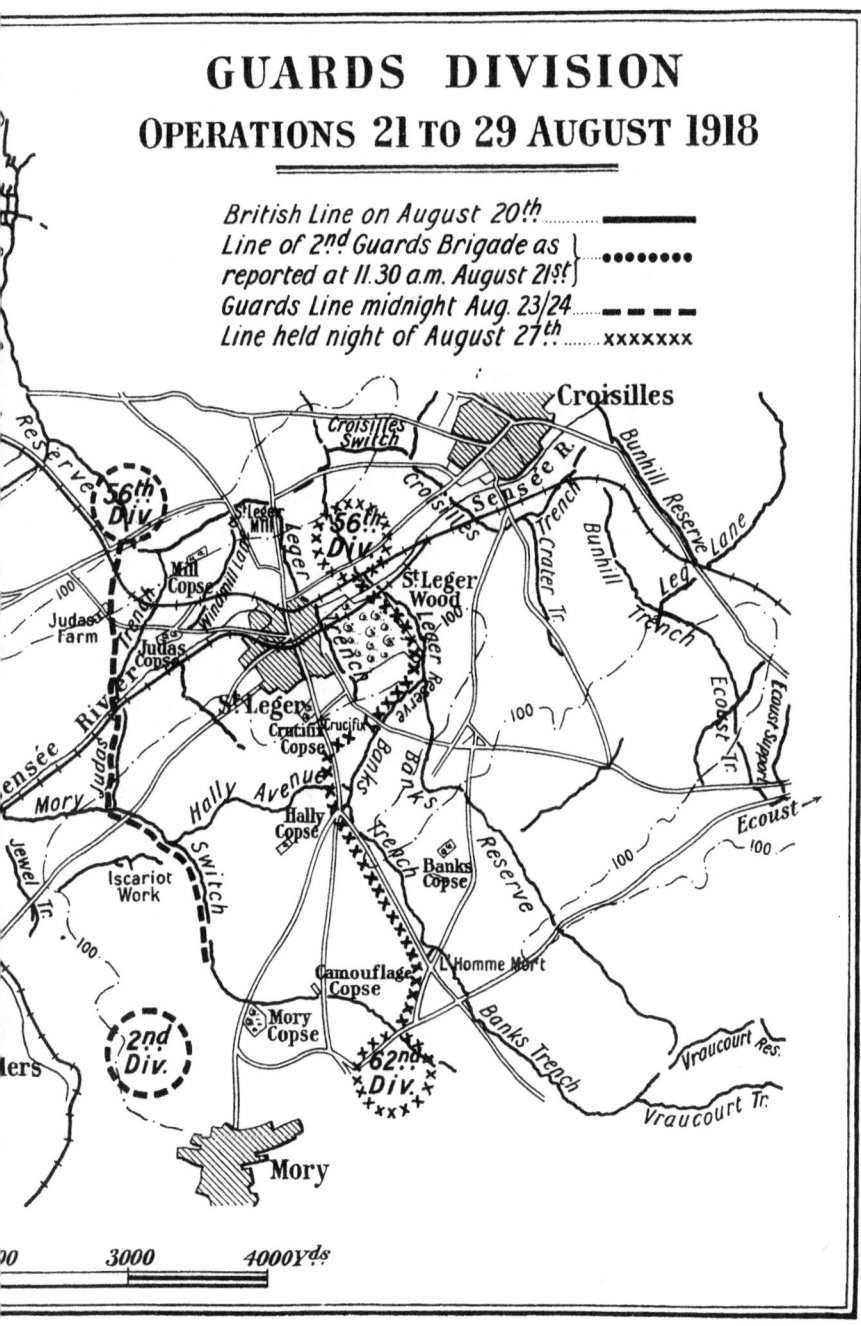

CHAPTER XVII

THE BREAKING OF THE HINDENBURG LINE—ADVANCE OF THE GUARDS TOWARDS THE CANAL DU NORD.

(1) EFFECTS OF THE ALLIED OFFENSIVE—THE GERMANS THRUST BACK ACROSS THE OLD BATTLE-FIELD OF THE SOMME—CAPTURE OF THE DROCOURT—QUÉANT LINE BY THE FIRST ARMY.

THE continuous pressure of the Allied advance gradually forced back the enemy's troops both south and north of the Somme. On the 29th of August Bapaume was evacuated by the Germans, and, by the night of the 30th of August, "the line of the Fourth and Third Armies ran from Cléry-sur-Somme past the western edge of Marrières Wood to Combles, Lesbœufs, Bancourt, Frémicourt and Vraucourt, and thence to the western outskirts of Ecoust, Bullecourt and Hendecourt." * South of the Somme the troops of the Allies by the same date had reached the left bank of the river from Nesle northward to Péronne, which town was held by the enemy in strength. On the 31st of August the 2nd Australian Division effected the passage of the Somme and stormed Mont St. Quentin, the high ground immediately to the north of Péronne, and, the following day, as a direct consequence of this brilliant feat of arms, the Australian Corps took possession of that town.† The same day the left

---

* *See* " Sir Douglas Haig's Despatches," p. 270.

† " Péronne fell on September 1, and north of that town the enemy, who had evacuated Bapaume early in the morning of August 29, was forced back to a line the southern portion of which corresponded roughly with that held by him during the winter of 1916, while its northern sector linked up with the powerful branch system known as the Drocourt—Quéant line." *See* " Sir Douglas Haig's Command," vol. ii. p. 299.

of the Fourth Army, and the Third Army farther to the north, were heavily engaged. The former gained possession of Bouchavesnes, Rancourt and Frégicourt, while the latter " held Sailly-Saillisel, Morval, Beaulencourt and Riencourt-les-Bapaume, and were established on the ridges east of Bancourt, Frémicourt, Vaulx Vraucourt and Longatte.*

The enemy had thus been thrust back across the whole of the old battle-field of the Somme, and the second stage in the great British advance to victory had been triumphantly brought to a conclusion.†

Meanwhile, the next stage in the offensive was already in progress. On the 26th of August, the First Army had moved forward east of Arras with the object of turning the enemy's positions on the Somme battle-field and thus cutting his railway communications running south-westward across this front.‡ By the end of the month the troops of the First Army " had gained the high ground east of Chérisy and Haucourt, had captured Eterpigny, and cleared the area between the Sensée and Scarpe rivers west of the Trinquis Brook. North of the Scarpe, Plouvain was held by us." §

The Third and First Armies had now reached a line from which they could assault the Drocourt—Quéant network of defences,‖ and, on the 2nd of September, " the whole of the

* *See* " Sir Douglas Haig's Despatches," p. 271.

† " The 1st September marks the close of the second stage in the British offensive. Having in the first stage freed Amiens by our brilliant success east of that town, in the second stage the troops of the Third and Fourth Armies, comprising 23 British divisions, by skilful leading, hard fighting and relentless and unremitting pursuit, in ten days had driven 35 German divisions from one side of the old Somme battle-field to the other, thereby turning the line of the river Somme. In so doing they had inflicted upon the enemy the heaviest losses in killed and wounded, and had taken from him 34,000 prisoners and 270 guns." *Ib.* p. 271.

‡ It will be remembered that the attacks made by the Guards on the 25th and 27th–28th of August were designed to assist the advance of the XVII Corps and Canadian Corps on the right of the First Army. *See* p. 138.

§ *See* " Sir Douglas Haig's Despatches," p. 274.

‖ " Our progress brought our troops to within assaulting distance of the powerful trench system running from the Hindenburg Line at Quéant to the Lens defences about Drocourt, the breaking of which would turn the whole of the enemy's organized positions on a wide front southwards." *See* " Sir Douglas Haig's Despatches," p. 274.

THE GUARDS AGAIN IN THE LINE

elaborate system of wire, trenches and strong points " which constituted this line was broken through by the Canadian Corps [1st and 4th Canadian Divisions and the 4th (British) Division] belonging to the First Army, and the XVII Corps (57th and 63rd Divisions) belonging to the Third Army.

The effect of this new success, following so rapidly the capture of Péronne, was instantaneous. The enemy, on the night of the 2nd–3rd of September, fell back rapidly on the whole front of the Third Army and on the right flank of the First Army.*

(2) THE GUARDS RELIEVE THE 3RD DIVISION WEST OF LAGNICOURT—ADVANCE OF THE 2ND AND 3RD GUARDS BRIGADES TOWARDS THE CANAL DU NORD, 3RD OF SEPTEMBER—RETREAT OF THE ENEMY TO THE HINDENBURG LINE.

In the morning on the 2nd of September the 3rd Division (VI Corps), which had pushed forward south of Ecoust St. Mein, was heavily engaged south-west of Noreuil. On the right its troops succeeded in occupying the high ground west of Lagnicourt, but in the centre their advance was checked by hostile machine-gun fire from the direction of Noreuil. On the left the division made steady progress in conjunction with the troops of the XVII Corps farther north.

Before noon of this day Major-General Feilding issued a warning order to the 2nd and 3rd Guards Bdes. to be in readiness to pass through the 3rd Division in order to continue the British advance.†

These two brigades had already moved up from the Ransart area to positions between Mory and Ecoust St.

---

* *See* " Sir Douglas Haig's Despatches," p. 275. " The enemy at once abandoned all hope of making good his resistance on the defensive line of which the river Somme south of Péronne formed the central sector. On the whole front from the Oise river to the Sensée his troops fell back, in the area of the British attack in haste and obvious disorder, to the positions immediately covering the Hindenburg Line and the Canal du Nord north of Havrincourt." *See* " Sir Douglas Haig's Command," vol. ii. p. 300.

† *See* W.D., Guards Division, September, 1918.

Mein, the 1st Guards Bde. remaining in divisional reserve south of St. Leger.*

Later in the day, the decision was made by the VI Corps commander to relieve the 62nd and 3rd Divisions in the line by the 2nd Division and the Guards Division respectively, and for these two latter divisions to carry on the attack the following morning. As soon as orders to this effect were received at divisional headquarters, Major-General Feilding instructed the 2nd and 3rd Guards Bdes. to move forward in order to relieve the 3rd Division.

The line on which the Guards now found themselves ran from a point on the Quéant—Vaulx Vraucourt road about 1,800 yards west of Lagnicourt, thence in a north-easterly direction across the Noreuil—Morchies road to a point on the Noreuil—Lagnicourt road just west of Lagnicourt. It then bent back abruptly along this road almost to the eastern outskirts of Noreuil whence it turned to the north-east again as far as the old British front line where it crossed the Noreuil—Quéant road, and linked up with the right of the XVII Corps.

This front was so singularly ill-adapted for the starting off line of an attack that it was decided to withdraw it for some little distance, the leading battalions of the 3rd Guards Bde. on the left of the divisional front forming up along the railway north-east of Ecoust St. Mein.†

At 5.20 a.m., zero hour, on the 3rd of September, the attack went forward covered by an artillery barrage supplied by the 74th and 75th Bdes., R.F.A. From the first it met with little or no opposition from the Germans, and the Guards had the pleasurable experience of being able to march steadily onward into the enemy's country without having to fight for every foot of ground—so strange and novel, indeed, was the sensation caused amongst officers and men by the unwonted absence of hostile machine-gun fire and the comparative silence of the enemy's guns, that the troops at first

---

* The 1st Guards Bde. remained in reserve during the first six days of September, moving forward in rear of the advance. A fair amount of training in open warfare was carried out during this period.

† See " The Grenadier Guards in the Great War," vol. iii. pp. 105, 106. " History of the Welsh Guards," p. 352.

AN UNOPPOSED ADVANCE 147

advanced with an unnecessary caution, suspecting some cleverly concealed trap—some new example of the Germans' skill in defensive warfare.* But as the morning wore on—an exceptionally warm one—it became apparent that the enemy had retreated all along the front and that the task before the Guards was to follow up his retirement with as little delay as possible. On the right, on the front of the 2nd Guards Bde., the 3rd Bn. Grenadier Guards † early in the afternoon reached the western outskirts of Boursies, while the 1st Bn. Scots Guards,‡ after consolidating the high ground immediately east of Lagnicourt, felt their way forward to the old British front line to the north-west of that village. The supporting battalion of the brigade, the 1st Bn. Coldstream Guards, followed up the leading battalions and reached the vicinity of Lagnicourt in the evening.

On the front of the 3rd Guards Bde., the 1st Bn. Welsh Guards on the right, and the 2nd Bn. Scots Guards on the

---

* " They (the 2nd and 3rd Guards Bdes.) ' went over the top ' under a creeping barrage . . . and—found nothing whatever in front of them save a prodigious number of dead horses, some few corpses and an intolerable buzzing of flies ! As they topped the ridge above Lagnicourt, they saw against the first light of the sun, dump after German dump blazing palely towards the east. That was all. They wandered, wondering, into a vast, grassy, habitationless plain that stretched away towards the Bapaume—Cambrai road. Not a machine gun broke the stupefying stillness from any fold of it. Yet it was the very place for such surprises. Aeroplanes swooped low, looked them well over, and skimmed off. No distant guns opened. The advance became a route-march, a Sunday walk-out, edged with tense suspicion. . . . Twice or thrice they halted and began to dig in for fear of attack. But nothing overtook them and they installed themselves, about dusk, in some old British trenches outside Boursies, four miles and more, as the crow flies, from Lagnicourt ! At midnight up came their rations, and the punctual home-letters, across that enchanted desert which had spared them." *See* " The Irish Guards in the Great War," vol. i. pp. 305, 306.

† A few days before this advance Lieut.-Colonel Thorne was appointed commandant of the IX Corps School. He was succeeded in the command of the 3rd Bn. Grenadier Guards by Major Viscount Lascelles, who remained its commanding officer until the end of the war.

‡ During the course of this advance the Grenadiers took 13 prisoners and themselves had 21 casualties. The Scots Guards record the capture of 35 Germans, 4 field guns, several machine guns and much material. Their casualties were 1 officer and 33 other ranks. *See* W.D's., 3rd Bn. Grenadier Guards and 1st Bn. Scots Guards, September, 1918.

left, moved forward in touch with troops of the 52nd Division. They had an equally easy task and reached the line of the Louverval—Inchy road in the course of the afternoon.* The 1st Bn. Grenadier Guards, the remaining battalion of the brigade, moved during the day from Noreuil to a position west of Lagnicourt where it spent the night.

Quite early in the morning of the 3rd of September it was clear to Major-General Feilding and his staff that, for the time being at any rate, the Germans were in full retreat, for, in addition to the news of the ease and rapidity with which the Guards were advancing, air reports were received at divisional headquarters stating first, that the enemy was burning the country in rear of his lines, and then, that Quéant and Pronville had been abandoned and that the Germans were no longer holding the Hindenburg Line south of those villages. At 10.15 a.m. orders were received from the VI Corps for each division to form an advanced guard of one brigade complete with the necessary detachments of R.F.A. and R.E.

Upon the receipt of these orders, Major-General Feilding instructed the 2nd and 3rd Guards Bdes. to establish a line along the old British front system of trenches from Boursies to the branch road running to Pronville, in a north-westerly direction across the spur of high ground, and thence along that road to the divisional boundary immediately south of Pronville. As soon as this line had been established, an advanced guard was to be formed for the purpose of forcing the crossings of the Canal du Nord in conjunction with the 2nd Division on the right.

But it was not until late in the evening that the line was actually established and an advanced guard formed. After their long march varying from four to five miles under a hot sun in full battle order the troops were much exhausted, and it took some little time to organize the new line. The enemy's artillery, too, became more active as the day

* The Welsh Guards took 14 prisoners, many machine guns and 4 anti-tank guns. The Scots Guards record the capture of a few German stragglers, one 8-in. howitzer, 3 H.V. guns of smaller calibre, 7 field guns and several machine guns. *See* W.D's., 1st Bn. Welsh Guards and 2nd Bn. Scots Guards, September, 1918.

THE APPROACH TO THE CANAL DU NORD

advanced, and retarded the work of the patrols which were sent to feel their way forward all along the front. There were few casualties, however, and the Germans made no attempt at a counter-attack.

Meanwhile, the two flanking divisions had also made good progress. At 3 p.m. reports reached Major-General Feilding that the 2nd Division on the right was in possession of Doignies and was advancing upon Hermies and Demicourt, and that the 63rd Division on the left had taken Inchy and was approaching Tadpole Copse and Mœuvres.

Upon receipt of this information, orders were sent to the 2nd Guards Bde. not to enter Boursies unless its troops were in touch with those of the 2nd Division, and to the 3rd Guards Bde. to gain touch with the 63rd Division at Tadpole Copse.

Reports of further progress were received as the day wore on, but a halt to the advance of the Guards was called at 8.15 p.m. Major-General Feilding then instructed Brig.-General Follett to form an outpost line consisting of one company across the spur of high ground west of the Louverval—Inchy road and to withdraw the remainder of his troops into bivouacs in the area between Lagnicourt and Louverval for the night, in readiness to pass through the 2nd Guards Bde. at dawn the following day. The 2nd Guards Bde. was ordered to hold the old British front line from the Bapaume—Cambrai road to the outpost line occupied by the 3rd Guards Bde. and to throw out patrols south of Boursies.*

The general advance of the VI Corps was ordered to be resumed at 5.30 a.m. on the 4th of September when the scheme of operations involved the turning of the crossings of the Canal du Nord and the locating—but not the assaulting —of the enemy's main line of resistance. This advance was to be carried out by the 3rd Guards Bde. which, after passing through the line of the 2nd Guards Bde., was to

---

* At this period in the evening of the 3rd of September the front of the VI Corps ran approximately from Hermies just west of Demicourt to Boursies, thence roughly due north to Tadpole Copse, the right of the XVII Corps being either in this copse or possibly in Mœuvres.

extend north through the troops of the 63rd Division in Tadpole Copse and Mœuvres.

The night of the 3rd–4th of September passed tolerably quietly, although the patrols of the 2nd Guards Bde. reported that their progress was checked by the enemy's machine-gun fire.*

(3) STIFFENING OF THE ENEMY'S RESISTANCE BETWEEN BOURSIES AND MŒUVRES—CONTINUOUS PRESSURE MAINTAINED ALONG THE LINE BY THE GUARDS DIVISION, 4TH–7TH OF SEPTEMBER.

It is no easy matter to give anything like a detailed account of the events of the next few days. Little definite information is to be gathered from the War Diaries and reports of the various battalions, but it is clear from the divisional record that little progress was made.

It was evident from an early hour in the morning of the 4th of September that the enemy's resistance had stiffened considerably since the previous evening, and that the Germans were holding the approaches to the western bank of the Canal du Nord in strength. The 3rd Guards Bde., with the 1st Bn. Welsh Guards on the right and the 2nd Bn. Scots Guards on the left, passed through the 2nd Guards Bde. shortly after 5 a.m. and was met with heavy machine-gun fire as soon as the troops approached the German positions

* Guards divisional railhead was moved to Boyelles on the 3rd of September. No real difficulty was experienced in getting forward both motor and horse transport during the day's advance although the latter, of course, had to be kept on the line of watering points, the establishment of which was found necessary. *See* W.D., Guards Division Train, September, 1918. The ground throughout the whole area of the advance was much cut up by shell fire, but it was possible to make use of numerous cross-country tracks which were in tolerably good condition. The main roads in villages were usually covered with from 2 to 3 feet of débris, but they were quickly cleared by working parties. The 4th Bn. Coldstream Guards (Pioneers) was almost exclusively employed upon the repair of roads and tracks. The Field Companies, R.E., were fully occupied in road reconnaissance and water supply. Water points were established at Noreuil, Ecoust, Quéant and Lagnicourt. At Louverval a demolished well was re-sunk. *See* W.D., C.R.E., Guards Division, September, 1918.

in front of the canal. The advance of the Welsh Guards was checked a little to the east of Boursies and the Scots Guards could make their way no farther than a point just south of Tadpole Copse. Attempts made by patrols of these battalions to move beyond these positions did not meet with any appreciable success.*

As soon as this information reached divisional headquarters, Brig.-General Follett was instructed to endeavour to open a way to the canal by clearing the enemy out of the intricate maze of trenches forming the front system of the Hindenburg Line south of Mœuvres.† Early in the evening, therefore, the 2nd Bn. Scots Guards with artillery support advanced to the attack and was successful in establishing posts south of Mœuvres. This appears to have been the extent of the advance on the 4th of September. At 8.20 p.m., that day, Major-General Feilding decided to make no attempt to advance the next day (5th of September), but he ordered the 3rd Guards Bde. to maintain a steady pressure on the enemy's positions and to explore the line of the canal for possible crossing places. His decision was influenced to a great extent by the fact that, on the night of the 4th, the situation on the northern flank of the Guards Division was somewhat obscure. It was known that the Germans had counter-attacked at Inchy, but no definite information as to the result of the engagement had reached divisional headquarters at 8 p.m.

During the night of the 4th–5th of September the enemy maintained an incessant machine-gun fire all along the Guards divisional front, whilst his artillery bombarded the line and the area in rear with gas-shell.‡

* See " History of the Welsh Guards," p. 241.

† See W.D., Guards Division, September, 1918. " Before an attack upon the Hindenburg Line proper could be undertaken, there were a series of covering positions which had first to be reduced. Taught, no doubt, by the experience of 1917, the enemy in his last retreat had stopped somewhat short of the line to which he had withdrawn in the spring of that year. Since that date, too, battle tactics had changed in the course of the ceaseless evolution of war, and he must have felt that greater depth was necessary to a sure defence. The middle weeks of September were therefore devoted to capturing these covering positions." See " Sir Douglas Haig's Command," vol. ii. p. 311.

‡ " . . . all through the night the enemy kept up a constant

On the 5th of September the northern boundary of the division was extended so as to include Mœuvres. During the course of the day the troops of the 3rd Guards Bde. made strenuous efforts to improve their positions, but the German defence was as obstinate and well-organized as on the previous day. Little could be effected in face of the fierce machine-gun fire which greeted any kind of movement. However, in the evening the Welsh Guards contrived to establish themselves in Goat trench and held on to their new position, although they were heavily shelled from Bourlon Wood and were not in touch with the troops of the 2nd Division on their right.*

The 2nd Guards Bde. relieved the 3rd Guards Bde. in the line during the night of the 5th–6th of September, the front which it took over extending from Goat trench due north to a point just west of Mœuvres.† This relief was by no means an easy one, and it was rendered still more difficult by the heavy condition of the ground, the result of soaking rain following a violent thunderstorm. The situation of the troops in the line was one of the utmost discomfort, matters being made worse for them by the constant gas-shelling to which they were subjected throughout the night. The 3rd Bn. Grenadier Guards, which had relieved the Welsh Guards on the right of the line, suffered most severely from the effects of the gas bombardment.‡ On the

machine-gun fire. In spite of this patrols tested the possibility of further advance, but found the whole front heavily wired. The Scots Guards found the same strong defence on the left. Shelling was constant, and the reserve company (Welsh Guards) was heavily gassed." See " History of the Welsh Guards," p. 241.

* The enemy's gunners in Bourlon Wood had direct observation over this part of the line. *See* " History of the Welsh Guards," p. 242.

† On the 2nd of September the D.A.C. supplied wagons and limbers for a mobile section formed from the trench-mortar batteries. Two 6-in. mortars with 120 bombs were thus moved forward and went into action on the night of the 5th–6th of September on the left of the line. *See* W.D's., D.A.C. and T.-M.B., Guards Division, September, 1918.

‡ This battalion lost 6 officers and 91 other ranks casualties. " For an hour the Germans bombarded the valley with sneezing-gas shells, and all the officers and men kept on their masks, but when the gas bombardment appeared to cease and was succeeded by one of H.E. shells, every one incautiously took off his mask. The new bombardment proved to be one of mustard gas. By the time this

6th of September patrols of the 2nd Guards Bde. were busily employed in endeavouring to push back the enemy from his positions west of the canal, but little success was achieved. The Grenadiers, however, established a strong post at their junction with the 2nd Division, thus securing the right flank of the brigade which had hitherto been more or less in the air.*

In view of the increase in the volume of the German artillery fire, it was now considered advisable by the VI Corps commander to organize a line of resistance on the corps front in readiness for any eventuality. The organization of this line was completed on the 6th of September,† but, although the enemy's guns continued to be very active, no hostile infantry attack was attempted on the Guards front. At nightfall, on the 6th, the Guards divisional Artillery, which had followed the infantry closely on the 3rd of September, and occupied positions in the valley west of Louverval, again moved forward, taking up positions between Louverval and Boursies. During the next few days it carried out a regular programme of harassing fire according to the usual routine of trench warfare, and suffered a good deal from the vigorous gas and high explosive shelling of the enemy's guns.‡ As a precaution against hostile counter-attacks the Guards Machine-Gun Regiment was entrusted with the task of covering the battery positions.

was realized every one was being sick, and all the officers and N.C.O.'s were casualties." *See* " The Grenadier Guards in the Great War," vol. iii. pp. 129, 130.

* During the course of the 6th of September ground was gained on both flanks of the VI Corps. In the morning the 63rd Division on the northern flank of the Guards Division was reported to be across the canal at a point west of Bois de Quesnoy, and, at about noon, the IV Corps informed the VI Corps that the enemy had vacated Havrincourt Wood. *See* W.D., Guards Division, September, 1918.

† This line ran east of Doignies, thence across the Bapaume—Cambrai road west of Boursies in a north-easterly direction to the old British front line which it followed to a point west of the Louverval—Inchy road. Here it turned north-east again along the spur of high ground to the Hindenburg Line east of Tadpole Copse to a point north-west of Mœuvres.

‡ On the 8th of September D/75, R.F.A., was very severely shelled. Its commander, Major E. J. Housden, was wounded. *See* W.D., 75th Bde., R.F.A., September, 1918.

On the 7th of September the 1st Guards Bde. relieved the 2nd Guards Bde. in the line,* the latter brigade being withdrawn to the Lagnicourt area where the training of its troops was much interfered with by the bad weather.

During the next few days the attempts to open a way to the canal crossings on the VI Corps front by infantry action were continued, but, except for a short length of trench gained on the 8th of September by the 1st Bn. Irish Guards on the left of the divisional line,† no progress was made by the Guards. The in and out skirmishing in the trenches south of Mœuvres was reminiscent of the unpleasant days spent in the Hohenzollern Redoubt in the autumn of 1915; the fighting was well nigh as intricate, and, to those who were actually concerned in it, it appeared to be equally unprofitable.

(4) ORGANIZED ATTACK BY THE TROOPS OF THE VI CORPS— RÔLE OF THE GUARDS DIVISION IN THE BATTLE OF HAVRINCOURT, 12TH OF SEPTEMBER—MAJOR-GENERAL FEILDING LEAVES THE DIVISION ON HIS APPOINTMENT TO COMMAND THE LONDON DISTRICT—MAJOR-GENERAL MATHESON APPOINTED TO COMMAND THE GUARDS DIVISION.

It was now clear to the higher authorities that the enemy could not be dislodged from the very strong defensive positions in which he had taken refuge along the Canal du Nord north of Havrincourt and southward to Epéhy without a properly organized attack, and that these outworks of the Hindenburg Line must be captured before the final attack on the main

---

* *See* W.D., Guards Division, September, 1918. The same day the 57th Division relieved the 63rd Division on the left of the Guards.

† *See* W.D., 1st Bn. Irish Guards, September, 1918. The following day, at 1 p.m., the Germans made a silent raid on the extreme left of the sector held by the Irish Guards and in the ruined houses just south of Mœuvres succeeded in capturing and carrying off "two unarmed stretcher-bearers and three men who had not been in the line before." *See* "The Irish Guards in the Great War," vol. i. p. 307.

defensive system in rear could be satisfactorily launched.* Orders were issued, therefore, by the Third Army to the IV and VI Corps to attack on a front of about five miles in the Havrincourt sector on the 11th and 12th of September.

On the 9th of September the operation orders of the VI Corps for this attack reached Guards divisional headquarters.† The rôle of the Guards in the coming operation was to be more or less a passive one, as the attack was to be delivered on the southern portion of the corps front by the 2nd and 62nd Divisions. The tasks assigned to the Guards Division were (1) the covering of the left flank of the 2nd Division, and (2) the establishing, if practicable, of bridgeheads east of the canal opposite the divisional front. The divisional Artillery was to assist the attacking troops by firing smoke-shell to screen the ridge running north and south to the west of Graincourt, and the Guards Machine-Gun Regiment was to fire an overhead barrage into Havrincourt.‡ In addition to the advance on the VI Corps front, the 57th Division (XVII Corps) on the immediate left of the Guards was to endeavour to gain possession of Mœuvres on the 11th of September. This latter operation necessitated the taking over by the 57th Division of the northern portion of the Guards' front, and, consequently, on the night of the 9th–10th of September, the 1st Bn. Irish Guards was relieved in the line by a battalion of the 57th Division. The relief

---

* " North of Havrincourt, the Canal du Nord, behind which the enemy had taken shelter, with the open slopes leading down to it swept by the fire of the German positions on the east bank, could scarcely be taken except by a carefully organized attack." *See* " Sir Douglas Haig's Despatches," p. 276. A local attack carried out by troops belonging to the III Corps on the 10th of September at Epéhy ended in failure.

† *See* W.D., Guards Division, September, 1918.

‡ Major-General Feilding considered that the position allotted to the machine gunners in the corps orders was too much exposed. It could only be occupied the night before the attack and consequently the satisfactory laying of the guns would be a matter of some difficulty. The Major-General raised this objection because he was particularly anxious that any assistance rendered by the Guards to any other division should be as valuable and reliable as possible. The corps commander was unable to agree with any change in the original orders. *See* W.D., Guards Division, September, 1918.

was a long and tedious one, as it was carried out in total darkness and drenching rain.*

During the following day the necessary preparations were made on the Guards' front for the opening of the offensive which was to bring about the forcing of the Hindenburg Line. But it was ordained that the division was no longer to be led along the road to victory by the leader who had commanded it for so long and with so much success. On the 11th of September Major-General Feilding bade farewell to his troops and left divisional headquarters on his appointment to succeed Lieut.-General Sir Francis Lloyd in the command of the London District. His departure was genuinely regretted by all ranks. He had commanded the division for a period of two years and eight months. Under his leadership its troops had toiled and fought heroically and achieved glory in some of the hardest fighting in the war. His fearless and unselfish efforts on behalf of his men, his fine courage, his power of leadership, his invariable coolness in critical circumstances, had won for him the confidence, and secured for him the respect of all who served under him.†

His place was taken by Major-General T. G. Matheson (Coldstream Guards), G.O.C. the 4th Division, an officer of conspicuous ability and great experience, whose record in the war as battalion, brigade and divisional commander justified in every way his selection to command the Guards Division.

(5) The Battle of Havrincourt—Local fighting on the front of the VI Corps, 12th–27th of September.

In the evening of the 11th of September the 2nd Division pushed forward on the right of the Guards to try and obtain a footing east of the canal for its main attack to be delivered

---

* *See* W.D., 1st Bn. Irish Guards, September, 1918.

† "Lord Cavan had the honour of first commanding the division, and Major-Gen. Matheson that of commanding in the very last phase of the Great War, but Major-Gen. Feilding may be looked upon, from the length of time he commanded and the number of engagements he went through, as the commander of the Guards Division." *See* "History of the Welsh Guards," p. 247.

the following morning.* The attacking troops, whose left flank was covered by the Guards divisional Artillery, succeeded in establishing posts in the enemy's trenches east of the canal.

On the left of the Guards the 170th Infantry Bde. (57th Division) attacked Mœuvres at 6.15 p.m. and occupied part of the village. The Guards protected the right flank of this attack with trench-mortar and machine-gun fire, whilst a platoon of the 2nd Bn. Grenadier Guards on the extreme left of the divisional line assisted the advance of the 170th Infantry Bde. by forming a forward post.†

During the night the 3rd Guards Bde. relieved the 1st Guards Bde. in the line. The relief of the 2nd Bn. Grenadier Guards on the left by the 2nd Bn. Scots Guards was a comparatively simple affair, but the 1st Bn. Grenadier Guards, which went in on the right of the line, had many difficulties against which to contend. The battalion was called upon to take over an extended front from troops of the 2nd Division in the midst of the confusion consequent upon the fighting earlier in the evening, and it was not until the morning of the 12th that Lieut.-Colonel Viscount Gort succeeded in establishing the line to his satisfaction.‡

On the 12th of September the main attack by the IV and VI Corps was delivered and resulted in the capture of the villages of Trescault and Havrincourt, while north of the

---

* The enemy's main line of resistance opposite the front of the VI Corps lay on the eastern side of the Canal du Nord along the high ground west of Graincourt, thence southward to Flesquières. But between the network of trenches and strong points which formed the Hindenburg support system and the canal in this area lay a forward system of great strength, admirably adapted for machine-gun defence. Opposite the front of the Guards Division the canal cutting was dry, but the enemy still held some trenches on the western side of the canal where the formation of the ground greatly assisted the defence.

† See W.D's., Guards Division and 1st Guards Bde., September, 1918. During the night 8 prisoners belonging to the 226th R.I. Regiment (49th Reserve Division) and 2 belonging to the 2nd Guard Reserve Regiment (1st Guard Reserve Division) were taken and sent back through the divisional line.

‡ See W.D., 1st Bn. Grenadier Guards, September, 1918. Cf. "The Grenadier Guards in the Great War," vol. iii. p. 113.

Guards' front the troops of the 57th Division completed the capture of Mœuvres.

The infantry of the Guards Division was not required to participate in this day's advance—the rôle of the division in these operations, as in those of the previous day, being to stand fast—but, nevertheless, the 1st Bn. Grenadier Guards seized the opportunity to advance its positions in conjunction with the forward movement of the 2nd Division on its right whose troops consolidated a line in the enemy's trenches beyond the canal. The Grenadiers had several encounters with the Germans in the course of the day in which they successfully defended their new positions and killed or captured a good many of the enemy. They also materially assisted the troops on their flank.*

The divisional Artillery took part in the barrage covering the advance of the 2nd Division in the morning and was actively engaged during the remainder of the day in harassing the enemy's communications and firing upon any movement visible in his lines.† The Guards' machine gunners covered the 62nd Division during and after its attack and their assistance was greatly appreciated.‡

The days which followed the battle of Havrincourt to the 27th of September, when the battle of the Canal du Nord

---

* The prisoners belonged to the 226th and 72nd Reserve Infantry Regiments. The enemy's artillery fire was heavy throughout the day. The Grenadiers' casualties amounted to 2 officers and 15 other ranks. *See* W.D., 1st Bn. Grenadier Guards, September, 1918. On the 15th of September Brigadier-General Follett received the following letter from Brigadier-General W. S. Osborn, commanding the 5th Infantry Bde. :—" The 5th Infantry Bde. much appreciates the support given them on their left by the 1st Batt. Grenadier Guards. . . . The counter-attack repulsed by Grenadier Guardsmen would have fallen on their weakened companies . . . Will you please thank Colonel Lord Gort from me on behalf of the 5th. I.B."

† *See* W.D., 75th Bde., R.F.A., September, 1918.

‡ The G.O.C. the 62nd Division sent the following message to Major-General Matheson :—" I must send you a line to say how much we are indebted to your Machine-Gun Company for its invaluable assistance on 12th and 13th inst. By their rapid change of position forward on the afternoon of the 12th, they were able to take a most effective share in repulsing the German counter-attack on that evening, after having given me a splendid barrage in the morning." *See* W.D., Guards Division, App. 1127.

began, were full of local interest on the front of the VI Corps. The British troops gradually pushed forward their posts in order to improve their line for the coming offensive, while the enemy's artillery kept up an almost incessant fire and his infantry made desperate efforts to regain the ground which it had lost.

On the front of the Guards Division the 1st Bn. Grenadier Guards was able to report, at 2.30 p.m. on the 15th of September, that posts had been established on the line of the canal. From this date onwards careful reconnaissances of the canal were made by the battalions which successively held the line.

The reports received at divisional headquarters varied somewhat as to the width and depth of the dry waterway opposite the divisional front, but the necessity for the employment of light ladders for the scaling of the sides of the canal was generally recommended. The walls were almost perpendicular and, except in places where they were damaged by shell fire, the brickwork afforded but a poor foothold.*

During the night of the 15th–16th of September the 2nd Guards Bde. relieved the 1st Guards Bde. in the line, and also took over the northern sector of the front held by the 3rd Division on the right.† From this date to the night of the 22nd of September the divisional front was definitely divided into two sectors—the Mœuvres sector north of the Bapaume—Cambrai road and the Demicourt sector south of that road. Each of these sectors was held by a brigade, each brigade having one battalion in line, one in support and one in reserve. The front of the left brigade was covered by the 74th and 75th Bdes., R.F.A., formed into a group under the

---

* *See* W.D's., 1st Bn. Grenadier Guards and 1st Bn. Scots Guards, September, 1918. " The only part (of the canal) where a crossing was at all practicable was in a narrow sector about Mœuvres. Here the canal cutting was dry, but deep and wide as a modern London road when viewed from the house tops. Further, the ground west of the canal in this sector dropped gently down to the canal bank in long open slopes, destitute of cover and liable to be swept at any moment by the enemy's artillery and machine-gun fire." *See* " Sir Douglas Haig's Command," vol. ii. p. 321.

† This division took over the line of the 62nd Division as well as part of that vacated by the 2nd Division this same night.

command of Lieut.-Colonel Vickery,* while that of the right brigade was protected by the artillery of the 2nd Division.

In the evening, on the 17th of September, the enemy made a vigorous counter-attack on Mœuvres, which he succeeded in wresting from the 57th Division. A post of the Welsh Guards on the left flank of the 3rd Guards Bde. sector was attacked during this raid. The Germans bombed their way up a communication trench, but were driven back, the post holding firm.† The next day, in the afternoon, a heavy hostile barrage was put down along the Guards' front and the forward battery positions. The British artillery replied, but about three hours later the enemy's infantry attacked the positions of the 3rd Division on the right of the 2nd Guards Bde. The Germans succeeded in regaining a little ground before they were driven back, but their losses were heavy, the 1st Bn. Coldstream Guards being in a position to take them in enfilade as they advanced and also as they retreated.‡

* See W.D., C.R.A., Guards Division, September, 1918. The group zone of fire was shifted slightly to the north so that the batteries were made to cover 500 yards on either side of the Bapaume—Cambrai road and thence eastward.

† See W.D., Guards Division, September, 1918. This attack took place just as the Welsh Guards were being relieved by the 2nd Bn. Coldstream Guards, the 1st Guards Bde., taking over the sector in the evening.

‡ The 3rd Division completely re-established its line on the 19th of September and the same day the 57th Division regained Mœuvres.

GUARDS
OPERATIONS,

IVISION
SEPT. 1918

Line taken over by 2nd &
3rd Guards Brigades on
night 2/3rd September

Line taken over by
2nd Guards Brigade on
night 5/6th September

Corps Boundary

Corps Boundary on North
altered 5th September to

CHAPTER XVIII

THE BREAKING OF THE HINDENBURG LINE (*continued*)—
THE BATTLE OF THE CANAL DU NORD, 27TH OF SEPTEMBER, 1918.

(1) FINAL PREPARATIONS FOR THE CROSSING OF THE CANAL DU NORD AND ASSAULT ON THE HINDENBURG LINE.

THE first orders for the impending attack by the Third Army were issued on the 19th of September and the final preparations for its attack on the enemy's main defensive positions in the Hindenburg Line were now energetically proceeded with by the Guards Division.*

The frequent reliefs of the various battalions in the line during the course of the month had enabled all units to gain a fair knowledge of the approaches to the Canal du Nord, in addition to which the troops whilst in support positions in rear of the line had been given as much instruction as was possible in the actual tactics which would have to be employed in the coming operations. A list of the crossings over the canal was circulated among brigades as well as a topographical description of the ground on its eastern side (with much of which the Guards were already fairly familiar), together with elaborate details respecting

* The object of the British Commander-in-Chief in forcing the passage of the Canal du Nord and breaking through the Hindenburg Line opposite the Third and First Armies was to gain possession of the high ground lying between the Canal du Nord and the Scheldt, and so to make possible the advance of the Fourth Army farther to the south. " The lie of the ground was such that on the front of the Fourth Army adequate artillery fire could not be developed to support the assault or to deal with the cross-fire of German batteries to the north-east on what was known as La Terrière plateau, till the Third and First British Armies had got forward sufficiently to bring effective fire to bear upon those batteries from the north and north-west." *See* " Sir Douglas Haig's Command," vol. ii. pp. 320, 321.

the wire, trenches and dug-outs in the Hindenburg support system. A list, too, was provided of the units cooperating on the flanks of the division and of the positions they should reach during the various stages of the advance. Nothing, indeed, was omitted that careful staff work could anticipate for the successful conduct of the attack.*

The R.E. provided the attacking battalions with a number of portable ladders to assist the troops in scaling the walls of the deep cutting across which they would have to make their way, and, with the help of the 4th Bn. Coldstream Guards (Pioneers), made their preliminary arrangements for the subsequent bridging of the canal. Dumps of the necessary materials were formed as far forward as possible, bridges were constructed of salved material, and the approaches from Demicourt to the points on the canal selected for their construction were reconnoitred and made ready so far as circumstances permitted.†

On the 19th of September the gunners began the reconnoitring of forward gun positions east of the Demicourt—Mœuvres road, the arranging of their communications and the bringing forward of ammunition.‡ On the 20th, began the work of wire-cutting in the Hindenburg support system,§ and, during the nights of the 20th-21st and the 21st-22nd, the enemy's lines astride the Bapaume—Cambrai road were subjected to gas projector attacks.

On the night of the 22nd-23rd of September a final readjustment of the divisional line took place. The 2nd Guards Bde., which was to lead the way when the attack was launched, now took over the whole of the Guards front,‖

---

* See W.D., Guards Division, Apps. 1148, 1151.

† See W.D., C.R.E., Guards Division, App., September, 1918. Two 24-feet span bridges—one with girders as bearers and one with round logs—and also a trestle bridge, were constructed and taken forward. These bridges were put together and dismantled several times, so that the *personnel* could be sure of erecting them quickly.

‡ See W.D's., 74th and 75th Bdes., R.F.A., September, 1918.

§ On the 21st of September some sections of the artillery were withdrawn to their wagon lines for a brief rest and this plan was continued the following days until the evening of the 26th.

‖ The 1st Bn. Welsh Guards, which had relieved the 3rd Bn. Grenadier Guards in the line on the 21st of September and come under the

the 52nd Division (XVII Corps) extending its right as far as the Bapaume—Cambrai road.

The line from which the Guards were to attack thus extended southward from the Bapaume—Cambrai road to a point a little south-west of Lock 7 on the Canal du Nord.

(2) Tasks of the Guards Division and flanking divisions in the General Scheme of Operations.

On the 27th of September began the great battle by which the British Army was to break its way through the last and strongest of the enemy's organized defensive systems. On that day the Third and First Armies were ordered to attack on a front of about 13 miles from a point east of Metz-en-Couture opposite Gouzeaucourt to a point on the Canal du Nord a little to the north-west of Sauchy Lestrée.*

In the initial stage of this offensive the VI Corps commander decided to employ two divisions in the front line— the 3rd Division on the right and the Guards Division on the left.

The task assigned to the Guards was to force their way across the Canal du Nord, to carry by assault the Hindenburg support system, and then to advance along the spur of high ground running east and north-east of Flesquières. The final objective given to the division was a line, known as the "blue line," running from a little north of Marcoing along the western edge of Bois des Neuf northward to a point on the Marcoing—Cantaing road just south of Cantaing.

From the line of this objective patrols were to be pushed forward towards the Scheldt river and the St. Quentin Canal, until such time as the troops of the 2nd Division, who were to carry on the advance on this part of the line, had come up and passed through the Guards.†

orders of the 2nd Guards Bde., held the whole divisional front until the night of the 23rd–24th, when it was relieved by the 3rd Bn. Grenadier Guards and moved back into support positions in rear.

* *See* " Sir Douglas Haig's Despatches," p. 280.

† " The success of the northern part of the attack depended upon the ability of our troops to debouch from the neighbourhood of Mœuvres,

On the right of the VI Corps front the attack of the 3rd Division was directed on Ribécourt and Flesquières, and, after the capture of these villages, the 62nd Division was to pass through the 3rd Division and to continue the advance.

The operations of the XVII and Canadian Corps on the front of the First Army north of the Bapaume—Cambrai road were of a rather more intricate nature.* The 52nd Division, immediately to the north of the Guards, moving south from Mœuvres, was ordered to clear the front system of the Hindenburg Line west of the Canal du Nord as well as the trenches immediately east of the canal. It was calculated that this attack would meet the left flank of the Guards whose first objective lay among these same trenches.

Meanwhile, the 63rd Division was to cross the canal east of Mœuvres and to advance upon Graincourt and Anneux, its right flank being instructed to gain touch with the Guards at a later stage in the operations. Finally, the 57th Division was to pass through the 63rd Division in order to capture Cantaing and link up with the Guards or the 2nd Division, as the case might be, to the south of that village.

(3) PLAN OF OPERATIONS ON THE GUARDS DIVISIONAL FRONT.

Major-General Matheson, who carefully explained the scheme of operations to all commanding officers at a conference on the 25th of September, ordered Brig.-General Sergison-Brooke, 2nd Guards Bde., to launch the attack on the Canal du Nord. His objective, known as the "red line," was roughly the Hindenburg front and support systems of trenches in the triangle formed by the Demicourt—Graincourt, Demicourt—Flesquières and Havrincourt—Graincourt

and to secure the crossings of the Canal du Nord in that locality. The northern portion of the canal was too formidable an obstacle to be crossed in the face of the enemy. It was therefore necessary for the attacking divisions to force a passage on a comparatively narrow front about Mœuvres, and thereafter turn the line of the canal farther north by a divergent attack developed fanwise from the point of crossing." *See* "Sir Douglas Haig's Despatches," pp. 280, 281.

* The exact line on which the 2nd Division was to pass through the Guards would of course depend upon the amount of resistance encountered by the latter in the earlier stages of the battle.

TASK OF THE GUARDS OUTLINED

roads. As soon as this line of objectives had been gained the 2nd Guards Bde. was to form a defensive flank westward from the Havrincourt—Graincourt road until the troops of the XVII Corps were in possession of the trenches in the Hindenburg Line north of the divisional sector of the attack and of Graincourt.*

An hour and fifty minutes after zero hour, Brig.-General de Crespigny, 1st Guards Bde., was ordered to pass through the 2nd Guards Bde. and to capture the " brown dotted line," and such part of the " brown line " as lay to the south of it—roughly the Hindenburg support system running south-eastward from the Havrincourt—Graincourt road just north of Flesquières to Beet trench on the Flesquières—Premy Chapel road. The brigade was then to swing forward its left from the " dotted brown line " to the " brown line " north-east of Flesquières in conjunction with the attack of the 63rd Division upon Graincourt.†

Brig.-General de Crespigny was further instructed to continue his advance, if possible, in a north-easterly direction from Flesquières in order to form a defensive flank across the Flesquières—Cantaing road until the 57th Division was in possession of Cantaing. In the event, however, of the 1st Guards Bde. meeting with a vigorous resistance, the further advance was to be delayed until the 3rd Guards Bde. came up.‡ This latter brigade was to pass through the 1st Guards Bde. on the southern portion of the " brown line "—that is to say, east of Flesquières—at zero+four hours and thirty minutes, and was then to advance eastward along the high ground to Premy Chapel and to gain the " blue dotted line." If little opposition were encountered by his brigade Brig.-General Follett, upon reaching the line of the final objective—the " blue line "—was ordered to push out patrols towards the Scheldt and the St. Quentin Canal.§

---

* *See* W.D's., Guards Division and 2nd Guards Bde., September, 1918.
† This latter movement was timed to take place at zero+3 hours and 45 minutes.
‡ *See* W.D., 1st Guards Bde., September, 1918.
§ *See* W.D., 3rd Guards Bde., September, 1918.

(4) ARTILLERY ARRANGEMENTS.

Five brigades, R.F.A., were detailed to provide a creeping barrage to cover the main attack of the 2nd Guards Bde. eastward across the Canal du Nord, while its subsidiary attack northward for the purpose of clearing the enemy's trenches west of the canal was to be covered by the guns of one brigade, R.F.A.

The advance of the 1st Guards Bde. was to be covered by three brigades, R.F.A., and the 14th Bde., R.H.A., was to assist in exploiting the situation towards Cantaing.

The Guards Machine-Gun Regiment and Trench-Mortar Batteries were also to take part in the barrage. The 74th and 75th Bdes., R.F.A., under the command of Lieut.-Colonel Vickery, were detached as a mobile force to support the advance of the 3rd Guards Bde., and received orders to be in readiness to move forward at zero+two hours, and at zero+two hours and forty minutes, respectively. Until the " brown line " was captured, barrages were to be put down by the British heavy artillery.*

(5) ASSEMBLY OF THE TROOPS ON THE NIGHT OF THE 26TH–27TH OF SEPTEMBER.

At 6.30 p.m. on the 26th of September the Guards battalions began to take up their positions. The 2nd Guards Bde., which, it will be remembered, was holding the line, concentrated in the vicinity of the front with the 1st Bn. Scots Guards on the right, the 1st Bn. Coldstream Guards in the centre and the 3rd Bn. Grenadier Guards on the left.

The 1st Guards Bde. moved up from the Lagnicourt area and concentrated south-east of Beaumetz-les-Cambrai and east of Louverval. It had the 1st Bn. Irish Guards in front, followed by the 2nd Bn. Grenadier Guards and the 2nd Bn. Coldstream Guards.

The 3rd Guards Bde. moved forward north of Louverval

---

* *See* W.D., C.R.A., Guards Division, September, 1918. By request of Major-General Matheson the entire artillery action of the Corps was coordinated by the C.R.A., Guards Division. *See* W.D., Guards Division, App. 1148.

and along the Louverval—Lagnicourt road, the 1st Bn. Grenadier Guards, the 2nd Bn. Scots Guards and the 1st Bn. Welsh Guards in the order named.

All the troops succeeded in reaching their positions of assembly in good time and without much difficulty, although the rain which fell steadily during the night and early hours of the morning, made the ground wet and slippery.

At 4.30 a.m. on the 27th, the preparations of the 2nd Guards Bde. were disturbed by a heavy hostile bombardment which caused some casualties among the 1st Bn. Scots Guards.* Luckily, however, it was of short duration and was not followed by any action on the part of the German infantry; it did not seriously interfere, therefore, with the arrangements for the attack which was launched punctually at 5.20 a.m., zero hour.

(6) Attack of the 2nd Guards Brigade, 27th of September.

On the right of the 2nd Guards Bde. the 1st Bn. Scots Guards, moving forward under a particularly effective barrage, had little difficulty in crossing the canal, the light ladders carried by the men proving useful for scaling its walls. East of the canal the Germans put up a stout resistance in the network of trenches which formed the Hindenburg support system, and their machine-gun fire, especially from the left flank, caused some casualties among the attacking troops. But the Scots Guards pushed steadily forward and reached their objective—the " red line "—at 7 a.m., the 1st Guards Bde. passing through them a quarter of an hour later. For the remainder of the morning, and, indeed, until about 3 p.m. by which time the British attack from the north had begun to make some headway, the Scots Guards were exposed to a galling machine-gun fire from the direction of Graincourt, but, as the enemy attempted no counter-attack, they were able to consolidate their new positions.†

---

* *See* W.D., 1st Bn. Scots Guards, September, 1918.

† *See* W.D., 1st Bn. Scots Guards, September, 1918. The battalion claimed 300 prisoners, 2 field guns, 1 howitzer, 90 machine guns and 2 trench mortars. Its casualties amounted to 6 officers and 107 other ranks.

The 1st Bn. Coldstream Guards,* in the centre of the 2nd Guards Bde., had some hard fighting on its extreme left almost immediately after its attack was launched, the garrisons of two German posts on the canal at the Demicourt—Graincourt road crossing offering a very stubborn resistance.† By the time this opposition had been overcome and the leading company of the Coldstream on the left had got across the canal the covering barrage had been lifted farther forward. The enemy was thus enabled to bring his machine guns into action in front and also on the flanks of the attackers. Nor did the Coldstream obtain much assistance in clearing the Hindenburg support system from the troops of the XVII Corps farther to the north whose progress was much slower. The battalion succeeded, however, in despite of rather heavy casualties and of the difficulty of communication from the leading companies to battalion headquarters, in reaching to within about 200 yards of its objective all along its front.‡

The 3rd Bn. Grenadier Guards carried out the northern attack on a one-company front, its objective being the " red line "—the enemy's trenches just north of the Demicourt—Graincourt road west of the canal. The battalion had gained its objective by 8 a.m. An attempt was then made to assist the left of the Coldstream whose advance, as already related, had been checked on the east bank of the canal. But no sooner did the Grenadiers begin to move forward in this direction than they, too, were subjected to a very heavy machine-gun fire and could do but little. Later in the morning, two trench mortars were sent up to assist the attacking troops in this area, but by the time they arrived the enemy

---

* The battalion was under the command of Major the Honble. E. K. Digby.

† It was owing to the courage and initiative of Captain C. H. Frisby and Lance-Corporal T. N. Jackson that this opposition was overcome. They were each awarded the Victoria Cross. *See* Appendix III.

‡ *See* W.D., 1st Bn. Coldstream Guards, September, 1918. *Cf.* " Reminiscences of a Grenadier," pp. 212–214. The Coldstream record the capture of 300 prisoners—including 8 officers—30 machine guns and 10 trench mortars. Their own casualties amounted to 9 officers and 149 other ranks.

had already begun to retire as the result of the pressure on his northern flank and they were not brought into action.*

(7) ATTACK OF THE 1ST GUARDS BRIGADE, 27TH OF SEPTEMBER.

The task of securing the " brown dotted line " and the southern portion of the " brown line " was entrusted by Brig.-General de Crespigny to the 1st Bn. Irish Guards, and he instructed Lieut.-Colonel Baggallay to cooperate in the attack of the 63rd Division on Graincourt by swinging forward his left to the northern portion of the " brown line."

The 2nd Bn. Grenadier Guards, under the command of Major G. F. C. Harcourt Vernon,† was ordered to pass through the Irish Guards and to carry on the advance north-east of Flesquières towards Cantaing in order to establish the line on the northern portion of the " blue dotted line " south-west of the latter village.‡

The 2nd Bn. Coldstream Guards was kept in brigade reserve. The Irish Guards, accompanied by one section of machine guns and two Stokes mortars,§ advanced at zero

---

* *See* W.D., 3rd Bn. Grenadier Guards, September, 1918. Soon after midday Lance-Corporal Parry and Private Parry of this battalion accomplished a very gallant performance, crossing the canal and capturing a German officer and 7 men as well as a machine gun. *See* " The Grenadier Guards in the Great War," vol. iii. p. 134. The battalion took 83 prisoners and 28 machine guns. Its own casualties were only 17.

† Lieut.-Colonel G. E. C. Rasch had returned to England to take command of the 1st Provisional Bn. The command of the 2nd Bn. Grenadier Guards devolved upon Major Harcourt Vernon until the arrival of Major C. F. A. Walker on the 2nd of October.

‡ As already related, this line was to be held as a defensive flank until the 57th Division had gained possession of Cantaing. *See* p. 165.

§ Only one Stokes gun kept in touch with the battalion in the advance, but this proved useful against the enemy's machine-gun posts. " Then No. 1 Company reported they were getting more than their share of machine-gun fire, and the 1st Guards Brigade Trench-Mortar Battery, reduced to one mortar, one officer, one sergeant, four men, and ten shells, bestowed the whole of its ammunition in the direction indicated, abandoned its mortar and merged itself into the ranks of No. 3 Company. It had been amply proved that where trench-mortars accompany a first wave of attack, if men are hit while carrying two Stokes shells apiece (forty pounds of explosives), they become dangerous mobile mines." *See* " The Irish Guards in the Great War," vol. i. p. 315.

hour in rear of the 1st Bn. Scots Guards. Making their way through the enemy's artillery and trench-mortar barrage, which became very severe soon after zero hour, the leading companies of the Irish Guards followed the Scots Guards across the canal. On its eastern side they, too, were caught by the enfilade machine-gun fire from the north, and it was only after a strenuous struggle and at the cost of many casualties that they succeeded in making their way through the Hindenburg support system to the " red line." * But punctually at 7.6 a.m. the Irish Guards passed through the Scots Guards and went forward to their next objective, fighting their way along the trenches which led from the Hindenburg support system to Flesquières. They made slow but steady progress. On the right, after gaining touch with the Gordon Highlanders (3rd Division) who were attacking Flesquières, they drove the enemy out of the northern outskirts of that village. They gained Silver street and Sherwood switch, and then pushed forward again, getting as far as the cross-roads south-west of the beet factory at about 9 a.m. Here the enemy's artillery and machine-gun fire checked them for the time being. The Germans were still holding Graincourt and the Graincourt line in force and some of their guns on the low ground west and south-west of Orival Wood, firing over open sights, caused the Irish Guards many casualties. The battalion, however, with the assistance of a tank which came up from the south, appears to have been in possession of the greater part of its objective by about 11 a.m.†

The 2nd Bn. Grenadier Guards, which followed the Irish Guards, had little difficulty in crossing the canal, the men making use of the ladders that had been left by the preceding battalions. East of the canal some of the platoons lost

* Six officers were casualties before the Irish Guards deployed on the " red line " to pass through the Scots Guards.

† *See* Narrative, 1st Guards Bde. The Irish Guards claim to have reached the whole of their objectives by this hour in the morning, but whether the beet factory was actually in their possession as early as 11 a.m. seems to be open to doubt. *See* p. 174. *Cf.* " The Irish Guards in the Great War," vol. i. p. 315, and " The Grenadier Guards in the Great War," vol. iii. p. 118. The casualties of the Irish Guards amounted to 8 officers and 180 other ranks.

2ND GRENADIER GUARDS IN ORIVAL WOOD 171

direction and went too far to the left. This brought them under the enemy's machine-gun fire from the north and caused some slight confusion; nevertheless, the battalion was well up to time in its advance to the "brown line." As the Grenadiers approached Flesquières they, like the Irish Guards, suffered severely from the fire of the German guns and machine guns in the neighbourhood of Orival Wood. Upon reaching the line held by the Irish Guards, the Grenadiers sent out patrols to gain ground towards this wood while they formed up for the attack with their right in the vicinity of the beet factory. No advance, however, was considered possible so long as the Germans held Graincourt and the Graincourt line which entirely commanded the situation on this part of the battle-field.

The time at which the village of Graincourt and the western portion of the Graincourt line were captured is given as 4.30 p.m., and at that hour troops of the 2nd Division were advancing in a north-easterly direction down the Flesquières—Cantaing road. Operating on the left of this advance, the 2nd Bn. Grenadier Guards moved forward towards Orival Wood. The company on the left got to within a short distance of the western edge of the wood before its progress was checked by machine-gun fire; the centre company drove the enemy out of the wood, but could not advance beyond its northern edge; the company on the right succeeded in prolonging its line to the east in touch with the troops of the 2nd Division on the Flesquières—Cantaing road.

The position remained like this until about 6.15 p.m., when the 172nd Infantry Bde. (57th Division) succeeded in clearing the Graincourt line to a point about due north of Orival Wood. This, in conjunction with the attack of the 3rd Guards Bde. towards Premy Chapel, forced the enemy to beat a retreat and enabled the 2nd Bn. Grenadier Guards to advance its line east of the wood in touch with the 57th Division on the left and the 2nd Division on the right.*

* *See* Narrative, 1st Guards Bde., also "The Grenadier Guards in the Great War," vol. iii. p. 126. In the attack on Orival Wood the 2nd Bn. Grenadier Guards took 7 field guns and 8 howitzers. Eight

172 BREAKING OF HINDENBURG LINE

Comparatively little is recorded of the doings of the 2nd Bn. Coldstream Guards, commanded by Major I. Bullough, during the day's fighting. But when the 2nd Bn. Grenadier Guards moved forward from the Hindenburg support system, the Coldstream relieved it.* At this period in the day's fighting the Germans, encouraged no doubt by their successful defence of Graincourt, were renewing their resistance in the trenches west and south-west of that village, and it was deemed advisable to employ the Coldstream to watch the left flank of the 1st Guards Bde. and to clear the trenches in rear of the advance until quite late in the afternoon.†

(8) ATTACK OF THE 3RD GUARDS BRIGADE, 27TH OF SEPTEMBER
—BRIG.-GENERAL FOLLETT KILLED.

The 3rd Guards Bde. moved forward in two columns—the 1st Bn. Grenadier Guards followed by the 1st Bn. Welsh Guards forming the right, and the 2nd Bn. Scots Guards the left column. The leading troops reached the canal at 7.20 a.m., and its passage was accomplished without many casualties although the hostile shell fire was very heavy.‡ Once across the canal the advance became difficult owing mainly to the congestion of the troops in the trenches due to the enfilade machine-gun fire from the left flank. But, in spite of many hindrances, the leading battalion—the 1st Bn. Grenadier Guards—reached the " red line " at 8.30 a.m., which was well within the allotted time. About this hour brigade headquarters crossed the canal and soon afterwards Brig.-General Follett was mortally wounded by a machine-

---

other guns 400 yards away were put out of action, but could not be reached. Forty prisoners were captured. The casualties of the battalion amounted to 4 officers and 97 other ranks.

* By this time the Coldstream had already lost 5 of their officers, killed or wounded.

† *See* Narrative, 1st Guards Bde. W.D., 2nd Bn. Coldstream Guards, September, 1918. The Coldstream captured 5 officers and 50 other Germans. They had 7 officers and 55 other ranks casualties.

‡ The crossing of the canal by the 3rd Guards Bde. was much facilitated owing to the fact that the 2nd Guards Bde. had marked the best crossing places.

gun bullet. He was carried back in an unconscious condition to a dressing station near the canal, where he died. His loss was sincerely mourned by all ranks who served under him. He was a keen and experienced regimental officer, and had proved himself a thoroughly capable and very gallant brigade commander.*

About the time of the Brig.-General's death, at 10 a.m., all communications had broken down and 3rd Guards Bde. headquarters was temporarily out of touch both with the division and also with its own troops.† But the advance continued with clock-like precision and punctuality. The 1st Bn. Grenadier Guards, followed by the Welsh Guards, began moving forward from the "red line" at 9.35 a.m., and reached the sunken road east of Flesquières. This was its forming up position for the attack along the ridge towards Premy Chapel.

On the left, the exposed flank of the advance, the 2nd Bn. Scots Guards was obliged to make its way forward along the already overcrowded trenches, and, as Graincourt and the Graincourt line were still in the possession of the Germans, the battalion took up positions in readiness to face a possible counter-attack from the north. Its further advance, consequently, was delayed until the left of the 1st Guards Bde.

---

* "He (Brigadier-General Follett) was a good friend of the battalion [1st Bn. Welsh Guards], hard-working himself, and considerate for others. As a soldier he was very sound, with long experience with his battalion before he was promoted to the brigade. When he approached Company Officers he knew what he was talking about, and what they were talking about, two points greatly appreciated by those concerned. He was, too, a charming, kind-hearted man. Every one who knew him felt his loss deeply." *See* "History of the Welsh Guards," p. 258. "His death was mourned by the whole Division, for there was no braver man in the Army." *See* "The Grenadier Guards in the Great War," vol. iii. p. 110. As soon as he heard the news of Brig.-General Follett's death, Major-General Matheson sent orders for Lieut.-Colonel Lord Gort to take command of the 3rd Guards Bde., and, pending his arrival, for Brig.-General de Crespigny to command the brigade as well as his own.

† Communications were far from satisfactory throughout the day's fighting. This was largely due to the long and exposed left flank of the Guards Division. The wireless system was damaged and visual signalling was extremely difficult so long as it was exposed to the enemy's shell and machine-gun fire from Graincourt. Most messages, therefore, had to be sent by runners.

could be swung forward according to the plan of operation. It remained, therefore, in and about Shingler trench on the left of the 2nd Bn. Grenadier Guards, which was at this time holding Silver street. Later in the day, however, when the Germans were seen withdrawing from Graincourt, the Scots Guards were able to bring rifle and Lewis-gun fire to bear upon them as well as that of a captured field gun which was worked by one of their sergeants.*

To return now to events on the right of the 3rd Guards Bde. front where, as already related, the 1st Bn. Grenadier Guards had arrived in the neighbourhood of Flesquières with the Welsh Guards in close support and was forming up for the attack towards Premy Chapel. In a report timed 11.30 a.m., which reached divisional headquarters at 12.40 p.m., the 1st Bn. Grenadier Guards states that when the message was dispatched the Germans were still in the beet factory and the trenches surrounding it, and also that Flesquières was being heavily bombarded by the enemy.† Shortly after this message was sent three tanks appeared upon the scene and were at once directed upon Beet trench. Two of them were put out of action by the enemy's artillery fire

---

* *See* Narrative, 3rd Guards Bde. The Scots Guards only lost 1 officer and 15 other ranks during the day's fighting. Some idea of the congested state of the trenches on the narrow front occupied by the Guards north of Flesquières during the afternoon of the 27th of September may be gathered from the following picturesque description given by Mr. Rudyard Kipling of Shingler street and Silver street:—
" About noon, after many adventures, the 2nd Grenadiers arrived to carry on the advance, and Silver street became a congested metropolis. . . . Meantime, a battalion of the Second Division, which was to come through the Guards Division, and continue the advance, flooded up Silver street, zealously unreeling its telephone wires; machine-gun Guards were there, looking for positions; the 2nd Grenadiers were standing ready; the Welsh Guards were also there with intent to support the Grenadiers; walking wounded were coming down, and severe cases were being carried over the top by German prisoners, who made no secret of an acute desire to live and jumped in among the rest without leave asked. The men compared the crush to a sugar-queue at home. To cap everything, some wandering tanks which had belonged to the Division on the right had strayed over to the left." *See* " The Irish Guards in the Great War," vol. i. p. 316.

† This report does not tally with the account of the action given by the Irish Guards. They state that they captured the " brown line " beyond the beet factory at 11 a.m. *See* p. 170.

and the third was obliged to retire. But their presence seems to have diverted the attention of the Germans to some extent and Lord Gort was quick to seize the opportunity to push forward a platoon of Grenadiers up the road towards Orival Wood with orders to wheel to the right and to attack from the flank the enemy holding the trenches in rear of the beet factory. This manœuvre was attended with complete success and led to the surrender of 200 Germans. In despite of the fact that the troops who were to have cooperated in the movement on either flank were nowhere to be seen, Lord Gort, whose splendid courage and brilliant powers of leadership were a source of inspiration to his troops,* then decided to proceed with the attack on Premy Chapel with the assistance of the Welsh Guards. It was a daring decision and the gallant manner in which the two battalions carried out the operation was beyond all praise. The Grenadiers led the way along the ridge, the Welsh Guards covering both flanks.

The whole area of the advance was swept by machine-gun and close-range artillery fire, but, skilfully led and moving forward with dogged determination, the leading troops, after capturing Premy trench, succeeded in reaching Labour trench soon after midday. Here more prisoners were taken as well as two field guns.

Meanwhile, No. 3 Company, Guards Machine-Gun Regiment, had arrived on the eastern edge of Flesquières, its advance having been delayed owing to the difficulty of bringing forward its pack animals across the canal and the broken ground beyond it. Three of its guns were soon brought into action to cover the right flank of the Grenadiers, while three more were kept in reserve and afterwards utilized to bring effective fire to bear upon the enemy in Orival Wood.†

* Lord Gort was awarded the V.C. for his conspicuous gallantry in this day's fighting. *See* Appendix III.

† The 74th and 75th Bdes., R.F.A., which were to have covered the attack towards Premy Chapel did not succeed in getting into action until dusk. They moved forward as soon as the opening barrages had been fired, but their progress was slow, only one crossing place over the canal—the ramp south-east of Hermies—being available. Positions had been selected on the western side of Flesquières, but these were untenable during the daylight owing to the intensity of the enemy's machine-gun fire. In the evening the two brigades covered the left of

Early in the afternoon troops of the 62nd Division were observed on the outskirts of Marcoing, but they were forced to retire and the positions of the 1st Bn. Grenadier Guards and of the 1st Bn. Welsh Guards, whose advance had driven a wedge into the enemy's line, thus became dangerously exposed. It was decided, therefore, to discontinue the attack until the flanks had been secured. The advanced troops were, consequently, slightly withdrawn and the defence organized in depth. The command of the Premy ridge was thus secured and maintained, and undoubtedly facilitated the British attack upon the Graincourt line later in the day.

The account given by the Welsh Guards of this fighting does not tally in all respects with that given by the Grenadiers.* The action was a confused one and platoons and companies of the two battalions were much mixed up. The credit for a magnificent day's work clearly belongs to all the troops concerned. Lord Gort was severely wounded in the early stages of the advance towards Premy Chapel and obliged, much against his will, to go to the rear. Lieut.-Colonel Luxmoore Ball, commanding the Welsh Guards, was therefore the senior officer on the spot and it was he who was responsible for the actual conduct of the operation and the skilful handling of the attacking force.†

---

the 3rd Guards Bde. and found some excellent targets as the Germans retreated from Graincourt. *See* W.D's., 74th and 75th Bdes., R.F.A., September, 1918. Narrative, 3rd Guards Bde.

* *See* W.D., 1st Bn. Welsh Guards, September, 1918. According to this account the 1st Bn. Grenadier Guards advanced towards Premy Chapel at 12.15 p.m. On the right the attacking troops bore too far to the south and made but little progress, eventually occupying Beet trench about 2 p.m. with some of the Welsh Guards in support. On the left the Grenadiers succeeded in getting as far as Premy trench, but were then forced to take cover from the heavy machine-gun fire which opened from Premy Chapel. At 3 p.m. a withdrawal of the leading troops took place to the beet factory. The Welsh Guards echelonned in rear to the left, also withdrew, but left out three Lewis-gun posts. One company of the Welsh Guards was then disposed in trenches north-west of the factory facing Orival Wood. Every attempt to advance from this position in the direction of Cantaing met with failure and the greater part of the Welsh Guards eventually withdrew to Silver street, posts being pushed forward as soon as it became dusk.

† *See* "History of the Welsh Guards," p. 254. Captain J. H. C.

It is not easy to fix exactly the positions occupied by the advanced units of the 1st and 3rd Guards Bdes. in the evening of the 27th of September, but, from reports received at 7.30 p.m. at divisional headquarters, it would appear that the 1st Bn. Grenadier Guards was in Premy trench in touch with the 62nd Division on the right; the 1st Bn. Welsh Guards in Beet trench; the 2nd Bn. Grenadier Guards in the neighbourhood of the beet factory and on the line to the east of Orival Wood; and the 1st Bn. Irish Guards in Silver street.

An hour later—8.30 p.m.—the line of the 3rd Guards Bde. was given as running north-west and south-east through the cross-roads in rear of the beet factory with advanced posts thrown out about 400 yards in front of the main line. But some troops—presumably belonging to the 1st Bn. Grenadier Guards—were reported still to be occupying Premy trench.*

(9) Work of the Divisional R.E. and 4th Bn. Coldstream Guards (Pioneers) throughout the day's fighting.

The chief task of the sappers and pioneers on the 27th of September was to get the artillery across the Canal du Nord with as little delay as possible.† It had, of course, been out of the question actually to begin work on the immediate approaches to, and the crossings of, the canal before the day of the battle, but everything which could be done in the way of preparation had been put in hand before the attack was launched.‡

The 55th and 76th Field Companies, R.E., to each of which was attached a company of the 4th Bn. Coldstream Guards (Pioneers), moved forward in rear of the 2nd Guards Bde., and, notwithstanding that all the approaches to the

---

Simpson took over the command of the 1st Bn. Grenadier Guards after Lord Gort was wounded. The casualties of the Welsh Guards during the day amounted to 2 officers and 87 other ranks.

* See W.D., Guards Division, 27th of September, 1918.
† See Narrative, C.R.E., Guards Division.
‡ See p. 162.

canal were heavily shelled by the enemy, set about their work with splendid energy, the drivers of the wagons which brought up material from the forward dumps behaving with wonderful coolness and determination.*

By 9.30 a.m. each Field Company had a crossing for pack animals ready for use. Meanwhile, the construction of the bridges for the artillery was already well in hand. One of the selected crossing places was at the point on the Demicourt—Flesquières road, where a German light railway had traversed the canal. The causeway here had been blown up by the enemy, leaving a deep crater in the centre from 35 to 40 feet across. The 55th Field Company erected a 24-feet span bridge over this crossing, and at the same time half of the *personnel* of the 76th Field Company was employed to construct a ramp just south of the bridge. Both these pieces of work were successfully completed with the result that the first six guns were across the canal at about 11.30 a.m.

A 24-feet girder bridge was put up across Lock No. 7, but it was only possible to use this route for infantry traffic on the 27th of September as the approaches to the lock were much damaged and had to be repaired.† It was, however, in general use the following day.

The 76th Field Company repaired a ramp at a point south of the Demicourt—Flesquières crossing and succeeded in getting a single plank road through to the eastern side of the canal, making a skilful diversion to avoid a crater. This route was open for traffic by 1 p.m. But the gallant attempts made by the 55th Field Company to erect a trestle brigade at the Demicourt—Graincourt road crossing met with no success. The approaches in this area were swept by heavy hostile machine-gun fire and it was found impossible to bring forward the wagons with the trestles. Eventually, a ramp was utilized and a way was opened soon after 1 p.m.; but

---

* "As soon as the line of the canal had been secured our engineer troops commenced the construction of bridges, completing their task with remarkable speed and working with great gallantry under the fire of the German guns." See "Sir Douglas Haig's Despatches," p. 281.

† A German charge exploded at Lock No. 7, but did little damage.

it was not until about 4 p.m. that traffic could be sent forward by this route.

As soon as the men could be spared, a reconnaissance party was sent forward by each Field Company. These parties secured valuable information with regard to dugouts, roads and tracks, and water supply in the captured area. They also took 38 prisoners in the neighbourhood of Flesquières. Throughout the day, in addition to its strenuous work on roads and bridges, the 4th Bn. Coldstream Guards (Pioneers) had four Lewis guns in action on the canal bank against the enemy's aeroplanes which at one period in the day were very active.*

(10) RELIEF OF THE DIVISION BY THE 2ND DIVISION ON THE NIGHT OF THE 27TH OF SEPTEMBER—THE ACHIEVEMENTS OF THE GUARDS IN THE BATTLE OF THE CANAL DU NORD.

At about 7.30 p.m. on the 27th of September the relief of the Guards Division began, the 2nd Guards Bde. moving back across the Canal du Nord. The two other brigades withdrew from their positions in the line as their battalions were relieved by the advancing units of the 2nd Division, which were to carry on the attack the following day. The relief was successfully completed by 10.15 p.m., when the command of the Guards' sector of the VI Corps front passed to the G.O.C. the 2nd Division.†

* *See* W.D., 4th Bn. Coldstream Guards (Pioneers), September, 1918.
† The divisional Artillery remained in action after the infantry was withdrawn into reserve and supported the advance of the 2nd Division. Both the 74th and 75th Bdes., R.F.A., took part in the fighting on the 28th of September, firing from positions near Orival Wood. The following day they moved forward into Noyelles-sur-l'Escaut, where the 74th Bde. occupied the foremost positions of all the artillery in action on the bank of the Scheldt. Here the two brigades remained for the next ten days until the general advance was resumed on the 8th of October. The guns were under the direct observation of the enemy and the batteries at first suffered numerous casualties both in men and horses. But the spirit of the gunners was very high. All ranks thoroughly appreciated the change to mobile warfare, rations

At 10 a.m. on the 28th, divisional headquarters was opened at Lagnicourt, the 1st Guards Bde. being located in the trenches north-east of Demicourt, the 2nd Guards Bde. in and around Boursies, and the 3rd Guards Bde. in the trenches in the Hindenburg Line west of the canal.

The part played by the Guards in the battle of the Canal du Nord was a brilliant one. The attack which the division was called upon to make across the canal, through the strong defences of the Hindenburg support system and over the exposed area of country between Graincourt and Marcoing was an arduous undertaking in itself, but the long, open flank on the north and the narrowness of the front at Flesquières added immensely to the difficulties of the attacking troops, cramping their offensive action and rendering their advance unusually dependent upon the movements of other divisions. Yet the Guards succeeded in gaining the second line of their objectives in the face of a very stout resistance on the part of the enemy, whose gunners and machine gunners held on to their positions with great determination.* Nor is there any reason to suppose that had the progress of the flanking divisions been as rapid as that of the Guards, the " blue dotted line " would not have been secured by the 1st and 3rd Guards Bdes. It was almost entirely the hostile fire from the village of Graincourt and the northern portion of the Graincourt line which checked the impetus of the Guards' advance. This was proved the following day when the attacking troops made rapid progress,† but their success was also due to the fine achievement of the Guards the previous day by which the command of the Premy ridge had been gained.

The division received a message of congratulation from

---

were good and easily obtainable and the supply of ammunition seemed to be unlimited. *See* W.D's., 74th and 75th Bdes., R.F.A., September–October, 1918.

* The German order of battle opposite the Guards was as follows :— 2nd/226th Reserve Infantry Regiment, 228th Reserve Infantry Regiment, 79th Reserve Infantry Regiment, from north to south. The support battalions of the 226th and 228th had many men in the front line as reinforcements, all battalions being very weak. *See* W.D., Guards Division, September, 1918.

† On the morning of the 28th of September the 62nd Division took Marcoing Copse and the 2nd Division Noyelles with many prisoners.

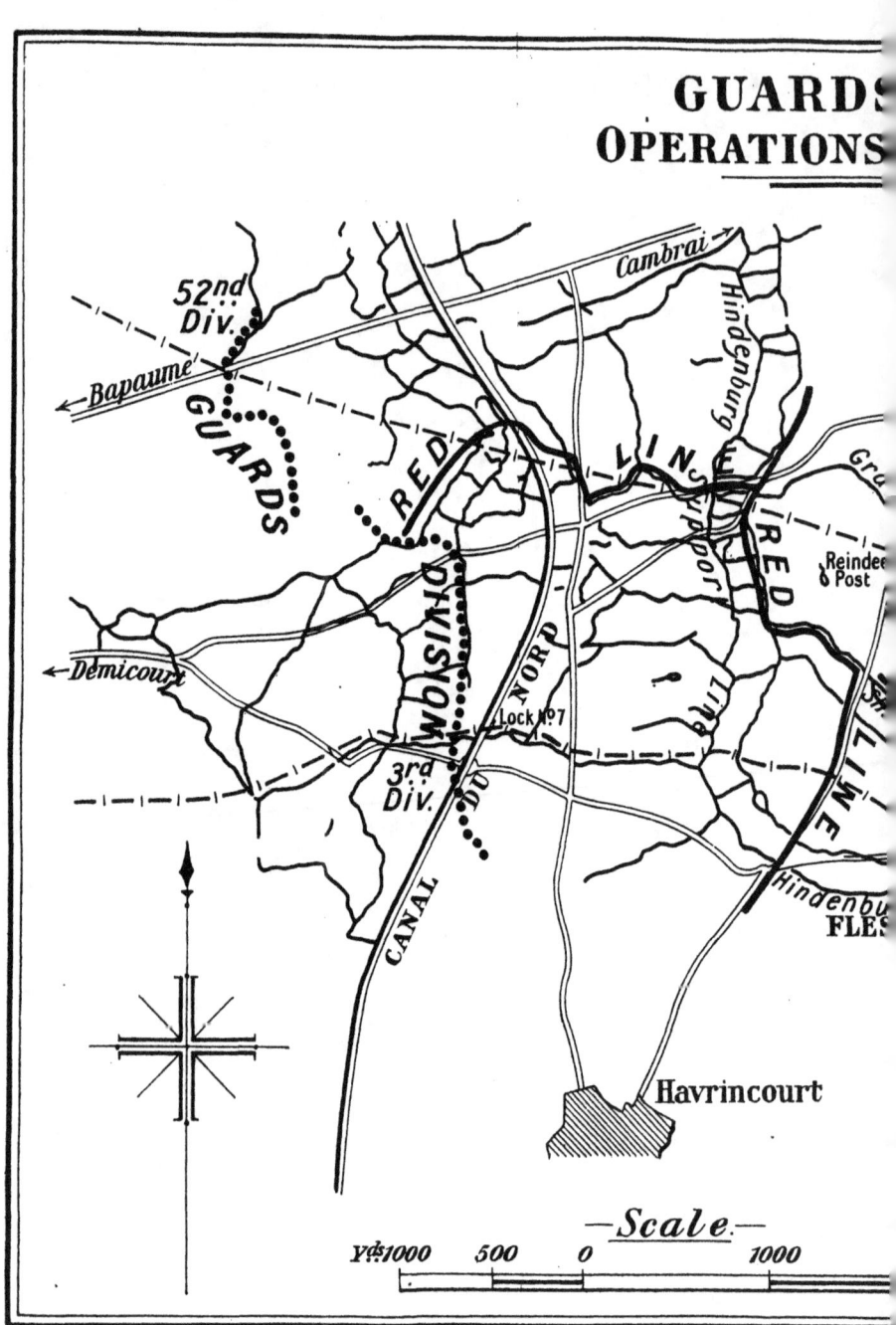

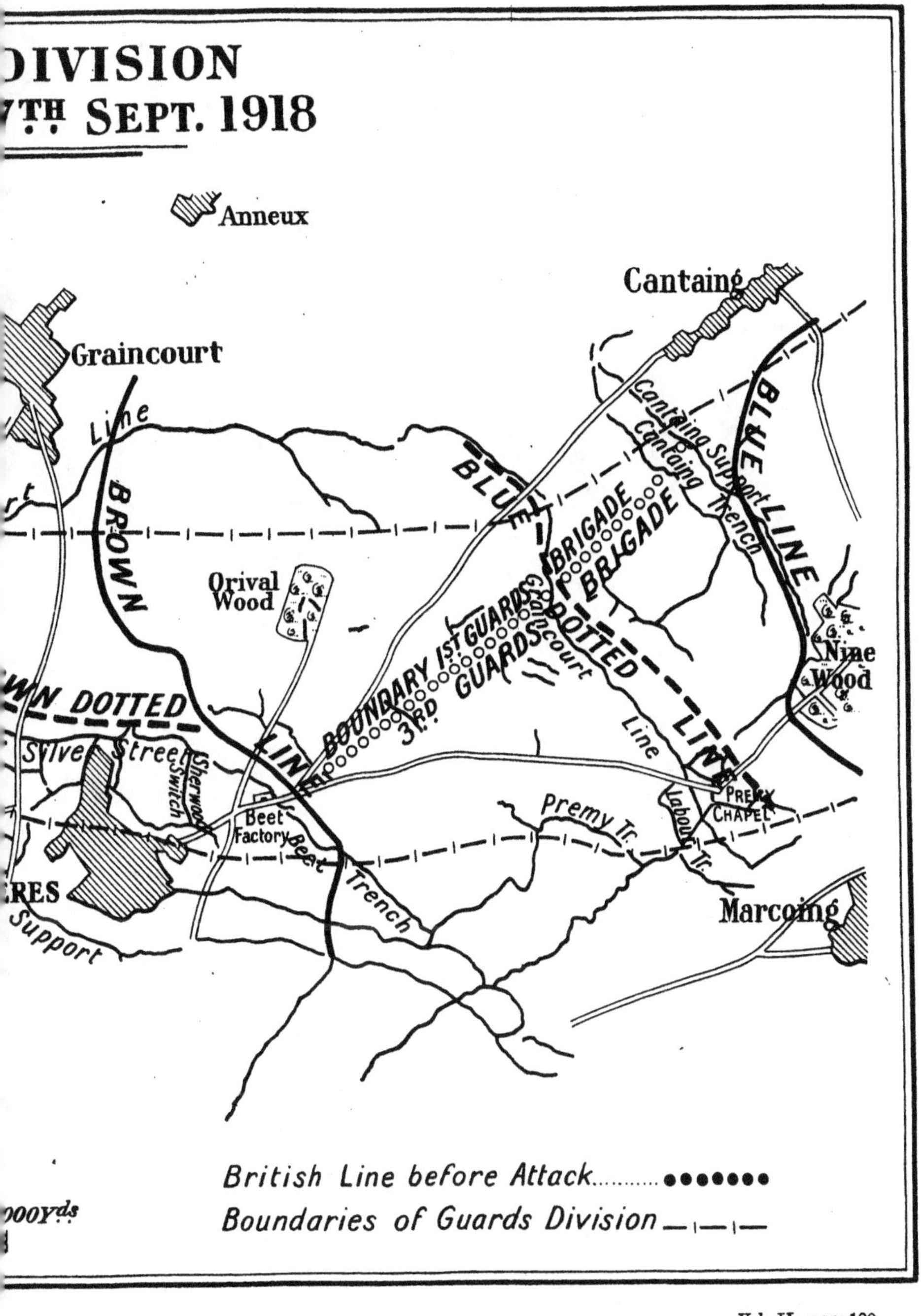
DIVISION
7TH SEPT. 1918
Anneux
Cantaing
Graincourt
Line
BROWN
BLUE
BLUE LINE
Cantaing Support
Cantaing Trench
BRIGADE
1ST GUARDS BRIGADE
3RD GUARDS
BOUNDARY
Graincourt
DOTTED
LINE
Orival Wood
Nine Wood
WN DOTTED
Silver Street
Sherwood Switch
Beet Factory
Beet Trench
Premy Tr.
Line
Labour Tr.
PREMY CHAPEL
RES
Support
Marcoing
British Line before Attack
Boundaries of Guards Division
000Yds

DIVISIONAL COMMANDER'S MESSAGE

the VI Corps commander,* and, in circulating it to his troops, Major-General Matheson took the opportunity of recording his own appreciation of the fine fighting qualities which had been displayed by all units :—

"The Major-General wishes his own thanks also to be expressed to all ranks for their fine achievement in yesterday's battle. He was much pleased with the handling of the artillery; with the rapid work of the engineers on tracks and crossings over the canal which he inspected personally; and with the spirit shown by all three Guards brigades in driving home a difficult attack over unfavourable ground against strongly organized positions.

"He was greatly impressed with the manner in which the 2nd Guards Brigade captured the Hindenburg Support Line against a very stout defence, and with the vigour and determination shown by the 1st and 3rd Guards Brigades in closing up in turn behind the leading brigade and carrying through their share of the advance. He fully realizes the exacting conditions by which the whole operation was marked, owing to the long open flank on the left and the narrowness of the front at Flesquières. He wishes particularly to convey to all ranks of the 1st Grenadier Guards and 1st Welsh Guards his admiration of the splendid gallantry of their advance along the Premy Chapel ridge. The complete capture of Premy Chapel ridge and of Nine Wood this morning is mainly due to the fine fighting spirit of these two battalions. He deeply regrets the loss by the 3rd Guards Brigade of its commander, Brig.-General G. B. S. Follett, D.S.O., M.V.O., during this action." †

The Guards captured 25 officers and 703 other German prisoners during the day's fighting and their own casualties were returned as 59 officers and 948 other ranks.‡

---

* "The corps commander desires you to express to all ranks of the Guards Division his admiration of the brilliant manner in which they carried out their share of to-day's operations." *See* W.D., Guards Division, App. 1163.

† *See* W.D., Guards Division, September, 1918.

‡ *Ib.*, September and October, 1918.

CHAPTER XIX

PURSUIT OF THE ENEMY TO THE SELLE RIVER—THE BATTLE OF THE SELLE, 17TH TO 25TH OF OCTOBER, 1918.

(1) PROGRESS OF THE ALLIED ADVANCE DURING THE EARLY DAYS OF OCTOBER.

THE various units of the Guards Division on their withdrawal from the battle were rested and reorganized in readiness to resume the advance when called upon.* Commanding officers also seized the opportunity of practising their men in open warfare exercises, but the work of training the troops was considerably interfered with as one battalion in each brigade was continuously employed on road construction during the short period during which the division was out of the line.†

It now seems advisable before proceeding further with the narrative to record very briefly the progress of, and the results achieved in, the battles of the Canal du Nord, of the St. Quentin Canal and of the Beaurevoir Line between the 27th of September and the 5th of October, for without some such summary the reader would not be in a position to

* Lieut.-Colonel J. C. Brand, 1st Bn. Coldstream Guards, assumed the temporary command of the 3rd Guards Bde. until the arrival of the new commander, Brig.-General C. P. Heywood. Lieut.-Colonel Viscount Gort was succeeded in the command of the 1st Bn. Grenadier Guards by Major the Honble. W. R. Bailey. Major E. T. C. Warner took over the command of the 2nd Bn. Scots Guards.

† *See* W.D., Guards Division, October, 1918. "The battalion faced the changed military situation by announcing that companies were 'at the disposal of their commanders for open warfare training,' after which they were instantly sent forward from their Demicourt trenches to help make roads between Havrincourt and Flesquières!" *See* "The Irish Guards in the Great War," vol. i. p. 319.

appreciate the situation when the Guards returned to the line on the 6th of October.

On the 27th of September the Third and First Armies reached "the general line Beaucamp—Ribécourt—Fontaine-notre-Dame—east of Haynecourt—Epinoy—Oisy-le-Verger," * and took 10,000 prisoners and 200 guns. The following day the advance in this area was continued and the Germans were driven out of Gouzeaucourt, Marcoing, Noyelles-sur-l'Escaut, Sailly and Palluel. On the 29th of September, after two days' incessant bombardment of the enemy's positions, the Fourth Army,† in conjunction with the French First Army farther to the south,‡ attacked on a front of 12 miles between Holnon, a village a little to the north-west of St. Quentin, to Vendhuille, while the Third Army carried on its advance farther north towards Gonnelieu and Welsh ridge. As a result of this day's fighting the Fourth Army reached the general line Gricourt—Le Tronquoy—Magny-la-Fosse—Nauroy—Bellicourt, and the Third Army captured Masnières and secured the crossings of the Scheldt between that village and the outskirts of Cambrai.§

During the next few days the work of driving the Germans out of their last prepared positions in the Hindenburg Line and in rear of it was steadily proceeded with along the fronts of the Fourth, Third and First Armies, with the result that, by the evening of the 7th of October, the British line ran from St. Quentin in a north-easterly direction to Beaurevoir, thence northward to the western outskirts of Cambrai, while north of that town the advance had reached Blécourt. The Hindenburg Line had become a British possession.‖

---

* See " Sir Douglas Haig's Despatches," p. 282.

† The attacking troops were the IX and III Corps and the II (American) Corps, assisted by a large force of tanks.

‡ The French occupied St. Quentin on the 1st of October.

§ See " Sir Douglas Haig's Despatches," pp. 282, 283.

‖ " The great and critical assaults in which during these nine days of battle the First, Third and Fourth Armies stormed the line of the Canal du Nord and broke through the Hindenburg Line mark the close of the first phase of the British offensive. The enemy's defence in the last and strongest of his prepared positions had been shattered. The whole of the main Hindenburg defences had passed into our possession, and a wide gap had been driven through such rear trench systems as

Meanwhile, farther to the north, the advance had been equally successful and, by the evening of the 7th of October, the First Army was in possession of Lens, from which town the British and Allied line ran northward to Armentières and thence east of Ploegsteert, Warneton, Houthem, Gheluwe and Dadizeele.*

The time had now arrived to exploit the successes gained in the battles of the Hindenburg Line and on the 8th of October the advance was resumed by the Fourth and Third Armies on a front of 17 miles between Sequehart, north-east of St. Quentin, to a point just south of Cambrai.†

had existed behind them. The effect of the victory upon the subsequent course of the campaign was decisive. The threat to the enemy's communications was now direct and instant, for nothing but the natural obstacles of a wooded and well-watered countryside lay between our Armies and Maubeuge.

"In the fighting of these days, in which thirty British and two American Infantry divisions and one British Cavalry division were engaged against thirty-nine German divisions, over 36,000 prisoners and 380 guns had been captured. Great as were the material losses the enemy had suffered, the effect of so overwhelming a defeat upon a moral already deteriorated was of even larger importance." *See* " Sir Douglas Haig's Despatches," p. 285.

* On the Flanders front the Allied forces, which consisted of the Second British Army, some French divisions and the Belgian Army, was placed under the command of H.M. the King of the Belgians.

† "The second and concluding phase of the British offensive now opened, in which the Fourth and Third Armies and the right of the First Army moved forward with their left flank on the Canal line which runs from Cambrai to Mons, and their right covered by the French First Army. This advance, by the capture of Maubeuge and the disruption of the German main lateral system of communications, forced the enemy to fall back upon the line of the Meuse and realized the strategic plan of the Allied operations. The fighting which took place during this period . . . falls into three stages . . . In the first of the stages, the battle of Le Cateau, certain incomplete defences still held by the enemy were captured, and his troops compelled to evacuate Cambrai and fall back behind the line of the Selle river. In the second stage, the Selle river was forced, and by a development of this operation our front pushed forward to the general line Sambre Canal—west edge of the Mormal Forest—Valenciennes, where we were in position for the final assault upon Maubeuge." *See* " Sir Douglas Haig's Despatches," p. 287.

ADVANCE RESUMED BY VI CORPS

(2) THE GUARDS DIVISION RETURNS TO THE LINE—ATTACK OF THE 3RD AND 2ND DIVISIONS TOWARDS THE SELLE RIVER, 8TH OF OCTOBER—ARRANGEMENTS FOR THE ATTACK ON WAMBAIX.

On the evening of the 6th of October the Guards moved forward to the Marcoing—Ribécourt area over cross-country tracks made heavy by recent rain, and, the following day, divisional headquarters was removed from Lagnicourt to Flesquières Château.*

The front of the VI Corps was now almost due south of Cambrai and the occupation by its troops of the Hindenburg Line east of the Scheldt considerably simplified the arrangements for the next advance. The task assigned to the corps in the scheme of operations of the Third Army was to attack on the front between Seranvillers and Niergnies and to push forward as rapidly as possible in conjunction with the IV Corps on the right and the XVII Corps on the left in a north-easterly direction towards the Selle river in the vicinity of Solesmes. The corps commander decided to

* In view of the reports and rumours which became current about this period in the Allied advance to the effect that the end of the war was in sight and that the German Government was about to ask for an armistice, Major-General Matheson, who feared that the enemy might seize the opportunity to attempt a fraternization with the troops, thought it advisable to issue the following order to the division before it returned to the line :—" (1) Rumours are current that the German Government intends to propose a suspension of hostilities, with a view to the discussion of Peace terms. It is possible that attempts at fraternization may in consequence be made by German troops in the line. (2) The German Army is hard pressed and the German High Command needs time to carry out its present withdrawal without heavy loss in men and material. German peace talk is therefore circulated in order to relax our pressure, gain time for the withdrawal, and prepare for a long defensive campaign next year. (3) All our troops will be warned against paying any attention to rumours of this kind. They are intended not to shorten the war, but to save the German Army from the consequences of defeat this year and to preserve its strength for the defence of German soil next year. Any attempt made by the enemy to fraternize in the field will also be disregarded absolutely. It is our intention to beat the enemy as fast as we can, not to allow him to recover his strength." *See* W.D., Guards Division, October, 1918.

carry out the attack on the 8th of October with the 3rd and 2nd Divisions which were in the line, his intention being, should little opposition be encountered, for the Guards Division to pass through the leading divisions during the course of the afternoon and to continue the attack. If, however, the enemy's defence proved to be formidable, the Guards were to take over the line as soon as darkness set in, and were then to attack Wambaix and the line of the Cambrai—St. Quentin railway the following morning.*

The attack of the 3rd and 2nd Divisions went so well at the outset in the early hours of the 8th of October, that at 9.25 a.m. the Guards were warned to be in readiness to carry on the advance that day, but shortly after this warning order reached divisional headquarters, the 2nd Division on the left of the attack and the left of the 3rd Division were counter-attacked by the Germans and driven back. Major-General Matheson was then informed that the 63rd Division, on the left of the 2nd Division, would capture Awoingt in the morning of the 9th of October and that the Guards Division was to cooperate in this operation. Upon the receipt of this information the Major-General discussed with the B.G.G.S. of the VI Corps, the advisability of the Guards continuing the attack of the 3rd and 2nd Divisions that day (8th of October) and taking the final objectives assigned to those two divisions. After some discussion, it was decided that this project was impracticable, first, because the field artillery had not succeeded in getting sufficiently far forward to cover effectively the advance of the infantry, and secondly, because it would not be possible for the Guards to reach the starting-off line in time to carry out the operation before the evening. The attack by the Guards, therefore, was fixed for the morning of the 9th, as originally planned †— the 3rd and 2nd Divisions were to complete the capture of their objectives and the Guards were to pass through them in order to attack Wambaix and the line of the railway.

Orders for the renewal of the advance by the Guards

* *See* W.D., Guards Division, App. 1189.
† This verbal arrangement was confirmed by a telegram from the corps received at divisional headquarters at 3 p.m.

ADVANCE OF 1st AND 2nd GUARDS BDES.

brigades were now issued without further delay from divisional headquarters. The attack was to be delivered by the 1st Guards Bde. on the right and the 2nd Guards Bde. on the left, the line of their first objective running from the cemetery south of Wambaix along the road to that village, thence—still following the line of the road—to the Halte on the Cambrai—St. Quentin railway, thence along the railway line to the outskirts of the village of Awoingt. The New Zealand Division (IV Corps) on the right was to advance at the same time as the Guards, but the attack upon Awoingt by the 24th Division (XVII Corps), which had replaced the 63rd Division on the left of the Guards, was arranged for a later hour.

Both the Guards brigades received orders to form up for the attack west of the Esnes—Niergnies road and to move forward to within 300 yards of that road before zero hour. It was realized that this line might not exactly coincide with the positions actually reached by the troops of the 3rd and 2nd Divisions who were being relieved by the Guards, but it was felt that any temporary loss of ground was of small importance and that the advance of the attacking battalions and also the artillery arrangements for the battle would be greatly assisted if the starting-off line were straight and clearly defined.* The artillery barrage, which was to be provided by nine brigades, R.F.A., was timed to come down along the line of the Esnes—Niergnies road at zero hour, 5.20 a.m.†

(3) ADVANCE OF THE 1ST AND 2ND GUARDS BRIGADES, 9TH OF OCTOBER—CAPTURE OF WAMBAIX—THE LINE FONTAINE AU TERTRE FARM—ST. HILAIRE REACHED.

The relief of the troops of the 3rd and 2nd Divisions was satisfactorily accomplished during the night of the 8th–9th

* The same policy, it will be remembered, had been adopted with complete success on the 3rd of September. *See* p. 146.
† *See* W.D., Guards Division, Apps. 1200, 1201.

of October,* and punctually at 20 minutes after zero hour the leading troops of the Guards Division crossed the Esnes—Niergnies road. They met with little or no opposition from the enemy during the early stages of their advance. On the right of the divisional front the 1st Guards Bde. attacked with the 2nd Bn. Coldstream Guards and the 2nd Bn. Grenadier Guards on the right and left of the line respectively. The 1st Bn. Irish Guards remained in reserve and spent the greater part of the day on the railway line between Wambaix and Cattenières.

The Coldstream, in touch with the New Zealanders on their right, captured Wambaix and then pushed straight forward over the railway line and seized the southern portion of Cattenières. The Grenadiers, after taking Seranvillers, assisted in the clearance of Cattenières and captured Estourmel.†

So far the German resistance had been negligible, but beyond Cattenières, which was in the possession of the 1st Guards Bde. by 9 a.m., the advance was checked by machine-gun fire from the beet factory at Boistrancourt and from east of Beauvois along the Cambrai—Le Cateau road. The country in which the Guards now found themselves was open and there was little or no cover from view or fire, so that the enemy's machine gunners, who were cleverly posted in groups of houses and in small clumps of trees, were able to fight a delaying action to the best advantage. After various unsuccessful attempts had been made to work round some of these posts, it was decided, therefore, to discontinue the advance until darkness set in. There was no need for useless waste of life.‡ A particularly gallant achievement

* " We got mildly gas-shelled on the way, and there was a horrible smell of stale gas about the streets of Rumilly, but it was not necessary to put on gas helmets; we found our assembly positions all right; the plan was for the 2nd Division to go back to rest as soon as we got into position." See " Reminiscences of a Grenadier," p. 219.

† See W.D's., 2nd Bns. Grenadier and Coldstream Guards, October, 1918. A few prisoners were taken as well as two howitzers, a field gun and some trench mortars and machine guns.

‡ " A certain amount of ground was gained by sectional rushes under extremely heavy machine-gun fire, but the complete lack of ' dead ' ground made real success impossible, and Major Walker [2nd Bn. Grena-

CAMBRAI—LE CATEAU ROAD REACHED

was performed during the course of this action by Private Edgar Holmes of the Grenadiers which must not pass unrecorded, for it gained him the Victoria Cross though unfortunately a posthumous one. He was acting as a stretcher-bearer and continued to carry out his duties after he had been dangerously wounded until he himself was killed.*

The 2nd Guards Bde. attacked with the 3rd Bn. Grenadier Guards on the right and the 1st Bn. Coldstream Guards on the left while the 1st Bn. Scots Guards was held in reserve. The Grenadiers, who were unfortunate enough to have 25 casualties from the British artillery barrage, were already east of Wambaix at 8.30 a.m.† Two hours later they reached Estourmel and patrols were pushed forward, in cooperation with their 2nd Battalion on the right, towards the Cambrai—le Cateau road in the direction of Igneul. But, although the battalion reached the close vicinity of this latter village before noon, it does not appear to have actually occupied it during this day's fighting. The enemy's long-range artillery fire was severe, especially in the afternoon, and this, combined with the incessant machine-gun fire, made any farther progress impossible for the time being. Lord Lascelles, therefore, ordered his men to dig themselves in and later in the day a line of posts was established along the eastern side of the Cambrai—Le Cateau road.

The 1st Bn. Coldstream Guards, on the left of the 2nd Guards Bde. line, at first made even quicker progress than the Grenadiers, although they, too, suffered from the fire of the British guns.‡ They reached the Cambrai—le Cateau

dier Guards] decided to postpone any further move until it could be made under cover of darkness." *See* "The Grenadier Guards in the Great War," vol. iii. pp. 153, 154.

* *See* Appendix III.

† "At the appointed hour our barrage came down, and we advanced; no opposition, no trouble at all, except for some of our own guns firing short; it seemed such a pity one couldn't switch off the barrage and just advance without it, but it was not possible. We saw our railway embankment, and could have got to it long before, but our barrage necessitated our going slow . . . as soon as our guns ceased firing on it, we took possession and had some breakfast." *See* "Reminiscences of a Grenadier," p. 220.

‡ *See* W.D's., 2nd Guards Bde., 3rd Bn. Grenadier Guards, 1st Bn. Coldstream Guards, October, 1918.

road without difficulty and here their Lewis gunners opened fire with some effect on the German gun-limbers as they retreated. The battalion then pushed forward, but the enemy's machine-gun fire now became so intense that the advance was checked, and the leading troops eventually dug themselves in on the eastern side of the road. A patrol of the Oxfordshire Hussars went through the battalion about 4 p.m., but it was unable to make any progress and was obliged to withdraw.*

During the morning the various sections of the Guards Machine-Gun Regiment, which accompanied the attacking infantry of the Guards brigades, had done much good service. Two sections in particular, which came into action in much exposed positions, had been most successful in reducing the enemy's resistance, although one of their guns had been destroyed by shell fire.†

At 9.30 a.m. when it was known how rapid was the advance that was being made by the Guards brigades, orders were issued for the 3rd Guards Bde. to move forward to the Seranvillers area and, at 4 p.m., divisional headquarters was transferred to Seranvillers Château. The outpost line for the night was then fixed to run from a point half a mile south-east of Cattenières, east of that village, east and north of Estourmel, west of Igneul, and thence along the Cambrai—le Cateau road to the left boundary of the corps front. The 1st Guards Bde. was ordered to push out patrols towards Boistrancourt, while the 2nd Guards Bde. was to work round Igneul from the north-west.‡

---

* *See* " The Grenadiers in the Great War," vol. iii. p. 161.

† Throughout the fighting in October the Guards machine gunners worked very closely with the infantry. Pack animals and limbers were kept as far forward as possible, and full discretion was given to the officers commanding sections to seize any opportunity of assisting the infantry that might present itself. The machine gunners were also in close touch with the artillery—when the fire of the guns had forced the enemy to retire from any position, the machine gunners were usually in a position from which they could bring an accurate and effective fire on the retreating Germans. This was notably the case at Haussy on the 16th of October.

‡ *See* W.D., Guards Division, October, 1918. The prisoners taken during the day belonged to the 163rd and 395th I. Regts. The

During the course of the evening the orders for the next day's operations were issued from divisional headquarters. The general advance was to be resumed the following morning in a north-easterly direction towards the Selle river.* The 1st and 2nd Guards Bdes. were to put their reserve battalions into the front line and were instructed to press the German rear guards as vigorously as possible, moving forward in a series of clearly defined "bounds." In view of the experience of the day's fighting on the 9th, when the artillery barrage rather delayed than expedited the advance, there was to be no preliminary barrage, but the 310th Bde., R.F.A., was detailed to support the 1st Guards Bde. and the 75th Bde., R.F.A., the 2nd Guards Bde. One 18-pdr. battery was ordered to advance in close support of each of the leading battalions, while two troops of the Oxfordshire Hussars and a platoon of the VI Corps Cyclists were to be in readiness should an opportunity arise for their employment.†

(4) CONTINUANCE OF THE ADVANCE OF THE 1ST AND 2ND GUARDS BRIGADES, 10TH OF OCTOBER.

The 1st Bn. Irish Guards, with three companies in the line, continued the advance of the 1st Guards Bde. at 5 a.m. on the 10th of October,‡ Except for the fire of an occasional German sniper, the battalion met with little opposition before it reached the line Fresnoy Farm—Carnières at 7 a.m. From this time until midday the enemy's artillery fire was severe, and a temporary check to the advance about 11 a.m. west of Bévillers was caused by the enemy's machine-gun fire. About noon, however, the German rear guards appear to have

approximate casualties of the Guards amounted to 7 officers and 120 other ranks.

   * The New Zealanders on the right of the Guards expected to have cleared Fontaine and Beauvois by the morning of the 10th and to be in a position to continue their advance from the line of the Cambrai—le Cateau road. On the left the 24th Division was already in touch with the 2nd Guards Bde. between Cauroir and Carnières.

   † *See* W.D., Guards Division, App. 1203.

   ‡ *See* W.D's., 1st Guards Bde., App. 530, and 1st Bn. Irish Guards, October, 1918.

withdrawn and during the afternoon the Irish Guards cleared the village of Quiévy which was found to be in a tolerably good state of repair and contained supplies of hay and straw. They reached their final " bound," the high ground north-east of Quiévy, about 10.30 p.m.

On the front of the 2nd Guards Bde., the 1st Bn. Scots Guards moved forward at the same time as the Irish Guards with three companies in the line.* They occupied Carnières, Boussières and St. Hilaire without any difficulty during the course of the day, and, when darkness set in, had established posts east of the Ereclin river.

As a result of the day's operations, the line of the Guards Division, at nightfall on the 10th, ran almost up to the St. Vaast road from Fontaine au Tertre Farm (where the division was in touch with the New Zealanders) to a point due east of St. Hilaire. Thence it bent back to meet the right of the 24th Division west of St. Vaast.† It will be seen, therefore, that the Guards had advanced about 8 miles in two days.

Major-General Matheson now issued his orders for the 11th of October. The 3rd Guards Bde., the troops of which were billetted in Estourmel and Cattenières, was to resume the advance and two machine-gun companies, a squadron of the Oxfordshire Hussars and a company of the Corps Cyclists were placed under the orders of Brig.-General Heywood.‡

(5) Advance of the 3rd Guards Brigade, 11th of October
—Capture of St. Vaast.

The 3rd Guards Bde. deployed for the advance at 5 a.m. on the 11th of October with all three of its battalions in the line—the 1st Bn. Grenadier Guards on the right, the 2nd

* *See* W.D., 1st Bn. Scots Guards, October, 1918.

† *See* W.D., Guards Division, October, 1918. In the evening of the 10th of October the New Zealand Division was east of Viesly and intended to cross the Selle river that night. *See ib.*, App. 1208.

‡ The cavalry and cyclists found no opportunity for independent action on the 10th of October.

A CHECK IN THE ADVANCE

Bn. Scots Guards in the centre and the 1st Bn. Welsh Guards on the left. As both the 1st and 2nd Guards Bdes. had made some progress during the night of the 10th–11th, the troops of the 3rd Guards Bde. had to march a considerable distance before they reached new ground. This necessitated the battalions leaving their billets soon after midnight, and in the darkness there was some little loss of direction, with the result that the Grenadiers and Scots Guards were not in touch when they crossed the railway line east of Quiévy. The countryside here was undulating with great fields of grass and stubble affording but little cover, and the patrols of the Grenadiers came under fire almost immediately they began to move forward. The German machine gunners were posted on the high ground beyond the railway and in the orchard north of Fontaine au Tertre Farm, although some New Zealanders had already reached the farm buildings. As the Grenadiers descended the slope towards the orchard they were also enfiladed by the enemy's machine-gun fire from the St. Vaast—Solesmes road. The Germans in front of them, however, retreated as they approached and the orchard was soon in their possession. Now fierce bursts of fire from machine guns posted on the north-eastern ends of the spurs of hill running down to the railway swept the crest of the high ground east of the orchard and effectually checked the progress both of the Grenadiers and also of the Scots Guards on their left. One company on the right of the former managed to push on to the forward slope southwest of Gourlain Chapel, but could get no farther, and the battalion was pinned to its ground until darkness began to set in.*

The 2nd Bn. Scots Guards, although it encountered heavy machine-gun fire, reached the high ground north of the orchard, where its right flank secured touch with the Grenadiers. Here for the time being its advance was brought to a standstill. Its left flank bent back along the St. Vaast—St. Python road, where it linked up with the right of the Welsh Guards whose advance had also been checked. The section of machine guns attached to the Scots Guards is reported

* *See* W.D., 1st Bn. Grenadier Guards, October, 1918.

to have been of the utmost assistance to the battalion in this rather trying situation, and B/74, R.F.A., was able to cover the front to some extent, although little direct observation could be obtained by the gunners.*

On the left of the Scots Guards, the advance of the Welsh Guards was directed upon St. Vaast. As the battalion went down the slope towards that village it became a target for the German machine gunners posted on the railway line near St. Aubert station. One company succeeded in working its way round St. Vaast in a south-easterly direction, while the Guards' machine guns engaged those of the enemy. This rendered the hostile fire less accurate, but did not by any means reduce its volume. Another company of the battalion reached the sunken road at the cemetery west of St. Vaast and engaged the enemy with fire. There were, however, no signs of any troops belonging to the 24th Division on the left, and so any continuance of the advance on this flank was temporarily out of the question. Meanwhile, the company which was pushing forward south-east of St. Vaast had been checked by hostile machine-gun fire from the railway sidings and had been compelled to dig in. But the village itself was found to be held in no great strength by the Germans and the Welsh Guards gained possession of the greater part of it quite early in the morning. A defensive flank was then formed astride the river to the north of the village, and a section of machine guns was posted south of the cemetery to cover the gap which existed between the left of the 3rd Guards Bde. and the 24th Division.†

At 9.20 a.m. an attempt was made to pass troops round the northern edge of St. Vaast, but this was frustrated by the enemy's machine-gun fire from the southern outskirts of St. Aubert and from the railway embankment.‡ The

* *See* W.D., 2nd Bn. Scots Guards, October, 1918.

† At least two efforts were made by the cavalry to push forward during the morning round the south of St. Vaast, but each attempt ended in failure.

‡ About this period in the day officers belonging to a battalion of the 24th Division arrived at battalion headquarters. They told the commanding officer that their battalion had been ordered to attack St. Aubert from the south and asked for covering fire from the Welsh

THE LEFT FLANK CLEARED

German gas-shelling was also very troublesome about this period of the day. At 10.15 a.m. the 18-pdr. battery attached to the Welsh Guards came into action, concentrating its fire upon the southern edge of St. Aubert and the railway embankment. Under cover of this fire it was found possible to link up the battalion line from the cemetery round the north-western portion of St. Vaast. The whole of the village was now occupied and the Guards' machine guns came into action at the cemetery.

No farther advance was attempted during the day and at night the line ran from the eastern outskirts of St. Vaast on the St. Python road round the north side of the village to the St. Aubert road. The left flank and the valley to the south were covered by machine guns.*

At 7.20 p.m. Major-General Matheson ordered the 3rd Guards Bde. to consolidate the line which it had reached and to push forward strong patrols during the night in order to establish, if possible, bridgeheads at St. Python and to secure the high ground about Arbre de la Femme.†

Later in the evening further instructions were issued from divisional headquarters stating that no attack was to be made by the Guards the following day if the enemy's resistance was found to be of an organized character. The New Zealanders on the right, however, who were already in Briastre and beyond the Selle river north-east of that village, were going to press their advance, whilst, on the left of the Guards, troops belonging to the 24th Division were to make an attempt to encircle St. Aubert from the north.‡

The patrols sent out by the 3rd Guards Bde. during the night of the 11th–12th of October reported no indications of a German retirement. On the contrary, the enemy was found to have moved forward his machine guns in some

---

Guards. Lieut.-Colonel Luxmoore Ball promised his assistance, but gave it as his opinion that the attack could not possibly succeed. This view of the situation was shared by Brig.-General Heywood who came up to see the position, and the operation in question did not take place. *See* " History of the Welsh Guards," p. 264.

* *See* W.D., 1st Bn. Welsh Guards, October, 1918.

† *See* W.D., Guards Division, App. 1210.

‡ *Ib.* App. 1211.

places and was clearly doing his best to hinder the work of reconnaissance.

(6) PROGRESS MADE BY THE GUARDS, 12TH OF OCTOBER.

At dawn on the 12th of October the enemy began a retirement opposite the 24th Division. Troops of this division, who crossed the Selle river north-east of St. Aubert, saw the Germans retreating towards Haussy. On the right of the Guards' front the 1st Bn. Grenadier Guards found that the enemy had withdrawn from his positions west of the railway, and when, at about 2.15 p.m., the Scots and Welsh Guards on the left were seen to be advancing, two platoons on the left flank of the battalion cooperated in the movement. The leading troops encountered some rather severe shell fire, but by the evening the Grenadiers had succeeded in establishing three posts along the line of the railway—one below Gourlain Chapel and the others farther up the line towards St. Python.*

The 2nd Bn. Scots Guards found little difficulty in reaching the high ground between Arbre de la Femme and a point south of the St. Vaast—St. Python road. From this line a view was obtainable over the valley of the Selle and patrols were pushed on to the railway west of the river.† The Guards' machine gunners, who came into action along the ridge, and B/74, R.F.A., which fired from positions in a hollow due north of the orchard at Fontaine au Tertre Farm, covered this forward movement.‡ The Welsh Guards, after they had verified the accuracy of an air report stating that St. Aubert and the railway embankment were no longer in the occupation of the enemy, also moved forward. They were greeted with machine-gun fire from the high ground north and south of Arbre de la Femme, which the fire of the

---

* *See* W.D., 1st Bn. Grenadier Guards, October, 1918.
† Early in the morning three bridges were sent up to the Scots Guards and the same number to the Welsh Guards for use in case the battalions were able to reach the Selle during the day's operations. *See* W.D., Guards Division, October, 1918.
‡ *See* W.D., 2nd Bn. Scots Guards, October, 1918.

THE 3RD GUARDS BDE. REACH THE SELLE

battery attached to the battalion did little to subdue. Some delay was caused by this opposition, but, at about 1 p.m., the advance was resumed, the Germans retiring before it. But as the leading companies topped the ridge at Arbre de la Femme a heavy hostile artillery barrage was put down all along the line, and patrols which were sent on down the slope located the enemy in some strength east of the Selle. The hostile shelling went on for the rest of the day, and, in view of the orders given to the battalion, no farther advance was attempted.*

In the evening Major-General Matheson issued the following order for the next day's operations :—

" Air reports indicate that enemy is evacuating both banks of the Selle between Solesmes and Haussy. The troops on the right have taken the high ground east of Briastre, those on the left are advancing on the high ground west of Haussy. The 3rd Guards Brigade will complete the capture of the high ground west of the river and ascertain if the river positions are still held. If not held, bridgeheads will be established and also posts on high ground east of the river." †

During the course of the night the Welsh Guards were successful in establishing one company east of the railway at a point nearly due east of Arbre de la Femme. Patrols ascertained that the Selle was from 16 to 20 feet broad and from 3 to 6 feet deep. A bridge, which they had taken forward with them, was found not to be long enough to span the stream, but this was of no great importance as a German foot-bridge was discovered to be still intact and a ford was also found farther to the north.‡

(7) EVENTS OF THE 13TH OF OCTOBER—RELIEF OF THE 3RD GUARDS BRIGADE.

Throughout the 13th of October the 1st Bn. Grenadier Guards was subjected to persistent and accurate hostile

---

* *See* W.D., 1st Bn. Welsh Guards, October, 1918.
† *See* W.D., Guards Division, App. 1212.
‡ *See* W.D., 1st Bn. Welsh Guards, October, 1918.

shelling. Solesmes and St. Python appeared to be strongly held by the enemy, and, at about 2 p.m., one of the battalion's posts which had been established on the railway was rushed by the Germans under the cover of an intense trench-mortar fire, only one survivor succeeding in making his way back.*

In the early hours of the morning a company of the 2nd Bn. Scots Guards penetrated into the northern end of St. Python and pushed out patrols as far as the river, capturing a few prisoners and some machine guns. Farther to the south, the Scots Guards occupied the railway junction and also entered the western end of the village. Both these operations were carried out in pitch darkness and in face of a considerable opposition, the eastern portion of St. Python beyond the river and the slopes northward towards Haussy being held by German machine-gun detachments posted in carefully sited positions.

As soon as there was sufficient daylight a firmer grip was secured upon the western side of the village. But the clearing operations were much hampered by the presence of many civilians and in the afternoon heavy hostile shelling added to the difficulties.† By the evening, however, the Scots Guards held most of St. Python west of the Selle, although every attempt to secure a bridgehead had failed.‡ All the river crossings, including the main road bridge, had been destroyed by the enemy, and débris of every description dammed the stream, making deep pools in some cases 30 feet

---

* *See* W.D., 1st Bn. Grenadier Guards, Narrative, October, 1918.

† There is a well authenticated story of one German being found dressed in civilian clothes. He shot the French civilian who pointed him out to a party of Scots Guards and killed a corporal before he himself was dispatched. The presence of civilians greatly complicated the difficulties of the attacking troops, and, on the 17th of October, Major-General Matheson asked for a corps ruling with regard to the employment of artillery in cases where, as in St. Python and Solesmes, the enemy had sited machine guns in villages still occupied by French citizens. The reply was that no such villages were to be bombarded by the heavy guns, but that shrapnel and machine-gun fire might be used to cover an advance as it might be presumed that the inhabitants would take shelter in their cellars. Where, however, hostile machine guns had been located in any particular houses, such houses might be bombarded. *See* W.D., Guards Division, Apps. 1232, 1245.

‡ The cavalry and cyclists again failed to cross the river.

or more in width. R.E. bridges, therefore, were sent for in readiness for further attempts at crossing the river during the night.

The heavy fighting among the houses in St. Python—in the course of which Corporal Wood led his platoon with such conspicuous gallantry that he was recommended for the Victoria Cross *—caused the enemy severe losses and drove his troops back in disorder, and the Guards' machine guns and the R.F.A. did considerable execution among them during the afternoon. On the whole, therefore, the Scots Guards had a highly successful day.†

Persistent hostile shell and machine-gun fire was maintained upon the positions held by the Welsh Guards throughout the 13th of October, and no general advance by the battalion was attempted. Patrols which were sent forward succeeded in crossing the river, but could make no farther progress. After darkness set in, the 2nd Guards Bde. relieved the 3rd Guards Bde. in the line.‡

During the operations between the 11th and 13th of October the Welsh Guards appear to have been dissatisfied with the support given to them by the battery R.F.A. attached to them. On the other hand, the War Diary of the 1st Bn. Grenadier Guards refers in eulogistic terms to the good work done by D/74, R.F.A., which assisted the battalion. The valuable aid given by the machine gunners is referred to by both battalions and the Welsh Guards reported that the cavalry did extremely good work, patrols always advancing till driven in by heavy machine-gun fire.§

* *See* Appendix III.
† *See* W.D., 2nd Bn. Scots Guards, October, 1918.
‡ During the three days in the line the 3rd Guards Bde. lost 10 officers and less than 200 other ranks. On coming out of the line the brigade was congratulated on its achievements in a special message from the divisional commander. *See* W.D., Guards Division, App. 1220.
§ *See* W.D.'s, 1st Bn. Grenadier Guards and 1st Bn. Welsh Guards, October, 1918.

(8) Events of the 14th and 15th of October.

The orders given to the two fresh battalions in the line—the 3rd Bn. Grenadier Guards and the 1st Bn. Scots Guards—were to make every endeavour to establish bridgeheads over the Selle and the R.E. and Pioneers were held in readiness to set about the bridging work as soon as an opportunity could be given to them.

In the early morning of the 14th of October a patrol of the 3rd Bn. Grenadier Guards crossed the Selle just north of St. Python and captured a prisoner who gave some valuable information. He stated that the enemy's main line of resistance was along the Solesmes—Valenciennes road and that the Selle was fordable opposite the sector of the front held by his battalion north of St. Python. His regiment had orders to retire through Vertain. The moral of the troops in his division was not good. He believed that there was another division in close support, but little defensive work was being done. The communications in rear were very bad and little or no news reached the front line troops. He quite realized that Germany was beaten, and said that the troops were aware that they were retiring from France. When questioned as to the condition of the civilian population, he stated that about 10 per cent. of the population had left St. Python, having been provided with the necessary transport by the Town Major who was "a lenient man." The remaining civilians had plenty of food.*

The day passed comparatively quietly on the divisional front and there was a noticeable decrease in the activity of the enemy's artillery. During the night the 1st Bn. Scots

---

* The situation, however, of the French civilians was by no means a pleasant one as is shown by the following incident which took place on the 17th of October and was brought to the notice of all ranks in the division. "A young French girl came out of her house in the western portion of St. Python and walked down the main street. The Germans at once turned a machine gun on her and wounded her in three places. She was brought into our lines by two men of the 3rd Grenadier Guards and taken to the main dressing station at Carnières, where everything possible was done for her. The girl is dying." *See* W.D., Guards Division, App. 1236.

Guards passed a company over the river. It dug in at a point near the junction of the St. Python—Haussy and Solesmes—Haussy roads. But here the German machine-gun fire was very severe, especially in enfilade from a house on the river bank farther to the north. The company commander was badly wounded, and eventually it was found necessary to withdraw the company.*

During the course of the 15th of October the enemy's artillery was active along the whole of the divisional front, and his infantry showed a more offensive spirit than on the previous day, the 3rd Bn. Grenadier Guards having some stiff fighting in St. Python.

It was now decided that the 24th Division should attack Haussy on the 16th, and orders were given to the 2nd Guards Bde. to assist in this operation by engaging the enemy's machine guns on the forward slopes south-east of that village. The Guards divisional Artillery was also to take part in the covering barrage.†

During the night of the 15th–16th of October the 1st Bn. Coldstream Guards relieved the 1st Bn. Scots Guards on the left of the divisional front.

(9) Haussy taken and lost—The 1st Bn. Coldstream Guards in action—Orders issued for the passage of the Selle river.

Early in the morning on the 16th of October the Germans were observed to be digging in on the St. Python—Haussy road. The 3rd Bn. Grenadier Guards at once withdrew its two platoons from the eastern bank of the Selle and the artillery was instructed to open fire on the enemy. The British guns accordingly began firing at 11.10 a.m., but the shells dropped short, and it was found advisable to order the cease fire after the Grenadiers had suffered five casualties.‡

---

* The company's casualties amounted to 2 officers and 29 other ranks.
† See W.D., Guards Division, App. 1224.
‡ See W.D., 3rd Bn. Grenadier Guards, October, 1918.

Meanwhile, on the left of the Guards, the troops of the 24th Division took Haussy, although their attack farther to the north made little progress. In order to link up with the advance on the left which caused a gap in the line, a company of the 1st Bn. Coldstream Guards moved off about noon to hold a position east of the river. Haussy at this time was being heavily shelled by the enemy, but three platoons of the Coldstream managed to reach and to occupy the sunken road on the south-east side of the village from the chapel to the cemetery, while the remaining platoon continued the line to the right as far as the river.

Almost as soon as these positions had been occupied, the enemy launched a strong counter-attack, endeavouring to envelop Haussy. His left was on the Haussy—St. Python road, and, as his troops advanced, they attempted to work round the right of the Coldstream. This movement exposed them to the concentrated rifle, Lewis-gun and machine-gun fire of the Guards. They suffered very heavy casualties and were driven back. But on the left of the Guards' divisional line the enemy was more successful and succeeded in entering Haussy from the east and north. The advanced company of the Coldstream was consequently in grave danger of being cut off if it remained where it was. It was accordingly withdrawn by the right across the river in order to regain touch with troops of the 24th Division along the railway line.*
This manœuvre was skilfully carried out under very heavy fire. All the officers became casualties, but the non-commissioned officers displayed great coolness and initiative in the emergency. The Germans made no serious attempt to press forward beyond Haussy throughout the remainder of the day.

In the afternoon the preliminary scheme of operations for the passage of the Selle river was issued from divisional headquarters. This operation, which was provisionally fixed for the early morning of the 20th of October,† was

---

* See W.D., 1st Bn. Coldstream Guards, October, 1918. The casualties of the advanced company of the Coldstream amounted to 9 killed, 13 wounded and 12 missing.

† The 19th–20th was the night of the full moon. Zero hour was to be between 2 a.m. and 4 a.m. on the 20th. In view of the fact that

to be carried out by the Guards and the 62nd Division—the latter division taking over from the Guards the right portion of the VI Corps front before the crossing of the river was attempted. The corps on the right and on the left of the VI Corps were also to participate in the operation. Infantry bridges were to be placed in position after darkness set in on the 19th, and bridges for the artillery were to be thrown across the river as soon as the first objectives had been taken.* In the initial attack the Guards were to cross the Selle river and advance to a line east of the Solesmes—Valenciennes road, while the 62nd Division was to attack Solesmes from the north and south, and then to gain possession of the high ground beyond that village. Until this latter objective was captured, the Guards would be compelled to hold a long defensive flank on their right.

(10) RESUMPTION OF THE GENERAL ALLIED ADVANCE.

The 17th of October was a quiet day for the Guards, but farther to their right, from Le Cateau southward, the general Allied advance was resumed,† and in the evening the 62nd

the enemy's artillery usually put down its counter-preparation at 4 a.m., Major-General Matheson pressed the corps commander to fix zero hour at 2 a.m. *See* W.D., Guards Division, App. 1227.

* It was at first proposed to make the establishment of these bridgeheads a separate operation preliminary to the actual crossing of the river. Major-General Matheson, however, was opposed to this policy and it was not pressed by the corps. He pointed out that it would probably lead to local fighting which would be costly in casualties, and add to the complications of the British artillery barrage. He also gave it as his opinion that if the bridgeheads were established in this manner, the enemy would shift his barrage to the actual line of the river and so increase the difficulties of bridge-making. *See* W.D., Guards Division, App. 1227.

† "Meanwhile, communications on the Le Cateau front were improving, and it was possible to recommence operations of a more than local character for the forcing of the Selle positions and the attainment of the general line Sambre et Oise Canal—west edge of the Forêt de Mormal—Valenciennes. This advance would bring the important railway junction at Aulnoye within effective range of our guns. Our operations were opened on the 17th October by an attack by the Fourth Army on a front of about ten miles from Le Cateau southwards, in conjunction with the French First Army operating west of the Sambre et Oise Canal." *See* "Sir Douglas Haig's Despatches," p. 291.

Division took over its battle front facing Solesmes and St. Python. The 1st Guards Bde., on relief, moved back to Boussières and St. Hilaire, while the 2nd Guards Bde. remained behind to hold the shortened divisional front, the 1st Bn. Scots Guards relieving the 3rd Bn. Grenadier Guards in the line.* The night of the 17th–18th was a peaceful one, and about 170 civilians from St. Python seized the opportunity to cross over into the British lines, where everything that was possible was done by the Guards to assist them.

Major-General Matheson's orders for the crossing of the Selle river were now issued to the troops, although the exact time for the opening of the attack was not fixed until the following day. The task of forcing the passage of the river was given to the 1st and 3rd Guards Bdes. on the right and left respectively. After the passage of the river had been safely effected, the leading battalions were to deploy for the advance on the road east of the river and to move forward to their first objective—a line running northward from Solesmes along the Solesmes—Haussy road to the cemetery south of Haussy—under a barrage provided by five brigades, R.F.A., whilst another brigade of artillery was to fire thermite on the enemy's machine-gun positions farther to the east.† As soon as the first objective had been secured, the advance was to be continued to the second objective—a line running from a point on the Solesmes—Vertain road about half-way between these two villages east of the Solesmes—Valenciennes road to the cross-roads at Maison Blanche. On the right and left of the divisional front the 62nd and 19th Divisions were to cross the Selle at the same time as the Guards, the former division being instructed to gain possession of le Pigeon Blanc before clearing Solesmes.‡

The following day, in the afternoon, a report was received at divisional headquarters that the Germans were retiring opposite the 4th Division on the right of the First Army

---

* The 1st Bn. Coldstream Guards remained in the line without relief from the night of the 15th–16th to the night of the 19th–20th.

† *See* W.D., Guards Division, App. 1240.

‡ *See* also p. 207.

north of the 19th Division. But patrols of the 1st Bn. Scots Guards, which were sent out as soon as this information had been received, drew fire from St. Python, and the troops of the 62nd and 19th Divisions also verified the continued presence of the enemy opposite their respective fronts. In view, however, of the possibility of a hurried retirement on the part of the Germans when once the passage of the Selle had been accomplished, Major-General Matheson warned his brigades to be in readiness to carry forward their advance.*

(11) THE CROSSING OF THE SELLE RIVER, 20TH OF OCTOBER.

At about 10 p.m. on the 19th of October the R.E. and the 4th Bn. Coldstream Guards (Pioneers), whose work was covered by patrols of the 2nd Guards Bde. on the eastern bank of the Selle, set to work to place bridges across the river. By dint of strenuous labour four infantry bridges were in a state of readiness on the front of each attacking brigade some little time before zero hour.† Tapes to assist the infantry to find the bridges were laid from the assembly positions over the railway line to the various crossing places.‡ The approach march of the 1st and 3rd Guards Bdes. was made in drizzling rain, but there were sufficient glimpses of moonlight to reveal such landmarks as existed and the troops reached their assembly positions in good time.

Punctually at zero hour, 2 a.m. on the 20th of October, a very effective British barrage was put down along the road east of the river,§ and after three minutes, during which the

* *See* W.D., Guards Division, App. 1246.

† On the front of the 1st Guards Bde. there were also two single plank bridges across the river left by the Germans. The average width of the Selle opposite the front of the Guards Division was 14 feet; its depth from 2 to 3 feet with a muddy bottom; its banks varied from 7 to 8 feet in height. The work of the R.E. in bridging the river is more fully dealt with on p. 213.

‡ It would appear that one at any rate of these tapes was an inaccurate guide, and one platoon of the 1st Bn. Grenadier Guards is reported to have been obliged to wade the river. *See* " The Grenadier Guards in the Great War," vol. iii. p. 148.

§ The barrage was placed on this road because it was thought that the Germans might have forward posts along it.

leading battalions were crossing the stream, was lifted on to the area east of the road.

The 1st Guards Bde. on the right of the divisional front, attacked with the 2nd Bn. Grenadier Guards, and the 1st Bn. Irish Guards on the right and left respectively. The 2nd Bn. Coldstream Guards was held in reserve with special orders to watch the right flank of the brigade.

The crossing of the Selle was effected without undue difficulty,* and the deployment for the attack was carried out smoothly. From the first the advance went well, for there was little hostile shell fire, the German gunners apparently being taken by surprise. Both battalions succeeded in reaching their first objective—the line of the Solesmes—Valenciennes road—well up to the scheduled time and with but few casualties.† After an hour's halt, the advance to the second objective—a line about half-way between the Solesmes—Valenciennes road and Vertain— was begun. It led over the crest of the high ground and thence down a slope towards some rifle pits and machine-gun emplacements defended by wire. The leading companies kept well up with the creeping barrage, and so ineffective was the enemy's resistance that both battalions were in possession of their second objectives by 4.40 a.m.‡

---

* " Very indifferent bridges had been erected by the Royal Engineers and the Pioneer Battalion of the Coldstream Guards, and it was no easy matter getting all the men across in single file on two extremely narrow planks. However, there were very few casualties and the leading companies deployed into waves and went forward, followed by the supports and reserves in artillery formation." *See* " The Grenadiers in the Great War," vol. iii. p. 156. It is difficult to see how in the circumstances and in the time at their disposal the R.E. could have provided wider bridges.

† Most of these casualties were caused by the British barrage. About 50 prisoners and some machine guns were captured before the first objective was reached. *See* W.D's., 2nd Bn. Grenadier and 1st Bn. Irish Guards, October, 1918.

‡ The number of prisoners was now considerably increased. The 2nd Bn. Grenadier Guards, one of whose platoons made a successful attack with the bayonet upon a party of Germans on the right rear of the battalion, alone claiming 200 prisoners in addition to 2 field guns. The 1st Guards Bde.'s captures of war material also included an anti-tank gun, some trench mortars and about 40 machine guns. *See* W.D., 1st Guards Bde., App. 530.

Meanwhile, the 2nd Bn. Coldstream Guards, which had moved forward about 40 minutes after zero hour, reached the line of the first objective about 3.30 a.m. and at once established the right flank of the 1st Guards Bde. from the road junction east of the Solesmes—Valenciennes road to the cross-roads west of le Pigeon Blanc.

On the left of the divisional front the advance of the 3rd Guards Bde. was led by the 1st Bn. Grenadier Guards. The Grenadiers, after crossing the river, succeeded in keeping well up with the creeping barrage despite the heavy ploughland on the side of the hill east of the Selle, and made rapid progress. There was little or no opposition to their advance and they reached the line of their first objective—the road running south-east from the cemetery on the outskirts of Haussy—almost before the appointed time.*

The 1st Bn. Welsh Guards on the right, and the 2nd Bn. Scots Guards on the left, then took up the advance, passing through the Grenadiers at 3.10 a.m. While still west of the Solesmes—Valenciennes road, the progress of both the attacking battalions was checked by the enemy's rifle and machine-gun fire, and for some little time the Welsh Guards were out of touch with the Irish Guards on their right.† But, at 6.30 a.m., when arrangements were being made at divisional headquarters for some further artillery preparation, the enemy's resistance gave way. The advance was at once resumed and half an hour later its second objective —a line a little to the east of the Solesmes—Valenciennes road—was in the possession of the 3rd Guards Bde.‡

---

* A few prisoners were taken, but the majority of the Germans appear to have fled as soon as the British barrage came down. The Grenadiers had a few men wounded by British shells.

† *See* " History of the Welsh Guards," p. 269.

‡ *See* W.D's., Guards Division, 2nd Bn. Scots Guards and 1st Bn. Welsh Guards, October, 1918. The Welsh Guards report that they took 23 prisoners, 1 trench mortar and 3 anti-tank guns. Their own casualties are given as 30 men. The Scots Guards, on the left, had the heavier fighting, as the enemy in Chapelle d'Haussy offered some resistance before they were driven from their positions. The 8th Bn. Gloucestershire Regiment (19th Division) on the left of the Scots Guards took Maison Blanche.

As soon as daylight came the enemy's artillery opened fire with guns of all calibres upon the ground which the Guards had captured earlier in the morning.* But by this time the attacking troops had dug themselves in and were already tolerably well entrenched. Although, therefore, any movement on the top of the ground was restricted throughout the remainder of the day, casualties were surprisingly few considering the volume of the gun fire.†

At 6 p.m. orders were received for each Guards brigade to push forward troops to occupy positions commanding the Harpies stream. As soon as it was dusk, accordingly, patrols were sent out all along the front. By this time the enemy had already begun to withdraw his artillery, but his infantry and machine gunners were found to be still holding the line, and on the right especially the patrols of the 2nd Bn. Grenadier Guards came under heavy fire and for some time could make but little progress.

From every point of view the day had been a highly satisfactory one for the Guards Division. The passage of the Selle, which might have been a task of great difficulty had the enemy's defence been at all vigorous, had been safely accomplished and the high ground beyond the river had been captured with but few casualties. The staff arrangements had been admirable, the work of the R.E. and Pioneers had been performed in the most efficient manner, and the conduct of the operation by the regimental officers and men had been carried out with great precision and skill.‡

* "By half-past five, however, they were all in place, and set to dig in opposite the village of Vertain. Then dull day broke and with light came punishment. The enemy, in plain sight, opened on them with everything that they had in the neighbourhood, from 7 a.m. to 10 p.m., of the 20th. . . . They were, in most places, only a hundred yards away from a dug-in enemy, bent on blessing them with every round left over in the retreat." *See* " The Irish Guards in the Great War," vol. i. p. 327.

† The casualties of the 1st Bn. Irish Guards, for instance, between the beginning of the attack on the 20th of October and its relief on the 22nd, only amounted to 55. *See* " The Irish Guards in the Great War," vol. i. p. 329. The worst discomfort during these days' fighting was due to the weather—the men were soaked through all the time.

‡ The following message was received by Major-General Matheson from the VI Corps commander :—" My best congratulations on the

By the morning of the 21st of October a substantial amount of ground had been made good by the patrols. On the right of the divisional front the 2nd Bn. Grenadier Guards had posts pushed out towards Vertain near which village the Irish Guards had also established a post; the Welsh Guards had a company in position near the orchard farther to the north; and a company of the 2nd Bn. Scots Guards was dug in on the western bank of the Harpies stream in touch with the 19th Division.* There was a good deal of hostile shelling throughout the day, but, although the enemy was observed to be in some strength in Vertain, no counter-attack was attempted. In the afternoon the divisional line was reorganized. The 2nd Bn. Coldstream Guards was sent back to Carnières, while the 1st Bn. Grenadier Guards took over the whole of the front of the 3rd Guards Bde., with the 2nd Bn. Scots Guards in support. The 1st Bn. Welsh Guards moved back to St. Hilaire.

During the night of the 21st–22nd of October, which was a very wet and cold one, the patrols of the 1st Bn. Grenadier Guards were extremely enterprising and the reports sent in by them regarding the enemy's dispositions east of the Harpies stream proved of much assistance to the troops of the 2nd Division who carried on the British advance on this part of the front the following day.†

The Guards were relieved in the line in the evening of the 22nd, and were withdrawn for rest and reorganization into the Carnières—Boussières—St. Hilaire area.‡

skilful manner in which the difficult task of to-day's date, involving the passage by night of an unfordable stream under the close fire of the enemy, was carried out. It reflects much credit on commanders, staffs and the gallant officers, non-commissioned officers and men of your division. I am particularly pleased with the admirable work of the Royal Engineers and Pioneers in overcoming the difficulty of the river passage, and with the artillery and machine gunners for their able support of the attack." In circulating this message to the division, the Major-General added his own expression of gratitude to his troops, alluding especially to the work of the R.E. and Pioneers. *See* W.D., Guards Division, App. 1249.

* *See* W.D., Guards Division, October, 1918.

† The G.O.C., the 2nd Division, expressed his appreciation of their services.

‡ The total number of prisoners taken between zero hour on the

(12) Work of the Divisional Artillery and Trench-Mortar Batteries during the month of October.

On the 1st of October the 74th and 75th Bdes., R.F.A., were in action in positions near Noyelles and Nine Wood, firing in the standing barrage which was designed to drive the Germans out of the machine-gun positions blocking the advance of the troops of the VI Corps between Rumilly and Proville.* The two brigades remained in the same positions until the 5th of October, when the 75th Bde. was withdrawn from the line and placed in mobile reserve. The following day new battery positions were reconnoitred just west of Rumilly, and ammunition was taken up to them under cover of darkness. These positions were occupied by the 75th Bde. On the 7th of October and the following day its batteries assisted in covering the attack delivered by the 2nd and 3rd Divisions between Seranvillers and Niergnies.† On the 9th of October the same brigade covered the advance of the Guards Division, being attached for this operation to the 2nd Guards Bde., and moving forward in close support of the infantry. As the line advanced batteries took up positions near the railway north of Wambaix, and, in the morning on the 10th, C/75 was practically in the front line, where its guns were so close to the enemy that not a round could be fired. The gun teams are reported to have used their rifles with good effect.‡

20th of October and 4 p.m. on the 21st of October appears to have been 8 officers and 284 other ranks. The casualties of the division during this same period did not amount to this number. *See* W.D., Guards Division, October, 1918.

* The record of the day's work is recorded as follows in the War Diary of the 74th Bde., R.F.A. :—" Fired barrage for the infantry who did not attack. Barrage lasted 3 hours and tired men for no material result."

† The 74th Bde., R.F.A., was employed with the troops of the XVII Corps on the left of the VI Corps from the 7th to the 10th of October. On the 8th of October the mobile section of the divisional Trench-Mortar Batteries, which had been resting at Noyelles since the the 1st of October, was moved up to Rumilly where it was heavily shelled, losing some of its *personnel* and most of its mules. The section did not get into action until the 12th. *See* note, p. 211.

‡ *See* W.D., C.R.A., Guards Division, Apps. I and II, and W.D. 75th Bde., R.F.A., October, 1918.

THE DIVISIONAL ARTILLERY

The advance of the 3rd Guards Bde. on the 11th of October was supported by both the 74th and 75th Bdes., R.F.A., under the command of Lieut.-Colonel T. Kirkland, the three 18-pdr. batteries of the 74th Bde. being allotted to the attacking battalions, with orders to move forward in close support of the infantry. The foremost batteries came into action between St. Hilaire and the Calvary south of that village, and, on the two following days, again advanced first to the neighbourhood of Quiévy and then to positions between the orchard and the St. Vaast—St. Python road. During the night of the 13th–14th of October, when, it will be remembered, the 1st and 2nd Guards Bdes. relieved the 3rd Guards Bde. in the line,* the 75th Bde., R.F.A., became the right group covering the front of the 1st Guards Bde., and one of its batteries was kept in close support in readiness for the resumption of the advance by the infantry. The left group, consisting of the 74th Bde., R.F.A., and the 76th Army Bde., was employed to cover the front held by the 2nd Guards Bde.

On the 14th of October, so heavy was the hostile shelling that A/75 and D/75 were obliged to shift their guns into less exposed positions; but, nevertheless, the brigade maintained its harassing fire upon the enemy's defensive positions and communications throughout the day. On the 16th, all the batteries of the Guards divisional Artillery cooperated in the attack made by the 24th Division on Haussy, their fire being directed upon the southern end of the village. The positions occupied by the batteries, however, were found to be too much exposed to the fire of the enemy's guns which was very accurate, and consequently, on the following day, the 18-pdr. batteries were slightly withdrawn.† On the 17th of October, the day on which the 62nd Division took over

---

* On the 12th of October the mobile section of the divisional Trench-Mortar Batteries came into action, firing 19 rounds into St. Vaast. The section then advanced with the infantry and was in action with the 1st and 3rd Guards Bdes. on the 15th, 16th and 17th of October, but it appears to have had few opportunities of distinguishing itself. It was relieved in the line when the 62nd Division took over part of the Guards' front.

† *See* W.D., C.R.A., Guards Division, App. VII.

part of the Guards' front preparatory to the crossing of the Selle river, the two brigades of the Guards divisional Artillery were grouped together in order to cover the front held by the 2nd Guards Bde. and during the next two days their batteries kept such of the enemy's defensive positions as were known continuously under fire.

In the attack on the 20th of October the 74th and 75th Bdes., R.F.A., with the 14th Army Bde., R.H.A., supported the advance of the 1st Guards Bde., forming the right group in positions near the Solesmes—Valenciennes railway.* All the artillery brigades were employed to fire in the creeping barrage with the exception of the 74th Bde., R.F.A., which maintained a standing barrage of thermite and shrapnel upon the German machine-gun posts and organized defences on the high ground east of the river. As soon as the bridges over the Selle had been placed in position, the 74th and 75th Bdes., R.F.A., each sent forward a section of guns to assist the infantry against hostile tanks and machine guns. The mobile section of the divisional Trench-Mortar Batteries was also sent across the river and succeeded in reaching Maison Blanche, from which position at night it opened fire on the enemy's machine guns in Ferme de Rieux.

In the morning on the 21st, the 75th Bde. and the 41st (2nd Division) Bde., R.F.A., crossed the river and came into action in positions south-east of Haussy.

When the infantry of the Guards Division was withdrawn from the line on the 22nd of October, the divisional Artillery remained in action as the right group and covered the advance of the 2nd Division on the 23rd and 24th. Both brigades were then relieved and withdrew to St. Hilaire for a week's much needed rest.

* The left group, covering the 3rd Guards Bde., consisted of the artillery of the 2nd Division and the 76th Army Bde. *See* W.D., C.R.A., Guards Division, App. XIX.

THE BRIDGING OF THE SELLE

(18) WORK OF THE DIVISIONAL R.E. AND 4TH BN. COLD-
STREAM GUARDS (PIONEERS) DURING THE MONTH OF
OCTOBER—THEIR SHARE IN THE CROSSING OF THE
SELLE RIVER.

During October the Field Companies, R.E., and the Pioneers were fully employed upon the usual tasks incidental to an advance. Roads were repaired, improved and maintained. Craters were filled in; culverts reconstructed; the local water supplies cleaned and inspected and watering points provided for the horses and mules. A great many land-mines, too, which had been left by the enemy, were found and destroyed. This work was so successfully carried out that no casualties resulted.*

The tasks allotted to the R.E. and Pioneers for the crossing of the Selle river were :—(1) the construction of footbridges for the infantry before zero hour on the 20th of October; (2) the construction of pontoon or trestle bridges as soon as possible after zero hour for the passage of field guns across the river to assist the infantry in the event of counter-attacks by tanks; and (3) the construction of a bridge at St. Python capable of carrying tanks and heavy vehicles. There was also the possibility that yet another bridge might be required to relieve any congestion of traffic there might be on the bridge at St. Python. It was anticipated that the provision of the footbridges would be the most difficult of these tasks as it involved a long carry down the slope from the railway line exposed to the close-range fire of the Germans. It was decided that eight footbridges were to be used—four on the front of each attacking brigade—and that each alternate bridge should be duplicated, if possible, and a spare pier and grid dumped at each bridge in case repairs were needed.

Two Field Companies, R.E. (the 75th and 76th), were employed upon the erection of these footbridges, one on the front of each brigade, and each was assisted by a company of the 4th Bn. Coldstream Guards (Pioneers). The bridges were

* *See* W.D., C.R.E., Guards Division, Narrative.

of various types, piers of cork, petrol tins and light barrels being used.

The work of construction began at 10 p.m. on the 19th of October.* Tapes were first laid due east from the railway to the various crossing places on the river and notice boards erected. This took until midnight, and from that hour onwards one bridge was carried down every ten minutes on the front of each brigade in strict accordance with a definite programme which had been laid down. Each carrying party had orders to erect its bridge if possible, but, should the enemy's fire be too severe, it was to lie down and to be in readiness to put up the bridge as soon as the British artillery barrage opened.

The most difficult part of the work was that of carrying the piers down the steep banks of the Selle, which, owing to the heavy rain, were very slippery, without making any noise calculated to attract the attention of the enemy. In despite of every difficulty, however, the R.E. and the Pioneers succeeded in placing the eight footbridges across the river just before 2 a.m., zero hour.† The absolute silence and perfect discipline which were preserved by all ranks, the excellence of the organization maintained by the commanders of the Field Companies, and the avoidance of any splashing when the piers were put into the water, all contributed to this splendid result.‡

Each of the Field Companies employed upon the footbridges was also ordered to make a pontoon or trestle bridge, its instructions being to get its bridge into position an hour

---

* Previous to this, R.E. patrols, each consisting of an officer and two men, had been sent forward to obtain information as to the crossing places. They were obliged to fight for their information and killed several Germans. On the night of the 20th of October similar patrols were dispatched to investigate the banks of the Harpies stream near Vertain.

† Two sappers remained at each bridge as a maintenance party and a small standing patrol of the 4th Bn. Coldstream Guards (Pioneers) was kept at each bridgehead.

‡ The Germans only appear to have discovered that work was in progress on the river bank when the last bridge was being put into position. Desultory fire was then opened on the working parties, but it was then too late for the enemy to make an organized effort to find out what was happening.

DIFFICULTIES OF HEAVY BRIDGING

before zero hour, or, if this were impossible, as soon as the British barrage opened.

On the right the 75th Field Company succeeded in getting their trestles fixed into the bed of the river, but one of them sank in a deep, muddy hole, and every attempt to extricate it or to adjust the bridge failed until daylight came. As soon as it was light enough to see, the bridge was quickly put into working order. On the left, the 76th Field Company was more successful and its trestle bridge was erected fifteen minutes before zero hour. A large part of the credit for this achievement was due to the working party of the 4th Bn. Coldstream Guards (Pioneers) whose men waded into the river in the dark with the trestle on their shoulders and up-ended it in exactly the right place.*

The construction of the bridge to carry heavy traffic turned out to be the most difficult of the tasks of the R.E. in the battle of the Selle. It was entrusted to the 55th Field Company. The only approach by which materials could be brought forward to the site chosen for the bridge was blocked by the ruined remains of a brick railway bridge which had been blown down into the road. The work of clearing away this obstacle was begun at 4 a.m. on the 20th of October under a heavy hostile bombardment of gas and high explosive shell which continued for four hours. It was not until the expiration of this time that the working parties could dispense with their gas masks. Nevertheless, the men worked with a will and determination beyond all praise. Their task was a very arduous one. Some of the larger blocks of fallen brickwork had to be blown up and then as much of the débris as possible was drawn away by a tank. At about 3 p.m. the route was sufficiently clear for a supply tank, laden with bridging material, to scramble its way through to the immediate vicinity of the river, and, about two hours later, the actual work of bridge construction began. Notwithstanding the enemy's artillery fire, which continued until midnight and necessitated the frequent putting on of their gas masks by the toiling sappers and pioneers, and although

* This bridge was in use very soon after the advance began for the passage of field guns and machine-gun limbers.

the wet and slippery condition of the timbers rendered the work of construction very difficult, the bridge was open for traffic at 8 a.m. on the 21st of October. Meanwhile, continuous reliefs had been working throughout the night in clearing away the remains of the old railway bridge, with the result that a route for single traffic was ready by the time the bridge across the river was in position. A double track was finished within the next twenty-four hours.*

During the month of October a great strain was naturally placed upon the divisional Signal Company, the advance, of course, necessitating constant changes in the various lines of communication. But the signallers appear to have carried out their arduous duties to the satisfaction of the divisional commander, the communications being well maintained throughout the course of the operations.†

* Another bridge designed to carry 60-pdr. guns was constructed by the 75th Field Company, R.E., on the 22nd of October. The work of construction was begun at 9 a.m. and the bridge was completed by 4 p.m.

† Major Hussey was evacuated sick on the 14th of October, and was succeeded in the command of the Signal Company by Major Ryan.

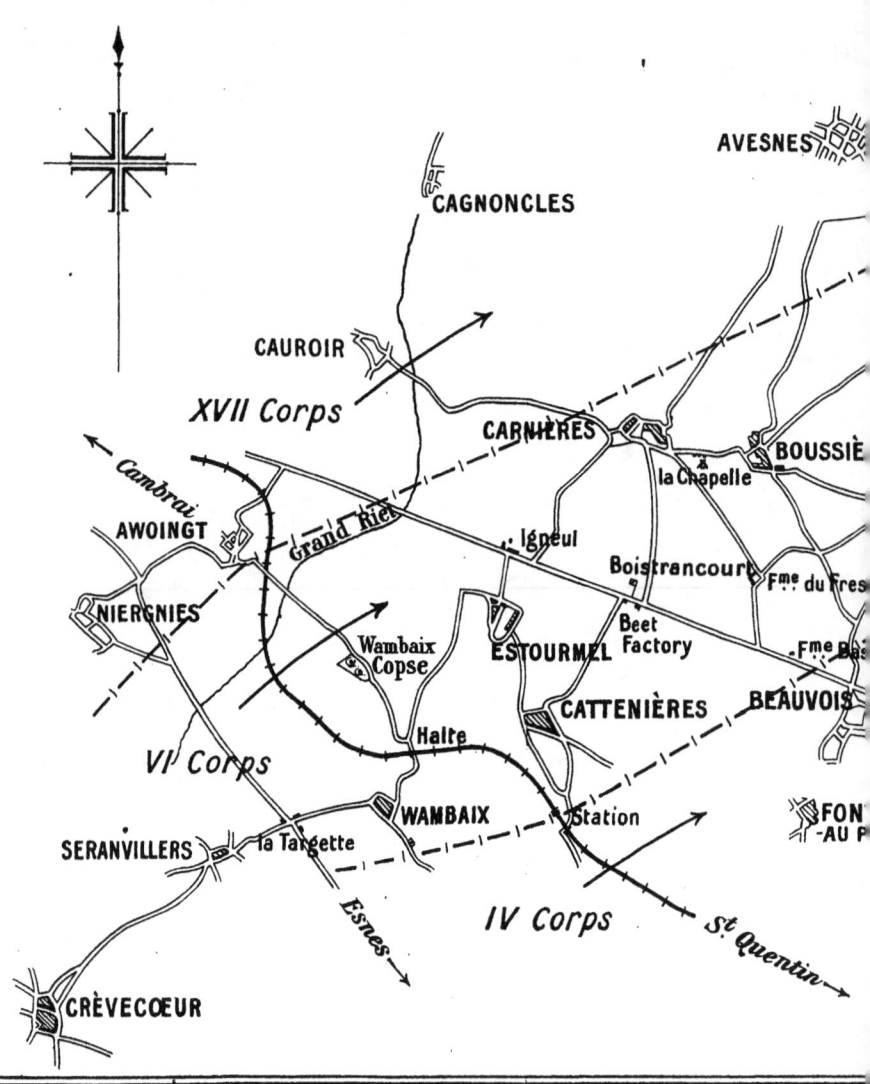

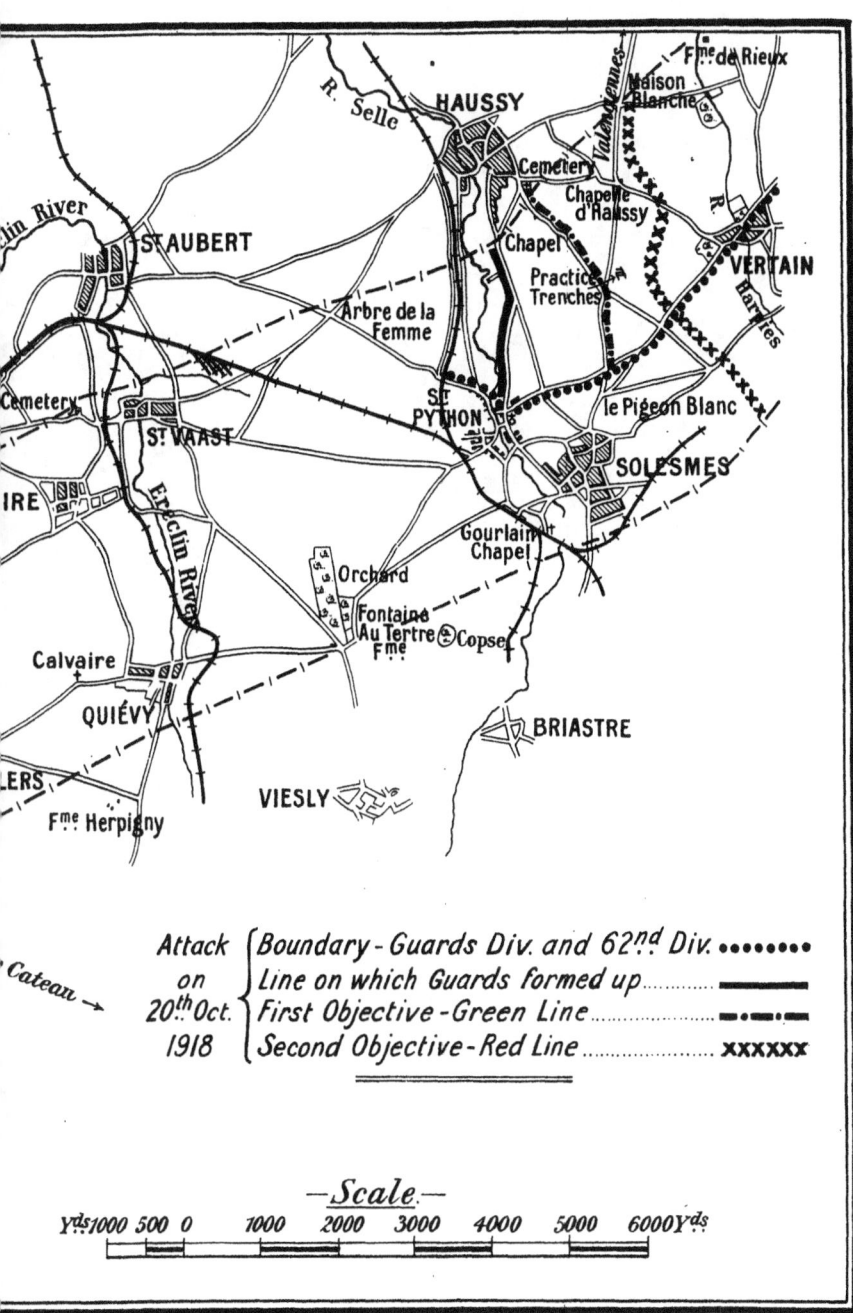

CHAPTER XX

THE BATTLE OF THE SAMBRE AND THE OCCUPATION OF MAUBEUGE, 4TH TO 9TH OF NOVEMBER, 1918—THE ARMISTICE.

(1) GROWING EFFECTS OF THE ALLIED VICTORIES—OPENING OF THE FINAL BRITISH ADVANCE.

AFTER their relief by the 2nd Division the Guards spent the remainder of the month of October in rest billets. In the area in which the troops now found themselves the villages had been little, if at all, damaged by shell fire, and it was possible, consequently, for all ranks to be in tolerable comfort.* This welcome change in the manner of life to which they had been so long accustomed brought home to officers and men more than anything else the amazing change which had come over the war. In other respects their time out of the line was spent much in the usual way—refitment, drill, company training, football †—and there were few who realized that they had reached the last stage in the war—that only one more period in the line lay before the division.

---

* " Since passing to the east of the Hindenburg defences a rest had some meaning for the battalion. Villages had scarcely been touched by shell fire—there were a few houses wrecked in each one, but by comparison with the devastated area they seemed in good repair—and the men had billets with a whole roof, and a board floor to sleep on. Dirt and filth were there in quantities, but that could be cleared away." *See* " History of the Welsh Guards," p. 271.

† " . . . they were washed and cleaned and reclothed with all speed, and handed over to their company officers for the drill that chases off bad dreams. The regimental sergeant-major got at them, too, after their hair was cut, and the massed brigade drums played in the village square of Carnières, and ere the end of the month, intercompany football was in full swing." *See* " The Irish Guards in the Great War," vol. i. pp. 329, 330.

The general impression which appears to have prevailed among the troops who were actually in contact with the enemy at the end of October—indeed, up to the 10th of November—was that the Germans were retreating to a shortened defensive line along the Meuse and that another winter campaign was in store for the Allies. Nor was this view at all a surprising one for men whose knowledge of the situation was practically limited to their own immediate front. The fine rear guard actions which the enemy had fought, and the methodical manner of his retirement opposite the Guards, gave little indication of the state of demoralization existing behind his lines.

To the Allied Higher Command, however, it was now apparent that the German Army was already virtually beaten.* By the end of October the British front ran approximately from south-east of Le Cateau northward along the western edge of the Forêt de Mormal to the western outskirts of Le Quesnoy; thence it bent back to a point just west of Valenciennes, and thence ran northward just west of the Canal de l'Escaut to its northern boundary. The British Commander-in-Chief, therefore, was in a position to strike a decisive blow at the enemy's Army before the German leaders could withdraw their troops to a new defensive line farther in rear.† Before, however, he resumed the general

* "By this time the rapid succession of heavy blows dealt by the British forces had had a cumulative effect, both moral and material, upon the German Armies. The difficulty of replacing the enemy's enormous losses in guns, machine guns and ammunition had increased with every fresh attack, and his reserves of men were exhausted. In the Selle battle the twenty-four British and two American divisions engaged had captured a further 20,000 prisoners and 475 guns from the thirty-one German divisions opposed to them, and had advanced to a great depth with certainty and precision." *See* "Sir Douglas Haig's Despatches," p. 293.

† "The capitulation of Turkey and Bulgaria and the imminent collapse of Austria—consequent upon Allied successes which the desperate position of her own armies on the western front had rendered her powerless to prevent—had made Germany's military situation ultimately impossible. If her armies were allowed to withdraw undisturbed to shorter lines, the struggle might still be protracted over the winter. The British Armies, however, were now in a position to prevent this by a direct attack upon a vital centre, which should anticipate the enemy's withdrawal and force an immediate conclusion." *See* "Sir Douglas Haig's Despatches," p. 293.

advance, Sir Douglas Haig deemed it advisable to capture the town of Valenciennes. Accordingly, on the 1st of November, the XVII Corps (First Army) and the XXII and Canadian Corps (Third Army) attacked on a front of six miles south of Valenciennes, and, in the course of two days' fighting, gained possession of that town, crossed the Rhonelle and established the British front two miles to the east of that river.*

The ground was now cleared for the resumption of the main offensive, and, on the 4th of November, the Fourth, Third and First Armies, from south to north, resumed the attack on a front of about thirty miles on the line Avesnes—Maubeuge—Mons.

(2) THE GUARDS RETURN TO THE LINE—THE NEW FRONT WEST OF VILLERS POL—ARRANGEMENTS FOR THE RESUMPTION OF THE ADVANCE ON THE 4TH OF NOVEMBER.

On the 2nd of November the Guards Division moved forward towards Villers Pol in order to relieve the 2nd Division in the left sector of the VI Corps front, divisional headquarters that day being established at Vertain.

The front now occupied by the Guards extended for about a mile and lay just west of Villers Pol. It was held by two battalions—the 1st Bn. Coldstream Guards (2nd Guards Bde.) on the right, and the 2nd Bn. Coldstream Guards (1st Guards Bde.) on the left.

As soon as the news of the capture of Valenciennes had been received, orders were issued for the resumption of the attack by the troops of the VI Corps on the 4th of November. Maubeuge was fixed upon as the ultimate objective of the Guards Division. The era of short objectives and limited advances was over for ever. Commanders and their staffs now calculated the movements of their troops in miles, not in yards. The enemy was no longer of much account. The only matters which seriously troubled the staff were the maintenance of communications and the supply of food and

* *See* " Sir Douglas Haig's Despatches," p. 294.

ammunition to the fighting troops. In their retreat the Germans displayed their usual thoroughness in the art of destruction; bridges and culverts were everywhere broken down or mined, and there were craters of varying dimensions along the roads. The R.E. and Pioneers, needless to say, had their hands full.*

For the operations on the 4th of November the divisional staff drew up two alternative plans—the decision as to which of them should be put into execution being made to depend upon the nature and extent of the enemy's opposition. The first plan contemplated an advance by the 1st and 2nd Guards Bdes. on the 4th of November to a depth of about three miles after which the 3rd Guards Bde. was to pass through them in order to carry on the advance for another three or four miles. The second plan, which was eventually adopted, was for the two leading brigades to move forward for a distance of about seven miles on the 4th and then for the 3rd Guards Bde. to continue the advance the following morning.

In the early hours of the 3rd of November the enemy's artillery became active on the front of the Guards Division, a heavy gas bombardment being put down in the area lying between the Quesnoy—Valenciennes railway line and the valley of the Rhonelle. This was probably to cover a German withdrawal farther to the north opposite the front of the First Army, news of which reached divisional headquarters about 10.45 a.m. Orders at once were sent to the brigades in the line to send forward patrols to find out whether or not the enemy was still in his positions opposite the Guards.

In the afternoon reports from the air stated that Villers Pol was deserted and that the advanced troops of the XVII Corps on the left of the Guards' front were already on the outskirts of Jenlain.

At about 4 p.m., however, a patrol of the 2nd Bn. Coldstream Guards, which had succeeded in reaching the Rhonelle river, was prevented by hostile shell fire from entering Villers Pol, and patrols of the 1st Bn. of the same regiment, which were feeling their way towards that village on the right

* See p. 234.

of the divisional front, also met with artillery resistance. Nevertheless, by about 5 p.m., the 2nd Guards Bde. was able to report that a patrol of the 1st Bn. Coldstream Guards had crossed the stream * and made its way into Villers Pol. The village at this period in the day was being bombarded both by the German and British guns, while the enemy's snipers were still in action in the neighbourhood of the church.

At 5.40 p.m. the troops of the XVII Corps were reported to be on the Le Quesnoy road south of Jenlain. An appreciable gain of ground, therefore, had been made during the day, which necessitated some alteration in the arrangements for the attack the following day. The first objective for the Guards had been fixed as the line of the Le Quesnoy—Jenlain road. It was now decided that the covering barrage for the Guards brigades, which was to be supplied by the divisional artillery on the left and the artillery of the 2nd Division on the right, should be put down on a protective line some way to the east of that road as, in view of the enemy's retirement, the positions actually reached by the Guards patrols at the time the attack was due to start might not be accurately known to the gunners.†

Zero hour was fixed for 6 a.m. on the 4th of November. On the right of the Guards the 62nd Division was ordered to advance from the line of the first objective—the Le Quesnoy—Jenlain road—an hour after zero, and during this hour the 2nd Guards Bde. was warned to take special measures to safeguard its right flank. On the left, the 24th Division (XVII Corps) was timed to begin its advance from the line of the first objective, without a covering barrage, half an hour before the Guards moved forward to the attack.

The night of the 3rd–4th of November was dark and wet, which made the movement of troops extremely difficult,

* The river was reported to be about 10 feet in width and fordable everywhere.

† *See* W.D., C.R.A., Guards Division, November, 1918. When the Guards Division relieved the 2nd Division in the line, the Guards divisional Artillery was formed into the left group, under the command of Lieut.-Colonel C. Vickery.

but, nevertheless, the leading battalions of the 1st and 2nd Guards Bdes. slowly felt their way forward.

The 1st Bn. Coldstream Guards of the latter brigade succeeded in making its way into Villers Pol about midnight. After some hand to hand fighting the few remaining Germans were driven out of the village. West of the Rhonelle, however, the Coldstream encountered a hostile artillery barrage and at 3.30 a.m. they reported that the advance of their leading companies had been checked mainly by machine-gun fire from the Le Quesnoy—Jenlain road.* At 5 a.m. the leading troops of the two brigades were reported to be on the line of the Orsinval—Villers Pol—St. Hubert road.

(3) Advance of the 1st and 2nd Guards Brigades, 4th of November.

The rain during the night was followed by a thick fog in the morning on the 4th of November, and, at 6 a.m., when the advance was begun, the troops had some difficulty in seeing their way and the high ground east of Villers Pol was entirely hidden from view. The fog, combined with the crowded state of all the roads which were blocked with advancing troops and traffic of every description, made the approach marches of the supporting battalions of the 1st and 2nd Guards Bdes. a difficult and laborious manœuvre. They contrived, however, to reach their respective assembly positions with more punctuality than might have been expected and the advance went forward without any noticeable delay.†

The British artillery put down an effective barrage at

---

* *See* W.D's., Guards Division and 2nd Guards Bde., November, 1918. The Coldstream asked for an artillery barrage to be put down west of the Le Quesnoy—Jenlain road, but this could not be provided in view of the operations later in the morning.

† " On the 4th the battalion (3rd Bn. Grenadier Guards) started to take up its assembly positions in rear of La Flaque Wood, and was much hampered on the approach march by the crowded state of the roads and the congestion of traffic." *See* " The Grenadier Guards in the Great War," vol. iii. p. 183. *See* also " The Irish Guards in the Great War," vol. i. p. 333.

zero hour beyond the Le Quesnoy—Jenlain road, and, at 7 a.m., the 74th and 75th Bdes., R.F.A., limbered up, forded the Rhonelle river and moved forward in support of the infantry, the 74th Bde. covering the 1st Guards Bde. on the left and the 75th Bde. the 2nd Guards Bde. on the right.

On the right of the divisional attack the 1st Bn. Coldstream Guards, after a certain amount of fighting, reached the first objective—the Le Quesnoy—Jenlain road—in good time.* The 3rd Bn. Grenadier Guards, which had crossed the Rhonelle by means of a single plank bridge under heavy hostile shell fire, then came up, and, passing through the Coldstream, continued the advance in touch with the 2nd Bn. Grenadier Guards on the front of the 1st Guards Bde. The area over which they were attacking was much enclosed and the Grenadiers were hampered in their advance by the enemy's machine-gun defence for which the country was admirably adapted. They succeeded, however, in driving the Germans out of Preux-au-Sart, where some prisoners were taken, and, by 4 p.m., their leading companies had reached the vicinity of Gommegnies. Here the progress of the battalion was temporarily checked by the fire of hostile machine guns posted in the houses in the village; but touch was well maintained with the troops on either flank, and, as soon as it became dusk, more ground was gained. The advance of the battalion throughout the day had been well supported by the 75th Bde., R.F.A.†

On the front of the 1st Guards Bde. the leading battalion, the 2nd Bn. Coldstream Guards, after some sharp fighting in which many Germans were killed, rather lost its direction in the fog and swung too much to the south-east. The 2nd Bn. Grenadier Guards, which followed the Coldstream, however, managed to keep its right direction and carried forward the attack towards Wargnies-le-Petit.‡ It met with a good deal of opposition. The enemy's machine gunners in a wood south-west of Wargnies-le-Petit held out very

---

* See W.D., 2nd Guards Bde., November, 1918. Eight German field guns were taken in this part of the field.
† See " The Grenadier Guards in the Great War," vol. iii. p. 180.
‡ Ibid.

stoutly and delayed the attack for some time and it was not until after some vigorous fighting, which resulted in the capture of some prisoners and 3 machine guns, that the advance could be resumed. The guns of A/74, R.F.A., which were brought up at a gallop to within a few hundred yards behind the infantry, proved of great assistance to the Grenadiers at this period in the day and materially aided their progress towards Wargnies-le-Petit.* The Guards' machine gunners were also particularly useful on the left of the attack, giving valuable support not only to the Guards, but also to the troops of the 24th Division.

At 6.30 p.m. the 1st Bn. Irish Guards, which had some difficulty in crossing the Rhonelle river in consequence of the congestion of traffic,† came up and continued the advance. As night came on, the enemy's defence appreciably weakened and the Irish Guards were able to establish a line east of Preux-au-Sart where, however, they do not appear to have been in touch with the troops of the XVII Corps on their left.‡

* The mobile section divisional trench-mortar batteries on the Wargnies-le-Petit—Villers Pol road also did good work, firing 40 rounds into the enemy's positions.

† " . . . when they reached the Rhonelle, its bridge being, of course, destroyed, and the R.E. working like beavers to mend it, they had to unship their Lewis-guns from the limbers, tell the limbers to come on when the bridge was usable, and pass the guns over by hand. While thus engaged the Scots Guards caught them up, went through them triumphantly, made exactly the same discovery that the Irish had done, and while they in turn were wrestling with their limbers, the Irish, who had completed their unshipping, went through them once more, and crossed the Rhonelle on the heels of the last man of the 3rd Grenadiers —' one at a time, being assisted up the bank by German prisoners.' " See " The Irish Guards in the Great War," vol. i. p. 333.

‡ See W.D., 1st Bn. Irish Guards, November, 1918. At 4 p.m. the number of prisoners reported by the division amounted to 2 officers and 119 other ranks belonging to the 4th, 206th and 216th Reserve Divisions. See W.D., Guards Division, November, 1918. But these figures are probably incomplete as the 2nd Bn. Grenadier Guards claims this number on the day's fighting in addition to 7 field guns and 8 machine guns, while the 2nd Bn. Coldstream Guards reports no less than 200 prisoners and 8 field guns taken. Cf. W.D's., 2nd Bn. Grenadier Guards and 2nd Bn. Coldstream Guards, November, 1918. The 3rd Bn. Grenadier Guards had 4 officers and 109 other ranks casualties; the 1st Bn. Scots Guards, which was in reserve all day, had 3 killed and

THE 3RD GUARDS BDE. ADVANCES

Meanwhile, at 9.40 a.m., a message had been received at divisional headquarters from an Intelligence officer at the VI Corps prisoners' cage stating that the enemy had no organized line of resistance west of Maubeuge. Orders were at once issued for the advance to be pressed energetically the following day, and cavalry and tanks were detailed by the VI Corps to act in cooperation with the infantry.*

(4) ADVANCE OF THE 3RD GUARDS BRIGADE, 5TH AND 6TH OF NOVEMBER.

The 3rd Guards Bde., whose battalions had spent most of the previous day in divisional reserve in Villers Pol, passed through the line of the 1st and 2nd Guards Bdes. and continued the advance at 6 a.m. on the 5th of November. The 1st Bn. Grenadier Guards was on the right and the 2nd Bn. Scots Guards on the left, the 1st Bn. Welsh Guards remaining in reserve.

Progress at first was easy and Amfroipret was captured without any difficulty. Some slight delay was then occasioned by the enemy's machine-gun fire, but the German opposition ceased as soon as the British field guns came into action and the troops were able to push on towards Bermeries.† In the afternoon the enemy made another stand, but, with the help of some tanks, the Guards drove him back and occupied Bermeries, establishing their line beyond it in touch with troops of the 62nd Division on the right and of the XVII Corps on the left.‡ The new front

---

30 wounded from shell fire ; the 2nd Bn. Grenadier Guards lost 3 officers and 108 other ranks and the 2nd Bn. Coldstream Guards, 5 officers and 85 other ranks.

* *See* W.D., Guards Division, November, 1918.

† The main difficulty against which the troops had to contend in this advance was the enclosed nature of the country. The maintenance of direction and connexion was no easy matter. " . . . when once a company or platoon had been sent off anywhere it could not be found again owing to the enclosed nature of the country. No communication between the various parties was possible, and the operations therefore developed into small isolated parties fighting independently of each other." *See* " The Grenadier Guards in the Great War," vol. iii. p. 174.

‡ By 4 p.m. the prisoners amounted to 1 officer and 192 other ranks.

was subjected to a good deal of hostile machine-gun fire from the railway crossing on the right and also from the spur of high ground just west of Buvignies, while the area in rear, especially the villages of Bermeries and Amfroipret, were shelled intermittently by the German heavy guns north-east of Bavai. Rain fell more or less continuously throughout the day, rendering the ground very heavy for the troops and the roads well-nigh impassable. This put a severe strain upon the horses of the artillery, but, nevertheless, the 74th and 75th Bdes., R.F.A., supported the advance of the infantry very effectively, forward sections of both brigades, located about 500 yards west of Bermeries, engaging the enemy's machine guns with much success.

The 1st Bn. Welsh Guards which, it will be remembered, was in brigade reserve, reached Amfroipret in the evening of the 5th of November. Here the battalion came in for a somewhat severe bombardment and had the misfortune to lose 31 men, one of the enemy's shells unluckily bursting in a barn where they were billetted.* Another shell struck brigade headquarters and Brig.-General Heywood was severely wounded. The command of the 3rd Guards Bde. devolved, therefore, upon Lieut.-Colonel J. Stirling, Scots Guards, until the arrival of Brig.-General J. Campbell, who assumed the command of the brigade on the 11th of November.†

At 6 a.m. on the 6th of November, a wet morning after a pouring wet night, the 3rd Guards Bde. resumed its advance. The 1st Bn. Grenadier Guards was still on the right of the line, but the 1st Bn. Welsh Guards had relieved the Scots Guards on the left.

The Grenadiers encountered no opposition until they reached the high ground north-west of Mecquignies where the fire of the German field guns and machine guns temporarily brought them to a standstill. By working along under cover of the houses and hedges which bordered the Amfroi-

---

* See " History of the Welsh Guards," pp. 276, 277.

† On the 5th of November the 1st Bn. Coldstream Guards lost its commanding officer, Lieut.-Colonel J. Brand having to be evacuated owing to sickness. His place was taken by Major the Honble. K. Digby.

pret—Mecquignies road, however, the company on the right succeeded in crossing the stream east of Bavisaux and in gaining touch with the advanced troops of the 62nd Division on the right. The enemy was then driven out of the grounds of Mecquignies Château, and at dusk a line was established just east of the village of Mecquignies in touch with the troops on each flank.*

The Welsh Guards, on the left of the divisional front, did not move forward until after the Grenadiers as they had to wait until the troops of the 24th Division on their left had drawn level with the Guards. When they did advance, however, they occupied Buvignies without meeting with much opposition, the field guns and machine guns † which accompanied them proving extremely useful in silencing the fire of the enemy's guns posted east of Bavai. As night set in posts were established on the Pont-sur-Sambre—Bavai road, with the left flank of the battalion thrown back towards Buvignies as there was as yet no sign of the approach of the 24th Division. On their right the Welsh Guards were in touch with the Grenadiers, and, by 2 a.m. on the 7th, their patrols were in Bavai. Here they took a few prisoners and were informed by the inhabitants, who welcomed them with embarrassing effusion, that the Germans had retired about two hours before their arrival to a line a few kilometres farther eastward.‡

* *See* " The Grenadier Guards in the Great War," vol. iii. p. 176.

† The Guards' machine gunners fired 3,000 rounds to cover the advance of the Welsh Guards towards Bavai and also carried out a useful area shoot later in the day.

‡ The following message from the VI Corps commander was received at divisional headquarters on the 6th of November :—" The Commander-in-Chief visited the corps commander to-day and expressed his high satisfaction at the manner in which the Guards and 62nd Divisions carried out the attack yesterday (the 4th of November), and the good progress which they have since made. He commended the good work of the commanders and staffs which had so greatly helped to bring about this result." *See* W.D., Guards Division, App. 1130.

(5) THE 2ND GUARDS BRIGADE RESUMES THE ADVANCE—EVENTS OF THE 7TH AND 8TH OF NOVEMBER—OCCUPATION OF MAUBEUGE.

In the early hours of the 7th of November the 2nd Guards Bde. passed through the 3rd Guards Bde., with the 1st Bn. Scots Guards on the right, the 1st Bn. Coldstream Guards in the centre and the 3rd Bn. Grenadier Guards on the left. The work of forming up for the advance was no easy matter owing to the mine craters which had completely destroyed the roads in many places. On the left, as the troops of the 24th Division had not put in an appearance at the time when the advance was due to go forward, the Grenadiers were called upon to form a defensive flank south-east of Bavai in the area of the XVII Corps. They were relieved here in the course of the afternoon and then advanced to Audignies Meanwhile, the Coldstream had pushed forward through that village and on towards La Longueville, cavalry patrols having reported that Malgarni was clear of the enemy. Between this latter village, however, and La Longueville hostile machine-gun fire checked their progress. On the right, the Scots Guards during the day gained possession of the high ground south of La Longueville and at dusk they were ordered to take that village. They pushed their way through it, but did not succeed in clearing it of Germans before darkness set in.*

Throughout the day's fighting the divisional Artillery was well forward with the infantry; B/74, R.F.A., on one occasion, coming into action at 700 yards' range and silencing some machine guns. The mobile trench-mortar section was unable to get into action until the following day.

During the afternoon an urgent message from the VI Corps reached divisional headquarters stating that a German officer carrying a flag of truce might be expected to make his appearance, and that, in the event of his doing so, he was to be conducted at once to the nearest divisional head-

---

* *See* W.D's., 2nd Guards Bde., 1st Bn. Coldstream Guards and 1st Bn. Scots Guards, November, 1918.

quarters.* This information was duly conveyed to the brigade in the line, but no such officer appeared. Later in the day, a telegram was received from the corps informing the divisional commander that the enemy appeared to be withdrawing opposite the whole length of the Third Army front, and that, if the infantry had lost touch with the German rear guards, the cavalry must regain it. The Guards were in touch with the enemy, but it was after the receipt of this message that the Scots Guards were ordered to take La Longueville. It was then too late in the evening to carry forward the advance that night, but Major-General Matheson gave the line of the Avesnes—Maubeuge—Mons road as the divisional objective for the next day.†

On the 8th of November the 2nd Guards Brigade still led the advance. The two battalions in the line—the 1st Bn. Scots Guards on the right, the 1st Bn. Coldstream Guards on the left—began moving forward at 6 a.m. The Scots Guards met with a stubborn resistance from the enemy's rear guards and made but slow progress, the company on the right suffering a good many casualties. The Coldstream, on the other hand, experienced no difficulty in driving the remaining Germans out of La Longueville. After emerging from that village, however, and passing through Les Mottes, their movements were considerably hampered by the fire of the enemy's machine guns posted south of Feignies. On their left the troops of the XVII Corps had made slower progress and at this period in the day were some distance in rear of the Guards' line. The Coldstream, therefore, were ordered to cooperate with the 24th Division which received instructions to work round Feignies.

After darkness set in, some more progress was made all along the line and the 2nd Guards Brigade reached the line of the Maubeuge—Valenciennes railway.

* *See* W.D., Guards Division, November, 1918.

† The Major-General circulated the following message to his troops in the evening of the 8th of November :—" The Major-General wishes to congratulate all troops and ranks of the Guards Division on splendid progress of last four days. He is confident that the Guards Division will capture Maubeuge." *See* W.D., Guards Division, App. 1299.

Such was the position at 6.15 p.m. when Major-General Matheson issued orders for the 1st Guards Bde. to take up the advance at 5 a.m. the following day and to capture Maubeuge. Soon afterwards, however, information was received at divisional headquarters to the effect that the next German line of resistance had been fixed west of Rouveroy—some distance east of Maubeuge—and that the enemy's rear guards had been ordered to hold back the British advance at all costs until the morning of the 9th of November.* The Major-General at once asked Brig.-General Sergison-Brooke whether his troops were equal to the task of pushing forward that night to Maubeuge. He was unwilling to ask the impossible, but the advisability of giving the Germans no respite was abundantly clear. The Brig.-General's reply was that his reserve battalion, the 3rd Bn. Grenadier Guards, had already been ordered to move on Maubeuge at 10 p.m. The battalion was to advance down the La Longueville—Maubeuge road, detaching troops to clear the suburbs as soon as it approached the town.†

Punctually at 10 p.m. in pitch darkness the 3rd Bn. Grenadier Guards, accompanied by two sections of machine gunners with their guns on pack animals, moved out of La Longueville, and, although their movements were much impeded by mine craters, the battalion marched steadily eastward towards Maubeuge. Except for a few desultory shots, they met with no opposition from the enemy and were in occupation of the citadel at Maubeuge shortly after 2 a.m. on the 9th of November. So rapid had been their advance that some German field guns which had been firing down the Maubeuge—Douzies road narrowly escaped capture. Only a few prisoners, however, were taken, as the bulk of the enemy's troops had made good their escape a few hours

---

* The 1st Bn. Coldstream Guards had captured near Feignies a runner belonging to the 2nd Bn. 86th Reserve Infantry Regiment. He was carrying orders for a German retirement at 6 p.m. through Feignies, Maireux, Bersillies and Villers Sire Nicole to Rouveroy. A rear guard consisting of one company was to hold the British at all costs until the morning of the 9th, in order to prevent them from feeling their way to the new positions during the 8th–9th.

† *See* W.D., Guards Division, November, 1918.

before the Guards entered the town.* The only inhabitant who could be found above ground when the relieving force entered Maubeuge was a priest, but later on in the morning the streets filled with excited men, women and children who welcomed the Guards with wild enthusiasm.

By 5 a.m., the leading troops of the 1st Guards Brigade †—the 1st Bn. Irish Guards on the right, the 2nd Bn. Coldstream Guards on the left—were crossing the railway through Douzies. A company of the former battalion ran into a party of the enemy, which surrendered after a few shots had been fired. This was the only resistance encountered on the road to Maubeuge, where, on their arrival, the two battalions moved straight through the town and took up a line beyond it.‡

At 10.50 a.m. a message from the 1st Guards Bde. was received at divisional headquarters stating that its troops were digging in on the road just west of Assevent and thence northward, with one battalion, the 2nd Bn. Grenadier Guards, astride the Maubeuge—Elesmes road as a defensive flank. At this period in the day the 24th Division was on the line of the railway north of Douzies and the cavalry reported that the country was clear of the enemy as far as Boussois, where German machine guns were still active.§

The Guards had now reached their final objective in the battle of the Sambre, ‖ but the Armistice had not yet been

* The town was searched for stragglers, but only 3 officers and 36 other Germans were collected. The task of the 2nd Guards Bde. was now ended. Since the 4th of November, the casualties in the brigade had amounted to about 25 per cent. of the infantry engaged. *See* W.D., 2nd Guards Bde., November, 1918.

† The brigade had been moving forward since the 7th of November in order to carry on the advance. It spent the 8th of November in billets on the southern outskirts of Bavai, where every cellar was packed with refugees.

‡ Major-General Matheson sent a special message of congratulation to the 1st Guards Bde. on the fine spirit which its troops had displayed in pushing through the town to take possession of the division's final objective on its eastern side.

§ *See* W.D., Guards Division, November, 1918.

‖ At 2 p.m. the following message was sent to the VI Corps :—
" Patrols of 3rd Grenadier Guards entered Maubeuge Citadel about 2 a.m. this morning, almost cutting off some enemy infantry and guns. Town clear of enemy by 3 a.m. About 50 prisoners captured. 1st Guards

signed and the task of continuing the pursuit of the enemy might yet lie before them. Patrols, therefore, were pushed forward behind the screen of cavalry and cyclists which now covered the front of the Third Army, and every precaution was taken to safeguard the new divisional line. Soon after 5 p.m. the 1st Guards Brigade reported that Elesmes, on the left of the Guards front, and the road running south-east of that village had been occupied early in the afternoon by troops of the XVII Corps, and that Boussois-la-Folie was clear of the enemy. The safety of the left flank of the division was thus secured, whilst on the right touch had been gained with the 62nd Division. Everything was in readiness, therefore, so far as the Guards were concerned, in the evening of the 9th of November, for the resumption of the advance. The R.E. and the 4th Bn. Coldstream Guards (Pioneers) had already begun the work of bridging the Sambre, and the infantry, although undoubtedly weary after its strenuous exertions, was fully capable of carrying on its pursuit of an enemy who was now plainly both beaten and demoralized. But the war was at an end. After a little over four years of bitter fighting the military power of Germany had been beaten to the ground. The acceptance of the Allied terms by her Government was the outward admission of her utter incapacity to continue the struggle which she had so wantonly provoked.*

Brigade is consolidating high ground north and east of town with outposts on Sambre and Salve bridges and east and north-east of Assevent. 62nd Division reported on high ground south-east of Maubeuge. No touch gained as yet as all Sambre bridges are destroyed. Our artillery in action north-east outskirts of Maubeuge. No sign of enemy this morning and no artillery fire. Infantry patrols have reached Assevent and Elesmes without gaining touch with enemy. Cavalry report enemy holding outskirts of Boussois. Maubeuge is very full of civilians. Maire is in charge. Am appointing Capt. Powell Town Commandant to assist him."

* " The strategic plan of the Allies had been realized with a completeness rarely seen in war. When the armistice was signed by the enemy his defensive powers had already been definitely destroyed. A continuance of hostilities could only have meant disaster to the German Armies and the armed invasion of Germany." *See* " Sir Douglas Haig's Despatches," p. 298. On the 11th of November " the British front extended over a distance of about 60 miles from the neighbourhood of Montbliart, east of Avesnes, to just north of Grammont." *Ib.* p. 311.

THE GUARDS' SHARE IN FINAL VICTORY

(6) THE ARMISTICE, 11TH OF NOVEMBER—ACHIEVEMENTS OF THE GUARDS DIVISION IN THE FINAL STAGES OF THE WAR.

Divisional headquarters was established in Maubeuge on the 10th of November, and, at 7 a.m. on the 11th, orders were received from the VI Corps with regard to the conditions of the Armistice.

When at 11 a.m. commanding officers announced the cessation of hostilities to their respective units, the news was received with the dignity and self-control which had marked the British soldier from the beginning to the end of the war. There was no exuberant outburst of enthusiasm, no wild scenes of rejoicing. Officers and men went quietly about their ordinary duties, scarcely realizing at first that the end had really come, that the long strain was over, and yet dimly conscious that they had lived through an epoch and that a great and wonderful success had crowned their efforts.* All ranks of the division were justly proud of their share in the final triumph, and greatly appreciated the congratulations which they received from their own commander and the VI Corps commander.†

Out of the eighty-one days which had elapsed since the 21st of August the Guards had spent fifty-four in the line, and twenty-nine of these had been days of hard fighting

* See "The Irish Guards in the Great War," vol. i. pp. 337, 338, in which Mr. Rudyard Kipling describes very fairly the first vague impressions made by the announcement of the Armistice on the mind of the fighting soldier. Cf. " Reminiscences of a Grenadier," p. 233, and " History of the Welsh Guards," p. 284.

† Major-General Matheson's address to the division is printed in full. See Appendix XI.

The following message was received from the VI Corps commander :—" My best congratulations to you all on the capture of Maubeuge and the dash displayed by the commander and troops who carried out the actual operation after previously fighting almost continuously for a week under difficult circumstances and in bad weather. The recovery by the Guards of the fortified city, whose name is associated with the stirring events of 1914, has come at a most important moment and, for this reason, is all the more a source of satisfaction to myself and all ranks of the VI Corps." See W.D., Guards Division, App. 1806.

against a determined and skilful enemy with his back to the wall. Between the Cojeul valley, from which the advance had started on the 21st of August and the fortress town of Maubeuge where it ended, the artillery and infantry of the division had captured a series of fortified ridges of great natural strength, and forced their way across the Canal du Nord and various rivers. In the first stages of their advance they had been called upon to cross great stretches of country which afforded but little cover against the organized defences of the enemy—in the later stages, when they had emerged into an area where the hostile trench systems no longer existed, they still encountered a tenacious resistance and had also to contend against conditions of ground and weather which taxed their powers of physical endurance to the uttermost. But throughout the advance from Moyenneville to Maubeuge—a distance of nearly 50 miles—the courage, the discipline and the endurance of all ranks never failed. The spirit of the division was indomitable. Officers and men of every unit, which belonged to it, had only one object in view—the maintenance of the glorious reputation which the Guards Division had won for itself at Loos and steadily augmented during its three years of strenuous existence. No troops, in the words of their commander, had " served their King and Country more devotedly in hard times as in soft; no troops had done more to win the prize . . . the victorious cessation of hostilities and the promise of a justly rewarding peace." *

(7) WORK OF THE DIVISIONAL R.E. AND 4TH BN. COLDSTREAM GUARDS (PIONEERS) AND THE DIVISIONAL SIGNAL COMPANY AND OF THE ADMINISTRATIVE SERVICES DURING THE CLOSING DAYS OF THE ADVANCE.

Enough has been said in the preceding narrative to give some faint idea of the magnitude of the task which fell upon the R.E. and 4th Bn. Coldstream Guards (Pioneers) during the concluding stages of the war.

* *See* Appendix XI.

ENGINEERING DIFFICULTIES OF THE ADVANCE 235

It is impossible to exaggerate the important bearing which their work had upon the rapidity of the advance and the successes achieved by the Guards. The destruction by the Germans of the railways and roads had been so systematic and effective that the British troops were called upon to move forward in an area which, to all intents and purposes, was without communications. The enclosed nature of the countryside with its large, cultivated fields, intersected with streams the bridges over which had been destroyed, also rendered difficult any extensive movement across country. The wet weather, too, that prevailed from the beginning of November onwards, intensified a hundredfold the work on the lines of communication. The roads and tracks were churned up by the ceaseless traffic into veritable morasses. It was only by the tireless labours of the R.E. and Pioneers that the various routes were kept open, and the supply of food and ammunition assured to the fighting troops. From the day the division returned to the line to the capture of Maubeuge on the 9th of November, work on the construction and maintenance of communications was kept up at high pressure both by day and night. The ford on the Rhonelle at Villers Pol was marked and the road through the village cleared very soon after the attack was delivered on the 4th of November. By 6 p.m. that day a trestle bridge had been placed across the Rhonelle despite the fact that the fire of some of the enemy's trench mortars had destroyed several of the wagons which were bringing up the materials, putting 2 men and 11 horses out of action.

After the passage of the Rhonelle had been effected, a bridge capable of carrying heavy traffic was erected over the stream at Wargnies-le-Petit. Craters in the existing roads were filled in with astonishing rapidity, while many new approaches and deviations for the facilitating of the traffic were constructed. Explosive charges left by the enemy under such culverts and bridges as he had not blown up before his departure were located and removed.

There can be no doubt that the Guards Division was well served by its R.E., and Major-General Matheson was only giving expression to the general opinion when he stated in his address to his troops on the 11th of November that " but for the determination shown by the Royal Engineers in overcoming the peculiar difficulties of a rapid advance in bad weather over natural and artificial obstacles of all sorts, the division could never have reached Maubeuge last week." The divisional Signal Company, to which the Major-General also alluded in his address, passed through the ordeal of the advance with great credit, successfully keeping up its communications by dint of much energy and determination on the part of all ranks.

The share of the Administrative Services in the final advance, as will have been already gathered by the reader, was an all-important one. In five days the Guards Division moved forward a distance of about nineteen miles, and throughout that period there were few, if any, cases of shortage in the supply of rations or of ammunition. Officers and men of the Army Service Corps and the D.A.C. worked with the same enthusiasm as the rest of the troops of the division. The organization of the R.A.M.C. also stood the test of mobile warfare, all ranks carrying out their arduous duties with great efficiency. The mobile dressing stations kept pace with the advance notwithstanding the many obstacles in their way, and the arrangements for the evacuation of the wounded worked with wonderful smoothness and celerity.

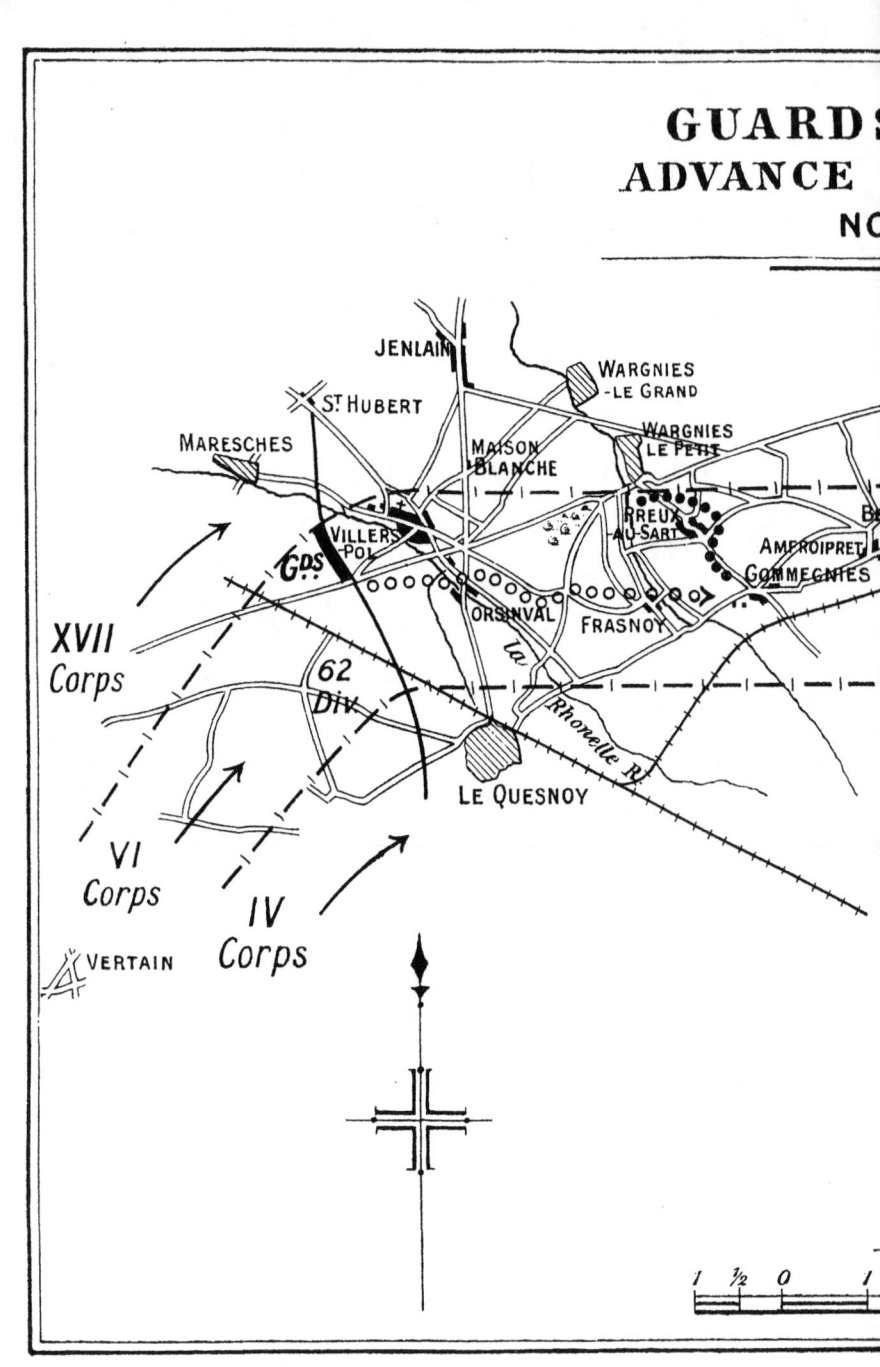

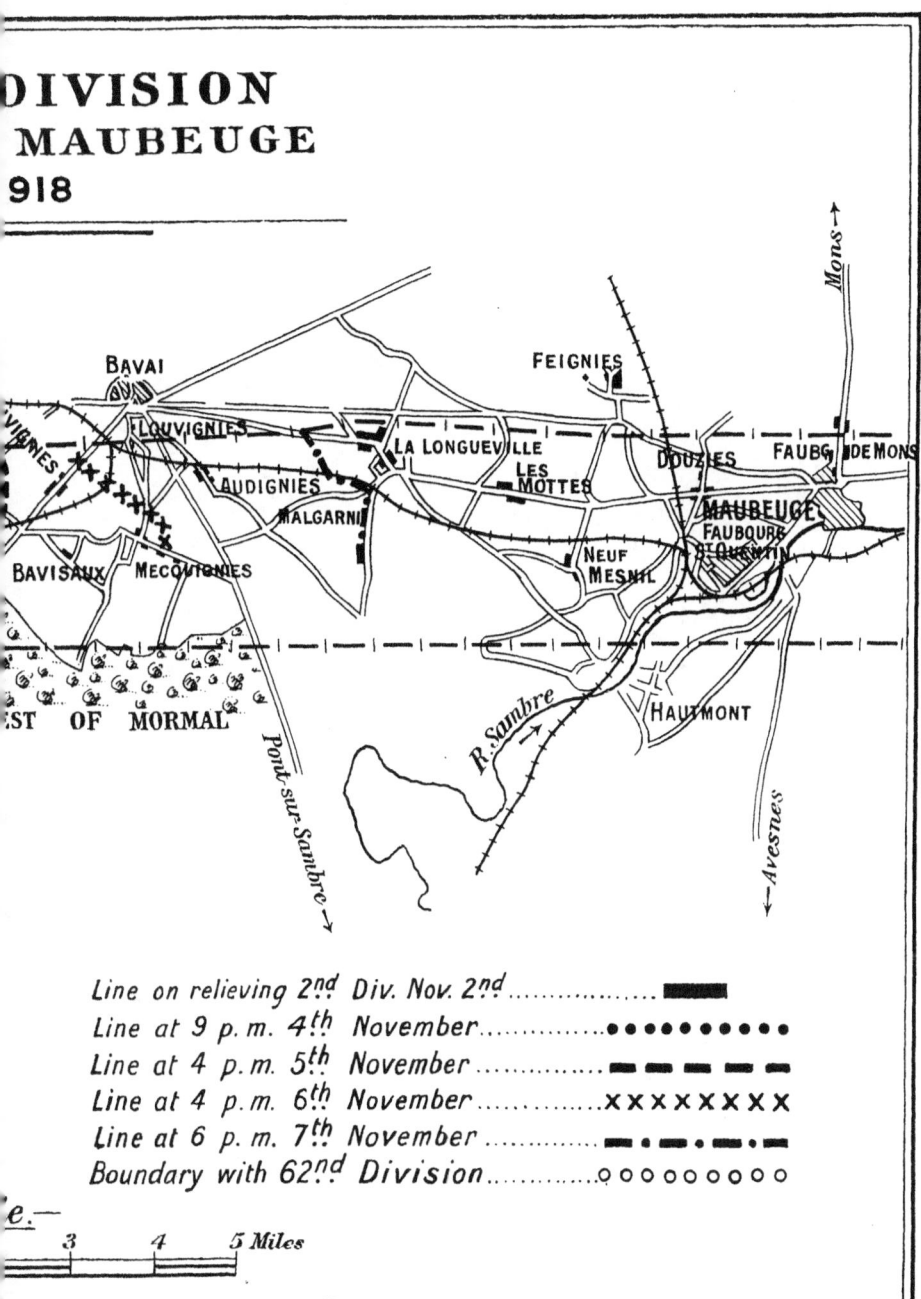

CHAPTER XXI

THE MARCH INTO GERMANY—THE GUARDS DIVISION AT COLOGNE—RETURN TO ENGLAND—THE TRIUMPHAL MARCH THROUGH LONDON.

The days in Maubeuge passed pleasantly for the Guards Division. The conditions were agreeable. The town was practically undamaged, and the inhabitants vied with each other in their hospitality and kindness towards their deliverers. The troops, who, it is scarcely necessary to say, behaved with their invariable courtesy and good nature, were immensely popular with all classes of the townspeople.

Every trace of the wear and tear of the recent fighting and of the long and muddy marches was speedily removed, and, in an astonishingly short space of time, the troops of the Guards Division had reassumed their customary parade ground appearance; the horses and mules their sleek, well groomed condition; the guns and vehicles their neatness and polish.

On the 14th of November a very impressive Mass and Service of thanksgiving was celebrated in the Collegiate Church. It was attended by Major-General Matheson and his Staff, the three Brigadiers, about 200 officers and the chaplains of the different denominations, and the Roman Catholic troops of the division. The sermon was preached by the Rev. J. Scannell, the senior Roman Catholic chaplain in the division, and the 1st Bn. Irish Guards provided a Guard of Honour in the Sanctuary. The band of the Coldstream Guards played the accompaniment of the hymns, and the trumpeters of the divisional Artillery sounded the salute at the Consecration. At the conclusion of this religious service, a civic ceremonial took place in the principal square of the town at which the Mayor presented a French flag to the Guards Division in commemoration of its relief of Maubeuge and Major-General Matheson gave a silver cup to the municipality. Subsequently, he entertained at luncheon the Mayor and municipal officials. The day concluded with a tattoo by the massed drums of the division in the square.

Two days later the division held its own Thanksgiving Service in the barrack square. The simplicity of this service, and the earnestness of the congregation, will always live in the memory of those who were present.*

The preliminary instructions with regard to the march into Germany were issued by the VI Corps on the 15th of November. The corps was to move forward in two columns. On the right the 62nd Division was to lead the advance, followed by the 3rd Division; on the left the Guards Division was to lead, with the 2nd Division in rear.†

In his orders for the march Major-General Matheson divided the division into the following 4 groups :—

"A" Group—1st Guards Bde.; 55th Field Company, R.E.; No. 2 Company Guards Machine-Gun Bn.; 74th Bde., R.F.A.; 280th A.T. Coy., R.E.; Section 174th Tunnelling Coy., R.E.; 4th Field Ambulance; 3rd Company Divisional Train.

"B" Group—2nd Guards Bde.; 75th Field Company, R.E.; 4th Bn. Coldstream Guards (Pioneers); 9th Field Ambulance; 4th Company Divisional Train.

"C" Group—3rd Guards Bde.; 76th Field Company, R.E.; Guards Machine-Gun Bn. (less No. 2 Co.); 3rd Field Ambulance; 2nd Company Divisional Train.

"D" Group—75th Bde., R.F.A.; 76th (Army) Bde., R.F.A.; Divisional Ammunition Column; 1st Company Divisional Train; 46th Mobile Veterinary Section.

* *See* "A Private in the Guards," by Stephen Graham, p. 295.
† The VI Corps was now posted to the Fourth Army, and subsequently to the Second Army when it was decided that the area in Germany allotted to the British troops was too narrow to admit of the employment of more than a single Army Command. *See* "Sir Douglas Haig's Despatches," p. 316.

RECEPTION IN BELGIUM

For the first few days of the march, it was judged necessary that a Pioneer sub-group should precede the division. This formation, which was placed under the command of the C.R.E., consisted of all the Royal Engineer units enumerated, the 4th Bn. Coldstream Guards (Pioneers) and the 1st Bn. Irish Guards.

Major-General Matheson, when issuing his orders for the advance, seized the opportunity of reminding all ranks that the march would be a trying one.

The communications in the country through which the division would pass were broken and disorganized, and the troops would be more dependent than ever upon good staff work. He stated that the higher authorities seemed " to be anxious lest the staff work of divisions and brigades should break down," but that he himself was confident that " the staff work of the Guards Division would be equal to the test." *

Late on the 17th of November the battalions of the 4th Guards Bde., which had been entrained at Criel Plage on the 14th and had reached Cambrai the following day, arrived in lorries at Maubeuge. Each battalion was reabsorbed in its own brigade.

The March to the Rhine began on the 18th of November in frosty weather, divisional headquarters being established at Binche the following day,† where an address of welcome was presented to the Major-General by the Burgomaster, and the townspeople gave the troops an enthusiastic welcome to Belgium. On the 20th the VI Corps commander, with

---

* *See* W.D., Guards Division, App. 1316. During the march the troops had to wear their steel helmets, and each man carried his gas mask, 120 rounds of ammunition, rifle and usual accoutrements.

† " It was misty and frosty, and it threatened to snow as we marched out in our long files. . . . The road was hard after several days' frost. We were all provided with gloves, which kept our fingers from being chilled, and the march was pleasant. We must have afforded a strange contrast, all rosy-cheeked, well-equipped, well-set-up, marching with decision and style, we and the returning British army of prisoners we met on the road, the haggard-faced soldiers, worn-out and emaciated, who in fives and sixes came struggling in from Namur and Charleroi, where they had been liberated in accordance with the Armistice conditions." *See* " A Private in the Guards," p. 299.

Major-General Matheson, led the division from Marchienne-au-Pont into Charleroi, and the Fourth Army commander took the salute in the front of the Hotel de Ville. The troops received a tremendous ovation from the crowd.*

Owing to the bad state of the roads the advance was not resumed until the 24th of November, but, by the 30th, the Meuse had been crossed and Trieu had been reached.† About this date it was decided at a divisional conference to send Colour Parties to England to fetch the Colours of each battalion. Plans were also discussed for the provision of recreation and amusements for all ranks during the coming winter in Germany.

Up to this period in the advance the R.E. and Pioneers had found a certain amount of work to do in facilitating the movements of the columns in rear, but it was now found possible to break up the Pioneer sub-group and its various units rejoined the groups to which they had been originally attached. The 74th Bde., R.F.A., joined the remainder of the divisional artillery and a heavy artillery group, consisting of the 63rd Mobile Bde., R.G.A., with a detachment of Lovat's Scouts, came under the command of the Guards Division. The Guards Machine-Gun Regiment from this time onwards marched as a complete unit with " C " Group.‡

As the division approached the German frontier the attitude of the civilian population became far less friendly,

* " On admirait la tenue irréprochable, la propreté, l'équipement, l'allure alerte, le flegme de ces troupes qui revenaient cependant du combat. . . . La foule enthousiasmée ne pouvait se lasser d'admirer nos libérateurs et surtout de les acclamer chaudement. Ce qui a surtout capté notre admiration enthousiaste, dans ce défile triumphal des troupiers britanniques, c'est le caractère de tenacité froide et indomptable, ce trait de volonté indémontable et d'inaltérable endurance que nous lisions sur ces faces rasées et energiques ; volonté, tenacité et endurance qui furent le principe de l'effondrement militaire de la Germanie et une des causes essentielles de l'écrasante victoire de nos armes." Extract from *Le Pays Wallon*, 21st of November, 1918.

† Whilst at Trieu two wild boar hunts were organized by the officers of the 1st Bn. Coldstream Guards. The Brigadier and staff of the 2nd Guards Bde. and many officers from the Guards battalions took part in these hunts. On the first day one pig and two hares were killed ; on the second day four pigs. *See* W.D., 1st Bn. Coldstream Guards, November, 1918.

‡ *See* W.D., Guards Division, December, 1918.

THE 2ND GUARDS BDE. REACHES COLOGNE

and in some villages there was a certain amount of difficulty with regard to billetting. In this part of the country the inhabitants had seen little of the war, and had prospered under German rule.* The weather, too, had broken by this time, and the triumphal march had become a somewhat long drawn out and wearisome procession, for the Guards were " treading on the tail " of the Canadian Corps in front of them, and there were blocks and delays on the road.

On the 11th of December, however, the leading Guards brigade crossed the frontier into Germany at Poteau, and the following day the 2nd Guards Bde. crossed it at Pont Brucken in the pouring rain. It was rather a dreary entrance into the Promised Land.†

Orders were now received for one brigade of the division to proceed to Cologne by train. The choice fell upon the 2nd Guards Bde., which was entrained at Weywertz on the 4th of December after the 4th Bn. Coldstream Guards (Pioneers) had joined the divisional Artillery and the 75th Field Company, R.E., the 3rd Guards Bde. The brigade reached Ehrenfeld station at 10.30 p.m. the same night. No guides had been provided, but the services of some German policemen were requisitioned and the troops found excellent accommodation in the Rhiel barracks near the Rhine in the northern suburbs of Cologne. When the Commander-in-Chief arrived in Cologne, on the 16th, the 3rd

---

* At Petit Han on the 6th of December the 2nd Bn. Irish Guards found that " the attitude of civilians was not very friendly. The billetting party had great difficulty in getting into some houses, especially into one house where the owner shook her fist, violently calling down curses on them the while, and was only persuaded to desist by being locked in her room for two hours." *See* W.D., 2nd Bn. Irish Guards, December, 1918.

† The 1st Bn. Coldstream Guards records that " the natives were very mild and, on the whole, ready to help." The 1st Bn. Scots Guards states that " the population were quite friendly with the exception of a pestilential priest who came to complain in the evening that one of the officers had a fox terrier in his bedroom—complaint summarily dismissed." *See* W.D's., 1st Bn. Coldstream and 1st Bn. Scots Guards, December, 1918. " The Germans seemed to be rather afraid of us, and servile, but very poor. Tottering old men insisted on shaking hands with us. The girls of the place seemed to be carefully kept out of our sight." *See* " A Private in the Guards," p. 321.

Bn. Grenadier Guards mounted a Guard of Honour and the massed drums of the 2nd Guards Bde. took part in the ceremonial.*

Meanwhile, the remainder of the division continued its march. The attitude of the Germans was marked throughout the advance by an apparent indifference to the arrival of the British troops, but in almost every village the inhabitants seemed anxious to please. On the march between Lechnich and Efferen some civilians appear to have been rude and ill-mannered,† but this seems to have been the exception, not the rule. Billets and other requirements were usually furnished without demur, and the good discipline and splendid appearance of the troops obviously impressed the people. They had witnessed and suffered from the disorderly return home of their own defeated army, and the contrast which was afforded by the behaviour of the Guards Division made them appreciate the military worth of the British Army.‡

On the 18th of December divisional headquarters was opened in the Excelsior Hotel at Cologne,§ and, by the 21st, on which day Major-General Matheson issued the following order to his troops, almost all the units of the division were located in their respective quarters in and round the city :—

---

* *See* W.D., 2nd Guards Bde., December, 1918.

† *See* W.D., 1st Bn. Grenadier Guards, December, 1918.

‡ A small landowner near Hallenthal stated that the German troops had looted the village as they retreated in great disorder. There were apparently numbers of deserters and discipline had ceased to exist. *See* W.D., Guards Division, App. 1401.

§ During their stay in Germany the units of the division were located as follows :—the 1st Guards Bde. and the Guards Machine-Gun Battalion, in the schools at Ehrenfeld which was the divisional railhead from the 25th of December onwards ; the 2nd Guards Bde. in the Rhiel barracks in the northern part of Cologne ; the 3rd Guards Bde. in the schools and gymnasium at Sulz on the western outskirts of Cologne ; the 4th Bn. Coldstream Guards (Pioneers) at Lindenthal to which place divisional headquarters was subsequently moved ; the divisional Artillery at Lövenich Königsdorf, Brauweiller and Widdersdorf ; the R.E. at Braunsfeld. The Trench-Mortar Batteries had been sent back to Solesmes when the march to Germany began. Their *personnel* were employed there in unloading duties until after Christmas, but then rejoined the division and were billetted at Mengenich.

"The Division has completed the march to the Rhine, on which it started from Maubeuge on Nov. 17th and 18th, 1918. The distance from Maubeuge by the route assigned to us was 180 miles. The actual distance covered by units in reaching their billets has been considerably greater. From Charleroi to Zulpich the route lay through the mountainous country of the Ardennes, the natural difficulties of which for troops were greatly aggravated by broken roads, heavy mud and constant rain. The good discipline shown through the march reflects great credit on the troops who had already been engaged in continuous fighting for two and a half months before.

"The greatest difficulties on the march have been connected with billetting and supply. My D.A.A.G., the Staff Captains of all Groups, and my Camp Commandant have had a very trying task to perform and I wish to acknowledge here the keenness and thoroughness with which, against great difficulties, their work has been done. I also owe special thanks to my D.A.Q.M.G., my Senior Supply Officer, and all ranks of the Army Service Corps for the manner in which they have dealt with the difficulties of supply.

"I have learnt from more than one source that the smartness and soldierly bearing of the troops of the Guards Division have made a deep impression on the population of those German towns and villages through which they have passed. All ranks of the Division will realize how important it is to maintain this impression, and to spread it through Germany as widely as we can. I count on all so to conduct themselves that the reputation of the Guards Division during the period of occupation in no way falls below its reputation during the war."

During their stay in Germany the Guards battalions returned to the ordinary routine of peace time. Officers and men alike understood that it was the duty of " the Brigade " to set an example of smartness and good discipline to the whole Army of Occupation, and to make the Germans appreciate to the full that British troops were just as well-versed in the details of drill and military training as were their own men in the days before the war. And so, throughout these weeks at Cologne, the Guards drilled, went their route marches, and carried out their guard-mounting duties with the steadiness and precision which are so familiar to the citizens of London—a demonstration of military efficiency which probably was not lost upon the German spectators who always crowded to watch them mounting guard.* In January, Colour Parties were sent to England for the Regimental Colours, and their return was the occasion of ceremonial parade at which H.R.H. the Prince of Wales presented a Union Colour to the 4th Bn. Grenadier Guards.† But although the division thus continued to uphold its reputation as a military machine, the energies of its commander and his staff were mainly devoted during this period to the task of tackling the many problems which arose in connexion with the demobilization of the army. The months which followed the Armistice were not easy ones for those responsible for the discipline and good order of the British fighting forces. The insistent scream raised in a large section of the English Press for their instant discharge not unnaturally had a most demoralizing effect upon the troops, and, in France at any rate, led to a certain amount of trouble, the consequences of which might have been far more serious than they were had it not been for the common sense and tact displayed by the authorities. In the Guards Division there was, it is needless to say, no kind of trouble or insubordination, but everything that was possible was done by the officers for the amusement of their men and for the keeping of their minds occupied during the trying period of waiting for their discharge.

The troops were comfortably lodged, and there were

---

* " We were very comfortable ; the civilians were civil, even cringing ; we had no trouble from anyone ; our methods were firm ; salutes were required from anyone in uniform, and civilians, if spoken to, had to remove their hats. When we were on the march anyone failing to comply with these rules was immediately arrested and taken for a walk. . . . Our daily work consisted of drill or a route march. . . . we were on guard three days out of every nine ; there were various guards on all the headquarters and all the bridges. . . . We used to go on guard as much like the King's Guard as we could, and tried to impress the inhabitants. I don't know if we did, but there was always a crowd to watch guard mountings." *See* " Reminiscences of a Grenadier," pp. 238, 239.

† *See* " The Grenadier Guards in the Great War," vol. iii. p. 195.

opportunities for recreation and entertainment in Germany which were sadly lacking in the devastated area in France. Much football was played in Cologne, and men, as well as officers, frequented the Opera and other places of amusement, where English pierrot shows and pantomimes were given. In Cologne, too, there were schools and colleges which could be requisitioned, and so it was really possible to carry on the educational courses which were intended to assist the troops on their return to civil life. Only those who are acquainted with the subject have any idea of the Herculean task imposed upon regimental officers by the scheme of education evolved by G.H.Q. in France after the Armistice. As a rule, they were called upon to make bricks without straw—to educate their men without the usual accessories of books, pens and paper, and, as often as not, in ruined villages in which there was no accommodation to hold their classes. But these drawbacks to efficiency did not exist, at any rate to the same extent, for the Army of Occupation in Germany, and the officers of the Guards Division, like those of other divisions, struggled manfully, and, it is hoped, successfully, with the new duties which the coming of peace had thrust upon them.

The demobilization of the division began soon after Christmas, and, by the middle of February, 1919, the numbers of the troops had been so much diminished that it was found necessary to break up the 4th Bn. Grenadier Guards, the 4th Bn. Coldstream Guards and the 2nd Bn. Irish Guards, in order to keep the remaining battalions up to strength.

At the end of the month the Guards began their return journey to England and by the middle of March all the battalions were home again. On the 22nd of that month the division, preceded by detachments of the Household Cavalry, had the honour of marching past His Majesty the King at Buckingham Palace, and then through the streets of London to the Mansion House. It was a triumphal procession, a fitting conclusion to the division's glorious record in the war. Thousands of spectators lined the streets and filled the windows, giving the troops an enthusiastic welcome.* At their head rode Lord Cavan, followed by H.R.H. the Prince of Wales and two members of the XIV Corps staff. And then came the battalions of the three Guards brigades, led by Major-Generals Feilding and Matheson, and the brigadiers and other leaders who had commanded them throughout the war. Demobilized officers and other ranks in plain clothes followed their respective battalions, and wounded men who could not walk and were conveyed in lorries shared in the triumphal progress. Representatives of the Artillery with their guns, and of the R.E., the R.A.M.C. and R.A.S.C. who had belonged to the Guards Division followed the Infantry.

After the march was ended every man who had taken part in it was given the following message from the King :—

"OFFICERS, NON-COMMISSIONED OFFICERS, AND MEN OF THE GUARDS DIVISION,—It is with pride and satisfaction that I take the Salute of the Guards Division on this memorable occasion of their triumphal march through London, and on the same spot where Queen Victoria in July, 1856, welcomed back three battalions of Guards from the Crimea.

"The Guards Division, first formed in 1915, practically served in every sector of the Western Front, and my visits to the British Armies in the field gave me opportunities of seeing the battle grounds on which it has made so great and enduring a name.

"The Division, which commenced its brilliant career at Loos, took a prominent part in 1916 in the hard fighting on the Somme, when on two occasions three Battalions of the same regiment were in the line together.

"At the third battle of Ypres the Division responded to the call of its Commander by capturing all allotted objectives in three separate attacks.

"The fighting round Cambrai, and the historical counter-attack which broke up a dangerous German thrust at Gouzeaucourt, will ever be remembered.

"During the critical days of 1918 an heroic resistance was offered to the vigorous assaults of an enemy numerically

* "In the City the crowds were, if possible, denser and more enthusiastic than in the West End, and the scene at the Guildhall was a sight that no one will forget." See "The Grenadier Guards in the Great War," vol. iii. p. 198.

stronger and elated by success, while during our subsequent rapid advance the efforts of the Division were crowned by the capture of Maubeuge, the flag of which is carried on parade to-day, a grateful tribute from its citizens.

"Nor do I forget the other Arms which enabled the three Brigades of Guards for the first time in the history of the British Army to fight as a Division. The Guards Division Royal Artillery, composed of the 74th and 75th Brigades of Field Artillery; the Guards Division Royal Engineers, formed of the 55th, 75th and 76th Field Companies; the 3rd, 4th and 9th Field Ambulances, constituting the Guards Division Field Ambulance, and the Guards Division Train and Supply Column.

"All these, inspired by the best traditions of their respective regiments and corps, fostered the invincible spirit and dogged determination of a Division which knew no defeat.

"Now, after three and a half years of close cooperation in the field, through the ever-changing fortunes of war, the units of the Guards Division are about to separate.

"As your Colonel-in-Chief I wish to thank you one and all for faithful and devoted services, and to bid you Godspeed. May you ever retain the same mutual feelings of true comradeship which animated and ennobled the life of the Guards Division.

"(Signed) GEORGE, R.I."

His Majesty's inspiring words are a fitting conclusion to this history of the Guards Division. They summarize the part which the division took in the Great War. Whatever their leaders demanded of them, the troops of the Guards Division did manfully and well. They gave an example of unflinching courage and endurance to the whole Army, and on more than one occasion—at Loos, at Gouzeaucourt, in front of Hazebrouck—their discipline and unyielding steadfastness saved a critical situation.* They proved on

---

* "The sterner the discipline the better the soldier, the better the army. . . . A strong discipline is the foundation of heroic exploits in the field. In time of necessity, when a thousand men must fight to the last though all be wounded or killed, in order that a much larger number may march into safety, it is only a strongly disciplined body that will not accept prematurely the chance to surrender." *See* "A Private in the Guards," p. 1.

many a stricken field the inestimable value in war of good training and *esprit de corps*.

Armies can be improvised, courage is the common heritage of the whole British race; but in the hour of trial, when defeat hangs in the balance, implicit reliance can only be placed in well-disciplined troops whose moral is based upon a feeling of mutual confidence between the officers and their men. And this confidence can only exist when all ranks are imbued with the same pride in their regiment and are inspired by an ideal of a great tradition and of a common patriotism. The individual may perish, but the regiment lives for ever.

> " Remember, then, whichever way the balance doth decline,
> If God is in His Heaven, and the Guards are in the line,
> All's well ! "

APPENDICES

APPENDICES

		PAGE
I.	Composition of the Guards Division on its Formation	251
II.	Succession of Officers, Staffs and Commands	253
III.	Victoria Crosses won by Officers and Other Ranks	269
IV.	Guards Division Operation Orders	278
V.	Note on the Reserve Battalions of the Guards Regiments	311
VI.	Origin and History of the Guards Machine-Gun Regiment	314
VII.	Household Brigade Officer Cadet Battalion	318
VIII.	Guards Entrenching Battalion	320
IX.	Guards Division Base Depôt at Harfleur	322
X.	Foreign Service of the Bands of the Regiments of Guards	324
XI.	Address by the Major-General Commanding the Guards Division on Armistice Day, 1918	326
XII.	Notes on Dress and Equipment of the Foot Guards during the War, 1914–1918	329
XIII.	Race Card. The Calais First Spring Meeting	333

APPENDIX I

COMPOSITION OF THE GUARDS DIVISION ON ITS FORMATION.

1st Guards Brigade ..
- 2nd Bn. Grenadier Guards.
- 2nd Bn. Coldstream Guards.
- 3rd Bn. Coldstream Guards.
- 1st Bn. Irish Guards.

2nd Guards Brigade ..
- 3rd Bn. Grenadier Guards.
- 1st Bn. Coldstream Guards.
- 1st Bn. Scots Guards.
- 2nd Bn. Irish Guards.

3rd Guards Brigade ..
- 1st Bn. Grenadier Guards.
- 4th Bn. Grenadier Guards.
- 2nd Bn. Scots Guards.
- 1st Bn. Welsh Guards.

Pioneer Battalion .. 4th Bn. Coldstream Guards.

Divisional Artillery ..
- *61st Howitzer Brigade, R.F.A.
- †74th Brigade, R.F.A.
- †75th Brigade, R.F.A.
- †76th Brigade, R.F.A.
- Guards divisional Ammunition Column.

Divisional Engineers ..
- ‡55th Field Company, R.E.
- †75th Field Company, R.E.
- †76th Field Company, R.E.
- †Guards divisional Signal Company.

Divisional Troops ..
- §Household Cavalry divisional Squadron.
- §Household Cavalry Cyclist Company.

Divisional Train and Supply Column ‖
- Nos. 436, 11, 124 and 168 Companies, A.S.C.
- 9th M.T. Company, A.S.C,

* From the 11th Division.
† From the 16th Division.
‡ From the 7th Division.
§ The Divisional Squadron and Cyclist Company were disbanded in the spring of 1916 and the *personnel* returned to their units. In July, 1917, the Guards Employment Company was formed in England and sent out to France to join the division.
‖ The Guards divisional Train Companies were numbered 1, 2, 3 and 4 G.D. Companies of the Train on joining the division. Their original numbers were 436, 11, 124 and 168 Companies, A.S.C. The Guards divisional Mechanical Transport Company which accompanied the division throughout the campaign was really a corps and not a divisional unit.

APPENDIX I

MEDICAL SERVICES	..	*4th Field Ambulance (attached 1st Guards Brigade). 9th Field Ambulance (attached 2nd Guards Brigade). 3rd Field Ambulance (attached 3rd Guards Brigade).
ORDNANCE SERVICE	..	A.O. Corps Detachment.
VETERINARY SERVICE	..	46th Mobile Veterinary Section.

* From the 2nd Division, where it had been attached to the 4th (Guards) Brigade.

APPENDIX II

SUCCESSION OF OFFICERS, STAFFS AND COMMANDS.

From the Formation of the Guards Division, August, 1915, to its Return to England, March, 1919.

(1) GENERAL OFFICERS COMMANDING.

Rank.	Name.	Unit.	From.	To.
Major-General	F. R. Earl of Cavan, K.P., C.B., M.V.O.	Grenadier Guards	6/8/15	2/1/16
Major-General	G. P. T. Feilding, C.B., C.M.G., D.S.O.	Coldstream Guards	3/1/16	30/9/18
Major-General	T. G. Matheson, C.B., C.M.G.	Coldstream Guards	1/10/18	To return of division to England.

(2) PERSONAL STAFF.

Rank	Name	Unit	From	To
Captain	C. M. Headlam	Bedfordshire Yeomanry	11/8/15	3/1/16
Lieut.	O. Lyttelton	Grenadier Guards	11/8/15	14/10/15
Captain	Hon. P. W. Legh	Grenadier Guards	11/12/15	2/1/16
Captain	R. Clutterbuck	Coldstream Guards	24/1/16	9/6/16
Lieut.	Hon. E. Elliot	Lothians & Border Horse (Scots Gds.)	—	—
Captain	G. A. C. Lane	Coldstream Guards	10/6/16	8/11/17
Lieut.	J. J. A. Viscount Holmesdale	Coldstream Guards	1/1/17	2/6/17
2/Lieut.	R. D. Gamble	Coldstream Guards	2/6/17	16/9/17
Lieut.	H. S. Morris	Coldstream Guards	16/9/17	—
Captain	F. F. Graham	Irish Guards	4/2/18	25/4/18
Lieut.	J. R. Saunders	Coldstream Guards	1/8/18	12/9/18
Lieut.	M. Duquenoy	Grenadier Guards	1/10/18	To return of division to England.
Lieut.	P. Guthrie	1st Life Guards	23/9/18	To return of division to England.

APPENDIX II

(3)
GENERAL STAFF.
GENERAL STAFF OFFICERS, 1ST GRADE.

Rank.	Name.	Unit.	From.	To.
Colonel	HON. W. P. HORE-RUTHVEN, C.M.G., D.S.O.	Scots Guards	25/8/15	6/3/16
Lt.-Colonel	C. P. HEYWOOD, D.S.O.	Coldstream Guards	21/3/16	4/9/17
Lt.-Colonel	HON. A. G. A. HORE-RUTHVEN, V.C., C.M.G., D.S.O.	Welsh Guards	5/9/17	25/12/17
Lt.-Colonel	R. S. McCLINTOCK, D.S.O.	Royal Engineers	26/12/17	31/3/18
Lt.-Colonel	E. W. M. GRIGG, D.S.O., M.C.	Grenadier Guards	1/4/18	3/2/19
Lt.-Colonel	W. H. DIGGLE, M.C.	Grenadier Guards	4/2/19	To return of division to England.

(4)
GENERAL STAFF.
GENERAL STAFF OFFICERS, 2ND GRADE.

Major	N. R. DAVIDSON, D.S.O.	Royal Artillery	25/8/15	2/8/16
Captain	E. SEYMOUR, M.V.O., D.S.O.	Grenadier Guards	3/8/16	26/8/17
Captain	M. B. BECKWITH-SMITH, D.S.O., M.C.	Coldstream Guards	27/8/17	2/1/18
Major	H. L. AUBREY-FLETCHER, M.V.O., D.S.O.	Grenadier Guards	3/1/18	5/12/18
Major	J. N. BUCHANAN, M.C.	Grenadier Guards	6/12/18	19/2/19
Major	M. B. BECKWITH-SMITH, D.S.O., M.C.	Coldstream Guards	20/2/19	To return of division to England.

(5)
GENERAL STAFF.
GENERAL STAFF OFFICERS, 3RD GRADE.

Captain	G. E. C. RASCH, D.S.O.	Grenadier Guards	17/8/15	1/12/15
Captain	A. F. SMITH, M.C.	Coldstream Guards	3/12/15	4/2/16
Captain	E. W. M. GRIGG, M.C.	Grenadier Guards	5/2/16	16/7/16
Captain	H. L. AUBREY-FLETCHER, M.V.O.	Grenadier Guards	17/7/16	27/12/16
Captain	R. O. HAMBRO	Coldstream Guards	28/12/16	26/2/18

OFFICERS, STAFFS AND COMMANDS

Rank.	Name.	Unit.	From.	To.
Captain	L. M. GIBBS, M.C.	Coldstream Guards	27/2/18	3/5/18
Lieut. (A/Capt.)	J. N. BUCHANAN, M.C.	Grenadier Guards	4/5/18	2/9/18
Captain	H. R. HELY-HUTCHISON, M.C.	Irish Guards	3/9/18	1/1/19
Captain	A. H. PENN, M.C.	Grenadier Guards	2/1/19	To return of division to England.

(6)

ADMINISTRATIVE STAFF.

A.A. & Q.M.G.

Lt.-Colonel	W. H. DARELL, D.S.O.	Coldstream Guards	16/7/15	23/12/16
Lt.-Colonel	F. G. ALSTON, D.S.O.	Scots Guards	25/12/16	5/12/18
Lt.-Colonel	H. L. AUBREY-FLETCHER, D.S.O., M.V.O.	Grenadier Guards	6/12/18	To return of division to England.

(7)

ADMINISTRATIVE STAFF.

D.A.A. & Q.M.G.

Major	F. G. ALSTON, D.S.O.	Scots Guards	15/7/15	24/12/16

D.A.A.G.

Captain	H. B. BALLANTINE-DYKES, D.S.O.	Scots Guards	25/12/16	17/3/18
Major	G. M. DARELL, M.C.	Coldstream Guards	18/3/18	4/2/19
Major	J. J. P. EVANS, M.C.	Welsh Guards	5/2/19	To return of division to England.

(8)

ADMINISTRATIVE STAFF.

D.A.Q.M.G.

Captain	A. F. A. N. THORNE, D.S.O.	Grenadier Guards	18/7/15	29/3/16
Major	R. H. HERMON-HODGE, M.V.O., D.S.O.	Grenadier Guards	30/3/16	24/6/17
Captain	SIR JOHN DYER, BART., M.C.	Scots Guards	25/6/17	31/7/17 *
Major	G. M. DARELL, M.C.	Coldstream Guards	8/8/17	17/3/18
Major	C. BEWICKE, M.C.	Scots Guards	18/3/18	To return of division to England.

* Killed.

APPENDIX II

(9)
GUARDS DIVISIONAL ARTILLERY.

GENERAL OFFICERS COMMANDING.

Rank.	Name.	Unit.	From.	To.
Brig.-General	C. E. GOULBURN, D.S.O.	R.A.	On Formation.	12/9/15
Brig.-General	A. E. WARDROP, C.M.G.	R.A.	13/9/15	28/2/16
Brig.-General	W. EVANS, D.S.O.	R.A.	1/3/16	27/5/17
Brig.-General	F. A. WILSON, C.M.G., D.S.O.	R.A.	13/6/17	To return of division to England.

BRIGADE MAJORS, R.A.

Major ..	D. LE P. TRENCH, M.C.	R.A.	On Formation.	19/2/17
Major ..	A. S. ARCHDALE, D.S.O.	R.A.	20/2/17	13/6/18
Major ..	P. G. YORKE	R.A.	24/6/18	2/10/18
Major ..	W. E. MANN, D.S.O.	R.A.	3/10/18	To return of division to England.

STAFF CAPTAINS, R.A.

Captain	W. E. MANN, D.S.O.	R.A.	28/8/15	12/1/16
Captain	J. A. BATTEN POOLL, M.C.	5th Lancers	13/1/16	19/12/16
Captain	B. WILLIAMS, M.C.	(late) 13th Hussars	26/12/16	To return of division to England.

(10)
ROYAL ENGINEERS.
C.R.E.

Lt.-Colonel	J. E. VANRENEN	R.E.	On Formation.	27/9/15
Lt.-Colonel	A. BROUGH, D.S.O.	R.E.	1/10/15	9/7/17
Lt.-Colonel	E. F. W. LEES, D.S.O.	R.E.	10/7/17	To return of division to England.

ADJUTANT TO C.R.E.

Captain	R. A. S. MANSEL	R.E.	On Formation.	7/12/15
Lieut.	H. G. EADY, M.C.	R.E.	8/12/15	6/12/16
Captain	G. H. S. KELLIE, M.C.	R.E.	7/12/16	5/10/17
Captain	J. STOPS	4/Coldstream Guards	7/10/17	4/7/18
Lieut. (A/Capt.)	J. W. LAWRIE, M.C.	R.E.	5/7/18	To return of division to England.

OFFICERS, STAFFS AND COMMANDS

(11)
GUARDS DIVISIONAL TRAIN.
OFFICERS COMMANDING.

Rank.	Name.	Unit.	From.	To.
Lt.-Colonel	J. C. L. BLACK, C.M.G.	R.A.S.C.	26/7/15	1/4/17
Lt.-Colonel	H. DAVIES, C.M.G.	R.A.S.C.	2/4/17	To return of division to England.

SENIOR SUPPLY OFFICERS.

Captain (T/Major)	A. W. JOHNS	R.A.S.C.	31/7/15	11/5/17
T. Major	C. W. LANDON, D.S.O.	R.A.S.C.	12/5/17	21/1/19
Captain	W. EDGINGTON	R.A.S.C.	22/1/19	—

ADJUTANT.

T. Captain	H. E. STANDAGE	R.A.S.C.	29/7/15	6/9/16
Lieut. (T/Capt.)	E. DOOLAN, M.C.	R.A.S.C.	18/9/16	To return of division to England.

(12)
MEDICAL SERVICES—GUARDS DIVISION.
A.D.M.S.

Lt.-Colonel (T/Colonel)	G. S. McLOUGHLIN, C.M.G., D.S.O., A.M.S.	R.A.M.C.	18/8/15	18/9/16
Colonel	S. GUISE MOORES, C.B., A.M.S.	R.A.M.C.	19/9/16	17/1/17
Lt.-Colonel (T/Colonel)	T. H. J. C. GOODWIN, C.M.G., D.S.O., A.M.S.	R.A.M.C.	21/1/17	16/4/17
Lt.-Colonel (T/Colonel)	H. B. FAWCUS, C.M.G., D.S.O., A.M.S.	R.A.M.C.	17/4/17	To return of division to England.

D.A.D.M.S.

Captain	F. D. G. HOWELL, D.S.O., M.C.	R.A.M.C.	18/8/15	17/3/17
Captain	W. F. McLEAN	R.A.M.C.	18/3/17	18/6/18
Captain (T/Major)	J. F. W. SANDISON	R.A.M.C.	19/6/18	—

O.C., No. 3 FIELD AMBULANCE.

Lt.-Colonel	A. W. COOPER, C.M.G., D.S.O.	R.A.M.C.	On Formation.	22/3/16
Captain (A/Lt.-Col.)	E. M. O'NEILL, D.S.O.	R.A.M.C.	23/3/16	To return of division to England.

APPENDIX II

O.C., No. 4 FIELD AMBULANCE.

Rank.	Name.	Unit	From.	To.
Major ..	P. A. LLOYD-JONES, D.S.O.	R.A.M.C.	On Formation.	14/12/15
Captain (A/Lt.-Col.)	J. J. O'KEEFFE, M.C.	R.A.M.C.	15/12/15	10/8/18
Lt.-Colonel	H. C. D. RANKIN	R.A.M.C.	11/8/18	

O.C., No. 9 FIELD AMBULANCE.

Lt.-Colonel	E. W. BLISS	R.A.M.C.	On Formation.	19/11/15
Captain (A/Major)	E. M. O'NEILL, D.S.O.	R.A.M.C.	20/11/15	22/3/16
Captain (A/Lt.-Col.)	A. D. FRASER, D.S.O., M.C.	R.A.M.C.	23/3/16	19/10/18
Captain (A/Lt.-Col.)	G. F. RUDKIN, D.S.O.	R.A.M.C.	20/10/18	—

(13)
DEPARTMENTS AND SERVICES.
A.D.V.S.

Major ..	F. C. O'RORKE, C.M.G.	R.A.V.C.	On Formation.	27/6/17
Major ..	P. D. CAREY (D.A.D.V.S.)	R.A.V.C.	29/6/17	18/2/19
Major ..	B. R. BODY (D.A.D.V.S.)	R.A.V.C.	19/2/19	—

D.A.D.O.S.

Major ..	W. BLADES, D.S.O.	R.A.O.C.	On Formation.	18/12/15
Major ..	R. H. V. KELLY	R.A.	19/12/15	11/1/16
Captain	G. FRASER	Suffolk Regiment	12/1/16	24/1/19

A.P.M.

Captain	EARL OF CLANWILLIAM, M.C.	Royal Horse Guards	On Formation.	1/11/17
Captain	C. B. GUNSTON, M.C., (D.A.P.M.)	Coldstream Guards	1/11/17	To return of division to England.

(14)
1ST GUARDS BRIGADE.
GENERAL OFFICERS COMMANDING.

Brig.-General	G. P. T. FEILDING, C.B., D.S.O.	Coldstream Guards	20/8/15	2/1/16
Brig.-General	C. E. PEREIRA, C.M.G.	Coldstream Guards	9/1/16	26/12/16

OFFICERS, STAFFS AND COMMANDS

Rank.	Name.	Unit.	From.	To.
Brig.-General	G. D. Jeffreys, C.M.G.	Grenadier Guards	30/12/16	21/9/17
Brig.-General	C. R. Champion de Crespigny, D.S.O.	Grenadier Guards	22/9/17	To return of division to England.

Brigade Majors.

Rank	Name	Unit	From	To
Captain	J. S. S. P. V. Viscount Gort, M.V.O., M.C.	Grenadier Guards	On Formation.	30/6/16
Captain	M. B. Beckwith-Smith, D.S.O.	Coldstream Guards	4/7/16	26/8/17
Captain	J. J. P. Evans, M.C.	Welsh Guards	27/8/17	3/2/19
Captain	J. A. D. Perrins, M.C.	Welsh Guards	4/2/19	To return of division to England.

Staff Captains.

Rank	Name	Unit	From	To
Captain	W. T. Towers-Clark, M.C.	Coldstream Guards	2/8/15	21/4/16
Captain	L. M. Gibbs, M.C.	Coldstream Guards	22/4/16	26/11/16
Lieut. (T/Capt.)	The Hon. H. B. O'Brien	Irish Guards	27/11/16	29/4/17
Captain	J. J. P. Evans, M.C.	Welsh Guards	30/4/17	26/8/17
Lieut. (T/Capt.)	Hon. A. N. A. Van-neck, M.C.	Scots Guards	27/8/17	22/1/19
Lieut. (A/Capt.)	Hon. A. G. Agar-Robartes, M.C.	Grenadier Guards	23/1/19	To return of division to England.

(15)

2nd GUARDS BRIGADE.

General Officers Commanding.

Rank	Name	Unit	From	To
Brig.-General	J. Ponsonby, C.M.G., D.S.O.	Coldstream Guards	23/7/15	19/11/16
Brig.-General	Lord H. Seymour, D.S.O.	Grenadier Guards	28/11/16	20/3/17
Brig.-General	J. Ponsonby, C.M.G., D.S.O.	Coldstream Guards	21/3/17	21/8/17
Brig.General	B. N. Sergison-Brooke, D.S.O.	Grenadier Guards	22/8/17	23/3/18 *
Brig.-General	G. B. S. Follett, M.V.O., D.S.O.	Coldstream Guards	25/3/18	25/4/18
Brig.-General	B. N. Sergison-Brooke, D.S.O.	Grenadier Guards	26/4/18	To return of division to England.

* Wounded (gassed).

APPENDIX II

BRIGADE MAJORS.

Rank.	Name.	Unit.	From.	To.
Major ..	B. N. SERGISON-BROOKE, D.S.O.	Grenadier Guards	18/8/15	25/11/15
Major ..	G. E. C. RASCH, D.S.O.	Grenadier Guards	2/12/15	15/7/16
Lieut. (T/Capt.)	E. W. M. GRIGG	Grenadier Guards	16/7/16	12/2/17
Captain	H. C. LOYD, M.C.	Coldstream Guards	13/2/17	8/3/18
Captain	W. H. WYNNE-FINCH, M.C.	Scots Guards	9/3/18	9/10/18
Captain	O. LYTTELTON, D.S.O., M.C.	Grenadier Guards	10/10/18	—

STAFF CAPTAINS.

Captain	H. B. BECKWITH-SMITH, D.S.O.	Coldstream Guards	27/8/15	3/6/16
Captain	SIR JOHN DYER, BART., M.C.	Scots Guards	4/6/16	23/6/17
Lieut. (T/Capt.)	O. LYTTELTON, D.S.O.	Grenadier Guards	24/6/17	7/2/18
Captain	W. H. WYNNE-FINCH, M.C.	Scots Guards	8/2/18	8/3/18
Captain	R. S. LAMBERT, M.C.	Grenadier Guards	9/3/18	22/4/18
Lieut. (T/Capt.)	C. E. M. ELLISON, M.C.	Grenadier Guards	2/5/18	21/1/19
Captain	G. FURZE	Coldstream Guards	22/1/19	1/3/19
Captain	HON. A. G. AGAR-ROBARTES, M.C.	Grenadier Guards	1/3/19	—

(16)

3RD GUARDS BRIGADE.

GENERAL OFFICERS COMMANDING.

Brig.-General	F. J. HEYWORTH, C.B., D.S.O.	Scots Guards	18/8/15	9/5/16 *
Brig.-General	C. E. CORKRAN, C.M.G.	Grenadier Guards	15/5/16	20/3/17
Brig.-General	LORD H. C. SEYMOUR, D.S.O.	Grenadier Guards	21/0/17	7/4/18
Brig.-General	G. B. S. FOLLETT, M.V.O., D.S.O.	Coldstream Guards	25/4/18	27/9/18*
Brig.-General	C. P. HEYWOOD, C.M.G., D.S.O.	Coldstream Guards	29/9/18	6/11/18†
Brig.-General	J. V. CAMPBELL, V.C., C.M.G., D.S.O.	Coldstream Guards	11/11/18	—

* Killed.   † Wounded.

OFFICERS, STAFFS AND COMMANDS

BRIGADE MAJORS.

Rank.	Name.	Unit.	From.	To.
Major ..	R. S. TEMPEST, D.S.O.	Scots Guards	23/8/15	17/2/16
Captain	E. C. T. WARNER, M.C.	Scots Guards	18/2/16	28/12/16
Captain	H. L. AUBREY-FLETCHER, M.V.O.	Grenadier Guards	28/12/16	2/1/18
Captain	F. G. BEAUMONT-NESBITT	Grenadier Guards	3/1/18	2/9/18
Captain	J. N. BUCHANAN, M.C.	Grenadier Guards	5/9/18	6/12/18
Captain	R. S. LAMBERT, M.C.	Grenadier Guards	6/12/18	To return of division to England.

STAFF CAPTAINS.

Captain	E. C. T. WARNER, M.C.	Scots Guards	18/8/15	17/2/16
Captain	H. BALLANTINE-DYKES, D.S.O.	Scots Guards	8/3/16	24/12/16
Lieut. (T/Capt.)	C. BEWICKE, M.C.	Scots Guards	25/12/16	18/3/18
Lieut. (T/Capt.)	F. P. ACLAND-HOOD, M.C.	Coldstream Guards	19/3/18	1/9/18
Captain	C. G. KEITH, M.C.	Grenadier Guards	2/9/18	To return of division to England.

(17)

ARTILLERY.

OFFICERS COMMANDING.

61ST (HOWITZER) BRIGADE, R.F.A.

Lt.-Colonel	G. N. CARTWRIGHT	R.A.	On Formation.	15/10/15
Lt.-Colonel	F. A. BUZZARD, D.S.O.	R.A.	16/10/15	Till reorganization.

74TH BRIGADE, R.F.A.

Lt.-Colonel	L. P. GARDEN	R.A.	On Formation.	Jan., 1916
Lt.-Colonel	C. RAVENHILL	R.A.	Jan., 1916	5/5/16
Lt.-Colonel	J. B. RIDDELL, D.S.O.	R.A.	6/5/16	15/11/16
Lt.-Colonel	F. A. BUZZARD, D.S.O.	R.A.	16/11/16	24/7/17 *
Lt.-Colonel	C. E. VICKERY, D.S.O.	R.A.	27/7/17	To return of division to England.

* Wounded.

APPENDIX II

75th Brigade, R.F.A.

Rank.	Name.	Unit.	From.	To.
Lt.-Colonel	F. R. Thackeray	R.A.	On Formation.	8/10/15
Lt.-Colonel	A. B. Bethell, D.S.O.	R.A.	9/10/15	16/3/18
Lt.-Colonel	J. B. Riddell, D.S.O.	R.A.	23/3/18	1/4/18
Lt.-Colonel	W. C. E. Rudkin, C.M.G., D.S.O.	R.A.	20/4/18	24/6/18
Lt.-Colonel	T. Kirkland, D.S.O.	R.A.	25/6/18	—

76th Brigade, R.F.A.

Rank.	Name.	Unit.	From.	To.
Colonel	R. D. Gubbins	R.A.	On Formation.	—
Lt.-Colonel	G. R. V. Kinsman, D.S.O.	R.A.	—	May, 1916.
Lt.-Colonel	F. C. Bryant, C.M.G.	R.A.	May, 1916.	Till Bde. became an Army Bde.

Guards D.A.C.

Rank.	Name.	Unit.	From.	To.
Lt.-Colonel	H. Fawcus	R.A.	On Formation.	15/5/16
Colonel	C. B. Watkins	R.A.	16/5/16	—

(18)
ROYAL ENGINEERS.
OFFICERS COMMANDING.

55th Field Company, R.E.

Rank.	Name.	Unit.	From.	To.
Major	A. Brough, D.S.O.	R.E.	On Formation.	30/9/15
Major	J. T. Heath, M.C.	R.E.	1/10/15	11/10/17
Major	H. M. S. Meares, M.C.	R.E.	22/10/17	—

75th Field Company, R.E.

Rank.	Name.	Unit.	From.	To.
Major	A. Rolland	R.E.	On Formation.	14/2/16
Lieut.	D. M. Fraser	R.E.	15/2/16	28/2/16
Captain	A. R. A. Iremonger	R.E.	29/2/16	2/3/16
Captain	H. J. Bulkeley	R.E.	6/3/16	6/5/16
Major	B. H. Fox	R.E.	17/5/16	10/6/17
Major	R. Briggs, M.C.	R.E.	11/6/17	—

OFFICERS, STAFFS AND COMMANDS

76TH FIELD COMPANY, R.E.

Rank.	Name.	Unit.	From.	To.
Major ..	M. O. C. TANDY	R.E.	On Formation.	27/9/15
Captain	W. C. RAMSDEN	R.E.	28/9/15	7/12/15
Captain	R. A. S. MANSEL	R.E.	8/12/15	24/12/15
Captain	W. C. COOPER	R.E.	3/1/16	17/6/16
Major ..	R. D. JACKSON, M.C.	R.E.	30/6/16	5/10/17
Major ..	G. H. S. KELLIE, M.C.	R.E.	6/10/17	14/7/18
Major ..	G. W. F. RIDOUT EVANS, M.C.	R.E.	15/7/18	—

SIGNAL COMPANY, R.E.

Captain	J. CLEMENTI	R.E.	On Formation.	3/10/15
Captain	W. E. PAIN, M.C.	R.E.	4/10/15	4/12/16
Major	L. G. PHILLIPS, M.C.	(Worcester Regiment)	5/12/16	15/9/18
Major ..	J. S. RYAN, M.C.	R.E.	16/9/18	—

(19)

COMMANDING OFFICERS.

1ST BATTALION GRENADIER GUARDS.

Lt.-Colonel ..	G. F. TROTTER, C.B., C.M.G., M.V.O., D.S.O.	On Formation.	17/3/16 *
Lt.-Colonel ..	A. ST. L. GLYN	17/3/16	9/7/16
Lt.-Colonel ..	M. E. MAKGILL-CRICHTON-MAITLAND, D.S.O.	10/7/16	7/3/18
Lt.-Colonel ..	J. S. S. P. V. VISCOUNT GORT, V.C., M.V.O., D.S.O., M.C.	8/3/18	27/9/18 †
Lt.-Colonel ..	HONBLE. W. R. BAILEY, D.S.O.	12/10/18	To return of division to England.

2ND BATTALION GRENADIER GUARDS.

Lt.-Colonel ..	G. D. JEFFREYS, C.M.G.	On Formation.	18/1/16 *
Lt.-Colonel ..	C. R. CHAMPION DE CRESPIGNY, D.S.O.	10/2/16	21/9/17 *
Lt.-Colonel ..	G. E. RASCH, D.S.O.	22/9/17	2/10/18

* To command an infantry brigade.
† Wounded.

APPENDIX II

Rank.	Name.	From.	To.
Captain (A/Lt.-Col.)	C. F. A. WALKER, M.C.	3/10/18	3/2/19
Major (T/Lt.-Col.)	M. E. MAKGILL-CRICHTON-MAITLAND, D.S.O.	3/2/19	To return of division to England.

3RD BATTALION GRENADIER GUARDS.

Rank.	Name.	From.	To.
Colonel	N. A. L. CORRY, D.S.O.	On Formation.	9/1/16
Lt.-Colonel	B. N. SERGISON-BROOKE, D.S.O.	9/2/16	14/9/16 *
Lt.-Colonel	A. F. A. N. THORNE, D.S.O.	18/9/16	7/6/17
Lt.-Colonel	G. E. C. RASCH, D.S.O.	23/6/17	11/7/17
Lt.-Colonel	A. F. A. N. THORNE, D.S.O.	13/7/17	1/9/18
Lt.-Colonel	H. G. C. VISCOUNT LASCELLES, D.S.O.	18/9/18	To return of division to England.

4TH BATTALION GRENADIER GUARDS.

Rank.	Name.	From.	To.
Lt.-Colonel	G. C. HAMILTON, D.S.O.	14/8/15	27/9/15
Lt.-Colonel	LORD H. C. SEYMOUR, D.S.O.	11/10/15	27/11/16 †
Lt.-Colonel	G. C. HAMILTON, D.S.O.	9/12/16	2/4/17
Lt.-Colonel	J. S. S. P. V. VISCOUNT GORT, V.C., M.V.O., D.S.O., M.C.	17/4/17	30/11/17 *
Lt.-Colonel	W. S. PILCHER, D.S.O.	1/12/17	To return of division to England.

1ST BATTALION COLDSTREAM GUARDS.

Rank.	Name.	From.	To.
Lt.-Colonel	J. PONSONBY, C.M.G.,	On Formation.	26/8/15 †
Lt.-Colonel	A. G. E. EGERTON	27/8/15	29/9/15 ‡
Lt.-Colonel	HON. G. V. BARING	2/10/15	15/9/16 ‡
Lt.-Colonel	G. B. S. FOLLETT, M.V.O., D.S.O.	24/9/16	12/11/16
Lt.-Colonel	E. B. G. GREGGE-HOPWOOD, D.S.O.	13/11/16	20/7/17 ‡
Lt.-Colonel	J. C. BRAND, M.C.	22/7/17	To return of division to England.

* Wounded.
† To command an infantry brigade.
‡ Killed.

OFFICERS, STAFFS AND COMMANDS

2ND BATTALION COLDSTREAM GUARDS.

Rank.	Name.	From.	To.
Lt.-Colonel	C. E. PEREIRA	On Formation.	17/5/15
Major	P. A. MACGREGOR, D.S.O.	18/5/15	24/5/15
Lt.-Colonel	J. M. STEELE	25/5/15	27/8/15
Lt.-Colonel	P. A. MACGREGOR, D.S.O.	28/8/15	24/3/16
Lt.-Colonel	G. B. S. FOLLETT, D.S.O., M.V.O.	25/3/15	18/7/16 *
Major	G. E. VAUGHAN	19/7/16	24/7/16
Lt.-Colonel	R. B. J. CRAWFURD, D.S.O.	25/7/16	12/11/16
Lt.-Colonel	G. B. S. FOLLETT, M.V.O., D.S.O.	13/11/16	24/11/16 *
Lt.-Colonel	L. M. GIBBS, M.C.	25/11/16	7/3/17
Lt.-Colonel	G. B. S. FOLLETT, M.V.O., D.S.O.	8/3/17	22/3/18 †
Lt.-Colonel	E. P. BRASSEY, M.C.	23/3/18	To return of division to England.

3RD BATTALION COLDSTREAM GUARDS.

Rank.	Name.	From.	To.
Lt.-Colonel	J. V. CAMPBELL, V.C., D.S.O.	On Formation.	28/11/16 †
Lt.-Colonel	R. B. J. CRAWFURD, D.S.O.	29/11/16	9/10/17
Lt.-Colonel	F. LONGUEVILLE, D.S.O., M.C.	10/10/17	24/4/18
Lt.-Colonel	R. B. J. CRAWFURD, D.S.O.	25/4/18	To return of division to England.

4TH BATTALION COLDSTREAM GUARDS
(PIONEERS).

Rank.	Name.	From.	To.
Lt.-Colonel	R. C. E. SKEFFINGTON SMYTH, D.S.O.	On Formation.	18/10/17
Lt.-Colonel	G. J. EDWARDS, M.C.	19/10/17	To return of division to England.

1ST BATTALION SCOTS GUARDS.

Rank.	Name.	From.	To.
Lt.-Colonel	S. H. GODMAN, D.S.O.	On Formation.	23/10/15 *
Lt.-Colonel	LORD E. C. GORDON-LENNOX, M.V.O., D.S.O.	24/10/15	19/6/16 †
Lt.-Colonel	S. H. GODMAN, D.S.O.	8/8/16	29/4/17

* Wounded.
† To command an infantry brigade.

APPENDIX II

Rank.	Name.	From.	To.
Lt.-Colonel	B. H. S. Romilly, D.S.O.	3/5/17	29/7/17 *
Lt.-Colonel	R. S. Tempest, D.S.O.	6/8/17	11/9/17 †
Lt.-Colonel	M. Romer	12/9/17	7/3/18
Lt.-Colonel	Sir V. A. F. Mackenzie, Bart., M.V.O., D.S.O.	8/3/18	To return of division to England.

2nd Battalion Scots Guards.

Lt.-Colonel	A. B. E. Cator, D.S.O.	On Formation.	28/3/16 *
Lt.-Colonel	R. S. Tempest, D.S.O.	29/3/16	15/7/17 *
Lt.-Colonel	N. A. Orr-Ewing, D.S.O.	16/7/17	24/8/17 †
Lt.-Colonel	J. A. Stirling, D.S.O., M.C.	25/8/17	To return of division to England.

1st Battalion Irish Guards.

Lt.-Colonel	G. H. C. Madden	On Formation.	11/10/15 ‡
Lt.-Colonel	R. C. A. McCalmont, D.S.O.	2/11/15	2/3/17 †
Lt.-Colonel	Hon. H. R. L. G. Alexander, D.S.O., M.C.	3/3/17	22/5/17
Lt.-Colonel	C. E. A. S. Rocke, D.S.O.	24/5/17	10/7/17
Lt.-Colonel	R. V. Pollok, D.S.O.	11/7/17	5/6/18 §
Lt.-Colonel	R. R. C. Baggalay, M.C.	6/6/18	To return of division to England.

2nd Battalion Irish Guards.

Lt.-Colonel	Hon. L. J. P. Butler, C.M.G.	On Formation.	4/5/16 †
Lt.-Colonel	P. L. Reid	4/6/16	11/1/17
Lt.-Colonel	E. B. Greer, M.C.	13/1/17	31/7/17 ‖
Lt.-Colonel	R. H. Ferguson	1/8/17	1/10/17
Lt.-Colonel	Hon. H. R. L. G. Alexander, D.S.O., M.C.	2/10/17	23/10/18
Lt.-Colonel	A. F. L. Gordon, M.C.	26/10/18	To return of division to England.

* Wounded.
† To command an infantry brigade.
‡ Died of wounds.
§ Acting commandant VI Corps School.
‖ Killed.

OFFICERS, STAFFS AND COMMANDS

1st Battalion Welsh Guards.

Rank.	Name.	From.	To.
Lt.-Colonel	W. Murray-Threipland, D.S.O.	On Formation.	26/12/16
Lt.-Colonel	G. C. D. Gordon, D.S.O.	27/12/16	13/2/18
Lt.-Colonel	H. Dene, D.S.O.	14/2/18	24/8/18
Lt.-Colonel	R. E. C. Luxmoore Ball, D.S.O.	8/9/18	To return of division to England.

4th Battalion Guards M.-G. Regiment.

Rank	Name		From	To
Lt.-Colonel	R. C. Bingham, D.S.O. (Coldstream Guards)		18/2/18 (On Formation of battalion.)	8/11/18 *
Lt.-Colonel	F. Penn, M.C. (2nd Life Guards)		9/11/18	To return of division to England.

(20)
GUARDS DIVISIONAL MECHANICAL TRANSPORT COMPANY.
(Formerly Guards Divisional Supply Column.)
Officers Commanding.

Rank	Name			From	To
T/Major	Sir W. E. T. Avery, Bart., M.C.		R.A.S.C.	On Formation.	15/11/18 †
T/Major	A. F. St. C. Collins, M.C.		R.A.S.C.	—	—

(21)
SENIOR CHAPLAINS TO THE FORCES.
Church of England.

Rank	Name	From	To
Rev.	R. J. Fleming, C.M.G.	On Formation.	28/12/15
Rev.	W. P. G. McCormick, D.S.O.	29/12/15	28/5/17
Rev.	F. W. Head, M.C.	29/5/17	1/2/19
Rev.	F. O. T. Hawkes	2/2/19	

* Wounded.
† Died of influenza.

APPENDIX II

OTHER DENOMINATIONS.

Rank.	Name.	From.	To.
Rev.	S. S. KNAPP, D.S.O., M.C. (R.C.)	—	31/8/17 *
Rev.	R. J. LANE-FOX, M.C. (R.C.)	16/9/17	7/12/17
Rev.	F. H. BROWNE, M.C. (R.C.)	8/12/17	29/2/18
Rev.	J. SCANNELL, M.C. (R.C.)	18/3/18	To return of division to England.

* Killed.

(22)

FRENCH MISSION.

OFFICERS IN CHARGE AT DIVISIONAL HEADQUARTERS.

August, 1915 : Capitaine de Reserve PRINCE AYMON DE FAUCIGNY-LUCINGE.
October, 1915 : Lieutenant COMTE POL DE LA CHESNAYE.
July, 1917 : Lieutenant CHARLES FURBY, D.C.M.

APPENDIX III

VICTORIA CROSSES WON BY OFFICERS AND OTHER RANKS OF THE GUARDS DIVISION.

1. " No. 6738 Lance-Sergeant OLIVER BROOKS, 3rd Battalion, Coldstream Guards.

" For most conspicuous bravery near Loos, on the 8th October, 1915.

" A strong party of the enemy having captured 200 yards of our trenches, Lance-Sergeant Brooks, on his own initiative, led a party of bombers in the most determined manner, and succeeded in regaining possession of the lost ground.

" The signal bravery displayed by this Non-commissioned Officer, in the midst of a hail of bombs from the Germans, was of the very first order, and the complete success attained in a very dangerous undertaking was entirely due to his absolute fearlessness, presence of mind and promptitude."—*London Gazette*, 26th of October, 1915.

2. " Major and Brevet Lieutenant-Colonel (temporary Lieutenant-Colonel) JOHN VAUGHAN CAMPBELL, D.S.O., Coldstream Guards.*

" For most conspicuous bravery and able leading in an attack.

" Seeing that the first two waves of his battalion had been decimated by machine gun and rifle fire he took personal command of the third line, rallied his men with the utmost gallantry, and led them against the enemy machine guns, capturing the guns and killing the personnel.

" Later in the day, after consultation with other unit commanders, he again rallied the survivors of his battalion, and at a critical moment led them through a very heavy hostile fire barrage against the objective.

" He was one of the first to enter the enemy trench.

* N.B.—The battalion concerned is the 3rd Coldstream Guards. The occasion is the attack at Ginchy, 15th of September, 1916.

"His personal gallantry and initiative at a very critical moment turned the fortunes of the day and enabled the division to press on and capture objectives of the highest tactical importance."—*London Gazette*, 26th of October, 1916.

3. "No. 13301 Lance-Sergeant FRED McNESS, Scots Guards.*

"For most conspicuous bravery. During a severe engagement he led his men on with the greatest dash in face of heavy shell and machine gun fire. When the first line of enemy trenches was reached, it was found that the left flank was exposed and that the enemy was bombing down the trench.

"Sergeant McNess thereupon organized a counter-attack and led it in person. He was very severely wounded in the neck and jaw, but went on passing through the barrage of hostile bombs in order to bring up fresh supplies of bombs to his own men.

"Finally he established a 'block,' and continued encouraging his men and throwing bombs till utterly exhausted by loss of blood."—*London Gazette*, 26th of October, 1916.

4. "No. 939 Sergeant ROBERT BYE, Welsh Guards † (Penrhiwceiber, Glamorgan).

"For most conspicuous bravery.

"Sgt. Bye displayed the utmost courage and devotion to duty during an attack on the enemy's position. Seeing that the leading waves were being troubled by two enemy blockhouses, he, on his own initiative, rushed at one of them and put the garrison out of action. He then rejoined his company and went forward to the assault of the second objective.

"When the troops had gone forward to the attack on the third objective, a party was detailed to clear up a line of blockhouses which had been passed. Sgt. Bye volunteered to take charge of this party, accomplished his object, and took many prisoners. He subsequently advanced to the third objective, capturing a number of prisoners, thus rendering invaluable assistance to the assaulting companies.

"He displayed throughout the most remarkable initiative."— *London Gazette*, 6th of September, 1917.

* N.B.—1st Scots Guards. Ginchy, 15th of September, 1916.
† N.B.—Advance from the Yser Canal, 31st of July, 1917.

VICTORIA CROSSES WON

5. "No. 15067 Private THOMAS WITHAM, Coldstream Guards * (Burnley).

"For most conspicuous bravery, when, during an attack, an enemy machine gun was seen to be enfilading the battalion on the right. Pte. Witham, on his own initiative, immediately worked his way from shell-hole to shell-hole through our own barrage, rushed the machine gun, and, although under a very heavy fire, captured it, together with an officer and two other ranks.

"The bold action on the part of Pte. Witham was of great assistance to the battalion on the right, and undoubtedly saved many lives and enabled the whole line to advance."—*London Gazette*, 6th of September, 1917.

6. "No. 7708 Lance-Sergeant JOHN MOYNEY, Irish Guards † (Rathdowney, Queen's County).

"For most conspicuous bravery when in command of fifteen men forming two advanced posts. In spite of being surrounded by the enemy he held his post for ninety-six hours, having no water and little food. On the morning of the fifth day a large force of the enemy advanced to dislodge him. He ordered his men out of their shell-holes, and, taking the initiative, attacked the advancing enemy with bombs, while he used his Lewis gun with great effect from a flank. Finding himself surrounded by superior numbers, he led back his men in a charge through the enemy, and reached a stream which lay between the posts and the line. Here he instructed his party to cross at once while he and Pte. Woodcock remained to cover the retirement.

"When the whole of his force had gained the south-west bank unscathed he himself crossed under a shower of bombs. It was due to endurance, skill and devotion to duty shown by this non-commissioned officer that he was able to bring his entire force safely out of action."—*London Gazette*, 17th of October, 1917.

7. "No. 8387 Private THOMAS WOODCOCK, Irish Guards † (Wigan, Lancashire).

"For most conspicuous bravery and determination. He was one of a post commanded by L./Sgt. Moyney which was surrounded.

---

* N.B.—1st Coldstream Guards. Advance from the Yser Canal, 31st of July, 1917.
† N.B.—2nd Irish Guards. North of the Broenbeek (near Ney Copse), 12th–13th of September, 1917.

The post held out for 96 hours, but after that time was attacked from all sides in overwhelming numbers and was forced to retire.

" Pte. Woodcock covered the retirement with a Lewis gun, and only retired when the enemy had moved round and up to his post and were only a few yards away. He then crossed the river, but hearing cries for help behind him, returned and waded into the stream amid a shower of bombs from the enemy and rescued another member of the party. The latter he then carried across the open ground in broad daylight towards our front line regardless of machine-gun fire that was opened on him."—*London Gazette*, 17th of October, 1917.

8. " No. 15122 Lance-Sergeant JOHN HAROLD RHODES, Grenadier Guards * (Tunstall, Staffs.).

" For most conspicuous bravery when in charge of a Lewis-gun section covering the consolidation of the right front company.

" He accounted for several enemy with his rifle as well as by Lewis-gun fire, and, upon seeing the enemy leave a ' pill-box ' he went out single-handed through our own barrage and hostile machine-gun fire and effected an entry into the ' pill-box.' He there captured nine enemy, including a forward observation officer connected by telephone with his battery. These prisoners he brought back with him, together with valuable information."
—*London Gazette*, 26th of November, 1917.

9. " No. 10053 Sergeant JOHN MCAULAY, D.C.M., Scots Guards † (Stirling).

" For most conspicuous bravery and initiative in attack. When all his officers had become casualties Sergt. McAulay assumed command of the company and under shell and machine-gun fire successfully held and consolidated the objective gained. He reorganized the company, cheered on and encouraged his men, and under heavy fire at close quarters showed utter disregard of danger.

" Noticing a counter-attack developing on his exposed left flank, he successfully repulsed it by the skilful and bold use of machine guns, aided by two men only, causing heavy enemy casualties.

" Sergt. McAulay also carried his company commander, who was mortally wounded, a long distance to a place of safety under

* N.B.—3rd Grenadier Guards. Near Houthulst Forest, 9th of October, 1917.

† N.B.—1st Scots Guards at Fontaine-notre-Dame, 27th of November, 1917.

very heavy fire. Twice he was knocked down by the concussion of a bursting shell, but, nothing daunted, he continued on his way until his objective was achieved, killing two of the enemy who endeavoured to intercept him.

"Throughout the day this very gallant Non-commissioned Officer displayed the highest courage, tactical skill, and coolness under exceptionally trying circumstances."—*London Gazette*, 11th of January, 1918.

10. "Lieutenant (A/Capt.) GEORGE HENRY TOTHAM PATON, M.C., late G. Gds.*

"For most conspicuous bravery and self-sacrifice.

"When a unit on his left was driven back, thus leaving his flank in the air and his company practically surrounded, he fearlessly exposed himself to readjust the line, walking up and down within fifty yards of the enemy under a withering fire. He personally removed several wounded men, and was the last to leave the village. Later, he again readjusted the line, exposing himself regardless of all danger the whole time, and when the enemy four times counter-attacked he sprang each time upon the parapet, deliberately risking his life, and being eventually mortally wounded, in order to stimulate his command.

"After the enemy had broken through on his left, he again mounted the parapet, and with a few men—who were inspired by his great example—forced them once more to withdraw, thereby undoubtedly saving the left flank."—*London Gazette*, 13th of February, 1918.

11. "Lieutenant (A/Capt.) THOMAS TANNATT PRYCE, M.C., G. Gds.†

"For most conspicuous bravery, devotion to duty, and self-sacrifice in command of a flank on the left of the Grenadier Guards.

"Having been ordered to attack a village, he personally led forward two platoons, working from house to house, killing some thirty of the enemy, seven of whom he killed himself.

"The next day he was occupying a position with some thirty to forty men, the remainder of his company having become casualties. As early as 8.15 a.m. his left flank was surrounded and the enemy was enfilading him.

* N.B.—4th Grenadier Guards at Gonnelieu, 1st of December, 1917.
† N.B.—4th Grenadier Guards at Vieux Berquin, 11th of April, 1918.

"He was attacked no less than four times during the day, and each time beat off the hostile attack, killing many of the enemy.

"Meanwhile the enemy brought up three field guns to within 300 yards of his line, and were firing over open sights and knocking his trench in. At 6.15 p.m. the enemy had worked to within sixty yards of his trench. He then called on his men, telling them to cheer and charge the enemy and fight to the last. Led by Captain Pryce, they left their trench and drove back the enemy, with the bayonet, some 100 yards. Half an hour later the enemy had again approached in stronger force. By this time Captain Pryce had only 17 men left, and every round of his ammunition had been fired. Determined that there should be no surrender, he once again led his men forward in a bayonet charge, and was last seen engaged in a fierce hand-to-hand struggle with overwhelming numbers of the enemy.

"With some forty men he had held back at least one enemy battalion for over ten hours. His company undoubtedly stopped the advance through the British line, and thus had great influence on the battle."—*London Gazette*, 22nd of May, 1918.

12. "Captain and Brevet-Major (A. Lt.-Col.) JOHN STANDISH SURTEES PRENDERGAST VEREKER, VISCOUNT GORT, D.S.O., M.V.O., M.C., 1st Bn. G. Gds.

"For most conspicuous bravery, skilful leading and devotion to duty during the attack of the Guards Division on 27th September, 1918, across the Canal du Nord, near Flesquières, when in command of the 1st Battalion Grenadier Guards, the leading battalion of the 3rd Guards Brigade.

"Under heavy artillery and machine-gun fire he led his battalion with great skill and determination to the 'forming up' ground, where very severe fire from artillery and machine guns was again encountered.

"Although wounded he quickly grasped the situation, directed a platoon to proceed down a sunken road to make a flanking attack, and, under terrific fire, went across open ground to obtain the assistance of a tank, which he personally led and directed to the best possible advantage. While thus fearlessly exposing himself, he was again severely wounded by a shell. Notwithstanding considerable loss of blood, after lying on a stretcher for awhile, he insisted on getting up and personally directing the further attack. By his magnificent example of devotion to duty and utter disregard of personal safety all ranks were inspired to exert themselves to the utmost, and the attack resulted in the capture of over 200 prisoners, two batteries of field guns and numerous machine guns. Lt.-Col. Viscount Gort then proceeded to organize the defence of the captured position until he collapsed; even then he refused to leave the field until he had seen the ' success signal ' go up on the final objective.

"The successful advance of the battalion was mainly due to the valour, devotion and leadership of this very gallant officer."
—*London Gazette,* 27th of November, 1918.

13. " Lieutenant (A./Capt.) CYRIL HUBERT FRISBY, C. Gds. (S.R.) attd. 1st Bn.

" For most conspicuous bravery, leadership and devotion to duty in action on the 27th September, 1918, across the Canal du Nord, near Graincourt, when in command of a company detailed to capture the Canal crossing, on the Demicourt—Graincourt road. On reaching the Canal the leading platoon came under annihilating machine-gun fire from a strong machine-gun post under the old iron bridge on the far side of the Canal, and was unable to advance, despite reinforcing waves. Capt. Frisby realized at once that unless this post was captured the whole advance in this area would fail. Calling for volunteers to follow him, he dashed forward, and, with three other ranks, he climbed down into the Canal under an intense point-blank machine-gun fire and succeeded in capturing the post with two machine guns and twelve men.

" By his personal valour and initiative he restored the situation and enabled the attacking companies to continue the advance.

" Having reached and consolidated his objective, he gave timely support to the company on his right, which had lost all its officers and sergeants, organized its defences, and beat off a heavy hostile counter-attack.

" He was wounded in the leg by a bayonet in the attack on the machine-gun post, but remained at duty throughout, thereby setting a splendid example to all ranks."—*London Gazette,* 27th of November, 1918.

14. " No. 20810 Private (L./Cpl.) THOMAS NORMAN JACKSON, late 1st Bn. C. Gds. (Swinton).

" For most conspicuous bravery and self-sacrifice in the attack across the Canal du Nord, near Graincourt.

" On the morning of the 27th September, 1918, L./Cpl. Jackson was the first to volunteer to follow Capt. C. N. Frisby, Coldstream Guards, across the Canal du Nord in his rush against an enemy machine-gun post. With two comrades he followed his officer across the Canal, rushed the post, captured the two machine guns, and so enabled the companies to advance. Later in the morning, L./Cpl. Jackson was the first to jump into a German trench which his platoon had to clear, and after doing further excellent work he was unfortunately killed.

" Throughout the day until he was killed this young N.C.O. showed the greatest valour and devotion to duty and set an inspiring example to all."—*London Gazette*, 27th of November, 1918.

15. " No. 16444 Corporal (L./Sgt.) HARRY BLANSHARD WOOD, M.M., 2nd Bn. S. Gds. (Bristol).

" For most conspicuous bravery and devotion to duty during operations at the village of St. Python, France, on the 13th of October, 1918.

" The advance was desperately opposed by machine guns and the streets were raked by fire. His platoon sergeant was killed, and command of the leading platoon fell to him. The task of the company was to clear the western side of the village and secure the crossing of the River Selle. Command of the ruined bridge had to be gained, though the space in front of it was commanded by snipers. Cpl. Wood boldly carried a large brick out into the open space, lay down behind it, and fired continually at these snipers, ordering his men to work across while he covered them by his fire. This he continued to do under heavy and well-aimed fire until the whole of his party had reached the objective point.

" He showed complete disregard for his personal safety, and his leadership throughout the day was of the highest order.

" Later, he drove off repeated enemy counter-attacks against his position.

" His gallant conduct and initiative shown contributed largely to the success of the day's operations."—*London Gazette*, 14th of December, 1918.

16. " No. 16796 Private WILLIAM EDGAR HOLMES, late 2nd Bn. G. Gds. (Didbrook, nr. Winchmere, Glos.).

" For most conspicuous bravery and devotion to duty at Cattenières on the 9th of October, 1918.

"Pte. Holmes carried in two men under the most intense fire, and, while he was attending to a third case, he was severely wounded. In spite of this, he continued to carry wounded, and was shortly afterwards again wounded, with fatal results. By his self-sacrifice and disregard of danger he was the means of saving the lives of several of his comrades."—*London Gazette*, 26th of December, 1918.

APPENDIX IV

GUARDS DIVISION OPERATION ORDERS.*

(a) ORDER FOR THE GUARDS' ATTACK AT LOOS, ISSUED 27TH OF SEPTEMBER, 1915.

See map facing p. 68, Vol. I.

G.R. 27   27th.

THE Guards Division will advance to the CITE ST ELIE—PUITS 14 BIS road as follows   2nd Bde. will attack—First objective CHALK PIT Second Objective PUITS No 14 BIS AAA 3rd Bde. will move to a position of readiness about the eastern edge of Loos in such time as to be ready to assault HILL 70 as soon as CHALK PIT & PUITS 14 BIS are in our hands AAA 2nd Bde. will be in position to assault CHALK PIT at 4 pm AAA 1st Bde. will protect left of 2nd Bde. by fire and as soon as CHALK PIT is in our hands will get touch with 2nd Bde. and will consolidate a new forward line roughly through G 24—d & b † to join present line about point 28 ‡ in G 18d AAA Pioneer Battn. will accompany 3rd Bde. and will be left in a position about G 30 c.I.I.§ ready to help with consolidation of line gained on receipt of orders from Divn. H. Qrs. AAA Artillery programme has already been communicated see my G.R. 270 AAA No advance will be made east of CITE ST ELIE—LENS road but the following line will be firmly consolidated and held HILL 70—PUITS 14 BIS—eastern edge of CHALK PIT—through G 24 d & b † to Point 28 ‡ in G 18 d AAA Reports to LE RUTOIRE AAA

ADVANCED GUARDS DIVISION
1.50 P.M.

(Sd) W. RUTHVEN, Lt. Col.

* These Orders are printed here exactly as they were issued. It has not been considered necessary to explain the system usually adopted of denoting positions on the squared maps by means of letters and figure coordinates, seeing that no squared maps have been reproduced in these volumes. All such references, however, have been made clear to the reader by means of footnotes.
† Approximately north-north-east from Chalk Pit.
‡ *See* Map facing p. 68. Vol. I.
§ North-east outskirts of Loos by Bénifontaine road.

OPERATION ORDERS

(b) ORDER FOR THE GUARDS' ATTACK ON THE 15TH OF SEPTEMBER, 1916.

See map facing p. 164, Vol. I.

No. 76.*

1. The Fourth Army will attack the enemy's defences between COMBLES RAVINE and MARTINPUICH on Z day † with the object of seizing MORVAL—LES BŒUFS—GUEUDECOURT and FLERS, and of breaking through the enemy's system of defence.

The French are undertaking an offensive simultaneously on the south and the Reserve Army on the north.

2. The attack will be pushed with the utmost vigour, all along the line, until the most distant objectives are reached. The failure of a unit on a flank is not to prevent other units pushing on to their final objectives, as it is by such means that these units, which have failed, will be assisted to advance.

3. *Preliminary bombardment:*

(a) Commencing on 12th September bombardment and wire cutting on hostile defensive systems will take place from 6 a.m. to 6.30 p.m. daily.

(b) The preliminary bombardment on the day of the attack will be similar to that on previous days, there being no further increase of fire previous to ZERO.‡

(c) At 6.30 p.m. each evening, from 12th September inclusive, night firing will commence and continue till 6 a.m. Lethal shells will be used.

4.—(a) The 6th Division is to attack on our right and the 14th Division on our left.

(b) The 2nd Guards Brigade will attack on the right of the Division—the 1st Guards Brigade on the left—the 3rd Guards Brigade will be in Divisional Reserve.

5. *Forming up areas.*

Forming up areas are shown on attached maps.§

---

* The times of attack from the "green" line onward and the times of the barrage movements are given as altered in an Amendment issued 13th of September.

† 15th of September. A notice to this effect was issued later on the evening of 12th of September, when zero hour was given as "probably between 6 and 6.30 a.m."

‡ Not definitely fixed till the morning of the attack.

§ *See* frontage of Guards Division on Map facing p. 164, Vol. I.

6. 1st and 2nd Guards Brigades will allot a forming up area for 75th and 76th Field Companies, R.E., respectively in their forming up areas.

Instructions as to movements of troops to their forming up areas will be issued separately.

7. Objectives allotted to Guards Brigades and neighbouring Divisions are shown on attached map.*

    First objective is marked GREEN.
    Second do.   do.   BROWN.
    Third do.   do.   BLUE.
    Fourth do.   do.   RED.

8. The Infantry will advance to the attack of the GREEN Line at ZERO †

to the attack of the BROWN Line at ZERO † +1 hour.
to the attack of the BLUE Line at ZERO † +2 hours.
to the attack of the RED Line at ZERO † +4 hours 30 mins.

9. *Artillery Barrages.*

(*a*) 50 per cent. of Field Artillery covering the Division will be used for creeping barrage, and 50 per cent. for stationary barrage.

(*b*) Details of stationary barrages will be issued later. In all cases the stationary barrage will lift back when the creeping barrage reaches it.

(*c*) At ZERO † the creeping barrage will open 100 yards in front of our front trenches, and will advance at rate of 50 yards per minute until it is 200 yards beyond the first objective when it will become stationary.

At ZERO † +1 hour the creeping barrage will become intense on a line 200 yards in front of first objective and will creep forward at rate of 50 yards per minute in front of that portion of the 1st Guards Brigade which is to advance to the second objective.

(*d*) At ZERO † +1 hour 10 minutes the creeping barrage will become intense on a line 200 yards in front of the first objective as far north as T 8 b 46,‡ thence on a line 200 yards in front of 2nd objective, and will advance at rate of 30 yards per minute

---

 * *See* Map facing p. 164, Vol. I.
 † Not fixed till the morning of the attack.
 ‡ Left boundary of Division. *See* Map facing p. 164, Vol. I.

until it has passed 200 yards beyond the third objective—when it will become stationary.

This barrage is to cover the advance of the Tanks.

There will be no creeping barrage in front of the Infantry during their advance to third objective which commences at ZERO *+ 2 hours.

(e) At ZERO *+3 hours 30 minutes the creeping barrage will become intense on a line 200 yards in front of the third objective—and will advance at rate of 30 yards per minute until it has passed 200 yards beyond fourth objective when it will become stationary. This barrage is to cover the advance of the tanks.

There will be no creeping barrage in front of the Infantry during the advance to the fourth objective which commences at ZERO *+4 hours 30 minutes.

(f) In the attack on first and second objectives, gaps of 100 yards wide will be left in the creeping barrage for the routes of the tanks.

10. The flow of troops of 2nd Guards Brigade and 1st Guards Brigade must be maintained so as to ensure a strong attack being pressed against each successive objective.

Sufficient men will be left in each line captured to clear it of the enemy. No troops of 2nd and 1st Guards Brigades will be detailed to remain behind in objectives after they have been passed, for purposes of consolidation.

The task of the two leading Guards Brigades is to press the attack through to their ultimate objectives with every means at their disposal.

11. The 3rd Guards Brigade will advance at ZERO *+1 hour 30 minutes until its leading troops reach the south-western outskirts of GINCHY, when the Brigade will halt and await orders.

Special instructions as to action of Reserve Brigade will be issued.

12. Tanks will be employed to cooperate with the attack. Instructions as to their employment are attached.

Instructions will be issued as to movement of tanks to their departure positions, and as to time of their advance to the various objectives.

* Not fixed till the morning of the attack.

13. *R.E.* (*a*) 76th Field Company, R.E., will be at disposal of 2nd Guards Brigade and 75th Field Company, R.E., at disposal of 1st Guards Brigade for the attack.

55th Field Company, R.E., will be in Divisional Reserve.

(*b*) Pioneer Battalion will act under orders of C.R.E. and will be employed on improvements of communications forward as attack progresses.

14. (*a*) 9th Squadron, Royal Flying Corps, will have two contact aeroplanes in the air from zero to dark on Z day, and again from 6.30 a.m. to 9 a.m. on Z+1 day.

(*b*) Flares will be lit as follows :—

    (i) On obtaining each objective.
    (ii) At 12 noon and 5 p.m. on Z day.
    (iii) At 6.30 a.m. on Z+1 day.

Red Flares will be used by Infantry, Green Flares by Cavalry.

15. Watches will be synchronized at 12.30 p.m. and 6.30 p.m. on Y day by telephone from Divisional Headquarters.

16. Special instructions will be issued on the following subjects :—

(*a*) Division of Artillery into groups, and which fronts they support.

(*b*) Liaison between Artillery and Infantry, also between neighbouring Infantry Brigades.

(*c*) Medical arrangements.

(*d*) Supply of Rations, Water, S.A.A., Light Trench-Mortar Ammunition, Hand Grenades.

17. All transport will be packed up, and ready to move forward at one hour's notice after zero+4 hours. An officer from each Brigade Transport will remain at Divisional Headquarters, Minden Post, from zero+2 hours onwards.

A channel of communication will thus be provided between Guards Brigades and their transport.

18. The Cavalry Corps is to be disposed in depth by 10 a.m. on Z day * with its head at CARNOY ready to move at short notice.

As soon as the final objectives have been captured by the

---

* 15th of September.

Infantry, the Cavalry will advance and seize the high ground ROCQUIGNY—VILLERS AU FLOS—RIENCOURT LES BAPAUME—BAPAUME.

The XIV Corps and also the XV Corps on our left will be prepared to support the Cavalry on the above line at the earliest possible moment.

19. *Prisoners.*

Prisoners will be sent to Divisional Collecting Station at CRATER POST, A 8. a. 6. 3.* when they will be taken over and searched under A.P.M. arrangements.

Receipts will be given for all prisoners and escorts will return to their units.

All captured documents should be sent with prisoners to Divisional Collecting Station, whence they will be forwarded under Divisional arrangements.

20. Advanced Brigade Headquarters will be established as follows :—

2nd Guards Brigade—T. 19. a. $\frac{1}{2}$. $3\frac{1}{2}$.†
1st Guards Brigade—S. 24. b. 6. $1\frac{1}{2}$.‡
3rd Guards Brigade—Dummy Trench.

Advanced Divisional Headquarters will open at BERNAFAY WOOD (S. 28. b. 4. 43) at 6 p.m. on Y day.

(Sd.) C. P. HEYWOOD,
Lieut.-Colonel,
General Staff, Guards Division.

12th September, 1916.
Issued to Signals at 7.30 p.m.

Instructions for Employment of Tanks.

(To accompany Guards Division Order No. 76.)

Nine tanks will be allotted to Guards Division to work partly in Guards Division and partly in 6th Division area.§

Three tanks will be employed in each group and will normally advance in file.

---

* About half a mile out of Carnoy on the Montauban road.
† North-west of Guillemont where the light railway crossed the Longueval road.
‡ At light railway " station," a little south-west of †.
§ The departure positions and lines of advance of the tanks were shown on a map attached to the instructions.

Attack of First Objective.

Tanks will start movement from their departure positions at a time so calculated that they reach their objective 5 minutes before the Infantry.

The Infantry will advance as usual behind a creeping barrage in which gaps, about 100 yards wide, will be left for the route of the tanks. The stationary barrage of both Heavy and Field Artillery will be timed to be lifted off the objectives of the tanks some minutes before their arrival at these objectives.

After clearing up the first objective a proportion of tanks should be pushed forward a short way to prearranged positions as defensive strong points. If necessary a tank may be sent to assist the Infantry in clearing such points in the line as may be holding them up.

The Attack of the 2nd Objective.

Tanks and Infantry will advance together under the creeping barrage. Tanks will move as before in column and on well defined routes. The pace will be regulated to tank pace (30–50 yards per minute), but Infantry must not wait for any tanks that are delayed.

The action of the tanks will be as for the first objective.

The Attack of the 3rd and Subsequent Objectives.

The tanks will start sufficiently far in front of the Infantry to reach the third and fourth objectives some time before the Infantry, being covered during their advance by a creeping barrage.

The tanks will move as before in column.

Their action will be arranged so as to crush wire and keep down hostile rifle and machine-gun fire.

The Infantry when they are advancing must not wait for any tanks that are delayed.

The following signals will be used :—
From Tanks to Infantry and Aircraft.

Flag Signals—RED Flag—Out of action.
                GREEN Flag—Am on objective.
                Other Flags—Are Inter-tank signals.

Lamp Signals—Series of T's—Out of action.
                  Series of H's—Am on objective.

A proportion of the tanks will carry pigeons.

If tanks get behind time table or get out of action, Infantry must on no account wait for them.

If the tanks succeed and the Infantry are checked the tanks must endeavour to help them.

General Notes.

Recent trials show that over heavily shelled ground a greater pace than 15 yards a minute cannot be depended on. This pace will be increased to 33 yards over good ground, and down hill on good ground it will reach 50 yards a minute.

N.B.—" Instructions for Tanks " (timed 11.55 p.m., 13th of September) contained more details of tank assembly, movements and tasks. It also said that Company Commanders would notify their requirements to the tanks.

" Guards Division Order No. 67 " (timed 6.30 p.m., 13th of September) contained information regarding R.E. Dumps and Traffic Regulations. Movements of Brigades to forming up areas were embodied in a March Table attached.

" Instructions as to action of Guards Brigade in Divisional Reserve " were issued separately on the 13th of September.

* * * * *

(*c*) ORDER FOR THE GUARDS' ATTACK ON THE 25TH OF SEPTEMBER, 1916.

See map facing p. 186, Vol. I.

No. 82.

1. (*a*) The Fourth Army will renew the attack on " Z " day in combination with attacks by the French to the South and the Reserve Army to the North.

(*b*) The objectives of the XIV Corps include MORVAL and LESBŒUFS and those of the XV Corps GUEUDECOURT.

(*c*) The attack of the XIV Corps will be carried out by the 5th Division on the Right, the 6th Division in the Centre and the Guards Division on the Left; the 56th Division will form a defensive flank on the South of the 5th Division.

The 21st Division will be attacking on our Left.

2. The 1st Guards Brigade will attack on the Right; and the 3rd Guards Brigade on the Left.

2nd Guards Brigade (less 1 Battalion) will be in Divisional Reserve.

1 Battalion, 2nd Guards Brigade, will be in Corps Reserve.

APPENDIX IV

2nd Guards Brigade will notify Divisional Headquarters the name of the Battalion detailed.

Preliminary Bombardment.

3. A steady bombardment of hostile positions will be commenced at 7 a.m. on " Y " day and will be continued to 6.30 p.m. It will recommence at 6.30 a.m. on " Z " day.

The ground in front and rear of the German trenches which are being bombarded will be searched occasionally with 18-pdr. shrapnel and H.E. shell.

There will be no intensive fire previous to the hour of ZERO.

Night firing will be carried out nightly between the hours of 6.30 p.m. and 6.30 a.m.

Forming up Areas.

4. Forming up areas are shown on attached map.*

1st and 3rd Guards Brigades will allot forming up areas to 75th and 55th Field Companies, R.E., respectively, within their areas.

Instructions for movements to forming up areas will be issued separately.

5. Objectives allotted to Guards Brigades and neighbouring Divisions, also dividing lines, are shown on attached map.*

    First Objective is marked   ..   .. GREEN.
    2nd Objective is marked   ..   .. BROWN.†
    3rd Objective is marked   ..   .. BLUE.

6. The Infantry will advance to the attack of the GREEN Line at ZERO
    to the attack of the BROWN Line at ZERO+one hour
    to the attack of the BLUE Line at ZERO+two hours.

Barrages.

7. (*a*) 50 per cent. of Field Artillery covering the Division will be used for creeping barrage and 50 per cent. for stationary barrage.

(*b*) In all cases the stationary barrage will lift back when the creeping barrage meets it.

8. (*a*) At ZERO the creeping barrage will commence 100 yards in front of our front trenches.

---

* Shown on a map attached to the order.
† A slight adjustment of the "brown" line on the fronts of the 3rd Guards Brigade and the 21st Division was made known on the 23rd of September.

It will advance at rate of 50 yards per minute until it is 200 yards beyond the GREEN Line when it will become stationary.

(b) At ZERO+one hour

The creeping barrage will commence 200 yards in front of the GREEN Line and will advance at the rate of 50 yards per minute until it has passed 200 yards beyond the BROWN Line when it will become stationary.

(c) At ZERO+two hours.

The creeping barrage will commence 100 * yards in front of the BROWN Line, and will advance at rate of 50 yards per minute, until it has passed 200 yards beyond the BLUE Line, when it will become stationary.

Details of stationary barrages will be notified later.

10. (a) The task of the two leading Guards Brigades is to press the attack through to the BLUE Line. A sufficient flow of troops must be maintained by 1st and 3rd Guards Brigades, from ZERO onwards, to ensure that the attack made from the BROWN Line is strong and well supported.

(b) Special arrangements must be made to deal with resistance in LESBŒUFS and thus prevent the possibility of the enemy cutting off our troops which have gained the BLUE Line.

(c) 1st and 3rd Guards Brigades will garrison and consolidate the BROWN Line with a portion of their Reserves when the attack pushes forward to the BLUE Line.

(d) On gaining the BLUE Line patrols will be sent forward, and any ground from which good observation can be gained will be occupied.

Such points will be consolidated and eventually joined up with our line.

11. **R.E.**

75th Field Company, R.E., and 55th Field Company, R.E., will be at disposal of 1st and 3rd Guards Brigades respectively for the attack.

76th Field Company, R.E., and Pioneer Battalion (4th Bn. Coldstream Guards) will be in Divisional Reserve.

12. One Contact Patrol will be in the air from ZERO till 6.30 p.m.

13. Flares will be lit by leading Infantry lines on obtaining each objective, and also at 6 p.m. on " Z " day.

14. Watches will be synchronized at 6 p.m. on " Y " day and at 8 a.m. on " Z " day by telephone from Divisional Headquarters.

* Subsequently altered to 200 yards.

15. Separate instructions will be issued on the following points :—
  (A) Division of Artillery into groups and the fronts they support.
  (B) Medical arrangements.
  (C) Supply of Rations.
      Water.
      S.A.A.
      Light Trench-Mortar Ammunition.
      Hand Grenades.

16. Ammunition portions of 1st Line Transport will be collected on the south-west side of BERNAFAY WOOD—to the south of the GUILLEMONT—MONTAUBAN road, and remainder of 1st Line Transport in the neighbourhood of MINDEN POST by 12 noon on " Z " day. An Orderly from each Brigade Transport will be in waiting at Advanced Divisional Headquarters, BERNAFAY WOOD, and an Officer from each Brigade Transport at Divisional Headquarters MINDEN POST from 12 noon on " Z " day to receive instructions.

17. *Prisoners.*

Prisoners will be dealt with as per paragraph 19, G.D.O. No. 76.

18. For the attack, Advanced Headquarters will be as follows :—

Divisional Headquarters	BERNAFAY WOOD (S. 28 b. 4. 4.) *
1st Guards Brigade	T. 19 a. ½. 3½ †
3rd Guards Brigade	S. 24 b. 6. 1½ ‡
2nd Guards Brigade	Dummy Trench (S. 23 b. 5. 2) §

19. " Z " day will be September 23rd.‖

Hour of ZERO will be notified later—it will probably be in the afternoon.¶

(Signed) C. P. HEYWOOD,
Lieut.-Colonel,
General Staff, Guards Division.

ACKNOWLEDGE
21st September, 1916.
Issued to Divnl. Signals at 12 noon.

* North-east portion.
† Outskirts of Guillemont on the Longueval road.
‡ West of 1st Guards Bde.
§ Just north-west of Trônes Wood.
‖ Altered later on this day to the 25th of September.
¶ Made known as 12.35 p.m. on the 24th of September. The French were to attack at the same hour.

Instructions for Tanks.

(Issued with Guards Divisional Order No. 82.)

1. Three tanks under Captain Hiscocks are allotted to the Guards Division for the operations on " Z " day. They will be kept in Divisional Reserve.

2. These tanks will be in their assembly positions at the south-west corner of TRÔNES WOOD by 5 p.m. on " Y " day, at which hour an orderly will be sent by Captain Hiscocks to Guards Divisional Headquarters.

3. At ZERO hour the three tanks will proceed from their assembly position to a point about T. 13 central,* avoiding the roads in getting to this point.

On arrival, Captain Hiscocks and two orderlies will report at 1st Guards Brigade Headquarters at T. 19 a. $\frac{1}{2}$. $3\frac{1}{2}$ † and will there await orders from Divisional Headquarters.

4. An advanced dump of petrol, 120 gallons, will be maintained at T. 13 central.*

5. From 5 p.m. on " Y " day, all orders from Divnl. Hdqrs. affecting tanks will be sent direct to Captain Hiscocks.

(Signed) E. SEYMOUR,
Captain,
General Staff, Guards Division.

ACKNOWLEDGE
21st Sept. 1916.
Issued to Signals at 2.30 *p.m.*

N.B.—On the 23rd of September Special Instructions were issued for the Brigade in Divisional Reserve (2nd Guards Brigade).

* * * * *

(*d*) ORDER FOR THE GUARDS' ATTACK ON THE 31ST OF JULY, 1917.

(Amended Copy.) ‡

No. 130. *See map facing p.* 254, *Vol. I.*
Plan.

1. (*a*) The XIV Corps in conjunction with Corps on our right and left will attack the enemy on " Z " day. §

---

* A point west of Ginchy.
† Outskirts of Guillemont on the Longueval road.
‡ This Order was issued *provisionally* on the 14th of July.
§ Postponed first from the 25th to the 28th of July and then to the 31st.

(b) ZERO will be at dawn.

The exact time of ZERO will be notified later.*

(c) The attack will be made in a series of bounds along the whole front of the attack.

Each bound is defined by a coloured line as drawn on Map " A " attached.†

First bound ..	..	.. BLUE line,
Second bound	..	.. BLACK line.
Third bound ..	..	.. GREEN line.
Fourth bound	..	.. DOTTED GREEN line.

(d) 38th Division will attack on our right, 1st French Divn. on our left.

Objectives.

2. (a) The final objective of the Division on " Z " day ‡ will be the GREEN DOTTED line between U. 28. a. 0. 7. and U. 20. c. 9. 5., thence the GREEN line to U. 20. c. 5. 8.§

(b) If opportunity offers, ground East of the final objective up to and including the RED line will be occupied.

Should the enemy be found strongly posted, no attack will be made to gain ground beyond the GREEN DOTTED line until adequate artillery preparation and support have been arranged.

Distribution.

3. The Division will attack from the front B. 12. d. 8. 7— B. 5. d. 80. 85.‖

2nd Guards Brigade will attack on the right.

3rd Guards Brigade will attack on the left.

1st Guards Brigade will be in reserve.

Map B attached shows Assembly position on night Y/Z.¶

Boundaries.

4. Divisional and Inter-Brigade boundaries are shown on Map " A " attached.**

---

* Fixed for 3.50 a.m.
† *See* Map facing p. 254, Vol. I.
‡ Postponed first from the 25th to the 28th of July and then to the 31st.
§ *See* Map facing p. 254, Vol. I.
‖ Altered by G.D.O. No. 134, 28th of July, to line reached by the 1st Guards Bde. on the 27th of July.
¶ Subsequently altered. *See* ‖ above.
** *See* Map facing p. 254, Vol. I.

Tasks of Guards Brigades.

5. (*a*) 2nd and 3rd Guards Brigades will be responsible for capturing the BLUE, BLACK and GREEN lines.

(*b*) 1st Guards Brigade (less 2 battalions) will be responsible for the capture of the GREEN DOTTED line, up to the RED line inclusive, as may be gained by patrols.

(*c*) 2 battalions 1st Guards Brigade will be in Div'l reserve.

Method of Attack.
2nd & 3rd Guards Bdes.

6. (*a*) 2nd and 3rd Guards Brigades will each attack on a front of 2 battalions.

The 2 leading battalions of the 2nd Guards Brigade, and the 2 leading battalions of the 3rd Guards Brigade prior to ZERO will capture the Eastern bank of the Canal (including CANAL SUPPORT)* and subsequent to ZERO will capture the BLUE and BLACK lines.

(*b*) No movement of troops of 2nd and 3rd Guards Brigades will be made between ZERO – 30 and ZERO.

(*c*) The capture of the Eastern bank of the canal on night Y/Z forms the subject of a separate order (Guards Div. Order No: 131).†

(*d*) The two reserve battalions of 2nd and 3rd Guards Brigades will capture the GREEN line.

These battalions will be east of the Canal by + 1 hour 45 minutes. Their leading wave will pass the line CANON FARM— SAUVAGE HOUSE not later than + 2 hours 30 minutes, and will reach the BLACK line by + 3 hours.

Movement of R.E. Group at zero.

7. (*a*) 76th Field Co. R.E. and 55th Field Co. R.E., followed by 75th Field Co. R.E. and 1 Co. Pioneers (4th Bn. C.G.) will move forward from assembly area in B. 7. c.‡ at zero.

(*b*) 76 Field Co. R.E. will move by tracks and trenches in 2nd Guards Brigade area; 55th Field Co. R.E. by tracks and trenches in 3rd Guards Brigade area. 75th Field Co. R.E. and 1 Coy. Pioneer Bn. (4th C.G.) will move by main ELVERDINGHE —BOESINGHE road.

(*c*) C.R.E. will issue orders for these movements.

* Subsequently amended by G.D.O. No. 134, 28th of July.
† Subsequently rendered inoperative by the advance across the Canal by the Guards Division on the 27th of July. G.D.O. No. 134, 28th of July was issued to meet the altered situation.
‡ West of Elverdinghe.

Method of Attack of 1st Guards Brigade.

8. (A) 1st Guards Brigade (less 2 battalions) will capture the GREEN DOTTED line.

(B) Movement from assembly area will commence at ZERO+10 minutes immediately in rear of R.E. group.

Two battalions concerned will be East of the Canal by + 2 hours 30 minutes. Their leading wave will pass the BLACK line not later than + 3 hours 55 minutes and will arrive at the GREEN line by + 4 hours 30 minutes.

(C) In the event of 2nd and 3rd Guards Brigades being held up on their whole front before reaching the GREEN line the two leading battalions 1st Guards Brigade will not become involved in the attack, until arrangements have been made to bring back the barrage. Their assistance will in this case be given, under orders of Divisional Headquarters to 1st Guards Brigade, in the form of a fresh attack supported by a fresh barrage.

The above does not preclude the two leading battalions 1st Guards Brigade from assisting to clear up a situation where a portion of the attack has been held up, and when the employment of one or two fresh companies may serve to readjust the advance.

(D) As soon as GREEN DOTTED line is captured, infantry patrols will be sent forward on the whole Divisional front by 1st Guards Brigade to ascertain the strength and location of the enemy. Cavalry patrols, if they succeed in getting forward, will assist in this reconnaissance. Detailed instructions dealing with action of Cavalry have been issued.

(E) Two companies 2nd Guards Brigade and 1 company 3rd Guards Brigade will be made available, if called for by 1st Guards Brigade, either (i) to hold the GREEN DOTTED line, should a considerable advance beyond this line be made by 1st Guards Brigade, or (ii) to support 1st Guards Brigade in case of heavy counter-attack.

These companies, if employed in front of the GREEN line, will come under tactical command of 1st Guards Brigade.

O.C. Companies of 2nd and 3rd Guards Brigades detailed for these tasks will gain touch with O.C. battalions of 1st Guards Brigade on the arrival of the latter in the neighbourhood of the GREEN line.

Should touch fail to be gained, these companies of 2nd and 3rd Guards Brigades will, without waiting for orders, act on their own initiative in carrying out the rôle given in sub-paras. (i) and (ii) above.

OPERATION ORDERS

Divisional Reserve.

(F) Two battalions 1st Guards Brigade will be in Divisional Reserve and will move so that their leading troops reach the neighbourhood of the 'X' line by plus 4 hours, moving thither by tracks 11 and 12, RAILWAY STREET, HUNTER STREET, CLARGES STREET and BRIDGE STREET, as convenient.†

Battalion Headquarters of these two battalions will, on arrival in neighbourhood of the 'X' line, be established in CHASSEUR FARM ‡ and B 11. a. 0. 2 § respectively.

Care will be taken not to block any Artillery traffic during this advance.

Liaison.

9. Special parties will be told off to gain touch with flank Divisions.

They will consolidate the positions to which they are detailed.

Each party will consist of not less than 1 officer, or N.C.O. and 6 men, and will be detailed as follows :—

2nd Guards Brigade.
    CABLE TRENCH at C. 7. a. 3. 4. ||
    CARIBOO TRENCH at C. 1. c. 9. 4 (*). ¶
    CHIMNEY HOUSE.
    GDE. BARRIERE HOUSE.
    Where GREEN line cuts railway (*).

By 3rd Guards Brigade.
    S.W. Corner of WOOD 14 (B. 6. a. 9. 9).
    POMPADOUR FARM (*).
    Eastern corner of WOOD 16 (U. 25. a. 4. 3).
    LOOBECK FARM.
    COLONEL'S FARM (*).

By 1st Guards Brigade.
    Where "DOTTED GREEN line" crosses the railway at U. 28. a. 0. 7 (*).

NOTE.—An officer to be with parties marked with an asterisk (*).

† Tracks and communication trenches leading forward to X Line.
‡ *See* Map facing p. 254, Vol. I.
§ West-south-west of Gouvy Farm.
|| Right boundary, included in the advance of the 27th of July.
¶ Where "blue line" crosses railway.

Consolidation.

2nd & 3rd Guards Brigades.

10. (*a*) 2nd and 3rd Guards Brigades will be responsible for consolidating the BLUE and GREEN lines.

(*b*) They will also be responsible for construction of the following Strong Points, in addition to any ordered by Brigadiers.

2nd Guards Brigade.

Not less than 2 strong points on the approximate lines: U. 26. c. 3. 3.—U. 26. c. 6. 7—a strong point on right flank of GREEN line.*

3rd Guards Brigade.

On the left flank of the Blue line (T. 30 d. 9. 8).
On the left flank of the GREEN line.
Not less than 3 strong points in the approximate line U. 26. c. 6. 7—ABRI FARM—MAJOR'S FARM.†
Garrisons for strong points will be detailed in advance.

1st Guards Brigade.

11. 1st Guards Brigade will be responsible for consolidating the GREEN DOTTED line, and will also be responsible for consolidating any ground forward of the GREEN DOTTED line gained by patrols.

In the event of occupation of positions considerably in advance of the GREEN DOTTED line, G.O.C. 1st Guards Brigade will hand over consolidation of the GREEN DOTTED line to the companies of the 2nd and 3rd Guards Brigades on which he will have a call, and will concentrate the work of his two battalions on consolidating the more forward positions gained.

Principles of Consolidation.

12. The lines consolidated will become the lines of resistance as gained.

Outpost lines of Advanced Posts will be established in front of the

    (*a*) GREEN line.
    (*b*) The DOTTED GREEN line.
    (*c*) Any line in front of the DOTTED GREEN line consolidated by 1st Guards Brigade.

---

* This line=ABRI WOOD—right boundary of " green line."
† A continuation of * to Major's Farm.

OPERATION ORDERS

Action in case Flanks held up.

13. In the event of a unit on either flank of the Division, or within the Division, being held up, adjoining units will on no account check their advance. They will drop small parties to form a defensive flank, while continuing to press forward to their objectives.

It is of vital importance that the barrage be followed closely by the Infantry.

Any nests of Germans left behind must be dealt with by reserves.

Artillery.

14. (*a*) Six brigades of Field Artillery will support the attack, and will form :
    (i) A creeping barrage.
    (ii) A standing barrage.

Sketch map showing times of lifts of the creeping barrage is attached—Map ' C.' *

The standing barrage will in all cases lift back when, or before the creeping barrage reaches it.

(*b*) The main points, as regards the creeping barrage, which affect the Infantry are as follows :—

(i) The barrage when moving will lift 100 yards at a time, pausing 4 minutes between each lift.

(ii) Where trenches exist, the creeping barrage has been so arranged that its 4 minutes' pause is on the trench.

(iii) The creeping barrage when lifting off the BLUE, BLACK and GREEN lines will lift back 100 yards, pause 4 minutes, then lift back another 100 yards and form a protective barrage.

(iv) The creeping barrage, which during the halts on the BLUE, BLACK, and GREEN lines will be temporarily stationary, will become intense for 4 minutes before it recommences to lift forward.

This will enable leading Infantry to get close up to the barrage.

(*c*) Smoke barrages will be made by barrage guns as follows, if wind is favourable :—

In front of BLUE line on 38th Division front from ZERO+50 minutes to ZERO+1 hour 5 minutes.

In front of BLACK line on 38th and Guards Division fronts from ZERO+2 hours 14 minutes to ZERO+3 hours.

    * This map showing barrage lines has not been reproduced.

In front of GREEN line on 38th and Guards Division fronts from ZERO+4 hours 21 minutes to ZERO+4 hours 45 minutes.

Movements of Artillery.

(i) When Infantry reach the GREEN line, the following movements of Artillery will take place :—

   84*th Brigade R.F.A.* To position just N. of WAALKRANTZ FARM.
   74*th Brigade, R.F.A.* To position N. of GOUVY FARM.

(ii) On capture of GREEN DOTTED line,

   5*th R.H.A. Brigade* moves to positions on general line of CARIBOO trench.

On arrival, this Brigade will come under orders of G.O.C. 1st Guards Brigade, to whom O.C. Brigade will report.

(iii) As soon as first battery 5th R.H.A. Brigade is reported East of the Canal,

15*th R.H.A. Brigade* will move to positions in C. 1. c.* On arrival, this Brigade will come under orders of G.O.C. 1st Guards Brigade, to whom O.C. Brigade will report.

(iv) 17*th Brigade, R.F.A.* will move on receipt of orders to a position in C. 1. b.† and will be under orders of Right Group.

Special Companies R.E.

15. (*a*) At zero+3 minutes, there will be a discharge of oil drums and of 4" Stokes Mortars firing Thermite.

This fire will cease at zero+6 minutes.

(*b*) Targets of these discharges will be
   CANAL DRIVE in C. 1. c., ARTILLERY WOOD, WOOD 15.‡

Machine Guns.

16. (*a*) The attack will be assisted by a Machine-Gun barrage.

The following Machine Guns are detailed for this task under Divisional Machine-Gun Officer.

   4th Guards M.-G. Co.
   2 sections 2nd Guards Brigade M.-G. Co.
   2 sections 3rd Guards Brigade M.-G. Co.
   88th Co. M.-G. Corps (29th Division).

(*b*) At + 2 hours 34 minutes 1 section 2nd Guards Brigade

---

* Vicinity of Canon Farm.
† Vicinity of Hey Wood.
‡ Cancelled by reason of the advance on the 27th of July.

M.-G. Co. and 1 section 3rd Guards Brigade M.-G. Co. will return under command of 2nd and 3rd Guards Brigades respectively.

At +3 hours 24 minutes, 88th Co. Machine-Gun Corps will be withdrawn into reserve West of ELVERDINGHE.

(c) Successive positions of barrage machine guns, and times of lifts are shown on Map ' D.' *

(d) On arrival in their final position about +7 hours barrage machine guns will come under orders of 1st Guards Brigade who will allot them tasks through the Divisional Machine-Gun Officer.

The latter will report at 1st Guards Brigade Advanced Battle Headquarters at +6 hours.

R.E. & 4th C.G. (Pioneers).

17. (a) 76th Field Co. R.E. (less 2 sections) will be attached to 2nd Guards Brigade.

55th Field Co. R.E. (less 2 sections) to 3rd Guards Brigade.

The primary tasks of above troops will be to assist in wiring the GREEN line and in superintending construction of Strong points.

(b) 2 sections 55th Field Co. R.E. and 2 sections 76th Field Co. R.E. will be attached to 1st Guards Brigade.

Their primary tasks will be to assist in wiring and consolidating positions gained by 1st Guards Brigade beyond the GREEN line.

(c) R.E. attached to Guards Brigades will not be sent up to commence their tasks until definite information of the situation is to hand.

In the case of 1st Guards Brigade, attached R.E. should not be sent forward until the line to be consolidated can be determined.

The above does not preclude Guards Brigadiers from moving forward their attached R.E. in rear of the attack to positions where they will be well placed to receive orders, and from which they can quickly commence their tasks.

(d) 75th Field Co. R.E. will be employed on construction of PONTOON BRIDGES under orders of C.R.E.

(e) Two companies 4th Bn. Coldstream Guards (Pioneers) will be responsible for running out and maintaining mat bridges and petrol tin bridges across the canal.

(f) Pioneer Bn. (less 1 company) will be responsible under orders of C.R.E. for construction of approaches to PONTOON

* This map has not been reproduced.

BRIDGES on both sides of the Canal, and for improving tracks East of the Canal.

(g) Such portions of companies mentioned in para. (e) as are not required to maintain mat and petrol tin bridges will be employed on task (f) as soon as task (e) is completed.

(h) One infantry battalion 29th Division will be attached to the division after Zero for work on Artillery tracks leading to and forward of the PONTOON Bridges. C.R.E. will arrange expert supervision of this work.

Communication with Aircraft.

18. (a) A contact patrol will fly over the Corps front at
   Zero+1 hour.
   Zero+2 hours 25 minutes.
   Zero+4 hours 20 minutes.
   Zero+5 hours 40 minutes.
   1.30 p.m.
   4.0 p.m.
   8.0 p.m.

(b) Leading troops will show positions to Contact aeroplanes when demanded,
   (i) By Klaxon Horn.
   (ii) By a series of White Lights.

Detailed instructions for Communication with Aircraft have been isssued.

S.O.S.

19. On ZERO day and subsequently, the S.O.S. Signal will be a Rifle Grenade bursting into two RED and two GREEN lights.

No other light signal will be employed except flares to show the position of Infantry to Contact patrols.

March to Assembly Area.

20. The march to Assembly Area is dealt with in Guards Division Order No. 133.*

Synchronization of Watches.

21. Watches will be synchronized on ' Y ' day from a watch brought round by a Divisional Staff Officer as soon as possible after 11.0 a.m. and 7 p.m.

---

* An amended March Table in accordance with the situation was issued on the 28th of July.

G.D.A., Guards Brigades and C.R.E. will similarly arrange to circulate a watch giving official time. In no circumstances will synchronization of watches be carried out by telephone.

Divisional Headquarters.

22. Divisional Headquarters will close at "J" Camp and open at ZOMMERBLOOM * at 6 p.m. on 'Y' day.

(Signed) C. P. HEYWOOD,
Lieut.-Colonel,
24th July, 1917.   General Staff, Guards Division.
Issued to Signals at 4.15 p.m.

[N.B.—On the 2nd of July a "Guards Division Instruction" announced that the XIV Corps attack was to be delivered, in conjunction with troops to north and south, "on a date to be communicated later." Boundaries, objectives and the tasks of the three Guards brigades were specified, and all preparations were ordered to be completed by the 20th of July. Further detailed instructions—some as the result of divisional conferences—were issued from time to time, special attention being paid to the method to be adopted in crossing the canal.

G.D.O. No. 130 was issued provisionally on the 14th of July.

Subsequent to the circulation of G.D.O. No. 130 (Amended Copy) on the 24th of July many additional orders and instructions were issued. The chief of these were:

July 25th—Regulation of trench traffic.
        Communications between the 1st Guards Bde. and the French.
July 26th—Message of appreciation of efforts of all ranks and units in preparing for the offensive.
        Policy as regards the maintenance of communication trenches.
        Notification of the French decision not to consolidate the BLUE line. The 3rd Guards Bde. ordered to join up its left on the BLUE line with the French on the BLACK line.
July 27th—Order for the advance of the 1st Guards Bde. across the canal. (Issued on receipt of aeroplane reports that the German front system was not held.)
July 28th—G.D.O. No. 134. This gives the line held by the

* North-west of Elverdinghe.

1st Guards Bde. east of the canal; states that the arrangements for the attack are to hold good with the exception that the offensive would start from the above line, and that the barrage at zero would start on a suitable line in front of this position; notifies as regards reliefs and assembly, that movement across the canal by day was not possible.

Order for the relief of the 1st Guards Bde. by the 2nd and 3rd Guards Bdes. on night 29/30th.

July 29th—Adjustment of artillery barrages consequent on the occupation by the Guards of German positions east of canal.

Instructions *re* siting and maintenance of infantry bridges over the canal.

Order that at +5 hours 50 minutes the protective field artillery barrage would cease in front of the GREEN DOTTED line, and that all the heavy artillery would lift on to or beyond the RED line. This fire would not lift back again without corps orders and reference to the 1st Guards Bde.]

* * * * *

(*e*) ORDER FOR THE GUARDS' ATTACK ON FONTAINE—NOTRE-DAME, ON THE 27TH OF NOVEMBER, 1917.

See map facing p. 322, Vol. I.

No. 165.

1. THE IV Corps will attack BOURLON and FONTAINE to-morrow morning.

2. The Guards Division will attack FONTAINE; the 62nd Division will attack BOURLON. The 186th Inf. Bde. will carry out the latter attack with headquarters at K. 4. d. 5. 5.*

3. Dividing lines between Divisions and Objectives are shown on attached map.

4. Zero hour will be 6.20 a.m.

5. The attack by the Guards Division will be carried out by the 2nd Guards Brigade.

6. The 3rd Guards Brigade less 1 battalion will be in Divisional reserve, one battalion (4th Bn. Grenadier Guards) to be ready to occupy the jumping off line as soon as vacated by the attacking troops, one battalion in the sunken road at about LA JUSTICE,† and one battalion in FLESQUIÈRES.

* S.W. of Graincourt.
† A mile east of Graincourt.

7. The attack will be made under a creeping barrage which will move at the rate of 100 yards in 5 minutes to the first objective, when a pause of ½ an hour will be made before the advance, which will be made at the same pace, to the second objective.

8. 14 tanks of ' F ' battalion No. 18 company will take part in the attack. These will be in position north and south of the FONTAINE—ANNEUX CHAPEL road to-night and will cross the jumping off line at Zero.

The tanks will move along all main streets in the village of FONTAINE and around the north and south ends of the village.

9. The D.M.G.O. will arrange for a protective machine-gun barrage in front of the outpost line.

The 7th Motor Machine-Gun Company will place 4 guns at the disposal of 2nd Guards Brigade.

10. The C.R.E. will detail a party, with explosives, to report to 2nd Guards Brigade H.Q. at noon to-morrow ready to move to FONTAINE as soon as situation permits to carry out demolitions.

IV Corps Cyclists will place 90 men at the disposal of the C.R.E. for carrying purposes.

11. 3rd Guards Brigade will be prepared to detail 50 men as extra stretcher bearers on demand by A.D.M.S. Guards Division.

12. Contact aeroplanes will fly over FONTAINE at intervals during the day.

13. Watches will be synchronized by an officer from Divisional Hd. Qrs. shortly after 6 p.m. to-night.

14. Hd. Qrs. 2nd Guards Brigade will be at LA JUSTICE.*
Hd. Qrs. 3rd Guards Brigade will be at K. 29. d. 2. 3.†
Divisional Hd. Qrs. will remain at FLESQUIÈRES.

ACKNOWLEDGE. (Signed) A. HORE-RUTHVEN,
26th Nov. 1917 Lieut.-Colonel,
Issued at 6 p.m. General Staff, Guards Division.

* * * * *

(*f*) ORDER FOR THE GUARDS' ATTACK ON THE FLESQUIÈRES—PREMY CHAPEL RIDGE, ON THE 27TH OF SEPTEMBER, 1918.

See map facing p. 180, Vol. II.

No. 222. 25.9.18.

1. (*a*) Guards Division is to attack and capture the FLESQUIÈRES—PREMY CHAPEL ridge in conjunction with other Divisions on both flanks.

---
* A mile east of Graincourt.
† About a mile west of Ribécourt.

(b) Corps and Divisional boundaries and the objectives of the attack in the area HAVRINCOURT—MARCOING—BOURLON WOOD * are shown in the attached map.

(c) The date of the attack has been notified to all concerned.†

2. *Flanks.*

(a) *On the Right.*

(i) 3rd Division is to capture the RED and BROWN Lines.

(ii) 62nd Division is then to pass through 3rd Division and capture the BLUE Line.

(iii) On each of the above lines the advance of 3rd and 62nd Divisions is synchronized with that of Guards Division.

(b) *On the Left.*

(i) 52nd Division is to capture the HINDENBURG Line west of the CANAL DU NORD, and to clear the ground between the CANAL and the HINDENBURG Support Line.

(ii) 63rd (R.N.) Division is to capture the HINDENBURG Support Line east of the CANAL DU NORD and the villages of GRAINCOURT and ANNEUX.

(iii) 57th Division is then to pass through 63rd (R.N.) Division and to capture the BLUE Line east of the villages of CANTAING and FONTAINE-NOTRE-DAME.‡

(iv) The times at which these objectives are to be reached are shown on the attached map.§

3. *Guards Division.*

The attack of Guards Division will be carried out by 2nd, 1st and 3rd Guards Brigades in the above order.

4. *Action of 2nd Guards Brigade.*

(a) 2nd Guards Brigade will capture the RED Line.

(b) It will then hold the RED Line from HAVRINCOURT—GRAINCOURT road westward as a defensive flank for the Division until the HINDENBURG system north of the VI Corps boundary ‖ and GRAINCOURT village have been cleared by 52nd and 63rd Divisions.

---

* Immediately north and north-east of Anneux.
† Announced on the 26th of September as the 27th of September, with zero hour 5.20 a.m.
‡ On the Bapaume—Cambrai road, one mile north of Cantaing.
§ These times are not on the map reproduced.
‖ The left boundary of the Guards Division.

OPERATION ORDERS

5. *Action of 1st Guards Brigade.*

(*a*) 1st Guards Brigade will pass through 2nd Guards Brigade on the RED Line at zero plus 1 hour and 50 minutes. It will capture the trench system north-west and north of FLESQUIÈRES (Brown Dotted Line) in K. 17. b. K. 18. a. and b and the BROWN Line in L. 13.*

(*b*) It will then move north-east along the FLESQUIÈRES—CANTAING spur in accordance with instructions issued separately (Instructions No. 5) and will establish itself on BLUE DOTTED LINE south-west of CANTAING.

(*c*) It will clear the low ground north of FLESQUIÈRES up to the northern VI Corps boundary † in conformity with the advance of 63rd and 57th Divisions on the left.

(*d*) It will continue to hold the BLUE DOTTED LINE as a defensive flank for 3rd Guards Brigade until 57th Division has captured CANTAING.

6. *Action of 3rd Guards Brigade.*

(*a*) 3rd Guards Brigade will pass through 1st Guards Brigade on the BROWN LINE in L. 13 at zero plus four hours and 30 minutes. It will advance at that hour along the spurs running eastward towards L. 16 * and north-east towards L. 9,‡ and will capture the BLUE DOTTED LINE.

(*b*) Separate instructions are issued (Instructions No. 5) regarding the action to be taken after capture of the DOTTED BLUE LINE.

(*c*) 2nd Division is to close up in rear of 3rd Guards Brigade on the BLUE DOTTED LINE and to pass through it on that line which 3rd Guards Brigade may have occupied in accordance with above instructions.

7. *Action of Artillery.*

(*a*) The attack will be supported by six Brigades, R.F.A., which will form creeping barrages up to the RED LINE.

(*b*) Barrage maps and detailed artillery instructions (Instructions No. 6) are issued separately—(distribution to companies).

---

* *I.e.* ground forward of the " red line " between the right boundary of the division and the " brown dotted line," up to and including the " brown line " within the same limits.

† The left boundary of the Guards Division.

‡ These map references merely give the general direction of advance to the " blue dotted line."

(c) The attack will also be supported by Heavy Artillery.

The action of Heavy Artillery (apart from counter-battery) is shown in the above instructions (Instructions No. 6).

8. *Machine Guns.*

(a) Three Machine-Gun Companies will cover the attack up to the RED LINE by barrage fire.

(b) One Company will be attached to 1st Guards Brigade and one to 3rd Guards Brigade for their advance east of the RED LINE.

(c) Detailed instructions are issued separately (Instructions No. 4).

9. *Contact Patrols.*

(a) Contact Patrols will call for flares at the following hours:—
    (i) Zero plus 1 hour 30 minutes.
    (ii) Zero plus 3 hours 30 minutes.
    (iii) Zero plus 6 hours.
    (iv) Zero plus 8 hours.

(b) Brigades will inform Division if a contact patrol is required at any other time.

10. *Synchronization.*

A Divisional Staff Officer will take round a watch to Guards Divisional Artillery, Guards Brigades and 4th Battalion Guards Machine-Gun Regiment between 4 p.m. and 5 p.m. on " Y " day.

11. *Headquarters.*

(a) Guards Brigades will establish their Headquarters by zero at positions in K. 7. a.* shown in attached map.

(b) 1st and 3rd Guards Brigades will move to positions within 200 yards of Forward Divisional Report Centres (Instructions No. 2) under orders from the Division.

(c) Divisional Headquarters will open at J. 10. a. 3. 1.† at 10 p.m. on " Y " day.

ACKNOWLEDGE   (Signed) E. W. M. GRIGG,
                                           Lieut.-Colonel,
25th September, 1918.   General Staff, Guards Division.

    * Trenches north-east of Demicourt.
    † Near Bapaume road, about one and a half miles west of Demicourt.

[N.B.—A Warning Order, containing many of the above details, had been issued on the 19th of September. This was amplified by Guards Division Instructions No. 1 (22nd of September).]

"Amended List of Crossings over Canal," "Notes on Flesquières Sector," and a notice giving the identity of the troops on the flanks of the Guards were all issued on the 23rd of September.

The following were published on the 24th of September:
"Guards Division Instructions No. 2"—Communications special instruction, reports of Guards Division Intelligence Squad.
Information, depth of the Canal du Nord.

Following G.D.O. No. 222 there were also issued on the 25th of September:
"Guards Division Instructions No. 3"—Concentration and approach march with march table.
"Guards Division Instructions No. 4"—Machine guns: detailed orders for each company.
"Guards Division Instructions No. 5"—Detailed orders for advance of the 1st and 3rd Guards Brigades from "brown" line.
Special instruction, balloons and signals.

And on the 26th of September:—
Special instruction, cooperation of R.A.F.
"Guards Division Instructions No. 6"—Artillery action.
"Guards Division Instructions No. 7"—Action of tanks.]

* * * * *

(g) ORDER FOR THE GUARDS' ATTACK ACROSS THE RIVER SELLE ON THE 20TH OCTOBER, 1918.

See map facing p. 216, Vol. II.

No. 228. 18.10.18.

1. *Plan.*

(a) Guards Division will capture the high ground north of SOLESMES on a date which has been communicated to those concerned.*

---

* The date (20th of October) was made known on the 19th of October.

(b) 62nd Division, on the right, is first to clear SOLESMES and afterwards to advance on to the high ground east of that village.

(c) 19th Division, on the left, is to capture HAUSSY and the high ground north-east of that village.

(d) Boundaries and objectives for the attack are shown in the attached map.*

2. *Attack of Guards Division.*

(a) The attack will be carried out by the 1st Guards Brigade on the right and 3rd Guards Brigade on the left.

(b) 2nd Guards Brigade will hold the line until zero † minus two hours.

Command of their respective sectors will then pass to G.O's.C. 1st and 3rd Guards Brigades.

(c) On relief 2nd Guards Brigade will concentrate in ST. HILAIRE and ST. VAAST, and will come into Divisional reserve.

3. *Method of Attack.*

Method of attack will be as follows :—

(a) 1st and 3rd Guards Brigades will cross the river at zero, and will form for attack on the road from V. 30. a. 5. 0 to the Chapel at V. 18. c. 3. 9.‡

(b) Both Brigades will advance together at zero plus 23 minutes and will capture the first objective or GREEN Line.

(c) 3rd Guards Brigade will resume the advance at zero plus 1 hour and 10 minutes, the troops on the right forming to the right behind the barrage on the SOLESMES—VALENCIENNES road as they reach it. This movement will be complete by zero plus two hours and 6 minutes.

(d) At zero plus 2 hours and 6 minutes 1st and 3rd Guards Brigades will advance simultaneously and will capture the second objective or RED Line.

4. *Flanks.*

62nd *Division.*

(a) The attack of 62nd Division on the right is to be carried out as follows :—

(i) One Battalion, 186th Infantry Brigade, will cross the

---

* *See* Map facing p. 216, Vol. II.
† Made known on the 19th of October as 0200 hours.
‡ For the forming up line, *see* Map facing p. 216, Vol. II.

river simultaneously with Guards Division, will capture LE
PIGEON BLANC, and will establish posts on the northern and
eastern outskirts of SOLESMES.

(ii) A second Battalion will follow the above Battalion and
will clear SOLESMES from the north.

(iii) A third Battalion will cross the river south of SOLESMES
and will attack the village from the south.

(iv) The Brown Line in the attached map shows the line east
of SOLESMES on which posts are to be established.*

(v) At zero plus 5 hours 185th Infantry Brigade is to pass
through 186th Infantry Brigade and capture the second objective
or RED Line.

(b) The right flank of 1st Guards Brigade will therefore be
unprotected

(i) While the left front Battalion, 186th Infantry Brigade, is
capturing LE PIGEON BLANC.

(ii) Until the 185th Infantry Brigade has captured the RED
Line.

G.O.C., 1st Guards Brigade, will therefore take measures to
hold a defensive flank along the road from W. 20 central to V. 30 d,†
so long as necessary.

19th *Division.*

(c) 19th Division on the left will be advancing simultaneously
with Guards Division throughout the operation.

5. *Bridging.*

(a) Light Infantry Bridges will be thrown on the front of each
attacking Brigade at zero.

(b) These bridges will be thrown by specially detailed parties
of R.E. and 4th Bn. Coldstream Guards (Pioneers) and will be
numbered from right to left consecutively.

(c) Tracks will be made from the road east of the railway to
the bridges, each track being marked with the number of the
bridge to which it leads.

(d) Instructions for the throwing of Artillery bridges after
zero will be issued later.

* Right boundary of the VI Corps.
† The right boundary of the Guards Division as far as the second
objective.

6. *Liaison Posts.*

Liaison Posts will be established with flank Divisions as follows :—
  (*a*) *Right Flank.*
    (i) Cross-roads in V. 30. d. 7. 7.*
    (ii) Le Pigeon Blanc—W. 25. d. 2. 8.
    (iii) Road junction—W. 20. c. 1. 0.†
    (iv) Cross-roads—W. 20. c. 7. 7.‡
  (*b*) *Left Flank.*
    (i) Road junction V. 12. c. 8. 1.§
    (ii) Road at W. 7. a. 2. 1.‖
    (iii) Maison Blanche—W. 1. d. 5. 3.

7. *Action of Artillery.*

(*a*) The attack will be supported by a creeping barrage of five Field Artillery Brigades. This barrage will be put down on the line of the road V. 30. a. 5. 0. to V. 18. c. 3. 9 ¶ from zero to zero plus 3 minutes.

It will then lift to a line 200 yards east of the road, and will remain on this line from zero plus 3 minutes to zero plus 23 minutes.

It will then advance by lifts of 100 yards every 4 minutes to a line 300 yards east of the first objective.

It will remain stationary on this line in the sector of the 1st Guards Brigade until zero plus 126 minutes.

In the sector of the 3rd Guards Brigade it will lift from this line at zero plus 70 minutes and will advance by lifts of 100 yards every 4 minutes to the line of the SOLESMES—VALENCIENNES road, building itself upon this road from south to north as it reaches it.

At zero+126 minutes the barrage will advance on the whole Divisional front by lifts of 100 yards every 4 minutes to a line 300 yards east of the Second Objective. It will remain upon this line for four minutes, and will then cease.

(*b*) Barrage tables will be issued for distribution to Battalions to-morrow.

(*c*) One Field Artillery Brigade will fire thermite shell on machine-gun nests east of the creeping barrage during the advance.

---

* The cross-roads west of le Pigeon Blanc.
† North-east of le Pigeon Blanc.
‡ Farther to the north-east towards Vertain.
§ By the Cemetery at Haussy.
‖ Where the boundary cuts the road from Chapelle d'Haussy.
¶ The forming up line of the infantry.

It will then be available to put down a barrage, if required, on the right flank of 1st Guards Brigade east of the BROWN LINE.

(d) The Field Artillery barrage will be 50 % shrapnel and 50 % H.E.

(e) The Corps Heavy Artillery will be engaging targets during the operation as follows :—

(1) 40 %—Machine-gun nests and trenches in depth east of Field Artillery barrage.

(2) 60 %—Counter-battery.

(f) Two sections of field guns will be pushed forward in close support of the infantry for anti-tank defence.

(g) On completion of the operation the Field Artillery will be organized in two Groups of 3 Brigades each covering the Right and Left Guards Brigades respectively.

8. *Action of Machine Guns.*

(a) Two Companies, 4th Bn. Guards Machine-Gun Regt., will be affiliated to 1st and 3rd Guards Brigades respectively with the following tasks :—

(i) To cover the flanks of the advance north of SOLESMES and south of HAUSSY.

(ii) To assist consolidation of the Second Objective in depth.

(b) O.C. 4th Bn. Guards Machine-Gun Regt., will detail guns for the above purposes in consultation with G.O's.C., 1st and 3rd Guards Brigades.

(c) The company in the line will be withdrawn at zero minus two hours, and will be concentrated in reserve in St. Hilaire.

A fourth company will also remain in reserve in St. Hilaire.

9. *Consolidation.*

(a) The Second Objective or RED Line will be the Main Line of Defence of the Division.

(b) Outposts will be established well in advance of this line, and the line itself will be consolidated in depth.

(c) The Field Artillery S.O.S. Line will be arranged by 1st and 3rd Guards Brigades with Group Commanders, and notified to the Division.

10. *Time.*

(a) Zero hour will be notified separately.*

(b) A Divisional Staff Officer will take a watch round to

---

* 0200 hours, 20th of October, announced 1200 hours 19th of October.

C.R.A., C.R.E., Guards Brigades, and 4th Guards Machine-Gun Regt. between 1500 and 1600 hours on " Y " day.

11. *Contact Patrols.*

(*a*) Success signals will be fired from each objective as soon as captured.

(*b*) Contact patrols will fly over the Divisional front at—
  Zero plus 5 hours.
  Zero plus 6 hours.
  Zero plus 7 hours.

(*c*) Contact patrols will be sent out at any other time required on demand to these Headquarters.

12. *Headquarters.*

(*a*) Headquarters of 1st and 3rd Guards Brigades will be established at zero in St. Hilaire.

(*b*) Instructions for the advance of Brigade Headquarters will be issued to-morrow.

(*c*) Divisional Headquarters will remain at Boussières.

(Signed) E. W. M. Grigg,
Acknowledge. Lieut.-Colonel,
Issued through Signals at 1930. General Staff, Guards Division.

[N.B.—The above Order cancelled a preliminary Order, called " Guards Divn. Instructions No. 1," issued on the 16th of October.

On the 18th of October were also issued detailed instructions for the crossing of the river Selle, and for communications.

A warning that the Guards Division might have to continue the advance on the 21st was issued on the 19th of October.]

APPENDIX V

NOTE ON THE RESERVE BATTALIONS OF THE GUARDS REGIMENTS.

A RESERVE battalion was formed by each regiment of Guards as soon as the Regular battalions went abroad, in order to take men who were left behind either because they were under age or unfit for active service, and reservists who were surplus to immediate requirements. Throughout the war recruits were sent to the Reserve battalions as soon as they had been passed out of the Guards Depôt, as well as sick and wounded men on their return to duty.*

The main task of the Reserve battalions was to equip, to train and to provide the necessary drafts of officers and other ranks for the battalions in the field. The training both of officers and men was very thorough, and, in addition to drill and other routine work, included instruction in musketry and the Lewis gun, all forms of open warfare, trench warfare, bombing, etc.

Recruits were sent to the Reserve battalions in batches usually varying from 200 to 300 men. The average period passed by them at the depôt was about twelve weeks, and it was found by experience that their standard of training on joining the Reserve battalions was about the same as in time of peace when the period at the depôt was seventeen weeks.

Grenadier Guards.—The Reserve Battalion was first quartered in the buildings of the London University, Prince Consort Road, S.W., but was moved to Chelsea Barracks on the 15th of August where it remained until it was disbanded in the spring of 1919. The strength of the battalion on the 31st of August, 1914, was 47 officers and 3,367 other ranks, and 25,112 men were passed through it during its existence. Training was carried out in

---

* In October, 1915, all sick and wounded men on their discharge from hospital who were not likely to be fit for service abroad within three months were sent to Command Depôts. The Command Depôt of the London District, to which Guardsmen were sent, was first at Seaford, then at Shoreham.

London and at the camp of instruction at Tadworth. The battalion was originally organized in 4 companies, but, in September, 1915, owing to the large number of men on the strength the formation of 5 additional companies was authorized. They were organized as follows :—4 to take and train recruits for active service ; 4 to take convalescents until again fit for service ; 1 to take employed men and men permanently unfit for service abroad.

Coldstream Guards.—The Reserve Battalion was quartered at Windsor throughout the war. It was at first styled the 4th Reserve Battalion Coldstream Guards, but, upon the formation of the 4th (Pioneer) Battalion, it became the 5th Reserve Battalion. From 1915 onwards the battalion was organized in 8 companies, 4 of which were utilized as training companies for recruits, while 4 were set apart for men who had already been on active service. The Reserve Battalion was disbanded in April, 1919.

Scots Guards.—The Reserve Battalion was first known as the 3rd Reserve Battalion, Brigade of Guards, and absorbed the surplus men of the Irish Guards as well as those of the Scots Guards, each regiment forming 2 companies. On the 17th of August, 1914, however, the officers and other ranks of the Scots Guards moved from South Kensington to Chelsea Barracks and were formed into the 3rd Battalion Scots Guards, which later on, on the 22nd of October, was officially designated the 3rd (Reserve) Battalion. On the 31st of August the battalion was sent to Sandown Park, Esher. It remained there until the 2nd of October following, when it was transferred to Wellington Barracks, where it remained until its disbandment in the spring of 1919. 9,716 recruits passed through the battalion during its existence. At first the battalion was organized in 4 companies, but, as time went on, 4 other companies had to be formed owing to the large number of men on the strength.

Irish Guards.—When the 1st Battalion went to France on the 12th of August, 1914, the Irish Guards were at once confronted with the difficulty of forming an entirely new battalion, a difficulty which had not to be faced by the three other regiments of Guards. The absence of officers and non-commissioned officers was the chief handicap with which the commanding officer had to contend. The other regiments of the brigade, however, were able to lend a certain number of officers and non-commissioned officers, who were gradually returned to their own units as their services could be dispensed with. The 2nd Reserve Battalion was sent to Warley Barracks soon after its formation. Its strength was then 900 men, and by the summer of 1915 had increased to 1,500 men. In August, 1916, the battalion was sent to France to join the Guards Division, and a 3rd Reserve Battalion was formed at Warley. In 1915 and again in 1917, successful recruiting tours were made in Ireland, in which the band and drums of the Reserve Battalion took part. In March, 1919, the cadre of the 2nd Battalion and the 3rd Reserve Battalion were absorbed into the 1st Battalion.

Welsh Guards.—The Reserve Battalion was formed at Wellington Barracks as soon as the 1st Battalion went to France in August, 1915. In September of that year the Reserve Battalion went into camp at Marlow, until the 18th of October, and spent the winter of 1915–1916 at the Tower. In June, 1916, it went into camp at Tadworth, and after the summer training, moved to Orpington in Kent. After another summer at Tadworth, the battalion was sent to Ranelagh Club, Barnes, where it remained until the end of the war. During its existence it sent 185 officers and 4,451 other ranks to France. It was absorbed into the 1st Battalion on the 18th of March, 1919.

APPENDIX VI

THE ORIGIN AND HISTORY OF THE GUARDS MACHINE-GUN REGIMENT.

THE Guards Machine-Gun Regiment was formed on the 23rd of February, 1918, and its disbandment was completed on the 30th of April, 1920. When war broke out in 1914, and for some months after the commencement of hostilities, the establishment of the machine or maxim-gun section of an infantry battalion was limited to 2 guns and a *personnel* of 18 of all ranks (1 officer, 1 sergeant and 16 privates). It was not long, however, before it became evident that the machine gun was destined to play a very important part in the operations.

Already in the autumn of 1914 and early in 1915, the battalion machine-gun sections of infantry brigades were brigaded when necessary, and their action coordinated, but not commanded as yet, by a brigade machine-gun officer.

In September, 1915, after the formation of the Guards Division, the machine-gun sections of the battalions comprising the three Guards Bdes. were formed into companies and were definitely known as the 1st, 2nd and 3rd Guards Brigade Machine-Gun Companies, commanded respectively by Captains P. R. Lawrence, Coldstream Guards, C. Bartholomew, Scots Guards, and Viscount Bury, Scots Guards. The *personnel* for these companies were in the first instance taken direct from men of the battalions, composing the respective brigades; but, later on, machine gunners trained at schools in France and in England served as the main source of supply of reinforcements.

In November, 1916, a Guards Machine-Gun Training Centre was formed at CATERHAM, moving to EPSOM at the end of December.

On the 1st of February, 1917, a divisional Machine-Gun Officer (Major R. C. Bingham, Coldstream Guards) was appointed to supervise and to coordinate the action of the three machine-gun companies, and, during the following month, all machine gunners

THE GUARDS MACHINE-GUN REGIMENT 315

of the Guards Division became part of the MACHINE-GUN GUARDS, who were administered at home for record purposes by the Lieut.-Colonel commanding the Welsh Guards. Officers from the five regiments were either seconded or transferred, whilst other ranks of the brigade companies and Guards Machine-Gun Training Centre, which henceforth was called upon to supply drafts for service abroad, were transferred to the Machine-Gun Guards.

A fourth company, under Captain B. Birkbeck, Coldstream Guards, known as the 4th Guards Machine-Gun Company, left Epsom on the 17th of March, 1917, and joined the Guards Division on the 21st at BRONFAY FARM Camp, thus completing the four companies which, until the end of the war, formed the complement of machine gunners for every infantry division in the field.

On the 4th of February, 1918, the Guards Machine-Gun Training Centre moved from Epsom to Pirbright Camp. On the 23rd of February, orders were received at divisional headquarters for the formation of the 4th Battalion Machine-Gun Guards, in consequence of the decision to transform the three regiments of Household Cavalry into machine gunners, and on the 27th of February Major R. C. Bingham and Major R. M. Wright were appointed as commanding officer and second-in-command respectively of the 4th Battalion. On the 23rd of April Brevet Lieut.-Colonel A. R. Trotter, 2nd Life Guards, was appointed to command the regiment and regimental district, and, in order to complete the establishment, about 400 men were transferred to the regiment from line battalions.

A *Royal Warrant* was issued on the 10th of May, 1918, constituting the regiment under the designation of the SIXTH OR MACHINE-GUN REGIMENT OF FOOT GUARDS OR GUARDS MACHINE-GUN REGIMENT.

The regiment consisted of five battalions :—

1st (1ST LIFE GUARDS) BATTALION under Lieut.-Colonel E. H. Brassey, formed of the 1st Life Guards, who became dismounted and converted into a Motor Machine-Gun Battalion.

Strength of formation :—40 officers and 720 other ranks.

2nd (2ND LIFE GUARDS) BATTALION under Lieut.-Colonel Hon. A. F. Stanley, similarly formed.

Strength on formation :—31 officers and 822 other ranks.

3rd (ROYAL HORSE GUARDS) BATTALION under Lieut.-Colonel Lord Tweedmouth, similarly formed.

Strength on formation :—30 officers and 756 other ranks.

4th (FOOT GUARDS) BATTALION under Lieut.-Colonel R. C. Bingham, formed from the 4th Battalion Machine-Gun Guards.

Strength on formation :—59 officers and 983 other ranks.

5th (RESERVE) BATTALION under Lieut.-Colonel R. E. K. Leatham, formed from the Guards Machine-Gun Training Centre.

Strength on formation :—70 officers and 1,051 other ranks.

On the 19th of August the new offices at Buckingham Gate were taken over as regimental headquarters.

In September, 1918, Colonel A. R. Trotter, as Lieut.-Colonel commanding the regiment, took his turn on the roster and performed the duties of Field Officer in Brigade waiting.

On the 22nd of September the regiment was honoured by the appointment of His Majesty the King as Colonel-in-Chief.

On the 6th of November a new cap badge, collar badges, and buttons were approved for the regiment.

On the 8th of November Major F. Penn, 2nd Life Guards, was appointed acting Lieut.-Colonel to command the 4th Battalion, vice Lieut.-Colonel Bingham wounded.

After the Armistice the 1st, 2nd and 3rd Battalions remained in BELGIUM, except for a period when the 1st Battalion was ordered to proceed to CALAIS, in connexion with the disturbances in that town, while the 4th Battalion accompanied the Guards Division to Germany as part of the Army of Occupation.

On the 18th of December demobilization began.

On the 15th of February, 1919, orders were received for the conversion of the three Household Cavalry battalions of the Guards Machine-Gun Regiment to their original status, and on the 4th of March these battalions left DUNKIRK for TILBURY, and were followed a month later by the 4th Battalion.

The following extract from the Commander-in-Chief's Despatch of the 21st of March records their services in the field :—

" Very gallant and effective service has been rendered by all machine-gun units, and not least by the battalions of the Guards Machine-Gun Regiment."

On the 22nd of March the 4th Battalion took part in the Guards' triumphal march through LONDON. The battalion was commanded by Lieut.-Colonel R. C. Bingham, the demobilized men by Major R. M. Wright.

On the 28th of March Lieutenant-Colonel R. E. K. Leatham assumed the command of the 4th Battalion, and, the following day, the 5th Battalion was absorbed into the 4th Battalion.

On the 9th of April re-enlistment for the regiment was permitted and the following day recruiting was opened.

On the 29th of May 2 officers and 39 other ranks embarked at

Newcastle with the 201st Battalion Machine-Gun Corps to join the North Russian Expeditionary Force.

On the 3rd of June, the 4th Battalion furnished one guard at the Trooping of the Colour in Hyde Park on the occasion of the King's Birthday Parade. The battalion had already taken its share of duty in furnishing the public duties in the West End.

On the 19th of July, the regiment was represented by a detachment under Major G. M. Perry in the Victory March in LONDON.

Recruiting was closed for the regiment on the 27th of November, and on the 25th of February, 1920, a Royal Warrant was issued for its disbandment. The G.O.C., London District, carried out his final inspection on the 5th of March, and the regiment was disbanded between the 31st of March and the 30th of April.

The following SPECIAL BRIGADE OF GUARDS ORDER was issued by Major-General G. D. Jeffreys, commanding the Brigade of Guards :—

GUARDS MACHINE-GUN REGIMENT.

" On the disbandment of the Guards Machine-Gun Regiment, the Major-General desires to express his high appreciation of the services of the following officers and warrant officers, who have by their example and devotion to duty, upheld in the Guards Machine-Gun Regiment the high standard and traditions of the Brigade of Guards :—

" Colonel A. R. Trotter, D.S.O., M.V.O., commanding the Regiment.

" Lieut.-Colonel R. E. K. Leatham, D.S.O., commanding the Battalion.

" Major T. L. C. Curtis, Regimental Adjutant.

" Warrant Officer (Class 1) Superintending Clerk H. G. Shaw.

" Warrant Officer (Class 1) Regimental Sergeant-Major F. Speller, M.C."

APPENDIX VII

THE HOUSEHOLD BRIGADE OFFICER CADET BATTALION

The Household Brigade Officer Cadet Bn. was one of thirty-seven battalions organized by the War Office to supply the ever-growing need for officers. It was formed on the 17th of February, 1917 (A.C.I. No. 241), and quartered at the Hall, Bushey, near Watford. It was primarily intended for the training of the Special Reserve officers of the Household Cavalry, Household Battalion and Brigade of Guards, officers of the Household Cavalry being taken away for a short course at Netheravon.

The staff was furnished entirely by the Brigade of Guards, and the original establishment of the battalion consisted of 200 officer cadets,* who were formed into two companies under the command of Lieut.-Colonel R. S. Tempest, Scots Guards. The course at first lasted for four months, but was subsequently increased, first to five and then to six months.

In May, 1917, Lieut.-Colonel E. J. L. Pike, Grenadier Guards, succeeded Lieut.-Colonel Tempest in the command of the battalion.

In April, 1918, the scope of the school was extended by the institution of a special course for officers, known as the Bushey Senior Officers' Course. This course lasted for five weeks, and was conducted by Major A. F. Smith, Coldstream Guards, as Chief Instructor.

Most of the cadets at Bushey came straight from the Public Schools; the remainder were either men who had been sent home from the various Expeditionary Forces recommended for Commissions, or business and professional men of good standing. Their ages varied from seventeen and a half to fifty. They were formed into platoons, each of which was at a different stage of training. As soon as a cadet had passed out satisfactorily, he was gazetted to a Special Reserve Commission. By the end of the

* In October, 1917, the establishment was increased to 250, and, early in 1918, to 400 officer cadets.

war 1,000 cadets, of whom a large proportion were for the Regiments of the Household Brigade, had received their Commissions.

The existence of the battalion came to an end in the summer of 1919.

APPENDIX VIII

THE GUARDS ENTRENCHING BATTALION.

ENTRENCHING battalions were brought into existence in the autumn of 1915. They were composed of drafts from home whilst awaiting absorption in their respective units, and were utilized for the digging of trenches and other manual work in rear of the front line.*

At first Guardsmen were sent indiscriminately to these battalions, but in December, 1915, a special Guards Entrenching Battalion was formed and placed under the command of Major E. C. Ellice, Grenadier Guards. From the 23rd of December, 1915, to July, 1916, the battalion was billetted in villages west and south-west of Albert, with its headquarters in the Bois des Tailles just west of Bray-sur-Somme, and from January to May, 1916, was employed on the construction of a line of trenches, with dug-outs and artillery positions, between Melencourt and Etenham.

Between the 16th of May and the 16th of July the Battalion did much work in connexion with the Somme offensive, working on the trench lines between Albert and the Somme, and making new roads to Bray and Suzanne.

During the actual fighting in July the battalion moved its headquarters to the neighbourhood of Mametz, and was employed in making gun emplacements for the French artillery, in working on the forward roads in the Carnoy, Maricourt and Montauban area, and in constructing dug-outs in rear of the forward lines. In December, 1916, the battalion moved to Trônes Wood and was employed until the following April in making strong points in front of Ginchy, in digging new trenches and gun emplacements to the east of Combles, and in work connected with the water supply and telephone lines from Ginchy to the Lesbœufs area.

* " The staff of the Battalion was kept as permanent as possible, but the Battalion itself was used as a stepping-stone from the Base battalion to the battalions in the front line. The training the officers received was invaluable." *See* " The Grenadier Guards in the Great War," vol. iii. pp. 202, 203.

During April, 1917, the battalion kept in touch with the British advance and brought the water supply up to the front line.

From April to July, 1917, the battalion, whose headquarters was now at Nurlu, was employed in preparing for the Cambrai offensive, laying down Decauville lines, carrying the water supply forward from Manancourt to Sorel, and digging trenches in Havrincourt Wood.

In July the headquarters, which had been moved to Fins in June, was shifted to Roisel, and the work of preparation for the Cambrai operations continued.

In August, 1917, entrenching battalions were done away with throughout the B.E.F., but the Guards Battalion was kept in existence until the 20th of September, when it, too, was disbanded.*

In October, 1917, Major-General Feilding organized a new Reinforcements Battalion, which served much the same purpose. It consisted at first of about 3,000 of all ranks organized in three companies, but the German counter-attack at Cambrai depleted its strength to a great extent. When the Guards moved out of the line the Reinforcements Battalion went to Duisans near Arras. There it was soon brought up to strength again, but the higher authorities now wished to know what it was, and after a somewhat lengthy correspondence, it was decided to change its name to the Guards Works Battalion, and this for the time being appears to have been considered satisfactory. The battalion was located in Arras, where it remained until the German advance in the spring of 1918. It did a considerable amount of entrenching work round Fampoux, and in rear of Monchy in front of Arras.

During the retirement of the Guards Division in 1918, the battalion was heavily called upon, but a system of exchange was instituted between it and the front line battalions, and thus it was found possible to give a few days' rest to tired men. About the end of April, 1918, the higher authorities raised objections to the retention of the battalion by the Guards Division, and it was reduced to a cadre, which was retained until the final British advance began.

* During the course of its existence 344 officers and about 10,000 other ranks passed through the Guards Entrenching Battalion.

APPENDIX IX

THE GUARDS DIVISION BASE DEPÔT AT HARFLEUR.

THE divisional Base Depôt was established at No. 10 Camp in the Lezarde valley at Harfleur towards the end of August, 1915, with Major A. H. Royds, Scots Guards, as officer in command. All the Guards' drafts, and those of the Household Battalion until its disbandment, were sent to this depôt on their arrival from England,* and here also were collected all officers and other ranks discharged from hospitals and convalescent camps in France. On their arrival at the depôt all ranks were posted to the various battalions on orders received from the Third Echelon through the Reinforcement Officer.

In the earlier part of the war every man who came to France had to be passed by the O.C. Central Training School as fully trained and fit to join his unit in the field,† but subsequently this Training School was abolished, and the only test which a man had to pass before being sent to his unit was in gas drill.

A daily state was made out at the divisional depôt showing the number of men available for each battalion and giving the names of the officers. A copy of this was sent to the O.C. Reinforcements, Third Echelon, and to the headquarters of the Guards Division, and a weekly return was also sent to the regimental lieut.-colonels at home.

Up to a certain date in the war all Permanent Base men were sent to a separate camp at Havre, but, later on, this practice was discontinued and they remained at the depôt where they were employed in various routine duties.‡ All " casuals," *i.e.* men in

---

* Senior officers almost invariably and other officers in times of emergency, travelled *via* Boulogne and not by Havre.

† It is recorded that no Guardsman was ever found to be inefficient to join his unit.

‡ In 1918 leave was obtained for P.B. non-commissioned officers, if suitable for the purpose, to be sent back to England as instructors.

France who found their way to the Base from one reason or another, were posted direct from the depôt to their battalions.*

By degrees the depôt was converted into a smart and well-established camp, where everything that was possible was done to make the men comfortable and to amuse them. A dining-hall was fitted up as a theatre, and concerts and dramatic entertainments were frequently held. The garden was a special feature at the depôt, and ultimately was able to provide a regular and adequate supply of vegetables. In 1918 the depôt carried off twenty prizes at the Havre Flower Show and four out of six medals presented by the Mayor.

In the autumn of 1915 the depôt was honoured with a visit from H.M. the King and H.M. the Queen visited it in the summer of 1917. H.R.H. the Duke of Connaught and Sir John French and Sir Douglas Haig were also amongst its visitors.

* The posting by the Third Echelon of other ranks was rarely interfered with by the divisional staff, but, in the case of officers, the matter was different. It was necessary to utilize their services to the general advantage, and consequently the divisional commander, with the assistance of the A.A. and Q.M.G., used to post them to battalions and to transfer them from one battalion to another as he deemed best.

APPENDIX X

FOREIGN SERVICE OF THE BANDS OF THE REGIMENTS OF GUARDS.

Soon after the formation of the Guards Division it was decided that the regimental bands should in turn visit the division. The band of the Grenadier Guards, consisting of 32 musicians under the command of Captain A. Williams, Mus.Doc., was the first to arrive, joining the division at Sailly-la-Bourse in October, 1915. It remained in France for three months, and made two subsequent visits, one in 1917, the other in 1918.

The band of the Coldstream Guards, under the command of Captain Mackenzie Rogan, Director of Music, first went to the front towards the end of January, 1916, where it remained until the end of April. It was with the division from the beginning of June, 1917, to the end of August, 1917, and again from early in September, 1918, to January, 1919.

The band of the Scots Guards, under the command of Bandmaster F. W. Wood, was with the division from the 22nd of May to the end of July, 1916, and again from early in September to the 2nd of December, 1917. It joined the division at Cologne on the 24th of December, 1918, and returned to England with it in March, 1919.

The band of the Irish Guards, under the command of Bandmaster C. H. Hassell, had two tours of duty in France, the first from the end of July to the beginning of November, 1916, the second from the beginning of December, 1017, to the 8th of February, 1918.

The band of the Welsh Guards, under the command of Bandmaster A. Harris, paid one visit to the front from the 28th of October, 1916, to the 11th of February, 1917.

During their periods of duty with the division the various bands displayed the greatest energy and enthusiasm, and there is no doubt that their work was much appreciated by the troops and did much to promote moral.

FOREIGN SERVICE OF THE BANDS

In addition to their service at the front, the massed bands of the Brigade of Guards visited both Paris and Rome, the former in May, 1917, the latter in February, 1918. Both visits were extremely successful. The bands were given enthusiastic receptions in both capitals, and their visits gave a visible demonstration of the cordial relationship which existed between the Allied nations.

APPENDIX XI

ADDRESS ISSUED TO HIS TROOPS BY THE MAJOR-GENERAL COMMANDING THE GUARDS DIVISION ON ARMISTICE DAY, 1918.

To the Guards Division.

By your capture on the 9th of Maubeuge, the ancient strong place of the Low Countries, you have brought to a victorious conclusion a period of many weeks of almost incessant fighting in which your determination and discipline have overcome the most formidable obstacles. Between the valley of the Cojeul, from which you launched the advance on August 21st and the great fortress which you entered on the 9th, you have stormed and captured a succession of ridges of great natural strength, and several canals or streams. Of the former the strongest were, in my opinion, the ridges south of St. Leger and Croisilles and the high ground at Flesquières. Of the latter the two most formidable were the Canal du Nord and the River Selle.

Out of the 81 days which have elapsed since August 21st, the Guards Division has been a total of 54 days in the firing line. Of these 54 days, 29 have been days of strenuous fighting, in which you beat back and wore down a skilful, tenacious and desperate foe. The conditions in which you fought were always hard and latterly most severe. The ruined area through which you first advanced contained no cover of any kind. Latterly, since you have fought your way back into an area of still standing villages and farms, cover has been plentiful out of the line, but troops in action have been severely tried by cold and rain and mud. In spite of these obstacles you have pressed your advance without respite and you have won the important goal on which the Guards Division was finally directed last week. This achievement speaks eloquently of your valour, your endurance and your willing discipline.

During the period of the advance the Artillery of the Division has been in action longer than any other arm and has been called upon to face much hardship and hard work. It has had to fire difficult barrages at short notice, and has often come under heavy artillery and machine-gun fire in pushing up in close support of the firing line. I have nothing but praise for the cooperation of Artillery Brigade Commanders with Guards Brigadiers; their energy, quick grasp of situations and promptness to act have been of constant service during the advance. During the whole period the Forward Observing Officers have also shown a fine spirit in getting forward for their work, and have frequently sent back early information of great value on the dispositions of the enemy and the progress of our troops. For all this I wish to convey my warmest thanks to Brigadier-General Wilson, his Brigade and Battery Commanders and all ranks.

The conditions of the advance have called for all the skill and endurance which the Field Companies, R.E., and the 4th Bn. Coldstream Guards (Pioneers) could put forth. They have faced and overcome great difficulties, often under fire, often under the handicaps of darkness and bad weather, often under the strain of work for long hours at a stretch. I consider that the speed and precision with which they carried out the bridging of the River Selle reflects the greatest credit on Lieut.-Col. Lees, the Field Company Commanders and all ranks engaged. Their success on that occasion was only one striking example of the high level of their work. The struggle to restore destroyed communications has been particularly severe during the past week, and they have acquitted themselves in a manner of which I think they have every reason to be proud. The strain upon the Divisional Signal Company has also been very great. They, too, have had great difficulties to surmount, long hours of work and little rest. They have risen well to the occasion and I congratulate Major Ryan and all ranks on their success. But for the determination shown by the Royal Engineers in overcoming the peculiar difficulties of a rapid advance in bad weather over natural and artificial obstacles of all sorts, the Division could never have reached Maubeuge last week.

Nothing in the record of the Brigade of Guards is finer than the performance of the three Guards Brigades of this Division since August 21st. From Moyenneville to Maubeuge they have advanced a distance of almost fifty miles. In the first week of the advance, from August 21st to 28th, in the face of very heavy fighting they went forward a distance of $5\frac{1}{2}$ miles. In the second phase, from September 3rd to 27th, during which they stormed the deep ditch of the Canal du Nord, broke through the Hindenburg System and won the Flesquières ridge, they penetrated into the enemy's lines a further distance of 11½ miles. In the third phase, from October 19th to 22nd, at the end of which they forced the crossings of the River Selle, they advanced a distance of 14½ miles. And in their final advance, against still tenacious opposition and in constant rain and cold, they drove the enemy back a distance of 19 miles before they reached their final goal, Maubeuge.

This record speaks for itself. It has not been achieved without the loss of many comrades, amongst which the heaviest is that of Brigadier-General G. B. S. Follett, M.V.O., D.S.O., Coldstream Guards, commanding the 3rd Guards Brigade, who was killed in action at the Canal du Nord. To him, to the Commanders of the 1st and 2nd Guards Brigades, Brigadier-General de Crespigny and Brigadier-General Brooke, and to his successor, Brigadier-General Heywood, who was wounded last week, I owe the warmest appreciation and gratitude. They, their Staffs and their troops have added a distinguished page to the history of the Brigade of Guards, and I wish to express my thanks to them and all their officers, non-commissioned officers and men.

The difficulties faced by other troops have also beset the work of the R.A.M.C. who, under the able command of Colonel Fawcus, have not allowed them to reduce in any degree their high standard of efficiency and zeal. They have also hampered the Army Service Corps and all the Administrative Services, but by one and all they have been cheerfully met and successfully overcome.

Finally I wish to thank my own Staff for their untiring work since the beginning of the advance. They have been responsible for the coordination of plans, which is essential to success. The task has, at times, been very difficult; the strain has, throughout, been great. I am deeply grateful for their industry and forethought, which have well deserved this great result.

I am even prouder to have the honour to command the Guards Division to-day than I was when I first came to it two months ago. No troops have served their King and Country more devotedly in hard times as in soft; no troops have done more to win the prize which is announced to-day, the victorious cessation of hostilities and the promise of a justly rewarding peace.

T. G. MATHESON,
Major-General,
Comdg. Guards Division.

Nov. 11th, 1918.

APPENDIX XII

NOTES ON THE DRESS AND EQUIPMENT OF THE FOOT GUARDS DURING THE WAR, 1914-1918.

IN August, 1914, the non-commissioned officers and men of the Foot Guards, in common with the whole of the British infantry, wore drab serge (khaki) jacket, trousers, and puttees, with peaked cap of the same material, and brass cap-badges and shoulder-titles (G.G., C.G., etc.). Their equipment consisted of belt (with bayonet frog and attachment for carrying the light entrenching tool); braces (with pouches for ammunition); pack (containing mess-tin, drab great-coat, and spare shirt, socks, and necessaries); and small haversack, which was attached to the left side of the belt when the pack was worn, but which could be worn on the back in place of the pack, when the latter was not carried. A waterproof sheet was folded under the supporting straps of the pack, and a water-bottle was attached to the belt.

The whole equipment was made of stout webbing material, and when properly fitted rode fairly easily on the man, in spite of its weight. The infantryman's only arms were the rifle and bayonet, but each battalion had a machine-gun section with two Maxim guns.

The officers wore khaki serge jackets of a pattern differing slightly from that of the Line, and with the badges of rank on the shoulder-straps, instead of on the forearm, as in the Line. Khaki peaked caps, cord breeches of the " ride and walk " type, puttees and brown ankle boots completed the costume of the dismounted officer. Mounted officers wore brown leggings and ankle boots, or alternatively brown field boots. Every officer was equipped with a Sam Browne belt, haversack, water-bottle and field glasses, and was armed with a sword and revolver.

Each officer was allowed 35 lbs. of kit carried on the baggage wagons. As, however, the weight of his Wolseley valise, waterproof sheet, and blanket accounted for a considerable proportion of the 35 lbs., this allowance did not admit of much kit being carried, and most dismounted officers carried voluntarily on their backs a ruck-sack containing such articles as spare socks and shirt, cardigan, and washing and shaving kit. Mounted officers carried articles of this description in their saddle-bags or wallets. Every officer carried a rainproof coat on his person or his saddle.

The above continued to be the dress and equipment for the first four months of the war, the men not only marching but fighting, in their heavy packs, and the officers carrying (and on occasion using) their swords in action.

After the Battles of Ypres, 1914, officers discarded their swords, and carried walking-sticks instead, whilst, in view of the rigours of winter, still further impedimenta were added to the already overburdened infantry soldier.

In December, 1914, goatskin jerkins were issued. These had long sleeves and were worn over the service dress jackets with the equipment over all. Though warm, these jerkins had many disadvantages. A man when wearing one could not move or use his arms freely and was in fact almost completely immobilized, whilst the adhesive mud of the country stuck to the long hair and thus added to the weight of the jerkin and the general discomfort of its wearer.

After the first issue no more of these goatskin jerkins were issued to the Guards battalions, sleeveless leather jerkins, which, though equally warm, were lighter and easier to wear and keep clean, being substituted for them.

Gum boots for troops occupying wet trenches began to be issued about January, 1915, and it was now frankly recognized that the infantry occupying the front system of defences, loaded up as the men were with greatcoats, jerkins, gum boots, fuel, etc., was under winter conditions completely immobile.

About this time dismounted officers began to adopt loose knickerbockers instead of the cord breeches worn in the early months of the war. These knickerbockers, familiarly known as "plus-fours," continued to be worn throughout (and after) the war.

About December, 1915, primitive forms of bombs (or hand-grenades) began to be introduced into the British Army. Most of these were more dangerous to their users than to the enemy, but all alike resulted in extra weight having to be carried by the soldier.

The gas attack by the Germans in April, 1915, found the British Army without any means of protection against this new and deadly weapon. Various forms of gas masks or respirators were hastily improvised and every man was issued with one of some kind, the "P" smoke helmet being adopted as the standard pattern during the summer of 1915, and continuing to be used until the autumn of 1916. These helmets were carried in small satchels slung over the shoulder or attached to the belt.

Following the example of the French, it was decided to adopt a steel helmet for protection against shell-splinters, and the first of these were issued experimentally during the battle of Loos, and proved to be effective for their purpose. During the winter of 1915–1916 these helmets were gradually issued to all troops, and were ordered to be worn by them whenever they were in the forward area.

In the early months of 1915 the Maxim guns were gradually replaced by Vickers guns and the number of machine guns per battalion was increased from two to four. About July, 1915, these guns and their *personnel* were withdrawn from battalions, and brigaded in Brigade Machine-Gun companies. They continued, however, nominally to belong to battalions until they were incorporated in the newly formed Guards Machine-Gun Regiment in the early part of 1917.

On the eve of the battle of Loos the Lewis automatic gun made its appearance, and three of these weapons were issued to each battalion. As these guns proved their utility and the supply increased, they were issued in ever-increasing numbers, until in 1918 each platoon had two, in addition to two allotted to battalion headquarters for anti-aircraft work. About the same period (September, 1915), after many experiments with other types, the Mills bomb was adopted as the universal pattern.

In the early autumn of 1916 the last important change in equipment took place, the smoke helmet being replaced by the small "box-respirator" for gas protection.

The box-respirator, though affording far more effective protection was much more cumbrous and unwieldy than the small and non-rigid smoke helmet. When not required for instant use, it was carried slung like a haversack; when in the "alert" position, it was worn on the man's chest, a far from comfortable situation for the wearer.

In 1917 a modified pattern of waterproof sheet, shaped so as to admit of its being used as a cape, was introduced. From this time onwards to the end of the war no considerable change in dress or equipment took place.

Officers' dress for battle or the line consisted of steel helmet, service dress as described above, belt, box-respirator, haversack, water-bottle and revolver. From 1917 onwards it became usual for officers to wear for battle jackets and trousers of the pattern issued to other ranks, with only the badges of rank on the shoulder straps for distinction.

Other ranks for battle or the line wore steel helmets, box-respirators, web-equipment with haversack on back in place of the pack (which with the greatcoat and all surplus kit was left behind with the transport), water bottle, mess-tin, light entrenching tool, waterproof sheet or cape, rifle and ammunition. This was known as "fighting order." Bombs and rifle-bombs were carried in canvas carriers, and on going into action each man carried two bombs in his pockets, thus creating a reserve.

In the "trench to trench" attacks (with limited objectives) of 1916 and 1917 each man carried a heavy shovel slung over his back, but these heavy tools were discarded in the more mobile operations of 1918, and men went into action as lightly equipped as possible.

APPENDIX XIII

SUNDAY: MARCH 12TH, 1916.
THE CALAIS FIRST SPRING MEETING
2nd Guards Brigade

BY KIND PERMISSION OF BRIGADIER-GENERAL J. PONSONBY, C.M.G., D.S.O.

JUDGE: BRIGADIER-GENERAL J. PONSONBY.
STARTER: LIEUT.-COL. HON. G. V. BARING.
KEEPER OF MATCH BOOK, STAKEHOLDER AND RECEIVER OF ENTRIES: CAPTAIN G. MOORE.

FIRST RACE 2.30 P.M.

THE SURREY PLATE

By subscription of 5 francs.

(15 hands or under.)

Weights—12 stone or over.

FOUR FURLONGS STRAIGHT.

1	Brigadier-General Ponsonby's	BIMBASHI.
2	Captain Beckwith-Smith's	NO. 4.
3	Lieut.-Col. B. S. Brooke's	LINDHURST.
4	Captain E. Vaughan's	BLUE BELL.
5	Captain Norman's	PRETTY POLLY.
6	Lieut. C. Bewicke's	OLD FAIRY HOUSE.
7	Captain Hon. E. K. Digby's	MULLAH.
8	Captain Sutton's	FLYING FOX.
9	Major E. B. Hopwood's	KÜMMEL.
10	Captain J. B. Bird's	BEETLE.
11	Lieut. F. M. Harvey's	BEDSORE.
12	Captain C. Moore's	DALY'S.
13	Major E. B. Greer's	THE MULE.
14	The Rev. S. Knapp's	LEE WHITE.
15	Lieut. Higginson's	RATTY.

APPENDIX XIII

SECOND RACE 3.0 P.M.

THE PONSONBY PLATE

By subscription of 5 francs.

(15 hands or under.)

Catch weights.

FIVE FURLONGS STRAIGHT.

1	Brig.-General Ponsonby's	ST. CLOUD.
2	Captain Wolridge Gordon's	CALLER HERRIN'.
3	Captain E. C. Martin's	NO. 9.
4	Captain H. de Trafford's	MUSTANG.
5	Lieut. Lord H. Kennedy's	OLD STORY.
6	Captain Sir Ian Colquhoun's	THE TETRACH.
7	Captain H. Ross's	FIFINELLA.
8	Captain Smith's	THE DOPE.
9	Major E. B. Greer's	THE MULE.
10	Captain the Hon. H. R. Alexander's	LAURETTE.
11	Captain F. H. Witt's	CHARLIE CHAPLIN.
12	Lieut. Vernon's	NELLY.
13	Lieut. C. F. Purcell's	ZIG ZAG.

THIRD RACE 3.30 P.M.

THE BUTLER PLATE

By subscription of 5 francs.

Catch weights.

ONE MILE STRAIGHT.

1	Captain Guy Rasch's	BOUNDING BEN.
2	Lieut. A. C. Trench's	JUMBO.
3	Lieut. C. Green's	NO. 9.
4	Captain O. Lyttelton's	SHAITAN.
5	Major B. Hopwood's	THE HUN.
6	Captain H. E. de Trafford's	PRILUS.
7	Lieut.-Col. the Hon. G. V. Baring's	THE DUD.
8	Captain Hon. E. K. Digby's	SNIPER.
9	Captain Hon. E. K. Digby's	MULLAH.
10	Captain Kinlay's	ALLY SLOPER.
11	Lieut. A. G. Thompson's	SILVER TAG.
12	Lieut.-Col. Hon. L. Butler's	CRUMP.
13	Captain C. Bartholomew's	PURSLANE.
14	Lieut. G. Walter's	KITTY.
15	Lieut. C. Boyd Rochfort's	SYNFORD.

THE CALAIS FIRST SPRING MEETING

FOURTH RACE 4 P.M.

THE BARING STEEPLECHASE

By subscription of 5 francs.

Catch weights over course.

ABOUT ONE MILE AND A HALF.

1 Captain Guy Rasch's — BOUNDING BEN.
2 Captain Guy Rasch's — JAMES.
3 Captain E. Vaughan's — CATAPULT.
4 Captain Platt's — BLACK KNIGHT.
5 Captain H. E. de Trafford's — MUSTANG.
6 Lieut. Lord H. Kennedy's — OLD STORY.
7 Major B. Hopwood's — BARRALONG.
8 Lieut. Jackson's — APOLLO.
9 Captain Hon. E. K. Digby's — PRIDE OF THE PLAGE.
10 Captain Norman's — PRETTY POLLY.
11 Captain H. Ross's — FIFINELLA.
12 Captain Kinlay's — ALLY SLOPER.
13 Lieut. A. G. Thompson's — SILVER TAG.
14 Lieut.-Col. Hon. L. Butler's — CRUMP.
15 Major E. B. Greer's — THE MULE.
16 Capt. Hon. H. R. Alexander's — LAURETTE.
17 Captain J. B. Bird's — BEETLE.
18 Lieut. G. Stirling's — PUNKA WALLA.

FIFTH RACE 4.30 P.M.

A CONSOLATION RACE

Catch weights.

Open to any horse or pony which has not been placed in any other race.

FIVE FURLONGS STRAIGHT.

Post entries subscription 5 francs.

The whole of the stakes to go to the winner.
All weights are exclusive of saddle.

INDEX

Aa River, i. 30
Abbeville, Ordnance workshops at, i. 188
Ablainzeville, ii. 55, 63, 66, 101 n.
Abri Wood, i. 247, 282
Achiet-le-Grand, ii. 51 ; le-Petit, i. 295
Acland-Hood, Lieut. F. P., ii. 261
Adinfer Wood, ii. 56, 61, 98, 100, 140
Agar-Robartes, Capt. the Hon. A. G., ii. 259, 260
Agnez-les-Duisans, ii. 23 n.
Aire, i. 34 ; canal, 33
Aisne, the, i. 6, 15 ; attack on, 215, 217 ; ii. 102 n.
Albert, i. 136, 142
Alexander, Lieut.-Col. the Hon. H. R., commanding 1st Bn. Irish Guards, i. 81 n., 207 n. ; ii. 266 ; 2nd Bn. Irish Guards, ii. 37 n., 38 n., 79, 267 ; 4th Guards Brigade, 63 n.
Allenby, General Sir E. H., at the battle of the Somme, i. 137 ; commanding the Third Army, 217
Allouagne, i. 91
Alston, Lieut.-Col. F. G., A.A. and Q.M.G., i. 199 n. ; ii. 255
Amfroipret, capture of, ii. 225, 226
Amiens, battle of, ii. 107
Ammunition dumps, blown up, i. 219 n., 220
Ancre River, i. 128, 136 n., 137, 142 n., 203 n., 216 ; ii. 108
Anneux, i. 299, 305 ; ii. 164 ; Chapel, i. 301
Anthoine, General, commanding the First French Army, i. 259
Antwerp, defence of, i. 19
Anzac Corps II, i. 219
Ape Copse, ii. 117 n.
Arbre de la Femme, ii. 195, 196, 197
Arbuthnot, 2nd Lieut. G., killed, i. 171 n.
Archdale, Major A. S., ii. 256

Ardee, Brig.-Gen. Lord, commanding 1st Bn. Irish Guards, i. 5 n. ; wounded, 10 n. ; commanding 4th Guards Brigade, ii. 30, 37 ; Infantry Brigades, 59 ; gassed, 63 n.
Ardennes, the, ii. 241
Arderlu Wood, i. 202 n.
Arleux-en-Gohelle, ii. 38
Armentières, ii. 79, 184 ; evacuated, 79 n.
Armistice, the, ii. 233
Army, the First, ii. 144, 161 n. 183, 219 ; advance on Valenciennes, i. 37 ; operations, 80
Army, the Second, i. 114 n., 115, 218, 223 ; ii. 184 n. ; aggressive policy, i. 126 ; at the Ypres offensive, 265
Army, the Third, i. 114 n., 293 ; ii. 41, 108, 112, 143, 161, 183, 185, 219 ; at the battle of the Somme, i. 137 ; Arras, 217
Army, the Fourth, i. 223 n. ; ii. 108, 143, 161 n., 183, 219 ; at the battle of the Somme, i. 137
Army, the Fifth, i. 223 n., 235 ; ii. 41 ; at the Ypres offensive, i. 265
Army, the New, character, i. 88
Army, the Reserve, i. 167 ; battalions, ii. 311
Arques, i. 32, 218
Arras, ii. 23, 28, 144 ; offensive, i. 213, 217
Arrewage, ii. 81, 85 n., 86
Arrow Head Copse, i. 192
Artillery, Divisional, efficiency, i. 90 ; method of retaliation, 104 ; work of the, 108, 196–198 ; ii. 99, 109, 210–212 ; reorganisation, i. 124 n., 197 ; at Sailly-le-See, 139 n. ; in the operations on the Somme, 182–186 ; bombardments, 202 ; ii. 141 ; at Morlancourt, i. 210 ; the battle of Messines, 218–221 ; Ypres, 233–

INDEX

235, 259–261, 268, 282 ; advance on Gouvy Farm, 253 ; casualties, 267, 283 ; in the Cambrai operations, ii. 16–19 ; on the Scarpe, 35–37 ; at the battle of the Canal du Nord, 166
Artillery Wood, i. 238, 240
Asquith, Margot, "The Autobiography of," extract from, i. 124 n.
Asquith, Lieut. Raymond, extract from his letter, i. 124 n.
Assevent, ii. 232 n.
Aubers ridge, i. 93, 95, 97
Aubigny, i. 293
Aubrey-Fletcher, Lieut.-Col. H. L., i. 154 n. ; ii. 254, 261 ; A.A. and Q.M.G., i. 199 n. ; ii. 255
Auchy, i. 13
Auchy-lez-La Bassée, i. 40, 41, 73
Audignies, ii. 228
Aulnoye, ii. 203 n.
Australian Army, i. 191 ; ii. 85 n., 88 ; at the battle of Messines, i. 221 ; the Ypres offensive, 265 n. ; attack on Mont St. Quentin, ii. 143
Austria, military operations in the Trentino, i. 135 n. ; collapse, ii. 218 n.
Auxi-le-Château, ii. 93
Avery, Major Sir W. E. T., commanding divisional Supply Column, i. 101 ; death ii. 267
Avesnes, ii. 219, 232 n.
Avroult, i. 34
Awoingt, attack on, ii. 186, 187
Ayette, ii. 57, 58 ; attack on, 67, 70 ; sniping from, 70 ; captured, 94 n.
Ayres-Richie, Lieut. A. T., attack on the Chalk Pit, i. 57

Baden-Powell, Major B., commandant of the School of Explosives, i. 111
Baggallay, Lieut.-Col. R. R. C., commanding 1st Bn. Irish Guards, ii. 99 n., 266 ; at the battle of the Canal du Nord, 169
Bailey, Lieut.-Col. the Hon. W. R., commanding 1st Bn. Grenadier Guards, ii. 122, 182 n., 263 ; wounded, 125
Bailleul, i. 212, 218
Ball, Lieut.-Col. Luxmoore, commanding 1st Bn. Welsh Guards, i. 126 n.; ii, 195 n., 267 ; attack on Premy Chapel, ii. 176

Ballantine-Dykes, Capt. H. B., ii. 255, 261
Bancourt, ii. 143, 144
Bank Copse, ii. 47, 49, 55, 140
Banks trench, attack on, ii. 129, 130, 134, 137
Bapaume, i. 136, 147 ; evacuated, ii. 143
Barastri, i. 296
Barber, Private T., awarded the V.C., i. 24 n.
Baring, Lieut.-Col. the Hon. G. V., commanding 1st Bn. Coldstream Guards, i. 68 n. ; killed, 153 ; ii. 264
Barly, ii. 96
Barrage, the creeping, i. 169, 247 n., 282 ; the standing, 169
Bartholomew, Capt. C., commanding 2nd Guards Machine-Gun Company, ii. 314
Batten-Pooll, Capt. J. A., ii. 256
Baudimont, ii. 23 n.
Bauvin, i. 38
Bavai, ii. 226, 227, 228
Bavarians, 5th Reserve Division, capture of, ii. 31, 32
Bavincourt, ii. 96
Bavisaux, ii. 227
Bazentin-le-Grand, i. 138
Beaulencourt, ii. 23 n., 144
Beaulieu Farm, raid on, ii. 92
Beaumetz-les-Cambrai, i. 296
Beaumetz-les-Loges, ii. 100 n.
Beaumont Hamel, i. 128, 136 n. ; capture of, 203 n.
Beaumont-Nesbitt, Capt. F. G., ii. 261
Beaurains, ii. 45
Beaurevoir, ii. 183
Becelaere, i. 9
Beckwith-Smith, Capt. M. B., ii. 254, 259, 260
Becque, la, ii. 88
Behagnies, capture of, ii. 55
Belgians, King of the, inspects the 2nd Guards Brigade, i. 188 n. ; commanding the army, ii. 184 n.
Bellewaarde stream, i. 116, 118
Bellicourt, ii. 183
Berkshire Regiment, 8th Bn., i. 56 n.
Berles-au-Bois, ii. 93, 105 n., 110
Bermeries, ii. 225, 226
Bernafay Wood, i. 143, 145, 149, 196 ; depôt in, 180
Berneville, ii. 23 n.
Bertincourt, i. 322, ii. 7

INDEX

Bethell, Lieut.-Col. A., commanding Brigades R.F.A., i. 169, 219; ii. 262; attack on Ginchy, i. 184; at the battle of Ypres, 234
Béthune, i. 12, 18, 47
Beuvry, i. 47
Bévillers, ii. 191
Bewicke, Major C., ii. 255, 261
Biddulph, Lieut.-Col. J. B., killed, ii. 99 n.
Bienvillers, ii. 76
Binche, ii. 239
Bingham, Major R. C., commanding 4th Bn. Machine-Gun Guards, ii. 32, 267, 314, 315; wounded, 316; march through London, 316
Birkbeck, Capt. B., commanding 4th Guards Machine-Gun Company, ii. 315
Bixschoote, i. 16, 20
Black, Lieut.-Col. J. C. L., commanding Divisional Train, i. 212 n.; ii. 257
Black Watch, 1st Bn., i. 2 n., 4; annihilated, 16
Blades, Major W., ii. 258
Blaireville, ii. 53, 56 n., 110; caves at, 141
Blathwayt, Major, killed, ii. 18 n.
Blécourt, ii. 183
Blendecques, i. 31
Bléquin River, i. 30
Bleu, attack on, ii. 84, 87
Bliss, Lieut.-Col. E. W., ii. 258
Block-houses or pill-boxes, construction of, i. 224 n.
Bluet Farm, i. 234 n., 235 n.
Body, Major, B. R., ii. 258
Boeschepe, i. 7
Boesinghe, i. 116, 124, 222-225; Château, i. 253, 284
Boiry Becquerelle, ii. 44 n., 59
Boiry-St.-Martin, ii. 56, 58, 111, 113, 115
Boiry-St.-Rictrude, ii. 47, 50, 113
Bois d'Aval, ii. 89, 91
Bois de Crapouillots, i. 252, 259
Bois Hugo, i. 39, 45, 54, 67
Bois de Neufs, ii. 163, 210
Bois-de-Warnimont, i. 139
Boisleux-St.-Marc, ii. 44, 46, 72
Boisleux-au-Mont, ii. 48, 54, 64, 72, 110
Boistrancourt, ii. 188, 190
Bolton, Lieut.-Col., taken prisoner, i. 21
Bomb-fighting, principles of, i. 79; accidents, 116 n.

Bombing School or School of Explosives, i. 111
Bonavis, i. 293; capture of, ii. 2
Bonn, Capt. W., ii. 126 n.
Bonquemaison, i. 128
Booby traps, i. 209
Boraston, Lieut.-Col. J. H., i. 305 n.
Border Regiment, 2nd Bn., i. 2 n., 20; at the battle of Neuve Chapelle, 23
Borre, i. 221
Bouchavesnes, ii. 144
Bougnies, i. 3 n.
Bouleaux Wood, i. 143 n., 145, 168 n.
Bourlon Wood, i. 293, 294, 298, 305; attack on, 295, 300-303; ii. 2 n. 17; reasons against, i. 304-308
Boursies, ii. 147, 149, 153 n., 180
Boussières, ii. 192, 204
Boussois, ii. 231
Boussois-la-Folie, ii. 232
Boyd, Lieut. W. A., temporarily commanding 2nd Bn. Scots Guards, i. 159 n.
Boyelles, ii. 43 n., 44, 47, 59, 150 n.; attack on, 64; attack from, 72-75
Bradbury, Sergeant-Major, killed, i. 203
Braithwaite, Major-Gen. W. P., commanding 62nd Division, i. 308
Brand, Capt. D. H., enters the German trenches, i. 205 n.
Brand, Major J. C., commanding 1st Bn. Coldstream Guards, i. 238 n.; ii. 118 n., 264; in temporary command of 3rd Guards Brigade, ii. 182 n.; retires, 226 n.
Brassey, Lieut.-Col. E. H., commanding 1st Bn. Guards Machine-Gun Regiment, ii. 315
Brassey, Lieut.-Col. E. P., commanding 2nd Bn. Coldstream Guards, ii. 265
Bray-sur-Somme, i. 139; ii. 93
Bretencourt, ii. 46
Briastre, ii. 195, 197
Bridford, Major-Gen. R. J., inspects the 4th Guards Brigade, ii. 38
Briggs, Major R., ii. 262
British Expeditionary Force in France, i. 1
Broembeek, the, i. 259, 261; crossing the, 262, 271; advance on, 269; bridging the, 277, 281

INDEX 339

Broken Mill, ii. 35
Bronfay, i. 193, 200 n., 212
Broodseinde, i. 269
Brooks, Lance-Sergeant, i. 76; awarded the V.C., 77; ii. 269
Brough, Lieut.-Col. A., C.R.E. Guards Division, i. 29, 63; ii. 256, 262; extracts from Notes, i. 120 n., 121 n., 125 n., 180 n., 181 n., 189 n., 194 n., 199 n., 202 n., 209 n., 211 n.; D.D.G.T., 227 n.
Browne, Rev. F. H., ii. 268
Browne, Lieut. the Hon M. D., killed, i. 67 n.
Bryant, Lieut.-Col. F. C., commanding 76th Brigade R.F.A., i. 123 n.; ii. 262
Buchanan, Major J. N., ii. 254, 255, 261
Bucquoy, ii. 58, 63
Bulgaria, capitulation of, ii. 218 n.
Bulkeley, Capt. H. J., ii. 262; attack on Hill 70, i. 62
Bullecourt, ii. 42, 143
Bullough, Major I., commanding 2nd Bn. Coldstream Guards, ii. 172
Bunhill trench, capture of, ii. 136
Burge, H., i. x.
Burton, Major S., killed, i. 238 n.
Bury, Capt. Viscount, commanding 3rd Guards Machine-Gun Company, ii. 314
Bus-les-Artois, i. 128, 139
Bushey, Senior Officers' Course, ii. 318
Butler, Lieut.-Col. the Hon. L. J. P., commanding 2nd Bn. Irish Guards, i. 31; ii. 267; 4th Guards Brigade, ii. 78; in the Lys offensive, 81–89; gassed, 92 n.
Buvigines, ii. 226, 227
Buzzard, Lieut.-Col. F. A., commanding Brigades, R.F.A., i. 169, 183, 198 n.; ii. 261; at the battle of Messines, i. 221; wounded, 234 n.; ii. 261
Bye, Sergeant Robert, awarded the V.C., ii. 270
Byng, Gen. Sir Julian, commanding the Third Army, i. 294; ii. 112

Calais, i. 116, 117; ii. 316; "First Spring Meeting," i. 117 n.; ii. 333–335
Cambrai, ii. 183, 185; operations, i. 291–322; ii. 1–22; evacuated, ii. 184 n.
Cambrin, i. 13
Cameron Highlanders, 1st Bn., i. 15 n.
Camouflage Copse, ii. 132
Campagne, i. 218 n.
Campbell, Brig.-Gen. J. V., commanding 3rd Bn. Coldstream Guards, i. 14 n.; ii. 265; attack on Ginchy, i. 154, 156; awarded the V.C., 157 n.; ii. 269; advance on Lesbœufs, i. 170; commanding an infantry brigade, 190 n.; the 3rd Guards Brigade, ii. 226, 260
Canadian army, driven out of Hooge, i. 123; want of system, 124 n.; capture Vimy ridge, 217; relieve the 3rd Division, ii. 76; series of demonstrations, 103; at Drocourt, 145; attack on Valenciennes, 219
"Canal Chronicle," the, i. 130 n.
Canal de l'Escaut, i. 292, 293; ii. 218
Canal du Nord, i. 210, 292, 295; ii. 19; advance on, ii. 148–181; crossing the, 161, 172; plan of operations, 163–167; battle, 167–181; results, 182
Cantaing, i. 298, 305; ii. 163; shelled, i. 300
Caporetto, victory of, i. 291
Captain's Farm, i. 247
Cardoen Farm, i. 242
Carey, Major P. D., ii. 258
Carnegie, 2nd Lieut. D. L., signal officer of the 4th Guards Brigade, ii. 37 n.
Carnières, ii. 191, 192, 217 n.
Carnoy, i. 143
Cartwright, Lieut.-Col. G. N., ii. 261
Cassel, i. 116
Cator, Lieut.-Col. A. B. E., commanding 2nd Bn. Scots Guards, i. 24 n.; ii. 266; attack on Hill 70, i. 63; commanding 37th Infantry Brigade, 114
Cattenières, ii. 188
Caucourt, ii. 16
Caudescure, ii. 89
Cavan, Brig.-Gen. the Earl of, commanding 4th Guards Brigade, i. 2 n., 6 n.; tributes to the troops, 10 n., 12 n., 177 n., 255 n., 288 n.; commanding

340 INDEX

50th Northumbrian Division, 14 n.; the Guards Division, 28; ii. 253; reviews it, i. 33; memorandum to, 34; orders attack on the Chalk Pit, 52–55; on Hill 70, 58, 64 n.; visits Guards Brigades, 65; orders attack on the Puits, 66; on the battle of Loos, 66 n.; instructions, 72, 82, 85; memorandum on bomb-fighting, 79; scheme for holding the line, 98; regulations for the troops, 99–101; on the Croix Barbée system of defence, 102; on artillery retaliation, 104; offensive policy, 107; opinion of the divisional Artillery, 109 n.; commanding XIV Corps, 113, 223 n.; in hospital, 139 n.; congratulations to the troops, 241 n., 279 n.; at the march through London of the Guards Division, ii. 246
Cerny, village of, i. 15
Chalk Pit, i. 39; attack on, 52–58, 67–69; captured, 56
Chaplains, ii. 268; value of their work, i. 132–134
Charleroi, ii. 240, 241
.Chavonne, i. 6
Chelers, ii. 78
Chemin des Dames, i. 15
Chérisy, ii. 144
Chesnaye, Lieut. Comte Pol de, ii. 268
Cinema, purchase of, i. 101
Cité St. Auguste, i. 39, 41, 44
Cité St. Élie, i. 41, 44, 80
Cité St. Laureut, i. 41; attack on, 44
Clanwilliam, Capt. the Earl of, ii. 258
Clementi, Capt. J., ii. 263
Clery-sur-Somme, i. 139; ii. 143
Clutterbuck, Capt. R., ii. 253
Cockshy House, i. 94
Coigneux, i. 129 n.
Cojeul River, ii. 43 n.; valley, ii. 115, 234
Coke, Major the Hon. R., wounded, i. 159 n.
Colby, Major, killed, i. 20 n.
Coldstream Guards, band, ii. 324
Coldstream Guards, 1st Bn., i. 1, 14, 30; attack on the Chemin des Dames, 15; casualties, 15 n. 17 n., 18 n., 19 n., 67 n.; companies annihilated, 16; reorganised, 17; attack on the Puits, 67. See Guards Division.

Coldstream Guards, 2nd Bn., i. 2, 30; cross the Aisne, 6; casualties, 9 n., 12 n.; attacked by German bombers, 12. See Guards Division
Coldstream Guards, 3rd Bn., i, 2, 30; attack at Landrecies, 3; casualties, 3 n., 6 n., 8; attacked by the Germans, 5. See Guards Division
Coldstream Guards, 4th Bn. (Pioneers), i. 32; at Elnes, 32; work of the, 95, 120, 180–182, 189, 194 n., 200 n., 211, 225, 226 n., 251, 267, 276; ii. 141, 150 n., 177–179, 213–216; at Bailleul, i. 212 n.; at the battle of Messines, 218; Arques, 219; in the Cambrai operations, ii. 19–21; on the Scarpe front, 34; advance on Maubeuge, 234–236. See Guards Division
Coldstream Guards, Reserve Bn., ii. 312
Colincamps, i. 129 n.
Collins, Major A. F. St. C., ii. 267
Cologne, ii. 242
Colonel's Farm, i. 247; capture of, 250, 258
Colquhoun, Capt. Sir Ian, i. 158
Combles, i. 138, 142 n., 152, 192, 194 n.; ii. 143; capture of, i. 175
Condé, i. 2
Congreve, Lieut.-Gen., commanding XIII Corps, ii. 38
Connaught, H.R.H. Duke of, inspects the Guards Division, i. 188, 288; attends the sports at Bavincourt, ii. 104; at the Base Depôt at Harfleur, 323
Contalmaison, i. 138
Cooper, Lieut.-Col. A. W., ii. 257
Cooper, Capt. W. C., ii. 263
Corbett, Major F. H., killed, ii. 109 n.
Corbie, i. 196
Corkran, Lieut.-Col. C. E., commanding 1st Bn. Grenadier Guards, i. 24 n.; an infantry brigade, 25 n.; the 3rd Guards Brigade, 123; ii. 260; at Carnoy, i. 143; attack on Gueudecourt, 162–164; instructions, ii. 7
Cornet Perdu, ii. 81, 85
Coron de Maron, i. 80
Corons Alley, i. 53 n.
Corps I, i. 2, 7, 12, 18, 20, 37, 68 71, 73
Corps II, i. 2, 3, 223 n., 265 n.

INDEX

Corps III, i. 80, 293 ; ii. 1, 2, 3, 23, 183 n.
Corps IV, i. 19, 37, 43, 68, 73, 80, 293 ; ii. 1, 2, 54, 108, 153 n., 155, 185
Corps V, i. 265 n., 293, 294
Corps VI, ii. 42, 45, 47, 94, 108, 112, 145, 148, 149, 153, 154, 155, 185, 203, 219, 228, 238
Corps VII, ii. 3
Corps VIII, i. 118 n., 128
Corps IX, i. 218, 222 ; ii. 183 n.
Corps XI, i. 33, 34, 37, 68, 71, 73, 75, 80, 92, 106 ; at the battle of Loos, 45, 49 ; reconstituted, 70, 92 ; relieve the Indian Corps, 92, 97
Corps XIII, i. 139 ; ii. 38
Corps XIV, i. 113, 114 n., 167, 207, 223 n.; in Flanders, 116 ; ordered to relieve VIII Corps, 128 ; transferred to the Fourth Army, 189 ; composition, 139 n. ; Intelligence Summary, 239 n. ; tribute to, 255 n.
Corps XV, i. 146, 151, 167 ; ii. 81
Corps XVII, ii. 23, 42, 145, 149 n., 155, 163, 164, 185, 219, 221, 228
Corps XVIII, i. 223 n.
Corps XIX, i. 223 n., 265 n.
Corry, Lieut.-Col. N. A. L., commanding 4th Guards Brigade, i. 2 n. ; in temporary command of 1st Bn. Irish Guards, 5 n. ; commanding 3rd Bn. Grenadier Guards, 31 ; ii. 264 ; return to England, i. 114
Cour d'Avoué Farm, attack on, i. 13
Courageous, H.M.S., i. 188 n.
Courcelette village, i. 142
Courcelles, i. 129 n. ; ii. 63, 67 ; capture of, ii. 116 n.
Craonne Farm, i. 269
Crawford, Lieut.-Col. R. B. J., forms a theatrical company, i. 182 n. ; commanding 2nd Bn. Coldstream Guards, 190 n. ; ii. 265 ; crosses the Yser Canal, i. 238 ; commanding 4th Guards Brigade, ii. 92 n.
Crespigny, Brig.-Gen. C. Champion de, commanding 2nd Bn. Grenadier Guards, i. 114 n.; ii. 263 ; attack on Ginchy, i. 155 ; message to Gen. Pereira, 155 n. ; report by, 171 n. ; commanding 1st Guards Brigade, 290 ; ii. 259 ; attack on Gouzeaucourt,

ii. 4 ; at the battle of the Canal du Nord, 165
Crichton, Major the Hon. H., killed, i. 5
Criel Plage, ii. 239 ; school for young officers, 93
Croisilles, ii. 42, 44, 132, 135, 139
Croix Barbée system of defence, i. 102
Croix-du-Bac, ii. 79
Cropper, 2nd Lieut., i. 205 n.
Cross Roads Farm, i. 127
Cuinchy, i. 18
Cunninghame, Capt. A., killed, i. 171 n.
Curlu village, i. 136 n.
Curtis, Major T. L. C., ii. 317
Cuthbert, Capt. J. H., attack on the Puits, i. 57

Dadizeele, ii. 184
"Daily Dump," the, i. 130, 131 n.
Dainville, ii. 23 n.
Darell, Lieut.-Col. W. H., on the staff of the Guards Division, i. 28 ; D.A. and Q.M.G. IV Corps, 199 n. ; ii. 255
Davidson, Major N. R., G.S.O.2, i. 28, 68 n., 78 n. ; ii. 254
Davies, Lieut.-Col. H., commanding Divisional Train, i. 212 n. ; ii. 257
Decauville railway, i. 195, 258, 277 n.
Delville Wood, i. 138 ; capture of, 140 n.
Demicourt, ii. 149, 159, 162, 178, 180
Dene, Lieut.-Col. H., commanding 1st Bn. Welsh Guards, i. 126 ; ii. 267 ; wounded, ii. 126 n.
Despagne Farm, i. 220
Dessart Wood, ii. 7
Dewar, G. A. B., i. 305 n.
Digby, Major the Hon. E. K., commanding 1st Bn. Coldstream Guards, ii. 168 n., 226 n.
Diggle, Lieut.-Col. W. H., ii. 254
Dixmude, i. 7 n.
Doignies, i. 296 ; ii. 19, 149, 153 n.
Doolan, Lieut. E., ii. 257
Douchy-les-Ayette, ii. 66
Doullens, i. 114 n., 128
Douteuse House, i. 240
Douve River, i. 220
Douzies, ii. 231
Dranoutre, i. 219 ; ii. 102 n.
Drocourt, ii. 143 n.
Dromesuil, i. 188
Dronvin, i. 81

Duisans, ii. 23 n.
"Dundas, Henry, Scots Guards, a Memoir," i. 130 n.; ii. 13 n., 38 n., 44 n.
Duquenoy, Lieut. M., ii. 253
Dyer, Capt. Sir John, ii. 260; killed, 255

Eady, Lieut. H. G., ii. 256
Earle, Lieut.-Col. M., wounded, i. 22 n.
Ecoust, ii. 43 n., 132, 143
Ecoust-St.-Mein, ii. 42, 124, 145, 146
Ecques-le-Biberon, i. 218 n.
Ecurie Wood Camp, ii. 37
Edgington, Capt. W., ii. 257
Edmonds, Brig.-Gen. J. E., i. x; "History of the Great War," 3 n., 4 n., 5 n., 6 n., 7 n. *See* War
Edwards, Major G. J., commanding 4th Bn. Coldstream Guards (Pioneers), i. 193 n., 290; ii. 265
Egerton, Lieut.-Col. A. G. E., commanding 1st Bn. Coldstream Guards, i. 30 n., 67; ii. 264; killed, i. 67 n.; tribute to, 68 n.
Egypt House, i. 275, 277, 284
Elesmes, ii. 231, 232
Ellice, Major E. C., commanding Guards Entrenching Bn., ii. 320
Elliot, Lieut. Hon. E., ii. 253
Ellison, Lieut. C. E. M., ii. 260
Elnes, i. 32
Elverdinghe, i. 131, 234 n., 236 n.; Château, 226
Epéhy, ii. 154; attack on, 155 n.
Eperlecques, i. 281
Epinette, ii. 81, 85
Epinoy, ii. 183
Equancourt, i. 209 n.
Ereclin River, ii. 192
Ervillers, ii. 47, 48, 51, 117, 122; advance on, 52; captured, 123 n.
Esnes, the, ii. 187
Esquelbecq, i. 281; Château, 117, 123
Esquerdes, i. 31
Estaires, i. 96; ii. 79, 81
Estourmel, capture of, ii. 188, 189
Eterpigny, capture of, ii. 144
Etinghem, i. 139
Etreux, i. 15
Etriecourt, i. 207; wells destroyed, 210 n.
Evans, Major J. J. P., ii. 255, 259
Evans, Brig.-Gen. W., commanding Divisional Artillery, i. 114, 182 n.; ii. 256

Falfemont Farm, capture of, i. 140
Fampoux, ii. 26, 28, 35
Fanshawe, Lieut.-Gen. Sir E., commanding Corps V, i. 294
Faucigny-Lucinge, Capt. Prince A. de, ii. 268
Fauquissart, i. 93
Fawcus, Lieut.-Col. H., commanding D.A.C., i. 123 n.; ii. 257, 262
Feignies, ii. 229, 230 n.
Feilding, Major-Gen. Sir Geoffrey, i. ix; commanding 4th Guards Brigade, 2 n., 6, 14 n.; wounded, 8; commanding 1st Guards Brigade, 28; ii. 258; orders to the troops, i. 51, 162; ii. 122; report on the proposed attack on Chalk Pit, i. 53 n.; instructions from Lord Cavan, 72; commanding the Guards Division, 113; ii. 253; characteristics, i. 113; message from Lieut.-Gen. Haking, 115 n.; on the bombing accidents, 116 n.; system of signed parchments, 117 n.; on the importance of reconnaissance, 129; tribute to the work of the chaplains, 133 n.; at Bus-les-Artois, 139; special signalling courses, 140; conferences, 141, 148, 166, 223, 232; plan of operations, 142; instructions to his Brigadiers, 148; 166 n.; on the failure of tanks, 161 n.; extract from a letter, 174 n.; plan of operations for the Flanders offensive, 223; tribute to the Guards Division, 255; on the Cambrai operations, 294; reasons against the proposed attack on Bourlon Wood, 306-308; report to XVII Corps, ii. 21 n.; to III Corps, 23; on anti-tank defence, 31 n.; in the German offensive, 46; on the dribbling methods of advance by the Germans, 53 n.; protest against the length of front held by the Guards Division, 65; at Humbercamp, 97; congratulations to the 1st Guards Brigade, 138 n., 140 n.; on the position of the machine gunners, 155 n.; commanding the London District, 156; at the march through London of the Guards Division, 246
Ferfay, i. 47

INDEX

Ferguson, Lieut.-Col. R. H., commanding 2nd Bn. Irish Guards, ii. 267
Fergusson, Lieut.-Gen. Sir Charles, commanding XVII Corps, ii. 23
Ferme de Rieux, ii. 212
Festubert, ii. 79; battle of, i. 13, 24, 88 n.
Feuchy, ii. 35; Chapel, 44 n.
Ficheux, ii. 53, 56, 60, 111
Filmer, Capt. Sir Robert, i. 110
Fisher-Rowe, Lieut.-Col. L. R., commanding 1st Bn. Grenadier Guards, i. 23 n.; killed, 24 n.
FitzClarence, Brig.-Gen. C., commanding the 1st Guards Brigade, i. 2 n.; killed 2 n., 11
FitzGerald, Lord Desmond, wounded, i. 81 n.
Flanders, i. 7, 116; offensive, 213, 215–290
Fleming, Rev. R. J., i. 101; ii. 268
Flers, i. 142, 146
Flesquières, i. 293, 295, 297, 317, 322; ii. 18, 20, 163, 164, 165, 180, 181; attack on, i. 299; ii. 170, 173, 174; Château, ii. 185
Fleurbaix, ii. 79
Foch, Marshal, i. 137
Foley, Major, wounded, ii. 109 n.
Follett, Lieut.-Col. G. B. S., commanding 2nd Bn. Coldstream Guards, i. 190 n.; ii. 265; wounded, i. 190 n.; commanding 2nd Guards Brigade, ii. 44, 259; 3rd Guards Brigade, 99 n., 121; tribute to 1st Bn. Grenadier Guards, 123 n.; killed, 172, 181, 260; character, 173 n.
Fontaine au Tertre Farm, ii. 192, 193, 196
Fontaine-Notre-Dame, i. 293, 299 n.; attack on, 308–321
Fosse No. 8, i. 41; capture of, 44; loss of, 52, 53 n.; attack on, 70, 85, 92; failure to recapture, 85
Fosseux, ii. 15, 23 n.
Fouquières, i. 81
Fourche Farm, i. 247
Fox, Major B. H., ii. 262
Fraser, Capt. A. D., ii. 25
Fraser, Lieut. D. M., ii. 262
Fraser, Capt. G., ii. 258
Frégicourt, i. 142 n.; capture of, 173 n.
Frémicourt, ii. 140, 144
French Army, at Polygon Wood, i. 9; relieve I Corps, 18; advance on Lens, 37; at Loos, 69; Boesinghe, 116; defence of Verdun, 135; capture Frégicourt, 173 n.; capture Sailly-Saillisel, 191 n.; relieve IX Corps, 192; failure of the attack on the Aisne, 215; effect on the troops, 216; cross the Yser Canal, 239; occupy St. Quentin, ii. 183
French, Field-Marshal Viscount, i. 2, 36; Despatch, 4 n.; transfers his troops to Flanders, 74; "1914," 11 n.; on the battle of Ypres, 22 n.; letter from Lord Kitchener, 26 n.; failure of his plans at the battle of Loos, 46, 49; tribute to the Guards Division, 78 n.; at the Base Depôt at Harfleur, ii. 323
Fresneville, i. 188
Fresnoy, attack on, ii. 39; Farm, 191
Fricourt, i. 137
Frisby, Capt. C. H., awarded the V.C., ii. 168 n., 275
Fromelles, i. 23
Fryer, E. B. M., "Reminiscences of a Grenadier," i. 258 n. See Reminiscences
Fuller, Lance-Corp. W. D., awarded the V.C., i. 24 n.
Furby, Lieut. Charles, ii. 268
Furze, Capt. G., ii. 260

Gaapard, i. 221
Gamble, 2nd Lieut. R. D., ii. 253
Garden, Lieut.-Col. L. P., ii. 261
Gars Brugghe, ii. 81, 84
Gas attacks, i. 42, 242 n.; ii. 330; cylinders, instructions for the installation, 74, 80; cancelled, 75, 79; mustard, i. 235; ii. 29 n., 152; shells, discharge of, i. 59; losses from, ii. 32 n.
Gauche Wood, attack on, ii. 9
Gavrelle, ii. 26, 27, 41
General's Farm, i. 232, 233, 260
Genly, i. 3 n.
George V., H.M. King, accident, i. 91; visits the Guards Division, 129; at Herzeele, 231; congratulations to them, 289; witnesses their march past, ii. 245; message to the troops, 246; at the Base Depôt at Harfleur, 323
German aeroplane shot down, i. 279 n.

German army, military operations, i. 3–13, 15–25; strong position at Loos, 40–42, 52; lines of defence, 41; at the battle of Loos, 42–90; dug-outs, 43 n.; attack on the Hohenzollern Redoubt, 81–87; mining operations, 104; bombardment of trenches, 120, 123 n.; capture Hooge, 123; on the Somme, 135–186; retreat to Bapaume, 158; surrender, 171, 174, 272; routed, 173; at St. Pierre Vaast Wood, 201; bombing attacks, 202–204; withdraw to the Hindenburg line, 204–208; use of booby traps, 209; losses in the Arras offensive, 217 n.; at the battle of Messines, 218–222; construction of pill-boxes, 224 n.; raids, 231, 263; battle of Ypres, 233; attacks of " mustard " gas, 235; bombing aeroplanes, 261 n., 266; operations in Cambrai, 295–322; ii. 4–22; counter-attacks, ii. 1; trench warfare on the Scarpe, 29; attack on Fresnoy, 39; offensive of 1918, 41–77; dribbling methods of advance, 52, 59; use of *minenwerfer* fire, 72; advance on Lys Valley, 78–93; close of the offensive, 94–107; capture Kimmel Hill, 102 n.; attack on the Aisne, 102 n.; on Reims, 102 n.; defeated at Amiens, 107 n.; attack on Moyenneville, 118; evacuate Bapaume, 143; retreat, 148–150, 196, 204, 218–232; Hindenburg Line broken through, 143–183

German block-house, capture of, i. 241, 246

German prisoners, number of, i. 248, 249 n., 254 n., 269 n., 287, 295; ii. 22, 115, 117 n., 128 n., 131 n., 140 n., 144 n., 147 n., 175, 181, 200 n., 218 n., 224 n.

German trenches, attacks on, i. 108–110

Germany, armistice, ii. 233

Gheluvelt, i. 9, 21; attack on, 22

Gheluwe, ii. 184

Ghent, i. 19

Gibbs, Rev. E., killed, i. 133 n.

Gibbs, Capt. L. M., ii. 255, 259; commanding 2nd Bn. Coldstream Guards, i. 190 n.; ii. 265

Gillilan, Major, ii. 91 n.

Ginchy, i. 138, 142; attack on, 143–145, 149–157, 183; plans for the attack, 146–151; captured, 183

Gird trench, i. 172; capture of, 174

Givenchy, i. 12 n., 13; defence of, 18; second action of, 25

Gloucestershire Regiment, 1st Bn., i. 11; 8th Bn. ii. 207 n.

Glyn, Major A. St. L., commanding 2nd Bn. Grenadier Guards, i. 114 n.; 1st Bn. Grenadier Guards, 118 n.; ii. 263

Goat trench, ii. 152

Godman, Lieut.-Col. S. H., commanding 1st Bn. Scots Guards, i. 19 n., 154; ii. 266; wounded, i. 57 n.; ii. 266

Gomiecourt, ii. 53; capture of, 55, 56

Gommecourt, i. 136 n., 137

Gommegnies, ii. 223

Gonnelieu, i. 293, 295; ii. 183; capture of, ii. 2, 3; attack on, 10–13

Goodwin, Lieut.-Col. T. H. J. C., ii. 257

Gordon, Lieut.-Col. A. F. L., ii. 267

Gordon, Lieut.-Col. G. C. Douglas, commanding 1st Bn. Welsh Guards, i. 208 n.; ii. 267

Gordon Highlanders, 2nd Bn., i. 2 n.; 6th Bn., i. 2 n.

Gordon-Lennox, Lieut.-Col. Lord E. C., ii. 266

Gort, Lieut.-Col. Viscount, commanding 4th Bn. Grenadier Guards, i. 199 n.; ii. 125 n., 264; wounded, ii. 13 n., 176; commanding 1st Bn. Grenadier Guards, 57, 117, 122 n., 259, 263; at the battle of Havrincourt, 157; commanding 3rd Guards Brigade, 173; awarded the V.C., 175, 274

Gosnay, i. 91

Gough, General Hubert, divisional commander, i. 25; commanding the Reserve Army, 128; attack on Thiepval, 167; commanding Fifth Army, 223 n.; tribute to the Guards Division, 288 n.

Goulburn, Brig.-Gen. C. E., i. 29; ii. 256

Gourlain Chapel, ii. 193, 196

Gouvy Farm, i. 254

Gouvy-le-Catelet, ii. 93

INDEX

Gouzeaucourt, i. 209 n.; ii. 2, 7, 183; attack on, ii. 4–6, 13
Graham, Capt. A. C., killed, i. 145
Graham, Capt. F. F., ii. 253
Graham, Stephen, "A Private in the Guards," i. 134 n.; ii. 238 n., 239 n., 241 n., 247 n.
Graincourt, i. 298, 302; ii. 155, 164, 167; capture of, ii. 171; attack on, 173, 180
Grammont, ii. 232 n.
Greenland Hill, ii. 26
Greer, Lieut.-Col. E. B., commanding 2nd Bn. Irish Guards, i. 201 n.; ii. 267; killed, i. 245 n.
Gregge-Hopwood, Lieut.-Col. E. B. G., commanding 1st Bn. Coldstream Guards, i. 68 n., 190 n.; ii. 264; killed, i. 238 n.
Grenadier Guards, band, ii. 324
Grenadier Guards, 1st Bn., i. 2, 30; at Kruiseecke, 20; casualties, 20 n., 22 n., 24 n., 25 n.; at the battle of Gheluvelt, 22; Neuve Chapelle, 23; Givenchy, 25; tribute to, ii. 123 n. *See* Guards Division
Grenadier Guards, 2nd Bn., attacked by the Germans, i. 5; casualties, 6 n., 13 n.; tribute to, 10 n.; at the battle of Festubert, 13. *See* Guards Division
Grenadier Guards, 3rd Bn., in London, i. 30; at Esquerdes, 31. *See* Guards Division
Grenadier Guards, 4th Bn., i. 30, 31. *See* Guards Division
Grenadier Guards, Reserve Bn., ii. 311
"Grenadier Guards in the Great War," i. 4 n., 10 n., 11 n., 21 n., 22 n., 24 n., 27 n., 30 n., 31 n., 62 n., 110 n., 117 n., 144 n., 145 n., 153 n., 155 n., 156 n., 160 n., 171 n., 172 n., 173 n., 191 n., 192 n., 203 n., 238 n., 246 n., 247 n., 249 n., 250 n., 270 n., 303 n.; ii. 11 n., 12 n., 49 n., 53 n., 62 n., 80 n., 83 n., 86 n., 89 n., 91 n., 106 n., 116 n., 123 n., 125 n., 128 n., 129 n., 130 n., 134 n., 146 n., 153 n., 157 n., 169 n., 170 n., 171 n., 173 n., 189 n., 190 n., 205 n., 206 n., 222 n., 223 n., 225 n., 227 n., 244 n., 246 n., 320 n.
Grenay, i. 38, 39, 40
Gricourt, ii. 183
Grigg, Lieut.-Col. E. W. M., G.S.O.1, ii. 75 n., 254, 260; orders to troops, 304, 310
Grovetown, i. 208
Gruyterszale Farm, i. 269, 272
Guards, Brigade of, work of the, in France, i. 1
Guards Brigade, the 1st, battalions, i. 1, 2, 14, 30; at the battle of Langemarck, 16; trench warfare, 18; at St. Omer, 30; review of, 33; at Nœux-les-Mines, 48; construct a new fire trench, 69; at Mazingarbe, 69; congratulations from Lord Cavan, 241 n.; recapture Gouzeaucourt, ii. 4–6; attack on Quentin ridge, 8–10; plan of relief, 71; tribute to, 138 n., 140 n. *See* Guards Division
Guards Brigade, the 2nd, battalions, i. 30; review of, 33; at Houchin, 48; attack on the Chalk Pit, 55–58; on Puits, 65–67; at Verquingneul, 68; attacked by the Germans, 75–77; at Hooge, 124; attack on Fontaine-Notre-Dame, 308–318; casualties, 318; at Gouzeaucourt, ii. 7; attack on Moyenneville, 114. *See* Guards Division
Guards Brigade, the 3rd, battalions, i. 31; review of, 33; at Hallicourt, 48; attack on Hill 70, 58–65; at Labourse, 69; attack on Ginchy, 143–145; advance on Gueudecourt, 162–164; ii. 7; attack on Gonnelieu, ii. 10–13; casualties, 131 n. *See* Guards Division
Guards Brigade, the 4th, battalions, i. 2; casualties, 7 n., 40 n., 76; ii. 90, 92; tributes to, i. 12 n., 14 n.; ii. 90; join the Guards Division, i. 13, 14 n.; changes in the commands, 14 n.; formed, ii. 29, 37; inspection, 38; in the German offensive, 46; at Bienvillers, 76; in the Lys offensive, 78–89; subsequent history, 91–93. *See* Guards Division
Guards Division, formed, i. 26; ii. 251; changes in the commands, i. 28, 113, 123, 199 n., 289; training, 33, 112, 140, 187, 222, 227; ii. 103; memorandum to, i. 34; march to Nœux-les-Mines, 48; advance on Loos, 49–52; relieved, 69, 87, 165,

322 ; ii. 14, 33, 140, 217 ; relieve Infantry Brigades, i. 71–74 ; corporate unity, 78, 89 ; tributes to, 78 *n*., 107 *n*., 110 *n*., 115 *n*., 176, 214, 255, 287–289, 303 *n*. ; ii. 14, 181, 227 *n*. ; attacked by the Germans, i. 81 ; attack on the Hohenzollern Redoubt, 84 ; casualties, 85 *n*., 120 *n*., 122 *n*., 126 *n*., 128 *n*., 165, 176, 195 *n*., 259, 266, 278, 280, 285 ; ii. 21, 22 *n*., 32 *n*., 33 *n*., 77, 98 *n*., 101 *n*., 104, 134 *n*., 181 ; courage and discipline, i. 89 ; at Gosnay, 91 ; La Gorgue, 93 ; method of holding the line, 97–99 ; regulations for the well-being, 99–101 ; defence system, 101–103 ; method of accurate intelligence, 105 ; offensive policy, 107 ; raiding expeditions, 107–110, 126–128 ; ii. 31–33 ; Bombing School, i. 111 ; join the XIV Corps, 113, 114, 139 ; in Flanders, 116 ; in the Ypres salient, 118–128 ; at Beaumont Hamel, 128–130 ; social life at Poperinghe, 130–132 ; chaplains, 132–134 ; ii. 268 ; on the Somme, i. 143–186 ; objectives, 146, 168 ; disposal of the troops, 146–148, 150 ; attack on Ginchy, 148–161 ; length of front, 150 *n*. ; ii. 65 ; plans for the attack on Lesbœufs, i. 167–169 ; capture Lesbœufs, 169–173 ; inspection, 188 ; divided into two groups, 190 ; at Sailly-Saillisel, 192–198 ; condition of the ground, 192–194 ; Works Battalions formed, 193 *n*. ; ii. 321 ; at Corbie, i. 196 ; Maurepas, 198 ; warning to the Germans, 200 ; pursuit of them, 205–208 ; ordered to consolidate their positions, 208 ; construction of the roads, 210–212 ; at Heilly, 213 ; Renescure, 218 *n*. ; take over the Boesinghe sector, 222–225 ; preparations for the attack on Ypres, 225–228, 232 ; crossing the Yser Canal, 228 ; reconnaissance work, 230–232 ; advance to objectives, 243–250 ; at Herzeele, 258, 266 ; reorganized, 259 ; operations on the Ypres offensive, 261–285 ; summary of the work, 286 ; in the Cambrai offensive, 295–322 ; ii. 2–22 ; at Arras, ii. 23 ; joins XVII Corps, 24 ; defence of the Scarpe, 25–35 ; in the German offensive, 41–77 ; withdrawal, 55–57 ; position at Ayette, 62 ; repulse attack from Boyelles, 72–75 ; at Bavincourt, 96, 101–104 ; relieve 32nd Division, 97–101, 105 ; epidemic of Spanish influenza, 104 ; sports, 104 ; attack on Moyenneville, 113–115 ; advance to victory, 118–142 ; advance on the Canal du Nord, 145–181 ; at the battle of Havrincourt, 156–158 ; battle of the Canal du Nord, 163–167, 180 ; advance on the Selle River, 185–209 ; crossing the, 204–206, 208 ; advance on Maubeuge, 219–231, 234 ; congratulations from VI Corps commander, 227 *n*., 233 *n*. ; thanksgiving services, 237, 238 ; march into Germany, 238–242 ; at Cologne, 242–245 ; return to England, 245 ; demobilization, 245 ; march past Buckingham Palace, 245 ; message from the King, 246 ; Operation orders, 278–310 ; Base Depôt at Harfleur, 322 ; bands, 324 ; address from Gen. Matheson, 326–328 ; dress and equipment, 329–332

Guards Entrenching Bn., ii. 320
Guards Machine-Gun Companies, i. 177, 202 ; ii. 95, 314 ; in the operations on the Somme, i. 177–180 ; at Bronfay, 212 ; the battle of Ypres, 235 ; number of guns in action, 275 ; at the battle of Fontaine-Notre Dame, 317 ; casualties, ii. 69 ; assist the infantry, 130
Guards Machine-Gun Regiment, formed, ii. 32, 314–317 ; casualties, 77 *n*. ; valuable service, 190 ; disbanded, 317
Guards Reinforcement Bn., ii. 70, 321 ; reformed, i. 294 ; broken up, ii. 97
Guards Reserve Battalions, ii. 311
Guards Works Bn., i. 193 ; ii. 321
" Guards at Loos," i. 59 *n*.
" Guards Pioneer Battalion," i. 32 *n*.
Gubbins, Col. R. D., ii. 262
Guemappe, ii. 29
Gueudecourt, i. 142, 146, 190, 196 ; attack on, 145, 162–164 ; captured, 174, 186

INDEX

Guillemont, i. 192, 196 ; capture of, 140
Gunston, Capt. C. B., ii. 258 ; commanding 2nd Bn. Irish Guards, i. 245 n.
Guthrie, Lieut. P., ii. 253
Gwynne, Rev. Father, i. 133 ; killed, 81 n., 133 n.

Habareq, ii. 19
Haie Wood, i. 194 n. ; shelled, 202 ; railway from, 211
Haig, Sir Douglas, commanding I Corps, i. 2 ; the First Army, 14, 37 ; tribute to the 4th Guards Brigade, 14 ; commanding XI Corps, 46 ; plan of operations, 70, 80, 83, 135, 190, 291 ; memorandum on the training of the Army, 111 ; reasons for continuing operations, 305 n. ; congratulations to the Guards Division, ii. 14 ; at the Base Depôt at Harfleur, 323
"Haig's Command, Sir Douglas," i. 215 n., 216 n., 217 n., 261 n., 265 n., 266 n., 269 n., 279 n., 291 n., 292 n. ; ii. 143 n., 145 n., 151 n., 159 n. ; "Despatches," i. 136 n., 137 n., 138 n., 139 n., 142 n., 191 n., 204 n., 217 n., 218 n., 233 n., 236 n., 254 n., 279 n., 291 n., 295 n., 305 n. ; ii. 1 n., 37 n., 41 n., 48 n., 79 n., 80 n., 87 n., 90 n., 95 n., 102 n., 107 n., 108 n., 119 n., 143 n., 144 n., 145 n., 155 n., 163 n., 164 n., 178 n., 183 n., 184 n., 203 n., 218 n., 219 n., 232 n., 238 n.
Haisnes, i. 41, 44
Haking, Lieut.-Gen., G.O.C. XI Corps, reviews 1st Guards Brigade, i. 33 ; conference at Lillers, 34 ; orders to the troops, 49, 52, 68 n., 82 ; telegram from, 53 n. ; plan of attack on Fosse No. 8, 85 n. ; memorandum on "the Winter Campaign," 106 ; tribute to the Guards Division, 110 n., 115 n.
Haldane, Lieut.-Gen. Sir J. A. L., commanding VI Corps, ii. 42
Hallicourt, i. 48
Hally Avenue, ii. 124 ; Copse, ii. 48, 121, 125, 130, 134, 137, 140
Halte, ii. 116
Ham, i. 211

Hambro, Capt. R. O., ii. 254
Hamel Work, ii. 116, 118, 122 n.
Hamelincourt, ii. 48, 54, 55, 56, 111 ; attack on, 117 n., 119, 120 ; abandoned, 117 n.
Hamilton, Lieut.-Col. G. C., commanding 4th Bn. Grenadier Guards, i. 31, 199 n. ; ii. 264 ; attack on Hill 70, 59 ; gassed, 60
Hamilton, Major the Hon. L. d'H., commanding 1st Bn. Coldstream Guards, i. 16 n. ; killed, 17 n.
Hammerville trench, ii. 123
Haplincourt, i. 296
Happy Valley Camp, i. 145
Hardecourt-aux-Bois, i. 138
Harfleur, Base Depôt at, ii. 322
Harlech, Lord, i. 61 n., 65 n.
Harpies stream, ii. 209, 214 n.
Harris, A., bandmaster, ii. 324
Harveng, i. 3 n.
Hassell, C. H., bandmaster, ii. 324
Haucourt, ii. 144
Haussy, ii. 196, 197 ; attack on, 201, 202, 207, 211
Haute-Deule Canal, i. 37, 38, 42, 88
Havrincourt, i. 293 ; conference at, 307 ; battle of, ii. 156 ; captured, 157 ; Wood, ii. 7 ; evacuated, 153 n.
Hawkes, Rev. F. O. T., ii. 268
Haynecourt, ii. 183
Hazebrouck, i. 7, 117 ; advance on, ii. 85
H.E. shell, use of, i. 109 n.
Head, Rev. F. W., ii. 268
Headlam, Capt. C. M., ii. 253
Heath, Major J. T., ii. 262
Hébuterne, i. 128, 129 n., 136 n. ; capture of, ii. 58
Heilly, i. 213
Hely-Hutchison, Capt. H. R., ii. 255
Hendecourt, ii. 3, 18, 61, 143
Henin, ii. 49 ; Hill, capture of, ii. 43
Henin-sur-Cojeul, ii. 43, 44 n.
Hennois Wood, i. 208
Hermies, i. 295 ; ii. 149
Hermin, ii. 16
Hermon-Hodge, Major R. H., ii. 255
Hertfordshire Regiment, 1st Bn., i. 12
Herzeele, i. 230, 258, 266
Hesketh-Prichard, Capt. H., lecture on "The Art of Sniping," i. 112 n.
Hey Wood, i. 245

Heywood, Brig.-Gen. C. P., G.S.O.1, i. 118 n.; ii. 254; instructor of the Staff Course at Cambridge, i. 290; commanding 3rd Guards Brigade, ii. 182 n., 260; wounded, 226; orders to the troops, 283, 288, 299
Heyworth, Brig.-Gen. F. J., commanding 20th Infantry Brigade, i. 2 n., 23; 3rd Guards Brigade, 28, 54; ii. 260; attack on Hill 70, i. 58, 60–62; "Account of the Capture of Hill 70," 61 n.; killed, 123
Hickie, Major-Gen., tribute to the C.R.A., i. 183 n.
Higgins, Sergeant, i. 110
Hill 70, i. 39, 45, 49, 52; attack on, 58–65
Hindenburg, General von, "Out of my Life," i. 296 n.; Line broken through, ii. 143–183
Hohenzollern Redoubt, i. 41, 46; attack on, 72, 76, 81–87
Hollebeke, i. 20
Holmes, Private Edgar, awarded the V.C., ii. 189, 276
Holmesdale, Lieut. Viscount, ii. 253
Holnon, ii. 183
Hondeghem, ii. 92
Hooge, i. 18, 22, 116, 123
Hopley, Capt. J., i. 160 n.
Hore-Ruthven, Lieut.-Col. A. G. A., G.S.O.1, i. 290; ii. 254; B.G.G.S. VII Corps, ii. 25 n.; orders to troops, 301
Hore-Ruthven, Lieut.-Col. the Hon. W. P., commanding 1st Bn. Scots Guards, i. 16 n.; G.S.O.1, 19 n., 28 n.; ii. 254; B.G.G.S. VIII Corps, i. 118 n.
Horne, Major-General, commanding the Guards Division, tribute to the 4th Guards Brigade, i. 14 n.
Horses, inspection of, i. 188; casualties among, 266 n.; ii. 142
Houchin, i. 48
Houlle village, i. 30
Housden, Major E. J., ii. 99 n., 111 n.; wounded, 153 n.
Household Brigade Officer Cadet Battalion, ii. 318
Houthem, ii. 184
Houthulst Forest, i. 8, 224, 260, 269, 274
Hovil, Major R., commanding 75th Brigade, R.F.A., i. 184 n., 234 n.
Howell, Capt. F. D. G., ii. 257

Hulluch, i. 37, 38, 41, 46
Humbercamp, ii. 97, 110
Hussey, Major, ii. 216 n.

Igneul, ii. 189, 190
Inchy, ii. 149, 151
Indian Corps, i. 12; at the battle of Ginchy, 18; Neuve Chapelle, 23; relieved, 92
Infantry Brigades—
5th, ii. 112, 158 n.; relieved, i. 71; capture Ervillers, ii. 123 n.
6th, i. 3; at the battle of Neuve Chapelle, 13 n.; relieved, 71, 72
8th, ii. 52
20th, i. 2; battalions, 2 n.; at Ypres, 19; at the battle of Festubert, 24
21st, i. 20
22nd, at Ghent, i. 19
26th, ii. 15
37th, i. 73
47th, i. 143, 144
48th, captures Ginchy, i. 143 n.; relieved, 144
58th, i. 113
59th, i. 160
61st, i. 160, 162
62nd, i. 160
64th, i. 174
71st, failure of the attack on Ginchy, i. 149
76th, ii. 140
83rd, i. 73
92nd, ii. 48, 52 n., 59, 63
93rd, ii. 38, 50, 51, 57, 59, 63, 70
94th, ii. 38
96th, ii. 76
97th, at Ransart, ii. 66
119th, i. 301
142nd, i. 69
167th, i. 143 n., 175
170th, ii. 157
179th, ii. 118
183rd, ii. 14
187th, ii. 40
Infantry Brigades, reduction of battalions, ii. 37 n.
Influenza, Spanish, epidemic of, ii. 104, 110
Inglinghem, parade at, i. 287
Iremonger, Capt. A. R. A., ii. 262
Irish Guards, band, ii. 324
Irish Guards, 1st Bn., i. 2, 30; attacked by the Germans, 5; casualties, 6 n., 10 n., 11, 12 n., 13 n.; attack on Reutel spur,

INDEX 349

8; at the battle of Nonne Boschen, 11; attack on the Germans, 12; at the battle of Festubert, 13; inspection, 34. *See* Guards Division

Irish Guards, 2nd Bn., i. 30; at Lumbres, 31; raid on Krupp Farm, 127; casualties, 127 n.; failure of the attack on Ginchy, 149. *See* Guards Division

Irish Guards Reserve Bn., ii. 312

" Irish Guards in the Great War," i. 4 n., 10 n., 13 n., 31 n., 78 n., 117 n., 127 n., 149 n., 156 n., 160 n., 191 n., 193 n., 201 n., 204 n., 205 n., 206 n., 207 n., 211 n., 213 n., 228 n., 231 n., 264 n., 273 n., 293 n., 309 n., 316 n.; ii. 47 n., 52 n., 62 n., 80 n., 82 n., 86 n., 92 n., 102 n., 105 n., 106 n., 137 n., 147 n., 154 n., 169 n., 170 n., 174 n., 182 n., 208 n., 217 n., 222 n., 224 n., 233 n.

Irvine, Lieut. A. F., wounded, i. 171 n.

Italian army, defeated at the battle of Caporetto, i. 291

Jackson, Major R. D., ii. 263

Jackson, Lance-Corp. T. N., awarded the V.C., ii. 168 n., 275

Jacob, Lieut.-Gen., commanding II Corps, i. 223 n.

Jacotin, Private, ii. 87 n.

Jeffreys, Major-Gen. Sir George D., i. ix; ii. 317; commanding 2nd Bn. Grenadier Guards, i. 5 n.; ii. 263; 1st Bn. Irish Guards, i. 13 n.; 58th Infantry Brigade, 113; 1st Guards Brigade, 199 n.; ii. 258; 19th Division, i. 289

Jenlain, ii. 220, 221

Jewel trench, ii. 138

Joffre, General, commanding the French army, i. 7; plan of operations, 135; retires, 215 n.

Johns, Capt. A. W., ii. 257

Jones, Rev. Sydney, i. 132

Judas Copse, ii. 47; Farm, ii. 121, 122, 123; trench, ii. 138

Keith, Capt. C. G., ii. 261

Kellie, Major G. H. S., ii. 256, 263

Kelly, Major R. H. V., ii. 258

Kemmel Hill, i. 219; capture of, ii. 102 n.

Kerr, Lieut. C., ii. 89 n.

King, Private, interview with a German, i. 201

King's Own Yorkshire Light Infantry, 12th Bn., ii. 67, 70, 84, 87

Kinsman, Lieut.-Col. G. R. V., ii. 262; retires, i. 123 n.

Kipling, Sir Rudyard, " The Irish Guards in the Great War," i. 4 n. *See* Irish Guards

Kirkland, Lieut.-Col. T., commanding Brigades R.F.A., ii. 211, 262

Kitchener, Field-Marshal Earl, creation of the Guards Division, i. 26–28; letter from, 26 n.; order to raise a Welsh Regiment, 31; interview with Sir F. Lloyd, 32 n.; inspects the 1st Bn. Irish Guards, 34

Klein Zillebeke, i. 9, 11

Knapp, Father, i. 117 n., 133; ii. 268; killed, 133 n.

Koehuit, i. 16

Kortekeer Cabaret, capture of, i. 258

Kruiseecke, i. 20; attack on, 21

Krupp Farm, i. 127

La Bassée Canal, i. 12, 19, 37, 38, 40, 68, 92, 98

La Bazeque, ii. 104

La Boiselle, i. 138

Labourse, i. 50, 69

Labuissière, i. 47

La Clytte, i. 221

La Cour de Soupir Farm, i. 6, 7

La Couronne, ii. 81, 85, 86

La Fère, ii. 41 n.

La Flaque Wood, ii. 222 n.

La Folie Wood, i. 310, 312, 317

La Gorgue, i. 93, 94, 100; Soldiers' Club, 101

Lagincourt, ii. 145, 146, 147, 180

La Justice, i. 298, 317; ii. 20

La Longueville, ii. 228, 229

Lambert, Capt. R. S., ii. 260, 261

Land Drainage Company, work of the, i. 96

Landon, Major C. W., ii. 257

Landrecies, battle of, i. 3

Lane, Capt. G. A. C., ii. 253

Lane-Fox, Rev. R. J., ii. 268

Langemarck, i. 224, 249, 250; battle of, 16; captured, 260

Lannes Copse, i. 262; Farm, 272

INDEX

La Quinque Rue, i. 92
Larbret, ii. 96
Larkhill, i. 29
Lascelles, Lieut.-Col. Viscount, commanding 3rd Bn. Grenadier Guards, ii. 147 n., 189, 264
Lateau Wood, i. 293
La Terrière plateau, ii. 161 n.
Laventie, i. 92, 96, 100; ii. 79, 96 n.
Lawrence, Capt. P. R., commanding 1st Guards Machine-Gun Company, ii. 314
Lawrie, Capt. J. W., ii. 256
Leach, Second Lieut. C. de L.; awarded the Albert Medal in Gold, i. 141 n.
Leatham, Lieut.-Col. R. E. K., ii. 316, 317
Lebucquière, i. 297
Le Cateau, ii. 203, 218; battle of, 184 n.
Le Cauroy, i. 295
Lechelle, i. 207, 296; ii. 20
Le Drumez, system of defence, i. 102, 103
Lees, Lieut.-Col. E. F. W., C.R.E., i. 228 n.; ii. 256
Legh, Capt. Hon. P. W., ii. 253
Le Mesnil, i. 207, 208
Lens, coal mining district, i. 36, 38; ii. 184
Leopard trench, i. 269
"Le Pays Wallon," extract from, ii. 240 n.
Le Rutoire Farm, i. 51, 65
Lesbœufs, i. 142, 156 n., 190; ii. 143; plans for the attack on, i. 145, 167–169; advance on, 158, 164; captured, 169–173, 177
Les Charmeux, i. 93
Les Cinq Chemins, i. 274
Les Mottes, ii. 229
Lestrem, ii. 79
Le Tronquoy, ii. 183
Leuze Wood, i. 138, 142; capture of, 140 n.
Lewis, Lieut. Rupert, i. 63
L'Homme Mort, ii. 129, 134
Lillers, i. 91; conference at, 34
"Lilywhites," theatrical company, i. 132 n.
Lindenhoek, i. 219
Lisle, Lieut.-Gen. Sir Beauvoir de, commanding XV Corps, ii. 81; tribute to the 4th Guards Brigade, 90
Lloyd, Major-Gen. Sir Francis, G.O.C. London District, i. 26; interview with Lord Kitchener, 32 n.
Lloyd-Jones, Major P. A., ii. 258
Locre, i. 23, 218; capture of, ii. 102 n.
London Division, the 47th, at the battle of Loos, i. 43
Longatte, ii. 124, 132, 144
Long-Innes, Major P. S., commanding 2nd Bn. Irish Guards, ii. 63 n.
Longueval, i. 138
Longueville, Lieut.-Col. F., commanding 3rd Bn. Coldstream Guards, i. 290; ii. 37 n., 265
Loos, mining village, i. 39; battle of, 42–90; bombarded, 68, 69; attack at, ii. 278
Louverval, ii. 148, 149, 153, 166
Louvois Farm, i. 269, 277, 284
Lowther, Brig.-Gen. H. C., commanding 1st Guards Brigade, i. 2 n.; wounded, 16 n.; commanding 2nd Guards Brigade, 28; Military Secretary to Sir J. French, 28
Loyd, Capt. H. C., ii. 260
Ludendorff, General, "My War Memories," i. 268 n., 292 n., 300 n.; ii. 2 n.; on "the black day," ii. 107
Lumbres village, i. 29
Lyautey, General, Minister of War, inspects the Guards Division, i. 188 n.
Lys River, i. 95, 96; Valley of the, German advance, ii. 78–93; offensive, 96
Lyttelton, Capt. Oliver, i. 153 n., 158; ii. 253; report, i. 158 n., 159 n.; brigade-major of the 4th Guards Brigade, ii. 37 n., 260
Lytton, Neville, "The Press and the General Staff," ii. 17 n.

MacGregor, Major P. A., commanding 2nd Bn. Coldstream Guards, i. 30 n.; ii. 265
Machine-Gun Companies, i. 177; ii. 315. See Guards
Mackenzie, Capt. E. D., staff captain of 4th Guards Brigade, ii. 37 n.
Mackenzie, Major Sir V. A. F., commanding Guards Reinforcement Bn., i. 270 n.; 1st Bn. Scots Guards, ii. 266

INDEX

Madden, Lieut.-Col. G. H. C., commanding 1st Bn. Irish Guards, i. 14 n. ; ii. 266 ; killed, i. 81 n.
Magny-la-Fosse, ii. 183
Maison Blanche, capture of, ii. 207 n., 212
Major's Farm, i. 247
Makgill-Crichton-Maitland, Lieut.-Col. M. E., ii. 263
Malgarnie, ii. 228
Malzhorn Farm camp, i. 193
Manancourt, i. 208
Manchester Regiment, 10th Bn., ii. 66
Mann, Major W. E., commanding 74th Brigade, R.F.A., ii. 131 n., 256
Mansel, Capt. R. A. S., ii. 256, 263
Marchienne-au-Pont, ii. 240
Marcoing, ii. 2, 18, 163, 183, 293
Maricourt, i. 137, 196, 210 ; Wood, i. 136 n.
Marne, the, i. 6, 15
Marrières Wood, ii. 143
Martin, Major G. N. C., ii. 36
Martin Mill, i. 277
Martinpuich village, i. 142 n.
Marwitz, Gen. von der, ii. 1
Mary, H.M. Queen, at the Base Depôt at Harfleur, ii. 323
Masnières, i. 293, ii. 2, 17 ; capture of, ii. 183
Matheson, Major-General T. G., commanding 3rd Bn. Coldstream Guards, i. 6 n., 8 n., 14 n. ; the Guards Division, ii. 156, 158 n., 253 ; plan of operations in the battle of the Canal du Nord, 164 ; tribute to the Guards Division, 181, 231 n. ; warnings against fraternizing with the Germans, 185 n. ; orders to the troops, 197, 204, 230, 242 ; on crossing the Selle, 204 ; address to the Guards Division, 233 n., 234, 236, 326-328 ; attends a thanksgiving service, 237 ; at Cologne, 241 ; at the march through London, 246
Maubeuge, i. 37 ; capture of, ii. 184 n. ; advance on, 219-231, 234, 241
Mauquissart, i. 94
Maurepas, i. 198, 199, 200 n.
Maxse, Brig.-Gen. Ivor, commanding 1st Guards Brigade, i. 6, 15 ; XVIII Corps, 223 n.
Mazingarbe, i. 47, 69

McAulay, Sergeant John, awarded the V.C., ii. 272
McCalmont, Lieut.-Col. R. C. A., commanding 1st Bn. Irish Guards, i. 81 n. ; ii. 266 ; advance on Ginchy, i. 157 ; report by, 170 n. ; commanding an infantry brigade, 206 n.
McCarthy, Lieut.-Col., commanding Brigades R.F.A., i. 183
McClintock, Lieut.-Col. R. S., G.S.O.1, i. 78 n. ; ii. 25 n., 75 n., 254
McCormick, Rev. Pat, i. 101 n. ; ii. 268 ; report on the work of the chaplains, i. 133 n.
McLean, Capt. W. F., ii. 257
McLoughlin, Col. G. S., A.D.M.S., ii. 257 ; lectures to the troops, i. 100
McNess, Lance-Sergeant Fred, awarded the V.C., ii. 270
Meares, Major H. M. S., ii., 262
Méaulte, i. 139, 199
Mecquignies, ii. 226
Menin road, i. 16
Mercatel, ii. 43, 45
Merris, ii. 79
Merville, i. 93, 94, 100 ; ii. 78, 80
Messines, battle of, i. 218-222
Meteren, i. 12, 23
Metz, i. 209 n., 322
Metz-en-Couture, i. 321 ; ii. 3, 4, 7, 163
Meuse, the, ii. 184 n., 218, 240
Middle Copse, i. 168 n.
Middlesex Regiment, 21st Bn., ii. 51 n.
Miles, Capt. Wilfred, i. x.
Minden Post, i. 167
Miraumont, i. 203 ; ii. 112 ; capture of, i. 203 n.
Mœuvres, i. 295 ; ii. 149-154, 159 ; attack on, ii. 157, 160 ; captured, 158, 160 n.
Monchy-le-Preux, ii. 26, 43 n.
Mons, i. 2, 3 ; retreat from, 15
Mont St. Quentin, attack on, ii. 143
Montbliart, ii. 232 n.
Montenescourt, ii. 18
Montmirail Farm, i. 277
Moores, Col. S. Guise, ii. 257
Morlancourt, ii. 139, 210
Morland, Lieut.-Gen., commanding XIV Corps, i. 139 n.
Mormal Forest, ii. 184 n., 218
Morris, Lieut.-Col. the Hon. George,

commanding 1st Bn. Irish Guards, i. 4; killed, 5
Morris, Lieut. H. S., ii. 253
Morrison, Capt., attack on Hill 70, i. 56 n.
Morteldje Estaminet, capture of, i. 126
Morval, i. 142, 167; ii. 144; plans for the attack on, i. 145; battle of, 173 n., 176; shelled, 195 n.
Mory, ii. 47; attack on, 48, 52, 122 n.; Copse, ii. 125
Mouchoir Copse, i. 192, 198 n.
Moulin de Pietre, i. 23
Moulle village, i. 30
Mount Pleasant, ii. 34; Wood, 26, 27
Moyenneville, ii. 23 n., 55, 108 n.; attack on, 59, 113–115, 118
Moyney, Lance-Sergeant, awarded the V.C., ii. 271
Murray, Colonel, i. ix
Murray, Rt. Hon. Sir George, i. ix
Murray-Threipland, Lieut.-Col. W., commanding 1st Bn. Welsh Guards, i. 32; ii. 267; attack on Hill 70, i. 61–65; letters from, 61 n., 65 n., 127 n.; attack on Ginchy, 144; withdraws to Ginchy, 163 n.; retires, 208 n.
Mustard gas, i. 235; ii. 29 n., 152

Nauroy, ii. 183
Nesle, ii. 143
Neuf Berquin, ii. 80
Neuve Chapelle, i. 12 n.; battle of, 13 n., 23, 88 n.
Neuville, i. 322; ii. 7
Neuville Vitasse, ii. 44 n.
New Zealand, army, officers attached to Guards battalions, i. 187; ii. 103; at Wulverghem, i. 219 n.; Tunnelling Company, ii. 34; advance on the Selle, 191 n.; at Viesly, 192 n.
Newfoundland Regiment, i. 273
Ney, i. 261; Copse, 261–264; Wood, 261–264, 272
Nicholas II., Tzar of Russia, abdication, i. 216 n.
Nieppe Forest, ii. 81, 91; bombarded, 92
Niergnies, ii. 185, 210
Nivelle, General, commanding the French Army, failure of his operations on the Aisne, i. 215
Nœux-les-Mines, i. 47, 48

Nollot, General, commanding the French XXXVI Corps, i. 288
Nonne Boschen (Nun's Wood), battle of, i. 11
Noreuil, ii. 44, 145, 146
Norrent Fontes, i. 34
Northumbrian Division, the 50th, i. 14 n.
Noyelles, ii. 210
Noyelles-lez-Vermelles, i. 71, 73; shelled, 75
Noyelles-sur-l'Eseaut, i. 301; ii. 179 n., 183
Nurlu, i. 208

O'Brien, Lieut. Hon. H. B., ii. 259
Occohes, ii. 110
Oise River, ii. 145 n.
Oisy-le-Verger, ii. 183
O'Keeffe, Capt. J. J., ii. 258
O'Leary, Lance-Corp., awarded the V.C., i. 12 n.
O'Neill, Capt. E. M., ii. 258
Orival Wood, ii. 16, 170; attack on, 171, 173
O'Rorke, Major F. C., ii. 258
Orr-Ewing, Lieut.-Col. N. A., commanding 1st Bn. Irish Guards, i. 10 n.; the 45th Infantry Brigade, ii. 99 n.; 2nd Bn. Scots Guards, 266
Osborn, Brig.-Gen. W. S., commanding 5th Infantry Brigade, letter from, ii. 158 n.
Ostend, i. 2, 19
Oultersteene, ii. 79
Ovillers la Boisselle, i. 138
Oxfordshire and Buckinghamshire Light Infantry, 2nd Bn., i. 9
Oxfordshire Hussars, ii. 190, 191

Paillencourt, i. 294
Pain, Capt. W. E., i. 207 n.; ii. 263
Palissade Farm, i. 232
Palluel, ii. 183
Palmer, Capt., i. 63
Panther trench, i. 264, 269
Paris, Conference in, i. 217
Parnell, Lieut. the Hon. W. A. D., killed, i. 171 n.
Parry, Lance-Corporal, ii. 169 n.
Parry, Private, ii. 169 n.
Passchendaele, i. 8, 269, 283
Passerelle Farm, attack on, i. 260
Paton, Lieut. George Henry

INDEX

Totham, awarded the V.C., ii. 273
Paynter, Major G., commanding 2nd Bn. Scots Guards, i. 22; wounded, 24
Pearson, Lieut., commanding 45th Sanitary Company, i. 101
Pearson-Gregory, Capt., i. 203 n.
Peissant, i. 2
Penn, Capt. A. H., ii. 255
Penn, Major F., commanding 4th Guards Machine-Gun Regiment, ii. 267, 316
Pereira, Brig.-Gen. C. E., commanding Coldstream battalions, i. 9; ii. 265; an infantry brigade, i. 13 n.; the 1st Guards Brigade, 113; ii. 258; reply to Lieut.-Col. de Crespigny, i. 155 n.; G.O.C. 2nd Division, 199 n.
Péronne, i. 136, 211; ii. 143; fall of, ii. 143 n.
Perrins, Capt. J. A. D., ii. 259
Perry, Major G. M., ii. 317
Petit Han, ii. 241 n.
Petit Morin, i. 6, 15
Phillips, Major L. G., commanding the Signal Company, i. 207 n.; ii. 263
Picantin, i. 92
Pike, Lieut.-Col. E. J. L., commanding the Household Brigade, ii. 318
Pilcher, Lieut.-Col. W. S., commanding 4th Bn. Grenadier Guards, ii. 13 n., 37 n., 264; the composite battalion, 91 n.
Pilckem, i. 224, 232
Pill-boxes, construction of, i. 224 n.
Pinson Farm, capture of, i. 251
Pitt, Sergeant, i. 173 n.
Plateau, i. 195, 211; ammunition dump at, 198; bombed, 202
Ploegsteert, ii. 79, 184; Wood, i. 219
Plouvain, ii. 144
Plumer, Gen. Sir Herbert, commanding Second Army, i. 115; ordered to attack Messines, 218; tribute to the 4th Guards Brigade, ii. 90; presents medal ribbons, 92
Poelcappelle, i. 260, 269, 283
Poezelhock, i. 9
Pollok, Lieut.-Col. R. V., commanding 1st Bn. Irish Guards, i. 231 n.; ii. 266; commandant of the VI Corps School, ii. 99 n.

Polygon Wood, i. 9, 20
Ponsonby, Lieut.-Col. the Rt. Hon. Sir Frederick, "The Grenadier Guards in the Great War," i. 4 n. *See* Grenadier
Ponsonby, Brig.-Gen. J., commanding 1st Bn. Coldstream Guards, i. 15; ii. 264; wounded, i. 15 n.; commanding 2nd Guards Brigade, 28, 30 n.; ii. 259; orders to the troops, i. 55; ordered to attack the Puits, 66; tribute to Lieut.-Col. Egerton, 68 n.; initiates the "Daily Dump," 130; on sick leave, 199 n.; commanding the 40th Division, 263 n., 289; ii. 42 n.; thanks to the Guards Division, 303 n.
Ponsonby, Major the Hon. Miles, commanding 4th Bn. Grenadier Guards, i. 60; attack on Hill 70, 61; killed, 62 n.
Pont Arcy, i. 6
Pont Brucken, ii. 241
Pont du Hem, i. 93, 101
Pont Rondin, ii. 82; attack on, 83
Pont-sur-Sambre, ii. 227
Pont Tournant, ii. 84, 85
Pont-à-Vendin, i. 37, 38; advance on, 80
Poperinghe, i. 117, 118, 130; Canal, 224, 228; theatre, 131
Portuguese army, defeated, ii. 79, 91 n.
Poteau, ii. 241
Powell, Capt., appointed Town Commandant of Maubeuge, ii. 232 n.
Pozières, i. 138
Pradelles, i. 221
Premy Chapel, ii. 165; attack on, 171, 173–177, 181
Pres, Château des, i. 74
Preux-au-Sart, ii. 223, 224
Prieure, i. 81
Priez Farm, i. 199
Prouville, ii. 148
Proven, i. 258
Proville, ii. 210
Pryce, Lieut. T. T., ii. 83; awarded the V.C., 89, 273
Puiseux, i. 4, 128
Puits, No. 14 bis, i. 39, 45; attack on. 54–57, 60, 65–67; evacuated, 57
Puresbécques, ii. 82, 87

Pym, Lieut., i, 127
Pys, i. 203 ; capture of, 203 n.

Quadrilateral, i, 143 ; attack on, 145, 152 ; captured, 168 n.
Quarries, plan of attack on, i. 70–72 ; abandoned, 72
Quart, Gen. von, ii. 79
Quéant, ii. 144, 146, 148
Queen's Cross, ii. 4, 5
Quentin ridge, ii, 3, 6 ; attack on, 9
Quesnoy, ii. 218, 220, 223 ; Farm, 58, 98
Quévy le Petit, i. 3 n.
Quiévy, ii. 192, 193, 213

Rainy trench, i. 175 n.
Ramsden, Capt. W. C., ii. 263
Rancourt, i. 142 n., 198 ; ii. 144
Rankin, Lieut.-Col. H. C. D., ii. 258
Ransart, ii. 56, 61, 66, 110
Rasch, Lieut.-Col. G. E. C., i. 22, 23 n. ; ii. 254 ; commanding 2nd Bn. Grenadier Guards, i. 290 ; ii. 263 ; 1st Provisional Bn., ii. 169 n. ; 2nd Guards Brigade, 260
Ravenhill, Lieut.-Col. C., commanding 74th Brigade R.F.A., ii. 261 ; retires, ii. 123 n.
Rawlinson, Gen. Sir Henry, commanding the First Army, tribute to the Guards Division, i. 107 n., 176 n. ; at the battle of the Somme, 137 ; attack on Amiens, ii. 107
Reid, Lieut.-Col. P. L., commanding 2nd Bn. Irish Guards, ii. 267 ; attack of trench fever, i. 147 n. ; retires, 200 n.
Reims, attack on, ii. 102 n.
"Reminiscences of a Grenadier," i. 258 n. ; ii. 108 n., 114 n., 116 n., 120 n., 123 n., 168 n., 188 n., 189 n., 233 n., 244 n.
Renescure, headquarters at, i. 218 n.
"Report of the Battles Nomenclature Committee as approved by the Army Council," i. 7 n., 25 n., 176 n.
Reutel village, attack on, i. 8
Revelon, ii. 3
Rhiel barracks, ii. 241
Rhine, the, ii. 239
Rhodes, Lance-Sergeant J. H., awarded the V.C., ii. 272

Rhonelle, the, ii. 219, 220, 223, 224 n. ; bridge across, 235
Ribécourt, i. 297, 299, 321 ; ii. 16, 164
Richebourg l'Avoué, i. 12, 92
Riddell, Lieut.-Col. J. B., commanding Brigades R.F.A., i. 123 n. ; ii. 261, 262
Ridout-Evans, Major G. W. F., ii. 263
Riencourt-les-Bapaume, i. 147 ; ii. 144
Riley, Lieut. C. J. M., attack on the Puits, i. 67 ; wounded, 67 n.
Rivière des Laies, i. 95
Robertson, Field-Marshal Sir William, "From Private to Field-Marshal," i. 216 n.
Roche, Major C. E. A. S., commanding 2nd Bn. Irish Guards, i. 147 n. ; report on the attack on Ginchy, 149 n. ; commanding 1st Bn. Irish Guards, 207 n. ; ii. 266 ; accident, i. 231 n.
Roclincourt, ii. 37
Rocquigny, i. 147, 210
Roeux, ii. 30 ; caves at, 28, 33
Rogan, Col. Mackenzie, bandmaster, i. 132 n. ; ii. 324
Rogers, Lieut.-Col. W. L. Y., commanding 76th Brigade R.F.A., ii. 262
Rolland, Major A., ii. 262
Romer, Lieut.-Col. M., commanding 1st Bn. Scots Guards, i. 290 ; ii. 266
Romilly, Lieut.-Col. B. H. S., commanding 1st Bn. Scots Guards, ii. 266 ; wounded, i. 242 n.
Rond de la Reine, i. 4
Ross, Capt. Hugh, commanding 1st Bn. Scots Guards, i. 242 n.
Roulers, i. 19
Roussel Farm, i. 242
Royal Army Medical Corps, work of the, i. 251, 284 ; ii. 236
Royal Engineers, Field Companies, i. 29 ; work of the, 90, 120, 121, 125, 180–182, 189, 194, 200, 209, 211, 251–253, 267, 276 ; ii. 141, 177–179 ; in the Cambrai operations, ii. 19–21 ; on the Scarpe front, 34 ; constructs bridges over the Selle, 213–216 ; advance on Maubeuge, 234–236
Royal Munster Fusiliers, 2nd Bn., i. 2 n., 11 ; cut off at Etreux, 15
Royds, Major A. H., commanding

INDEX

the Base Depôt at Harfleur, ii. 322
Rudkin, Capt. G. F., ii. 258
Rudkin, Lieut.-Col. W. C. E., commanding 75th Brigade R.F.A., ii. 99 n., 262; 57th Division, 111 n.
Rue du Bacquerot, i. 95
Rue du Bois, i. 24, 92; disaster at, 18
Rue Tilleloy, i. 93, 95 n.
Ruggles-Brise, Brig.-Gen. H. G., commanding 20th Infantry Brigade, i. 2, 21; wounded, 2 n.
Ruisseau Farm, i. 249, 282, 284
Rumilly, ii. 210
Russian army, in Galicia, i. 135 n.; collapse, ii. 24
Ruthven, Major-Gen. Lord, i. ix.
Ruthven, Lieut.-Col. W., orders to the Guards Division, ii. 278
Ruyaulcourt, i. 322; ii. 7
Ryan, Major J. S., commanding the Signal Company, ii. 216 n., 263

Sailly, ii. 183
Sailly-au-Bois, i. 129 n.
Sailly-Labourse, i. 72, 74, 81
Sailly-le-See, i. 139 n., 181
Sailly-Sallisel, i. 142 n., 192, 198, 206; ii. 144; capture of, i. 191 n.
Sailly-sur-La Lys, ii. 79
St. Aubert, attack on, ii. 194
St. Auguste, mining village, i. 39
St. Hilaire, ii. 192, 204, 211
St. Jean, i. 7, 120
St. Leger, ii. 43, 46; attack on, 124–127, 136
St. Martin's Wood, i. 208
St. Omer, i. 29
St. Pierre Divion, i. 137
St. Pierre Vaast, i. 198, 201, 205 n., 206, 207; ii. 192–195
St. Pol. i. 293
St. Pry, i. 81
St. Python, ii. 195, 196, 198, 200; bridge at, 213
St. Quentin, occupied, ii. 183; Canal, 163
St. Sixte, convent of, i. 124
Sambre, the, ii. 203 n.; battle of, 231; bridging the, 232; Canal, ii. 184 n.
Sandison, Capt. J. F. W., ii. 257
Sapignies, capture of, ii. 55
Sauchy-Lestrée, ii. 163
Saulty, ii. 108, 113
Saunders, St. J. R., ii. 253

Scannell, Rev. J., ii. 237, 268
Scarpe, the, ii. 144; defence of, 26–35
Scheldt, the, ii. 161 n., 163, 179, 185
Scots Guards band, ii. 324
Scots Guards, 1st Bn., i. 1, 14, 30; casualties, 15 n., 17 n., 18 n., 19 n., 238 n.; attack at Cuinchy, 18. *See* Guards Division
Scots Guards, 2nd Bn., i. 2, 30; at the battle of Kruiseeck, 21; casualties, 21 n., 23 n., 24 n., 25 n.; at the battle of Gheluwelt, 22; Neuve Chapelle, 23; Festubert, 24. *See* Guards Division
Scots Guards Reserve Bn., ii. 312
Scottish Division, the 15th, at the battle of Loos, i. 48
Scott-Kerr, Brig.-Gen. R., commanding 4th Guards Brigade, i. 2; wounded, 2 n., 5
Selle River, ii. 184 n.; advance on, 185–209; passage of the, 202, 204–206; construction of bridges over the, 213–216
Sensée River, i. 293; ii. 48, 50, 124, 144; Valley, ii. 138
Sentier Farm, capture of, i. 251, 258
Sequehart, ii. 184
Seranvillers, ii. 185, 210; capture of 188
Sergison-Brooke, Brig.-Gen. B. N., commanding 3rd Grenadier Guards, i. 114, 152; ii. 264; wounded, i. 152 n.; commanding 2nd Guards Brigade, 263 n., 289; ii. 259; at the battle of Fontaine-Notre-Dame, i. 315; gassed, ii. 44 n.; resumes command, 99 n.
Serre, i. 129, 187
Seymour, Capt. E., G.S.O.2, ii. 254; instructions for tanks, 289
Seymour, Brig.-Gen. Lord Henry C., commanding 4th Bn. Grenadier Guards, i. 110; ii. 264; gassed, i. 110; attack on Ginchy, 144; extract from a letter, 172 n.; commanding 2nd Guards Brigade, 199 n.; ii. 259; relinquishes command, ii. 98 n.
Shaw, H. G., ii. 317
Shells, supply of, i. 43
Shingler trench, ii. 174
Shrewsbury Forest, ii. 9
Signal Company, value of, i. 77; visual stations, 207, 208; training runners, 222; use of pigeons, 278; work of the, ii. 141, 216, 236

Signal Farm, i. 249
Signalling, courses of instruction, i. 111, 140; School at Agnez-les-Duisans, ii. 24
Silver Street, ii. 174, 177
Simencourt, ii. 23 n.
Simpson, Capt. J. H. C., takes over command of 1st Bn. Grenadier Guards, ii. 177 n.
Skeffington-Smyth, Lieut.-Col. R. C. commanding 4th Bn. Coldstream Guards, i. 32; ii. 265; return to England, i. 290
Smith, Major A. F., G.S.O. 3, ii. 254; Instructor of Bushey school, 318
Smith, Lieut.-Col. W., commanding 2nd Bn. Grenadier Guards, i. 6 n.; killed, 13 n.
Smith-Dorrien, Sir Horace, commanding II Corps, i. 2
Smoke, use of, i. 56
Sniping, lecture on, i. 112 n.
Soissons, i. 4
Solesmes, ii. 185, 198, 203, 204, 206
Solferino Farm, i. 284
Somme, the, attack on, i. 128, 135–186; ii. 95, 143; winter on the, i. 192
Sonastre, ii. 58
Souchez, i. 40
Soucy, i. 4
Soupir spur, i. 6
Spanish influenza, epidemic of, ii. 104, 110
Speller, Sergeant-Major F., ii. 317
Standage, Capt. H. E., ii. 257
Stanley, Lieut.-Col. Hon. A. F., commanding 2nd Bn. Guards Machine-Gun Regiment, ii. 315
"Starr, Dillwyn Parrish, The War Story of," i. 151 n.
Steele, Lieut.-Col. J., commanding 2nd Bn. Coldstream Guards, i. 13 n.; ii. 265; the 22nd Infantry Brigade, i. 30 n.
Steenbeek, the, i. 233, 248, 256, 281; Valley, 277
Stepney, Major H. H., commanding 1st Bn. Irish Guards, i. 5 n.; killed, 10
Stirling, Lieut.-Col. J. A., commanding 2nd Bn. Scots Guards, ii. 99 n., 266; takes command of 1st Bn. Grenadier Guards, 125 n., 126 n.; of 3rd Guards Brigade, 226
Stops, Capt. J., ii. 257

Strazeele, i. 219; ii. 80, 81
Streatfeild, Col. Sir Henry, i. 12 n., 188
Style, 2nd Lieut. O. G., i. 67
Suez Farm, i. 274, 277

Tadpole Copse, ii. 149, 150, 151, 153 n.
Tandy, Major M. O. C., ii. 263
Tanks, use of, i. 147, 168, 310; ii. 9, 113, 115; number, i. 147 n.; failure, 161; instructions, ii. 283–285, 289
Tempest, Lieut.-Col. R. S., commanding 2nd Bn. Scots Guards, i. 114; ii. 266, 318; wounded, i. 159; commanding 43rd Infantry Brigade, 290
Thackeray, Lieut.-Col. F. R., commanding 75th Brigade, R.F.A., ii. 262
Thielt, i. 19
Thiembronne, i. 30 n.
Thiepval, i. 142; attack on, 167
Thorne, Lieut.-Col. A. F. A. N., commanding 3rd Guards Brigade, ii. 116, 264; Commandant of the IX Corps School, 147 n.
Thorne, Capt. T. F. J. N., killed, i. 62 n.
Thourout, i. 7 n.
Tilloy, ii. 44 n.
Tilques, musketry ranges, i. 222
Tortelle River, i. 208
Torwes-Clark, Capt. W. T., ii. 259
Transloy, i. 173, 174, 196
Trefusis, Lieut.-Col. the Hon. J., commanding 1st Bn. Irish Guards, i. 11 n.; an infantry brigade, 14 n.
Trench, Major D. Le P., ii. 256
Trench warfare, value of intelligence summaries, i. 105 n.
Trench-Mortar Batteries, at the battle of Messines, i. 221; work of the, 235 n.
Trenches, condition of, i. 71 n., 83, 94–97, 119, 124, 225 n.; ii. 28; drainage, i. 96
Trentino, the, i. 135 n.
Trescault, i. 297, 299, 322; ii. 7, 20; capture of, ii. 157
Treux, i. 139
Trieu, ii. 240
Trinquis Brook, ii. 144
Trônes Wood, i. 138, 145, 151, 196, 210

INDEX

Trotter, Lieut.-Col. G. F., commanding 1st Bn. Grenadier Guards, i. 25 n.; ii. 263; 27th Infantry Brigade, i. 118 n.; 4th Bn. Machine-Gun Guards, ii. 315
Tunnelling Company, work of the, i. 226, 227, 251, 252
Turkey, capitulation of, ii. 218 n.
Tweedmouth, Lieut.-Col. Lord, commanding 3rd Bn. Guards Machine-Gun Regiment, ii. 315

United States of America, Army of the, join the Guards Division, ii. 106; in the battle of the Selle, 218 n.

Valenciennes, ii. 218; advance on, i. 37; attack on, ii. 219; captured, 219
Vanneck, Lieut. Hon. A. N. A., ii. 259
Vanremen, Lieut.-Col. J. E., C.R.E. Guards Division, i. 29; ii. 256
Vauchelles, i. 139
Vauchelles-les-Authie, i. 128
Vaudricourt, i. 81
Vaughan, Capt. E. N., i. 144
Vaughan, Major G. E., commanding 2nd Bn. Coldstream Guards, ii. 265
Vaulx Vrancourt, ii. 43, 144, 146
Vaux Wood, i. 208
Vee Bend, i. 269, 272
Veldhoek, i. 22 n., 278, 279
Vendhuille, ii. 2, 17, 183
Vendresse Valley, i. 15
Verdun, attack on, i. 135
Vermelles, i. 13, 37, 38, 40, 47, 72; bombarded, 75; R.E. dump at, 90 n.
Vernon, Major G. F. C. Harcourt, at the battle of the Canal du Nord, ii. 169
Verquigneul, i. 69
Verquin, i. 81
Vertain, ii. 200, 206, 208 n., 219
Vickery, Lieut.-Col. C. E., commanding 74th Brigade R.F.A., i. 234 n.; ii. 131 n., 137, 160, 221 n., 261; extracts from his diary, i. 254 n.; ii. 36 n., 99 n., 137 n., 142 n.; attack on Moyenneville, ii. 113; at the battle of the Canal du Nord, 166
Vielle Chapelle, ii. 79

Vierhouck, ii. 82; advance on, 83
Viesly, ii. 192 n.
Vieux Berquin, ii. 81, 82; capture of, 87
Vieux Moulin, ii. 82
Vignacourt, i. 139
Villers Chatel, ii. 16
Villers Cottérêts, i. 2 n., 4
Villers-au-Flos, i. 147
Villers-Guislain, capture, of, ii. 2, 3
Villers Plouich, ii. 3, 7
Villers Pol, ii. 219, 220; attack on, 221, 222
Vimy Ridge, capture of, i. 217
Vivières, i. 4
Voormezeele, ii. 102 n.
Vrancourt, ii. 44 n., 134, 143
Vulcan Crossing, i. 250

Wales, H.R.H. Edward, Prince of, foreword, i. vii.; on the staff of the Guards Division, 28; visits Guards Brigades, 129; at Herzeele, 231 n.; presents a Union Colour to the 4th Bn. Grenadier Guards, ii. 244; at the march past through London of the Guards Division, 246
Walker, Major C. F. A. commanding 2nd Bn. Grenadier Guards, ii. 169 n., 188 n., 263
Wambaix, attack on, ii. 186; captured, 188
Wancourt, ii. 43, 44 n.
"War, History of the Great," i. 3 n., 4 n., 5 n., 6 n., 7 n., 15 n.
Ward, Major C. H. Dudley, "History of the Welsh Guards," i. 32 n.; extract from his diary, ii. 77 n.
Wardrecques, i. 218
Wardrop, Brig.-Gen. A. E., commanding Guards divisional Artillery, i. 29, 54 n., 90, 114; ii. 256; report on the work of his batteries, i. 109 n.
Wargnies-le-Petit, ii. 223; bridge across, 235
Warner, Major E. T. C., ii. 261; commanding 2nd Bn. Scots Guards, 182 n.
Warneton, ii. 184
Warsaw, fall of, i. 36
Watkins, Col. C. B., commanding D.A.C., i. 123 n.; ii. 262
Watts, Lieut.-Gen., commanding XIX Corps, i. 223 n.
Webber, Major, commanding 1st

VOL. II.   2 A

INDEX

Bn. Irish Guards, i. 10 n.; wounded, 11
Wedge Wood, i. 143
Welsh Guards, 1st Bn., i. 30, 31; at Arques, 32; tribute to, 65; capture Morteldje Estaminet, 126; casualties, 127 n., 144 n.; attack on Ginchy, 144; band, ii. 324. *See* Guards Division
Welsh Guards Reserve Battalion, ii. 313.
"Welsh Guards, History of the," i. 32 n., 33 n., 127 n., 144 n., 164 n., 188 n., 211 n.; ii. 57 n., 69 n., 71 n., 77 n., 97 n., 101 n., 103 n., 127 n., 146 n., 151 n., 152 n., 156 n., 173 n., 176 n., 195 n., 207 n., 217 n., 226 n., 233 n.
Westroosebeke, i. 283
Weywertz, ii. 241
White Château, i. 119, 120
White Hope Corner, i, 234 n., 252
Wieltje Farm, i. 116, 118, 124, 127
Wigram, Col. Clive, i. 289
Wijdendrift, i. 234, 259
Williams, Capt. A., bandmaster, ii. 324
Williams, Capt. B., ii. 256
Williams, Lieut. M. G., attack on Hill 70, i. 65
Williams, Capt. Rhys, attack on Hill 70, i. 61, 63
Wilson, Brig.-Gen. F. A., commanding Guards Divisional Artillery, ii. 256
Wiltshire Regiment, 2nd Bn., i. 20
Wisnes, i. 33
Witham, Private Thomas, awarded the V.C., ii. 271
Woesten, i. 223, 230
Wood, F. W., bandmaster, ii. 324

Wood, Corporal H. B., awarded the V.C., ii. 276
Woodcock, Private Thomas, awarded the V.C., ii. 271
Woods, Corporal, awarded the V.C., ii. 199
Woollcombe, Lieut.-Gen. Sir C. L., commanding IV Corps, i. 297
Works Battalions, i. 193; ii. 321
Wormhoudt, i. 117, 123
Wright, Major R. M., ii. 315, 316
Wulverghem, i. 219
Wyatt, Lance-Corporal G. H., awarded the V.C., i. 4 n.
Wynne-Finch, Capt. W. H., ii. 260
Wytschaete ridge, i. 218; ii. 79

Yorke, Major P. G., ii. 256
Yorkshire Regiment, 13th Bn., ii. 51 n.
Yper Lea, the, i. 230, 252
Ypres, i. 19, 224; battles of, 7, 22 n.; salient, 116–128; condition of the trenches, 119; plan of attack on, 225–228; preliminary bombardment, 233–235; postponement of the battle, 236; offensive, 236–285
Yser Canal, i. 125, 224; crossing the, 228, 236–239
Ytres, i. 208; ii. 23 n.

Zandvoorde, i. 20, 22 n.
Zeebrugge, i. 19
Zeggers Cappel, i. 117, 123 n.
Zillebeke, i. 9 n.
Zommerbloem, i. 236 n.
Zonnebeke, i. 7
Zulpich, ii. 243
Zuydochoote, i. 234 n.

THE END

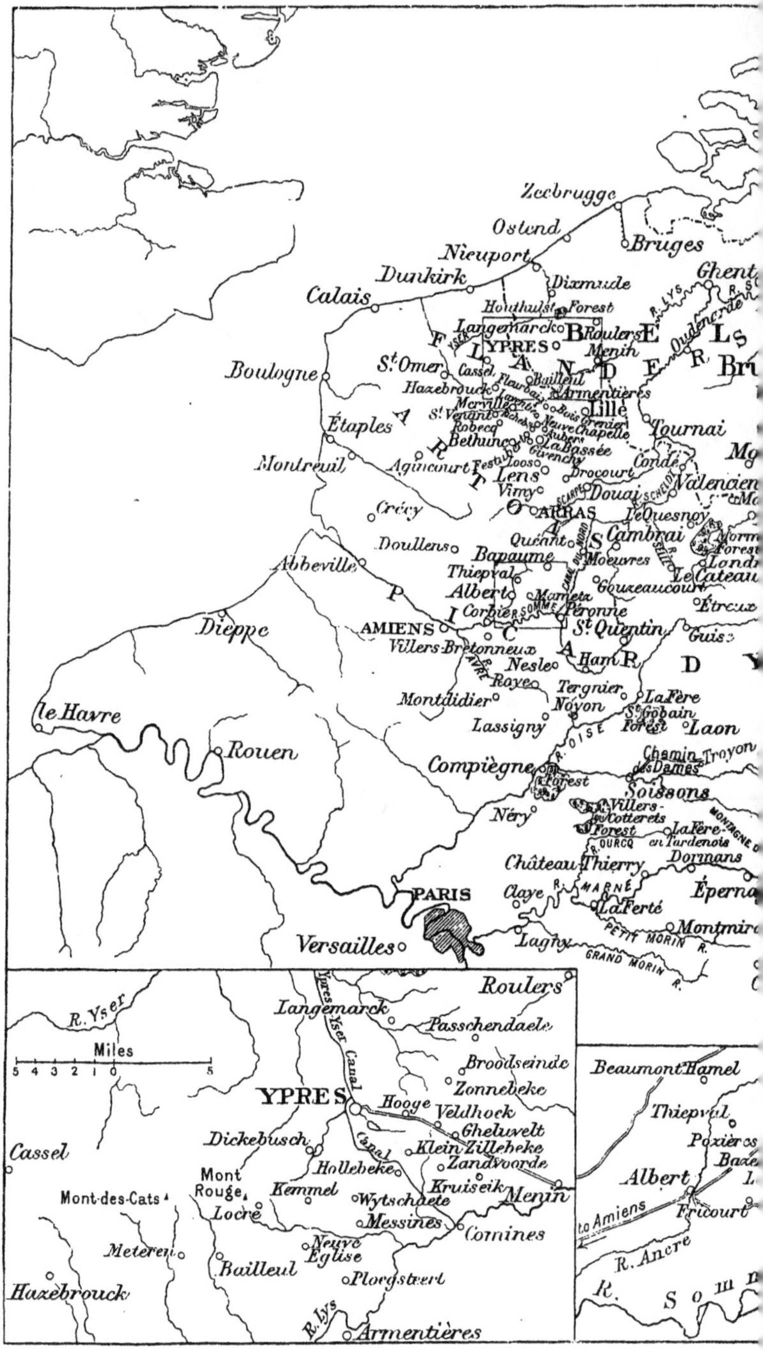
Zeebrugge
Ostend
Bruges
Nieuport
Dunkirk
Dixmude
Calais
Ghent
Houthulst Forest
Langemarck
YPRES
Roulers
Menin
R. Lys
Oudenarde
F L A N D E R S
Boulogne
St. Omer
Cassel
Bailleul
Hazebrouck
Armentières
Lille
Tournai
Merville
St. Venant
Robecq
Bethune
Neuve Chapelle
La Bassée
Givenchy
Étaples
A R T O I S
Montreuil
Agincourt
Festubert
Loos
Lens
Vimy
Drocourt
Condé
Douai
Scarpe
Crécy
ARRAS
Le Quesnoy
Quéant
Cambrai
Canal du Nord
Doullens
Bapaume
Moeuvres
Le Cateau
Abbeville
Thiepval
Albert
Mametz
Gouzeaucourt
P I C A R D Y
Corbie
Somme
Péronne
Étreux
Dieppe
AMIENS
St. Quentin
Villers-Bretonneux
Avre
Nesle
Ham
Roye
Tergnier
le Havre
Montdidier
Noyon
La Fère
St. Gobain Forest
Lassigny
R. Oise
Laon
Rouen
Compiègne
Forest
Chemin des Dames
Soissons
Néry
Villers-Cotterets Forest
R. Ourcq
La Fère-en-Tardenois
Château Thierry
Dormans
PARIS
Claye
Marne R.
La Ferté
Versailles
Lagny
Petit Morin R.
Grand Morin R.
R. Yser
Miles
5 4 3 2 1 0 5
Roulers
Langemarck
Passchendaele
Ypres Yser Canal
Broodseinde
Zonnebeke
YPRES
Hooge
Veldhoek
Gheluvelt
Dickebusch
Klein Zillebeke
Zandvoorde
Cassel
Hollebeke
Canal
Mont Rouge
Mont-des-Cats
Kemmel
Kruiseik
Wytschaete
Menin
Locre
Messines
Comines
Meteren
Neuve Eglise
Bailleul
Ploegsteert
Hazebrouck
R. Lys
Armentières
Beaumont Hamel
Thiepval
Pozières
Albert
Fricourt
to Amiens
R. Ancre

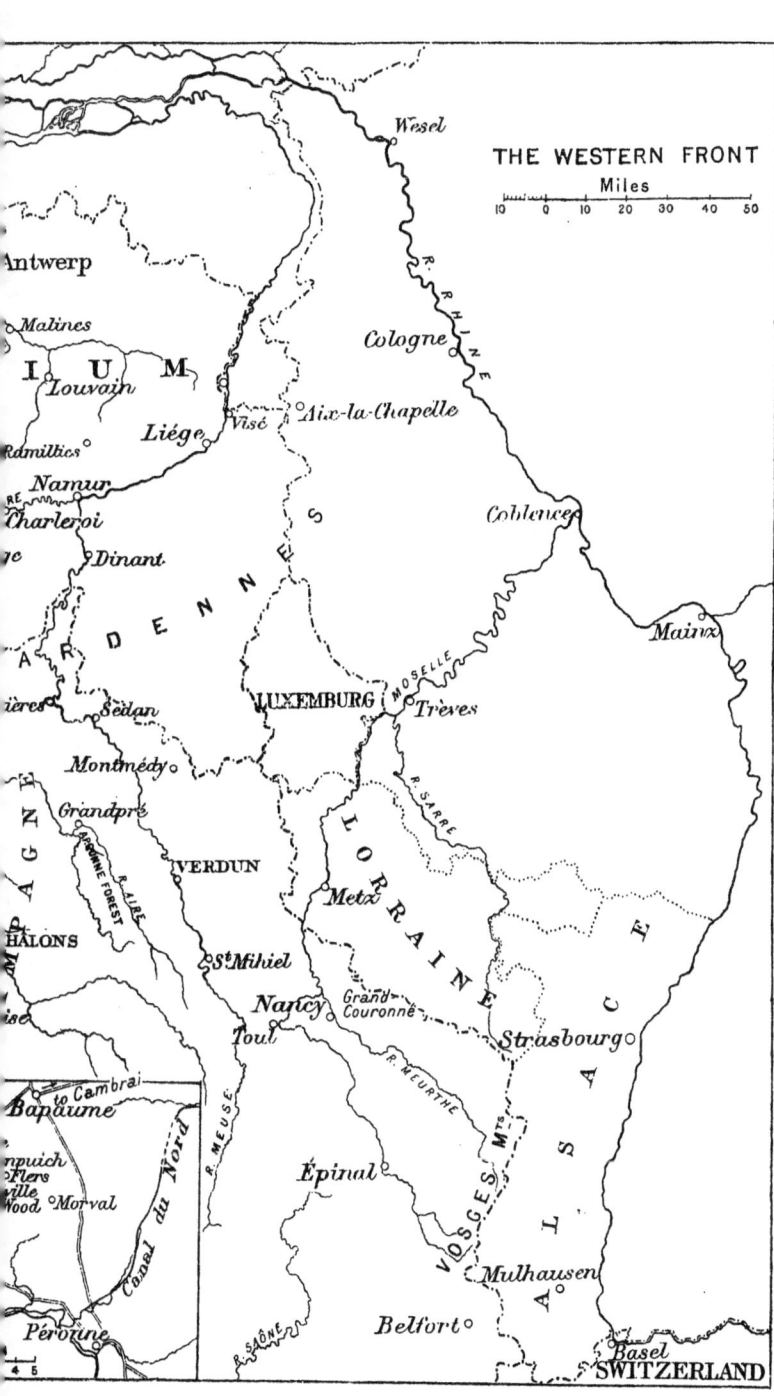

www.ingramcontent.com/pod-product-compliance
Lightning Source LLC
Chambersburg PA
CBHW061927220426
43662CB00012B/1828